# MISSIONARY CARE

12.55

# MISSIONARY CARE

## Counting the Cost for World Evangelization

Edited by

*Kelly O'Donnell*

**Consulting Editors**

*John Powell*
*Brent Lindquist*
*Kenneth Harder*
*Richard Gardner*
*Laura Mae Gardner*
*Michèle Lewis O'Donnell*

*William Carey Library*
Pasadena, California

# 26573795

Published by
William Carey Library
Post Office Box 40129
Pasadena, California  91114

ISBN 0-87808-233-6
Library of Congress C.I.P.# 92-72009

*Cover design by Katy O'Donnell-Filson*

Printed in the United States of America

# CONTENTS

## Part One: Missionary Care Overview

## Part Two: Counseling and Clinical Care

# Part Three: Team Development

# Part Four: Mission Agencies and Member Care

# Part Five: Future Directions

# Foreword

*Ralph and Roberta Winter*

We must confess that both of us were a bit ambivalent when the O'Donnells asked us to write the foreword to this book. It's not that we don't believe in member care. From the first day we started the U.S. Center for World Mission, we have stressed the need for a chaplain of sorts to care for our members. And early on, two of our staff, former missionaries who were wise in counsel, were appointed to be official counselors for the men and women respectively. Then, over rather long periods of time we have had half-day sessions of what we call "staff development"—a euphemism for member care done as a group.

Our reservations rather stemmed from the fact that in our day there has been an overemphasis on personal growth and psychological well-being. We are concerned that the mission community not become overly influenced by this inordinate focus on the "self." It once was that if you were not normal or had severe psychological problems, you went to a counselor. Now it almost seems that you cannot be normal without getting professional help somewhere along the way!

However, we must admit that more people than ever before really do need professional help. The number of missionary candidates, for example, who are children of alcoholics or who come from dysfunctional families is higher than ever before. Consequently, most mission agencies are finding it necessary to accept candidates who either need or may need psychological help. It is the astounding increase of family breakdown, divorce, and abuse in America and in Western societies in general which stands directly and indirectly behind the increase in personnel problems on the mission fields of the world.

Recently, Ralph was asked to speak at a conference of 175 pastors on the impact that the increased breakdown in American family life has had on the cause of missions. We spent a lot of time thinking and praying about this crucial theme. One part of his presentation addressed the proliferation of evangelical professionals involved in counseling, the "recovery movement," talking on evangelical radio stations, and authoring a myriad of books dealing with self-esteem, co-dependency, individual rights, addictive problems, and so on. And the question arises, which came first, the chicken or the egg? It is said that we have more lawsuits because we have more lawyers. Do we have more psychological turmoil because we have more counselors? It may work both ways.

Yet there certainly is an important place for the mental health professional and other member care workers in missions. The sane, balanced advice given by the twenty-three authors in this book makes that very clear. The authors, most of whom serve or have served as missionaries, understand the special stresses and strains that missionaries face. Complicating the situation, they are supposed to be saints, not just saints-in-the-making. They are lauded on leaving home, but on the field they are just another missionary, and one in culture shock at that.

Some missionaries, as a few authors admit, should never have gone to the field; perhaps they are not emotionally able to bear the stresses or flexible enough to adjust to the culture. Other missionaries who are eminently qualified sometimes end up so wounded that they are unable to function. And if not helped, the struggles which afflict them can disrupt the entire team.

The issue then becomes a larger one: how do you protect the integrity and mission of the whole while caring for those who have become hurt, angry, and even incapacitated? Further, how do we help them resolve their problems in a godly way, bringing them to a place of spiritual and psychological healing? How can we prevent such problems from arising in the first place? How could we determine if personal problems may not indeed spring from unhealthy organizational practices or one's spiritual need? Or could such problems rather stem from demonic oppression? How do we know, and what do we do?

Answering these types of questions is what this book is all about. We commend this book for tackling some of these tough issues which lie on the cutting edge of missionary care. Although we ourselves might not agree with every assumption made herein, on the whole the insights and suggestions given are superb. Whoever said it is easy being a missionary—especially in a pioneer field long held under Satan's sway? None of us are in missions because it is easy, but because we are committed to sacrificially obey the Lord who commanded us to make disciples of all nations. Missionary personnel, as this volume so aptly points out, must balance their divine call to service and self-denial with their realistic need for personal growth and supportive care.

So what really helps missionaries to survive and excel in missions? Devotion to the Lord, perseverance, inner strength, and a balanced member care program provided in the context of a supportive community. Especially important is having friends stand alongside you as you weather the challenges of missionary life together. This is also why the promise Christ gave in conjunction with his Great Commission is so precious: "Lo, I am with you always, even to the end of the age."

This book is a real treasure. It is one of those special and timely resources that can really help missionaries. It is absolutely essential for mission leaders and member care workers alike. We also highly recommend it for the ordinary missionary—the one who daily is out there each day "abounding in the work of the Lord." May God use it to enrich their lives and their ministries, we pray.

# Preface

*We are dwarfs mounted on the shoulders of giants, so that we can see more and further than they; yet not by virtue of the keenness of our eyesight, nor through the tallness of our stature, but because we are raised and borne aloft on that giant mass. Bernard of Chartres, 12th century*

Missionary care, for better or for worse, has been going on for centuries. It has, thankfully, been receiving considerably more attention of late within the evangelical missions community. In fact, as the above quotation suggests, the current practice of missionary care, like so many other of the Church's endeavors, is indebted to a host of predecessors who through sacrifice, courage, and obedience have formed the foundation upon which it stands.

This volume is a *missions* book which squarely rests upon the shoulders of such disciplines as missiology, anthropology, and psychology, as well as upon the contributions of those who over the last three decades have pioneered the "member care" field. I want to emphasize that this is a *missions* book since its primary goal is to aid the cause of world missions by helping missionary personnel remain healthy and effective.

Three underlying convictions have influenced my thinking in putting this book together: (a) a comprehensive, balanced approach to missionary care is an essential ingredient of mission strategy; (b) member care resources must be prioritized to support those who are targeting and working among the least evangelized; and (c) a variety of cooperative, innovative endeavors, directed by the Lord, are needed to support the growing number of missionary personnel around the world.

With regards to the first conviction, I write and edit from the perspective that mission personnel, in addition to their training, emotional stability, and spiritual maturity, require ongoing maintenance and further development. Indeed, my experience is that most people appreciate all the care and growth they can get as they weather the ups and downs of missionary life. I place missionary care on par with church planting strategies, language and culture mastery, and contextualization approaches.

My second conviction underscores the need for a systematic ranking of member care priorities. The criteria: Which mission organizations and missionary personnel are working among the least evangelized people groups? If the Great Commission is going to be fulfilled, then there needs to be a radical shift in the way mission resources—including member care workers and services—are being deployed. Member care resources must therefore be especially channeled to support those working among the least evangelized.

My third conviction, the need for cooperative endeavors, is reflected in the process of assembling this book—I have called upon a variety of authors to address crucial, relatively overlooked areas in the member care field. Like most joint ventures, coordinating the efforts of so many authors has been challenging, especially in trying to do this from afar. Nevertheless such combined efforts are the wave of the future; they will likely prove to be some of the most strategic, Spirit-led strategies for further developing and providing member care resources as well as for impacting unreached areas and people groups.

I would like to express appreciation to several people who have contributed significantly to this volume. I am grateful for the authors who carved out time in their busy schedules to pause, reflect, and write on their respective topics. I also appreciate having been able to call upon the collective wisdom of the six consulting editors. Their friendship has encouraged me, and their input has strengthened this book.

Special thanks to my YWAM colleagues on the Target 2000 Frontier Missions Project for their encouragement as I wrote and edited. Their computer wizardry, jovial countenances, and fervent prayers were frequent reminders that God's "good hand" was with me. Thanks also to Christine Alexander, who finely tuned the last draft, and the many friends and family members whose support makes it possible to continue my work in missions.

Finally, I am grateful to Michele, my wife, and our daughter Erin— giants in their own right—for their good cheer and patience that helped keep me going during the many phases of this project. They in particular have borne me up on their shoulders, steadying me during hard times and helping me to keep my eyes focused on the Lord.

Kelly O'Donnell
Amsterdam, The Netherlands
May, 1992

# List of Contributors

**Leslie Andrews**—Associate Professor, Ausbury Theological Seminary; PhD from Michigan State University and DMin from Columbia Theological Seminary.

**Barry Austin**—Pastoral Coordinator for Europe, Youth With A Mission, Nuneaton, England; Diploma from Victoria University, Wellington, New Zealand.

**Hans Finzel**—General Director Designate, Conservative Baptist Foreign Mission Society, Wheaton, Illinois; DMis from Fuller Theological Seminary.

**Laura Mae Gardner**—International Coordinator of Counseling Ministries and Personnel, Wycliffe Bible Translators, Dallas, Texas; DMin from Conservative Baptist Theological Seminary.

**Richard Gardner**—International Coordinator, Counseling Services, Wycliffe Bible Translators, Dallas, Texas; MA from Conservative Baptist Theological Seminary.

**Kenneth Harder**—Senior Management Development and Staffing Specialist, Compassion International, Colorado Springs, Colorado; PhD from Michigan State University.

**LeRoy Johnston, Jr.**—Psychologist, Christian and Missionary Alliance, Manheim, Pennsylvania; PhD from Florida State University.

**Becky Lewis**—Coordinator of Family Ministries, Frontiers, High Wycombe, England; BS from the California Institute of Technology.

**Tim Lewis**—Field Director and Deputy General Director, Frontiers, High Wycombe, England: MA from Western Conservative Baptist Seminary and MA from William Carey International University.

**Brent Lindquist**—President, Link Care Center, Fresno, California; PhD from California School of Professional Psychology, Fresno, California.

**Sandra Mackin**—Missionary, Campus Crusade for Christ International, Manila, The Philippines; MA from the International School of Theology, San Bernadino, California.

**Kathy Narramore**—Missions Pastor at Whittier Area Baptist Fellowship, Whittier, California; BA from Ausbury College.

**Kelly O'Donnell**—Psychologist, Youth With A Mission, Amsterdam, The Netherlands; PsyD from Rosemead School of Psychology, Biola University.

**Michele Lewis O'Donnell**—Psychologist, Youth With A Mission, Amsterdam, The Netherlands; PsyD from Rosemead School of Psychology, Biola University.

**John Powell**—Professor, Counseling Center, Michigan State University; PhD from the University of Missouri.

**Jarrett Richardson**—Psychiatrist, Mayo Clinic, Rochester, Minnesota; MD from John Hopkins University School of Medicine.

**Hans Ritschard**—Doctoral Candidate, Graduate School of Psychology, Fuller Theological Seminary; MA from Fuller Theological Seminary.

**Esther Schubert**—Consulting Physician in Missionary Psychiatry, Anderson, Indiana; MD from Indiana University, Department of Medicine.

**Peter Shedlosky**—Director of Human Resource Development, Youth With A Mission, Sunland, California; MA from Azusa Pacific University.

**Gary Strauss**—Associate Professor, Rosemead School of Psychology, Biola University; EdD from Northern Illinois University.

**Ruth Tucker**—Visiting Professor, Trinity Evangelical Divinity School; PhD from Northern Illinois University.

**Frances White**—Professor, Wheaton College Graduate School; PhD from the University of Maryland.

**Kenneth Williams**—International Counselor, Wycliffe Bible Translators, Idyllwild, California; PHD from United States International University.

# Introduction

We are immersed in an epoch of unprecedented opportunity for world evangelization. The missionary force is rapidly growing, with the number of missionaries from the Two-Thirds World expected to exceed that of Westerners within a few years. Major political and social changes are opening up opportunities for the gospel to penetrate previously unreached places and peoples; and there is a growing commitment of the Church to mobilize and coordinate its many resources to decisively thrust into unevangelized areas. These are exciting times indeed!

But these are also perilous times. Pushing back the frontiers of darkness that have enveloped whole people groups is fraught with difficulties. Sickness, burnout, and death are all real possibilities for missionaries—and in certain settings almost inevitable. Make no mistake about it: obeying the Lord's command to disciple the nations has and always will be costly. It is risky business.

The current effort to reach the world's unreached requires hardy folk who are willing to work together, make sacrifices, become vulnerable, and serve the Lord whole-heartedly in the midst of stressful, challenging situations. It also necessitates a concomitant, cooperative effort to support and nurture the missionary personnel involved in these new endeavors. Both are needed as we seek to put greater closure on the Great Commission.

## Member Care

It is encouraging to note the growing contributions to missionary care by agencies, consultants, and missionaries themselves. So much so in fact, that a field has now emerged devoted entirely to the care of mission personnel. *Member care*, a term which is frequently used to describe this field, refers to the commitment of resources for the development of missionary personnel by mission agencies, sending churches, and other missions-related groups. It is basically synonymous with *missionary care*, and I have chosen to use both terms interchangeably throughout this volume.

Member care is concerned with keeping mission personnel and their families healthy, resilient, and effective. Pre-field training, field orientation, field coaching, personnel departments, pastoral counselors, and reentry preparation are but a few of the many ingredients needed for a successful member care program. Member care serves as a handmaiden to the missions task, supporting missions personnel from candidacy through retirement. As such it is an ongoing and strategic means to help missionaries get their job done.

## Book Background

This book has been written with a wide audience in mind: missionaries, leaders, administrators, support staff, mission professors, and member care workers. It represents a collaborative effort to address some of the cutting edges concerning the care and development of mission personnel. Twenty-three authors were involved in writing the chapters of this volume, with six of these also serving as consulting editors for different sections.

For the most part I have selected topics that have not been written on extensively. One of my underlying desires in assembling this book was to fill in some of the gaps in both the literature on and practice of member care. Towards this end I have deliberately avoided emphasizing missionary families and missionary children (MKs), cross-cultural adjustment, reentry issues, and pre-field training. These are, of course, important topics, but ones which already take up a large portion of the extant literature and current focus of the member care field. My intent is to break new ground and stimulate innovative ideas.

As for the articles themselves, they are practical, easy to read, and filled with a variety of examples and case illustrations. There are five discussion questions at the end of each chapter to stimulate further ideas and help readers apply the material to their lives and mission settings.

My one regret is that I was not able to put together articles devoted entirely to member care issues and practices from the perspectives of missionary personnel from the Two-Thirds World. Nevertheless, several authors have been careful to discuss the cross-cultural relevancy of the material which they present.

## Book Overview

This volume is divided into five sections, with each section beginning with an introduction by the consulting editor or editors.

Part One, *Missionary Care Overview*, provides conceptual and historical perspectives on the practice of member care. It looks at the big picture, and includes articles on member care philosophy and models, basic issues for missionaries, and pastoral support structures.

Part Two, *Counseling and Clinical Care*, includes five articles on the prevention and treatment of serious problems. There is an update on missionary selection practices and a summary of the clinical disorders that can affect missionaries. Specific approaches and techniques for helping missionaries are described: stress management, short-term counseling, and crisis intervention.

Part Three, *Team Development*, explores the dynamics and care of teams. What does it take to work together effectively? How can members of multinational teams better understand and harmonize their differences? How can team building tools, field coaching, field leaders, and field consultation strengthen missionary teams?

Part Four, *Mission Agencies and Member Care*, looks at the crucial role that the mission agency plays in the care of its people. A framework is presented for understanding how organizations can function in a healthy manner. Also included are articles on career development, the ethical care of staff, and ways to support leaders.

Part Five, *Future Directions*, identifies both the upcoming challenges of member care and the opportunities to develop innovative services. Topics include training member care workers, the strategic role of sending churches, and setting up member care consultations and missionary support centers.

It is my hope that this volume will encourage missionary personnel around the world and further equip them for their work. May it be a source of blessing to those who have given so much of themselves to reach into the uttermost parts of the earth for the sake of the Lord Jesus.

# PART ONE
## MISSIONARY CARE OVERVIEW

# Part One
# Missionary Care Overview

*John Powell*

Consulting Editor

Missionary care—a means of encouraging and developing those on the front lines of world evangelization. This type of care was demonstrated by the Lord during His earthly ministry, is recorded of the early church in the Acts of the Apostles, and can be found in various forms throughout mission history. It is reflected in the wisdom of Proverbs and in the devotions of the Psalms. Missionary care, also referred to as *member care*, involves supportive relationships and services which promote ongoing adjustment and growth. It also acknowledges the reality of human frailties, the existence of spiritual warfare, and the need for God's sustaining grace.

We are all aware that missions is costly. Sacrifice and suffering are the frequent companions of missionaries. There are high risks and sometimes apparently low gains. World evangelization exacts a price in human resources that can only be balanced by the eternal results that it produces. Sensitive and continuing care are needed to support those called to this divine and demanding task.

But what types of care do missionaries need? How has it been provided in the past? And how can mission agencies develop balanced, effective member care programs for their people? Part One of this book addresses these important questions. Its five articles span the member care terrain, providing a bird's-eye view of its nature, practice, and relevance to missionary health and ministry effectiveness.

The first chapter, by Drs. Kelly and Michele O'Donnell, introduces the concept of member care and overviews its parameters. Kelly and Michele see member care as a commitment to develop missionary personnel throughout their entire careers. They describe proactive strategies for care and include specific applications for improving member care in an organization. The chapter finishes with a synopsis of the member care programs provided by three separate mission organizations.

No consideration of member care would be complete without some understanding of its historical development. In the next chapter, entitled "Historical Notes on Missionary Care," Dr. Ruth Tucker and Dr. Leslie Andrews review eight representative cases involving Protestant missionaries or their family members who experienced significant adjustment struggles at various times in their lives. Ruth and Leslie point out that attitudes and philosophies regarding member care have evolved over the years concurrent with changes in missiological convictions and strategies. A major part of the article is also devoted to surveying recent trends and resources that have shaped the current practice of member care. This chapter will be a stimulus for missionary personnel and member care workers alike to dig even deeper into the fascinating yet relatively uncharted history of member care in missions.

In the third article, Dr. Leroy Johnston expresses a number of practical concerns in missionary life and relates them to Abraham's experiences as described in Hebrews. He orients his comments around five primary issues of relevance for missionaries: obedience, perseverance, trust, perspective, and testing. LeRoy's thesis is that the preeminent issue in missionary care—and in missionary life—is the missionary's relationship with God. Many of the challenges facing missionaries can be subsumed under this primary concern. This article has a refreshing pastoral feel to it; the author encourages us onward in our missionary call and walk with God.

Mutual care—the building up of one another in love—is viewed by many to be the central ingredient in staff care. This is true for the author of the next chapter, Dr. Ken Williams, whose article "A Model for Mutual Care in Missions" explores the many ways that missionary personnel can uphold and support one another. Ken presents many helpful examples of how missionaries can encourage each other during pre-field preparation, on-field ministry, and assignment back home. The final section outlines a counselor training program offered by Wycliffe to further equip missionaries with important people-helping skills.

Chapter five, by Barry Austin, identifies several pastoral structures that are applicable to different mission settings: prayer partnerships, small groups, personnel departments, pastoral coordinators, and the local church. Barry offers several suggestions on the practicalities—the do's and don'ts—of setting up these structures. Last of all, he covers the important roles that leaders play in modeling and initiating staff care.

The member care terrain, as highlighted by the five articles in this section, is quite broad, ranging from the informal, mutual care that staff provide each other to the more formal, structured programs of care that often involve specialized services. As the opportunities and practical realities in missions shift, agencies will need to adjust their formal and informal efforts at member care accordingly. They must acknowledge the changing trends in missions and keep abreast with the needs and resources important for their members' personal growth, satisfaction, and effectiveness. How encouraging it is to see the growing number of mission agencies that are taking this exhortation to heart!

# 1

*Kelly O'Donnell*
*Michele Lewis O'Donnell*

# Perspectives on Member Care in Missions

What helps missionaries not only to survive but to excel in missions? How can agencies effectively support their missionaries? We would like to explore these two important questions by looking at the nature and scope of "member care."

Member care is the ongoing commitment of resources and potential resources by mission agencies, sending churches, and related mission organizations for the development of missionary personnel. It is an investment into everyone belonging to the mission—including adults as well as children, church planters as well as home office staff, candidates as well as those retiring from the field. It is also concerned with both personal and professional growth.

Member care is more or less synonymous with "missionary care." In the business world it is referred to as "human resource development" (McLagan, 1989); among the missions community it is often called pastoral care or personnel development. While the term *member care* is relatively new to missions, its practice is not. We are encouraged by the growing quality of missionary care services provided by mission agencies. Several examples of the current services and types of resources available for missionary personnel are described in chapters two and 21 of this book.

---

This chapter is a revision of the authors' article, "The Increasing Scope of Member Care" (1990, *Evangelical Missions Quarterly*, 26, 418-428). Used by permission.

## Five Facets of Member Care

There are many ways of looking at member care. First, member care can be viewed as a *structured program* that an agency sets up, involving different services (counseling, staff orientation) and different service providers (cross-cultural trainers, personnel directors). Member care within a mission agency, however, should be based on more than a formal program or a specialist function; neither is it embodied in a specific department. Rather it is founded upon the ongoing and informal mutual care that staff provide one another.

Second, member care involves a *philosophy of ministry* focusing on the care and growth of staff. This philosophy addresses the mutual benefits and responsibilities between members of the organization and the organization itself—that is, how members of the organization are to serve the organization and vice versa. The common element in any effective member care philosophy is a proactive commitment to staff *development*.

Next, member care is an *ethical necessity*. More than some optional commodity or benefits package, member care is an organizational responsibility. Members of a missionary community are valued and nurtured not just for their contributions, but primarily because it is the Biblical and right thing to do.

Fourth, member care is an *inter-disciplinary field*, drawing on the concepts and contributions from the behavioral and mental health sciences. It has a growing, recognized body of literature, specific types of practitioners/helpers, and various techniques for effecting staff development. Currently though, member care is still a young, somewhat amorphous field, and one which needs greater definition as to its parameters within a missions context.

Finally, member care can be seen as a *movement*, comprised of a growing number of missionaries, mission leaders, and member care workers. It is a trans-organizational, God-directed phenomenon, specifically designed to support the increasing number of missionaries and in preparation for the current and upcoming harvest of peoples throughout the earth.

## Signs of Member Care

Member care encompasses both visible structures and invisible processes within an organization. Some of the visible marks of member care include personnel assistance programs such as crisis counseling, as well as career guidance, pre-field and reentry orientation seminars, personnel development departments, and support groups. Member care is also invisible, in that it is an attitude, a posture, and a value woven into the fabric of organizational culture. As such, it reflects itself in the policies, practices, and "established ways of doing things" which characterize an organization.

While the primary responsibility for personal growth rests with missionaries themselves, the missionary agency and community also play important roles. Agencies and communities instill values, reinforce certain work habits, and establish social and work environments that can either help or hinder missionary growth and performance. Field leaders in particular are influential through their leadership styles and the behaviors they model.

We recall a certain group of missionaries which struggled with low morale, interpersonal strife, and a high drop-out rate as they provided primary health care services to the poor. This group excelled in missionary zeal, yet lacked a basic member care structure to help sustain them during their demanding daily schedules. The leaders valued hard work and perseverance but had difficulty showing empathy to members who needed time off or otherwise struggled with the work. Nor were there organized times set apart where team members could openly share their struggles and feelings with each other. This stoic approach to ministering in an inherently difficult mission setting, along with the crippling absence of pastoral care, resulted in needless staff casualties.

## Member Care in Proverbs

There is a straightforward piece of advice concerning member care in the book of Proverbs. While the context addresses the care of animals, an application can also be made to the care of humans, and in this case, missionaries.

*Know well the condition of your flocks*
*And pay attention to your herds*
*For riches are not forever*
*Nor does a crown endure to all generations.*
*(Proverbs 27:23,24 NASB)*

The admonition is to thoroughly understand the characteristics and condition of the people with whom we have been entrusted. In other words, what are the missionaries under our care like? What kinds of strengths, weaknesses, and personalities do they have? How are they doing? It also points to the importance of being alert to their needs and continually focusing on their well-being.

Note also the use of the terms "flocks" and "herds," both in the plural. Any given mission has different groupings of people such as departments, bases, families, and regions. Each group requires special and individualized care. Frontier church planters, for example, working in a restricted access country, will need different supportive services compared to clerical workers serving in the home office.

Finally, the rationale for such care is given. Riches (personnel) do not last forever. Nor does a crown (anointing) necessarily continue. The text goes on to describe how proper care will continue to yield results even during seasons of hardship and scarcity. What does all of this mean for mission agencies? Simply this. Without proper missionary care there will be no missionaries. And without missionaries there can be no missions.

## Questions about Member Care in Missions

Missionaries and leaders periodically express concerns about the philosophy and implementation of member care. Much of the concern seems to center not so much on the need for staff care, but on its possible overemphasis. Too much member care, it is felt, can become a distraction and ultimately make workers less resilient and effective.

Here are several questions that frequently surface when we have discussed the role of member care in missions. They raise important issues which a mission agency must resolve as it considers how it will provide member care for its people.

1. Will member care turn our staff into weak, dependent people, making them overly introspective, minimizing their need to develop strong character qualities and living by faith, and/or stirring up issues that they really do not need to address?

2. Is member care an attempt to recreate a comfortable Western suburban lifestyle on the field with its attendant perks and benefits, and thus minimize the legitimate place of sacrifice and suffering that is part of missions?

3. Will staff become demanding and expect the organization to do things that it either cannot do or is not responsible for doing?

4. Who determines which services are really necessary, the cross-cultural relevance and effectiveness of these services, and which people are qualified to provide member care?

5. Will member care set up a divisive dichotomy between task-oriented people and care-oriented people?

6. Do member care workers and advocates really understand the realities of adjustment and survival in missions, and do they have what it takes to really make it in missions themselves?

7. To what extent do staff project their unresolved, personal issues onto the organization, inappropriately viewing it as some type of parental figure that is not adequately caring for its "children?"

8. How realistic is it to assume that member care services will prevent the majority of staff casualties and attrition?

9. Is missionary life really more stressful than life back home, or that of missionaries of the past, requiring large doses of member care services to keep staff people going?

10. How appropriate is it to let our people serve in difficult and dangerous situations, especially when there are not sufficient member care resources to support them?

11. How do agencies develop the resources to improve and maintain their member care programs, as well as deal with agency policies, structures, and personnel that may resist improvement in such services?

## Member Care Strategies

In this section we describe a few member care approaches that can help staff become more healthy as people and effective in ministry. These approaches include: staff development, a life span emphasis, proactive interventions, resource development, and mutual support.

### Staff Development

Member care seeks to promote both the adjustment and development of staff. Adjustment implies being able to cope with the various challenges of missionary life. It involves a basic level of adapting to the new culture, relating harmoniously with colleagues, and performing adequately at one's job. Development, however, goes a step further to include the personal growth of missionaries through character formation, spiritual maturation, skill acquisition, and competence in cross-cultural living. Development, rather than adjustment, is the opposite of maladjustment. These distinctions may be diagramed along the following continuum.

| maladjustment | adjustment | development |
|---|---|---|
| (disease/disorder) | (maintenance/coping) | (competence/growth) |

Staff development is not automatic. Nor is it necessarily a by-product of missionary life. It must be worked at and carefully nurtured. While personal development is neither the goal nor the primary motivation for missions, it nonetheless plays a vital role in job satisfaction, performance, and length of service with the organization.

An underemphasis on development usually results in both individual and agency stagnation. An overemphasis, on the other hand, can lead to excessive self-absorption and drifting from the original purposes of the agency. A missionary need not be reluctant to ask, "How have I grown as a person through my missions experience?" Yet this must also be paired with, "How have I contributed to the development of my mission agency and the fulfillment of its goals?" Clearly a balance is needed.

## Life Span Emphasis

Member care is a commitment to the long-term care of staff over the course of their lives. One useful framework for understanding the experience of career missionaries is a life span approach which identifies and studies different developmental stages. The thought here is that missionaries and their families need special support as they deal with the various developmental tasks at each stage of their life (O'Donnell, 1987).

Consider, for example, the missionary family of four returning home on furlough where the parents are experiencing mid-life issues (questioning of career choice, re-working their marital roles), and where the two children have recently entered into adolescence (trying to fit into a peer group and establish a sense of group identity). Add to this the adjustment demands experienced during the reentry process (setting up house, deputation, schooling). The result is a considerable amount of stress for the family and its members as they seek to negotiate these simultaneous challenges.

All of these experiences and developmental tasks are normal, yet must be anticipated and understood. Support for the missionaries must thus be distributed throughout the entire life cycle (from infancy through old age) and throughout the various missionary stages (from recruitment through retirement), not just during candidacy school, annual retreats, or times of crises.

## Proactive Interventions

Proactive member care actively attempts to prevent problems and enthusiastically advocates missionary care. It is initiating and anticipatory, the opposite of "reactive" (Gardner, 1987). Here are a few proactive tools from our "bag of missionary development strategies" which we regularly use.

1. *Going into the community.* We seek out different individuals or teams at the locations where they minister, rather than waiting for them to come to our more formal and possibly threatening counseling offices. Our services are thus more accessible and acceptable to our staff.

2. *Action research.* We periodically initiate relevant organizational or program studies which will strengthen staff and improve the quality of life in the mission community. An example is studying reasons for missionary attrition, sharing the results with the leadership, and then encouraging change where possible. The goal of such research is change, not just new information.

3. *Needs and resource assessment.* This involves working with all or part of a missions community to assess their felt needs and then finding ways to meet these needs. One example would be creating a task force of concerned individuals to discuss and improve the training opportunities for non-Western missionaries within the mission agency.

4. *Identifying groups at risk.* Groups are identified within the mission or community that are susceptible to inordinate stressors or crises, and especially those who may not have access to important supportive resources. Some examples would be expecting parents who do not understand the system of prenatal medical care in the new culture, mission executives who travel frequently and are experiencing excessive work pressures, or missionary mothers who feel isolated from the mainstream work of the mission by virtue of their full-time role as parents.

5. *Advocacy.* This is a willingness to sensitively and openly support individuals, teams, or ministries that do not or may not have access to important organizational resources. For instance, toddlers may not have a well-staffed, day-care facility while their missionary parents work; or missionaries may leave the mission hurting and need additional follow-up care from the mission.

## Resource Development

We work from the assumption that enough resources exist, or potentially exist, within a mission organization to maintain and develop the well-being of its members. Given the reality of limited resources, however, creative investment of resources into staff, careful planning, and innovative services must be the rule (O'Donnell, 1986). For example, if there is a shortage of trained counselors within an agency, consider making referrals to missions-minded counselors outside the organization, or doing more group rather than individual counseling, or offering counselor training seminars to better equip missionaries in peer counseling. A little innovation goes a long way.

Oftentimes it is organizational policy which determines how available resources will be used. One of the most strategic ways to develop member care resources, then, is to influence the area of "policy-making." This is where some emotional sparks can fly. The goal here is not merely to "lobby" for more member care resources. Nor is it solely to push for policies which channel more money, additional staff, building space, or equipment into member care-related services. Rather the goal is first, to accurately represent the needs of staff and then second, to present and discuss creative ways to allocate and develop needed resources. Appropriate policies will hopefully flow out of this process.

### Mutual Support

Who is responsible for member care? Everyone! Missionaries, home office staff, mission executives, financial and prayer supporters, and one's sending church back home are all involved. Hebrews 3:13 exhorts us to "encourage one another day after day." Such mutual care is the essence and the medium of member care—the *sine qua non*. It is not confined to one specific department, such as the "Personnel Department," or one particular ministry, such as pastoral counseling. Member care is a mutual and inclusive process which ultimately affects and is affected by every member of the mission.

## Cross-Cultural Aspects of Member Care

Providing supportive member care services to staff from different cultures is always a challenge. Care is needed to ensure that one does not offend or even alienate another member, as what is an acceptable practice in one culture may not be so in another. For example, given a cross-cultural context, when is it appropriate to approach someone outside one's family for help ("bearing one another's burdens," Galatians 6:2), or to what degree can one be candid about his/her frustrations with team members ("speaking the truth to one another," Ephesians 4:25)? In most cases it takes getting to know both the different culture—keeping in mind the variations within that culture—and the staff members from the different cultures, in order to get a feel for how best to provide member care. Member care workers, especially those providing counseling and other mental health services, must also reflect upon their own cultural backgrounds as they seek to work in broad cultural contexts (Beck, 1990).

But how exactly does one begin to assess some acceptable ways to practice member care? What areas should a mission agency and member care workers consider? Here are three broad areas to help explore the cross-cultural relevancy of member care services. Use these items as a type of grid to guide the information you need in order to understand the person/culture in focus.

1. Identify the work style, leadership style, teaching style, and decision-making style with which individuals and their respective cultures feel most comfortable.

2. Identify the way they view problems, illnesses, causes and treatment of psychological disorders, ways to meet needs, and the role of helpers.

3. Identify the nature of their relationships with family/children, desired relationships with staff, and preferred level of involvement in the local community.

Working through these three areas takes some doing, and in some ways trying to come up with definitive answers is idealistic. Nonetheless, a determined attempt to develop member care services that are both acceptable to members from different cultures and responsive to their needs, is not only appreciated, but part of any effective member care program.

## Applications

What are some of the formal and informal avenues in which staff can be involved in providing and receiving member care? Here are some examples.

1. *Enhancing spiritual life*. Helping to organize special retreats, approaching leadership for personal prayer, holding weekly Bible studies.

2. *Children's ministries*. A creche for preschoolers, regular clubs or activities for children and teenagers, alumni follow-up programs for MK boarding schools.

3. *Increasing the sense of community*. Weekly small groups for support, community newsletters, community events such as picnics, meals together, and sports days.

4. *General supportive services*. A "pastoral care" team that monitors the needs of staff; career, financial, reentry, and retirement planning; professional counseling services; field pastoring and field coaching; visitation of sick members.

5. *Training opportunites*. Monthly seminars given by different staff members, programs for leadership development, correspondence courses for missionaries in remote areas.

How can a mission agency plan for the growth needs of its people? Basically, a commitment to an ongoing needs assessment process along with frank discussions among the leaders and staff are required. Keep in contact with each other. It is also helpful to appoint a member care task force or committee to oversee the various aspects of staff care and development. This team can meet and pray regularly. In short, prioritize member care, and integrate it into the life of your organization. Do not leave it up to chance!

## Examples of Member Care Programs

We have asked three mission agencies to briefly describe their perspectives on member care and the types of services that they provide. Here is what member care looks like for Wycliffe Bible Translators, the Foreign Mission Board of the Southern Baptist Convention, and The Evangelical Alliance Mission.

## Wycliffe Bible Translators

As a faith mission, Wycliffe (WBT) is a cooperative rather than a company. This means we have to take care of ourselves and each other. We do that in two general ways.

The first is *sequential care*, that is, all along the member's life cycle he or she is given full information in order to make wise choices. Early in their association with WBT, members are screened thoroughly and prepared as fully as possible in practical, technical, interpersonal, and cross-cultural areas. On-field care takes the form of orientation, allocation, supervision, workshops, seminars, and consultant help. Furlough care is expressed in advisory guidance. Though each member is responsible for his/her personal financial support, the organization has its own insurance coverage for health, life, and automobile, and a system of emergency funds when a member's funds do not come in.

The second is *specialized care*, types of help not needed by everyone. The Children's Education Department (CHED) places and supervises 350 to 400 teachers in 68 established educational programs around the world. CHED is developing an itinerant teacher program and working hard to internationalize aspects of the curriculum to meet the needs of member children from 36 countries. Six medical doctors serve the members in an advisory, record-keeping, and research capacity. Over 20 full-time and part-time counselors provide therapeutic, preventive, and consultant help from 10 locations. Thirteen career counselors work in nine countries. Spiritual encouragement is a responsibility assumed by each entity through a spiritual life committee, retreats, meetings, and so on, as well as by the ministry of the organization's counselors and chaplains.

Areas where we could improve are: pre-field preparation of families; pastoral care and spiritual life enhancement; reentry programs for young people and adults; ongoing help for adult MKs; more on-site training for field members whose tasks have changed; planning for retirement; housing and reduced assignment for elder members, of whom we have 322 over 65 years of age.

We need more funds and trained personnel to serve in all these areas. As Wycliffe has grown to its present size of 6,000 plus members, and 4,000 plus dependent children, the number of those prepared to serve as supportive personnel staff has not grown commensurately.

What is Wycliffe's ethos on member care? Basically, we seek for sturdy folk who will need minimal member care—hardy, resilient, godly individuals. Then we look in the mirror and down the roster of our colleagues and friends and realize that all of us are frail and need a Father's care and the care of our brothers and sisters within the organization, as well as the commitment of the organization to help us when our personal storm gets too strong. Our organization has made member care one of its top priorities and is moving in the direction of improving both our sequential and specialized care.

—*Laura Mae Gardner, International Coordinator,*
*Counseling Ministries and Personnel.*

### Foreign Mission Board, Southern Baptist Convention

Career missionaries are supported in keeping with the assumption that they are the core people in our foreign mission program. Auxiliary personnel have similar support while on the field. From initial correspondence to appointment, on through their career and retirement, a network of resources is intended to encourage spiritual, emotional, relational, and physical health.

Nine area directors and 18 associates overseas have regular field contact with missionaries. The associates particularly carry pastoral and counseling responsibilities. Two family consultants work from the home office and support orientation resources, personal and family needs, and resources for MKs. All staff are viewed as a support team and, of course, missionaries give care to each other through mission structures and informally. A network of Christian counselors and other professionals is used for referral and for furloughing missionaries. Some of them are asked to lead conferences and offer counseling on the field, from two weeks to several months.

The more structured care is extended in the following ways:

*Before Appointment*
1. Personal and group interviews for candidates.
2. Meeting with parents and family of candidates.
3. Follow-up letters to parents.

*Orientation for New Missionaries*
1. Seven weeks of field preparation.
2. Personal and family counseling.
3. Special children's orientation.
4. Personal development groups each week.

*On-Field*
1. Continued orientation.
2. Language program support.
3. Annual mission meetings for planning and fellowship with many missions, having a second meeting at mid-year for prayer and spiritual enrichment.
4. The mission organization provides a personal and family support system.
5. Local visits by field staff.
6. Occasional mission-regional MK retreats.
7. Work-related resource conferences.

8. Pre-furlough conference for each missionary with evaluation feedback and furlough planning.

*Furlough*

1. Financial support for continuing education and training.

2. Furlough conference (children included for those on their first furlough), with pre-retirement program for those on their next-to-last furlough.

3. Personal and family counseling available.

4. Educational assessment for children with assistance for special needs.

5. A number of furnished residences provided through local churches.

*Retirement*

1. Special celebration during a major meeting of our trustees where each is recognized, a monetary gift is given, three days of seminars on personal and family needs, and two days of seminars on financial and health information updates.

2. Each is added to the Mission Fellowship, a network of mission information and continuing mission support.

3. All missionaries, including those who have retired, are kept on a prayer calendar made available to all church members, that all will be specially held up in prayer on their birthdays.

*Missionary Children (MKs)*

1. Scholarships are provided to MKs to assist in university and other post-high school training.

2. A staff person makes visits to MKs at school for updates and support.

3. MKs are encouraged to attend reentry conferences and special retreats to meet additional needs.

—*Truman S. Smith, Senior Family Consultant*


## The Evangelical Alliance Mission

The Evangelical Alliance Mission (TEAM), which celebrated its 100th year in 1990, has had some components of member care in place for many years. Other programs are more recent, or still only emerging.

The ethos of the organization is generally supportive of people's needs. Administrative leadership works to promote a "family spirit" which makes the organization feel smaller than its active missionary force of 1,100.

Birthday cards, newsletters, and field visits by administrators promote warmth and a sense of belonging. Prayer retreats and annual conferences also contribute to a climate of mutual support and encouragement. Some fields have developed "Barnabas Programs" that team up first-term missionaries with experienced workers.

TEAM responded early as an organization to meet medical and retirement needs by providing a medical assistance program and a solid pension program. A staff medical doctor oversees health care needs and is also available for consultation.

Five years ago TEAM instituted furlough debriefing interviews designed to review and assist with personal, family, emotional, and reentry issues. The program has been well-received by the missionaries.

The office of Pastoral Care and Counseling is now in its eighth year. It provides counseling services, coordinates referrals, and acts as an advocate with mental health professionals. The range of services includes: spiritual encouragement; individual, marriage, and family counseling; conflict resolution; and personal problem-solving.

A recent development in TEAM's member care program is the establishment of the Franson Training Center. This resource center provides opportunities for training, personal growth, and individual research. TEAM believes that ongoing training and personnel development are essential to the health and well-being of its people.

The Evangelism and Church-Planting School, which has been organized since 1983, provides practical, continuing, professional development for the church-planting missionary.

Stress management workshops have been conducted on over half of our 30 fields during the past five years. These workshops focus on how stress affects various areas of life and provide practical, biblically-based coping strategies.

During the past few years we have conducted several overseas servant leadership and management skills workshops to train grassroots leadership within the organization. The workshop assists the individual in identifying and developing task and people skills specific to the missionary context. More than three hundred have attended to date.

Another new program is called "Explore." This career planning and personal development workshop is designed for people considering overseas experience. For three days we help people gather data on themselves. We then attempt to help them to assess their strengths and weaknesses, design a program for personal growth in areas of weakness, and think through the implications of pursuing a missionary career.

We believe there is much yet to do in member care and training. On the drawing board for the future are a furlough institute program and a reevaluation of portions of our candidate school to better prepare people for language learning and entering new cultures. A real danger exists for older agencies like TEAM to rest on "the way things have always been done." We must not assume past programs are sufficient for meeting current needs. We must remain sensitive to the needs of people as we serve them.

—*Lee Hotchkis, Pastoral Care Consultant*

## Questions for Discussion

Here are some important questions for an agency to consider as it seeks to improve its member care services. Be sure to discuss these questions thoroughly and pray to see how the Lord would guide you. 1. What is our overall philosophy of member care? How important is it really for us? How is member care reflected in our organizational culture and lifestyle?

2. Which services are already being provided, by whom, and where? Are they adequate, acceptable, and accessible?

3. What are the felt needs of our members? What groups may be at risk? How can we better prevent problems? What resources can we potentially develop to strengthen our missionaries?

4. How should we organize our services? Are our services sensitive to the cultural diversity reflected in our members?

5. How can we share member care resources with other agencies for each other's mutual benefit? What models for member care are being used by other agencies which might also be useful to us?

# References

Beck, J. (1990). Cultural reflection: A necessary task for the Christian psychotherapist. *Journal of Psychology and Theology, 18,* 123-129.

Gardner, L. (1987). Proactive care of missionary personnel. *Journal of Psychology and Theology, 15,* 308-314.

McLagan, P. (1989). Models for human resource development practice. *Training and Development Journal,* September, 49-59.

O'Donnell, K. (1986). Community psychology and unreached peoples: Applications to needs and resource assessment. *Journal of Psychology and Theology, 14,* 213-223.

O'Donnell, K. (1987). Developmental tasks in the life cycle of mission families. *Journal of Psychology and Theology, 15,* 281-290.

# 2

*Ruth Tucker*
*Leslie Andrews*

# Historical Notes on Missionary Care

In an age that has been termed the "Me Generation," it is difficult to imagine mission organizations not being actively involved in the mental and emotional well-being of their missionaries. From pre-appointment psychological testing and culture-shock seminars to re-entry debriefing and on-site marital counseling, mission boards directly and indirectly are more actively involved in personal and relational issues than virtually any other type of organization—religious or secular.

Historically, within Protestant missions, this was not the case. Mission societies held high the ideal of sacrifice. Strong faith in God, it was reasoned, was the prescription for a healthy mind and spirit. Dysfunctional families and co-dependent spouses had not yet been identified, and professional therapy was not an option. Self-reliance was the mark of a missionary—tempered only by dependence on God through prayer.

This perspective was not simply a product of Puritan piety or American frontier individualism. It is one that draws from the very essence of the Apostle Paul's message. His words in Philippians 4 sum up this outlook:

> *Do not be anxious about anything, but in everything, by prayer and petition, with thanksgiving, present your requests to God. And the peace of God, which transcends all understanding, will guard your hearts and your minds in Christ Jesus....I have learned to be content whatever the circumstances. I know what it is to be in need, and I know what it is to have plenty. I have learned the secret of being content in any and every situation whether well fed or hungry, whether living in plenty or in want. I can do everything through him who gives me strength....And my God will meet all your needs according to his glorious riches in Christ Jesus. (NIV)*

Yet, it is no secret that Paul himself had many needs and that he was often discouraged. In 2 Corinthians 1, he speaks of being "under great pressure, far beyond our ability to endure, so that we despaired even of life." Later on in chapter 11, he recounts physical abuse and dangers and deprivation of all kinds, and "besides everything else, I face daily the pressure of my concern for all the churches." Plain and simple, Paul was often stressed out. But the solution he offered was not rest—or even professional counseling.

But this happened that we might not rely on ourselves but on God, who raises the dead. He has delivered us from such a deadly peril, and he will deliver us. On him we have set our hope that he will continue to deliver us, as you help us by your prayers. (2 Cor. 1:9-11, NIV)

Paul's perspective here is instructive: personal dependence on God and collective prayer are essential for a missionary to be able to persevere in ministry.

It has been this biblical perspective that has dominated the attitude of missions over the centuries—a perspective that does not contradict the use of mental health professionals, but one that does not suggest a need for them either. It has not been until very recent times that mission societies have seriously considered the need for specially trained pastors, therapists, and counselors who can relate to the particular needs of missionaries.

In many respects mission boards have been influenced by the spirit of the times. They have bought into the contemporary focus on mental health. But it could also be argued that the modern advances in mental health do in fact aid the cause of missions much like the advances in other areas of health and medicine. Mission boards are deeply concerned that they do not repeat the errors of the past by ignoring the stress and strain associated with mission work.

Yet what actually did happen in the past with regards to the care of missionaries? How was member care practiced? And further, what are some of the trends in staff care that we are seeing today? This chapter will take a look at these questions and give some representative highlights of missionary care over the last 300 years and more recently during the last two decades.

## Early Examples of Missionary Adjustment and Care

One does not have to dig very deeply into Protestant missions heritage to find evidence of mental disorders. Indeed, some of the greatest names in the annals of missions history—including David Brainerd, David Livingstone, and C.T. Studd—would not have survived the battery of psychological tests most missionary candidates are now required to take. Other missionaries—both famous and obscure—suffered from serious depression and mental breakdowns.

## George Schmidt

In many instances mission board personnel or fellow missionaries made an effort to minister to the troubled missionary, but in some instances the mission exacerbated the problem by an utter lack of compassion and understanding. This was true for George Schmidt, a Moravian missionary who served as an itinerant evangelist in Europe following the great Moravian revival of 1727.

While serving in Austria, Schmidt faced harsh opposition from the Jesuits who deemed him a heretic deserving of punishment. He sought to elude his enemies to avoid arrest, but was captured and imprisoned in a dungeon cell for three years, during which time his companion died due to the mental and physical torment and deplorable prison conditions. Finally, after three more years of hard labor, Schmidt broke down under the pressure. He agreed to sign a revocation of his beliefs and was promptly released.

Here was a man who desperately needed the love and support of fellow Christians, but when he returned to the Moravian community of Herrnhut, he was shunned as an apostate. No sympathy or support awaited him there. He was seen as a failure. Devastated by the rejection, he returned to Austria in an effort to prove himself faithful, but was subsequently reassigned to South Africa in 1737.

In Africa, Schmidt faced opposition from Dutch Reformed ministers as he struggled to win converts among the Hottentots. At one point he was even chided by Count Nicolaus von Zinzendorf, the leader of the Moravians, for his harsh discipline: "You aim too much at the skin of the Hottentots and too little at the heart" (Kruger, 1967, p. 31). How sad that such advice was not heeded years earlier in Schmidt's own case. Perhaps he would have learned better how to deal with the native Africans.

## Dorothy Carey

The story of Dorothy Carey is another sad case of a mission board mishandling an individual who desperately needed understanding and moral support. Dorothy was married to William Carey, known as the "Father of Modern Missions." When he agreed to team up with Dr. John Thomas to serve as the Baptist Missionary Society's first missionaries, Dorothy was informed after the decision was made. She had three little children and was pregnant with the fourth, and felt no special call to spend the rest of her life in the disease infested interior of India. If her husband felt called, he would have to go alone.

But that solution was not satisfactory to Thomas or the board. After her fourth child was born, Thomas visited her and pressured her into going. To the director of the Baptist Missionary Society, he wrote: "I went back and told Mrs. Carey her going out with us was a matter of such importance

[that] her family would be dispersed and divided for ever—[that] she would repent of it as long as she lived" (Letter from John Thomas to Andrew Fuller, March 10, 1794, Baptist Missionary Society). She reluctantly agreed to go, fearing that God would punish her if she stayed home.

Thomas and the mission board failed to anticipate the consequences of forcing her to go against her will. Her first years in India were devastating for her. She endured poverty, loneliness, and debilitating illnesses, and worst of all, sorrow over the death of her five-year-old son. It was too much for her. She suffered a mental breakdown and was later described as being "wholly deranged."

### South Sea Islands

In some instances mission societies became very actively involved in the emotional well-being of their missionaries—though not always with the kind of advice and solutions we would expect today. Such was the case in the early nineteenth century when rumors of sex scandals began drifting back from the South Sea islands. It seems that some single male missionaries were not able to resist the lure of the beautiful island women. To insure such temptations would not taint their candidates, the directors of the American Board of Commissioners for Foreign Missions insisted the candidates marry before sailing to Hawaii. Six of the seven quickly found agreeable women and were married only days before departing in 1819.

Not all the hastily-arranged marriages worked. When the London Missionary Society learned that Henry Nott, a missionary to Tahiti, was co-habiting with a native woman, they insisted he abandon her for one of the four "godly young women" who had been sent out specifically to prevent such scandal. The woman chosen for Nott created more scandal than she alleviated, however. "When intoxicated she is absolutely mad and cares not what she does or says," observed the local missionary doctor. When she died some time later, he speculated that she "drank herself to death" (Gunson, 1978, p. 153). Whether she was troubled with alcoholism before she came to Tahiti or whether the problem surfaced after she arrived is not known, but for her and for many missionaries, the stress of culture shock and cross-cultural living, combined with loneliness, took its toll on their psychological well-being.

### David Brainerd

Depression was common—a problem often overlooked by mission societies. Consider the following accounts. David Brainerd, a missionary to the native Americans in the 18th century, was frequently tormented by loneliness and depression—a condition that is evident throughout his diary. Although he had been assigned to live and work with a veteran missionary couple who had seen success in their ministry, he chose to work alone and suffer the consequences: "I live in the most lonely melancholy desert, about eighteen miles from Albany," he lamented. Again, he wrote, "My heart was sunk....It seemed to me I should never have any success among the Indians. My soul was weary of my life. I longed for death, beyond measure" (Wynbeek, 1961, pp. 61-62).

### J. Hudson Taylor

Depression also plagued J. Hudson Taylor, the founder and director of the China Inland Mission. In 1868, after he and his family barely escaped from an angry mob of Chinese who burned their mission house in Yangchow, he faced public criticism, especially in the British press. In the months that followed, he became so discouraged that he succumbed to "the awful temptation...even to end his own life" (Pollock, 1962, p. 195). Today most mission agencies would be equipped to offer hospitalization or counseling, but in Taylor's day such was not an option. And there was no mission director to order him home; *he* was the director.

### A. B. Simpson

Another mission leader who suffered depression throughout much of his life was A.B. Simpson (1843-1919). According to his biographer, A.W. Tozer, just before he founded the Christian and Missionary Alliance, he plunged "into the slough of despond so deep that...work was impossible." It was a time of utter despair. "I wandered about," he later recalled, "deeply depressed. All things in life looked dark and withered" (Tozer, 1943, p. 71).

### Adoniram Judson

Sometimes periods of deep despair were caused by the death of a loved one—a trauma that was much a part of the mission experience in generations past. When Adoniram Judson, the great missionary pioneer to Burma, learned in 1826 that his wife Ann had died—soon to be followed by his baby daughter—his normal grieving process gradually turned into a mental disorder. He became a recluse and went out into the jungle and dug a grave, where he kept vigil, filling his mind with morbid thoughts of death. Spiritual desolation engulfed him: "God is to me the Great Unknown. I believe in him, but I find him not" (Anderson, 1972, p. 391).

Judson's recovery came not through psychiatric counseling or group therapy. Rather, it was aided by an outpouring of love and prayer from fellow missionaries. The years following that crisis were some of his most successful and productive years as a missionary.

## Mary Morrison

For Mary Morrison, the cause of her adjustment struggles—again, depression—was not as clear. She was the wife of Robert Morrison, the patriarch of China missions, and it is entirely possible that her frequent separations and loneliness contributed to her mental breakdown. Robert complained of lack of correspondence from friends and family back home, and Mary may have felt that neglect even more keenly. To a friend, Robert wrote: "Yesterday I arrived in Canton....I left my dear Mary unwell. Her feeble mind much harassed....My poor afflicted Mary....She walks in darkness and has no light" (Broomhall, 1924, p. 59). Her condition fluctuated back and forth in the years that followed until she died in 1821, after twelve years of marriage.

## Mary Livingstone

For Mary Livingstone, the wife of Africa's great missionary-explorer, David Livingstone, the problem was one of outright neglect. Because she and the little ones were not able to keep up the pace on his exploratory expeditions, he sent them back to England in 1852, where Mary found cheap lodging for herself and the children. It was a most distressing time for her, and the rumor among the mission community was that she had fallen into spiritual darkness and was drowning her sorrows in alcohol. When David finally returned five years later, he was a hero with no time for family. He made a quick visit home before launching a whirl-wind speaking tour.

One can only wonder where the directors of the London Missionary Society were during this time. Did they not recognize their responsibility in seeing that families such as the Livingstones were kept intact and in making sure that wives were not overwhelmed with depression? Perhaps they could be excused if Mary were off in some distant land, but she was right under their nose in London. Mary Livingstone was not an easy woman to deal with, but she deserved more attention than the mission gave her.

Not all missionaries, of course, suffered from such serious problems as those mentioned in the previous examples. Yet many of their needs were either overlooked by mission agencies or else could only be partially met by the fledgling member care services that were available. Missionaries were to depend on God for their well-being.

The early eras of Protestant missions were times of growth and experimentation for mission agencies. As they slowly matured, they developed better evangelistic strategies, clarified organizational structures and policies, and eventually in this century established more systematic services to care for their personnel.

# The Current Practice of Member Care

Significant shifts in member care practices have been occurring during the last 20 years. These shifts are reflected in several major trends, eight of which will be discussed in the remainder of this article. Specifically, we will be taking a look at trends in recruitment and selection, human service models, additional supportive services, flexible policies and programs, the care of missionary children, performance appraisals, local church involvement, and para-mission service agencies.

## Recruitment and Selection

Candidate screening has become an issue of great importance in the last two decades. Although it is tempting to assume that selecting the right candidates will guarantee their personal adjustment and success as missionaries, this is not always the case. With the rising incidence of abuse of all kinds within the general population, an increasing number of emotionally and psychologically bruised individuals are applying for missionary service. This current reality has required us to improve our testing and interview procedures. "How to screen for and reduce problems" continues as a major concern for personnel directors and leaders within mission agencies.

Candidates who may appear remarkably well-qualified for missionary service may have difficulty overseas, not only because of their background experiences, but because their ways of coping and achieving in their home culture simply do not work for them in their cross-cultural setting. No doubt this happened among missionaries of earlier generations, but usually the person became a "missionary drop out." Reducing missionary attrition and predicting missionary success are two goals to which more and more agencies are committing themselves.

## Human Service Models

Expectations and models for missionaries have changed. Under what can be referred to as the "missionary warrior model," earlier missionaries were called to endure hardship as "good soldiers of Jesus Christ." The mission's primary responsibility was to send them to the place of hardship, pray for them, and receive reports from them during furloughs.

More recently, however, there has been a growing interest by mission agencies to take responsibility for the holistic development of their people. For example, many mission agencies are now creating and filling member care positions in order to support and further equip their staff. In some instances, professional, in-house counselors are used to provide direct care to missionaries. In other cases, member care personnel refer missionaries to outside resource organizations. Although this "holistic" human service model is gaining respectability, funding these new services still poses a considerable challenge.

## Additional Member Care Services

Preventive pastoral care of field missionaries is one way in which missions are addressing the increasingly complex spiritual, emotional, and psychological needs of their missionary personnel. One mission identified pastoral care as the most prominent need facing its missionaries. In response to that need, the mission appointed "pastors to missionaries"—clergy couples who would visit the same field(s) year after year. In other instances, pastors, counselors, and/or psychologists are going to fields, some for short-term care and others for extended stays.

Many agencies are providing more opportunities for personal growth and in-service training. These opportunities are offered through retreats, team development sessions, workshops, and annual conferences.

Missions are also confronting the need to restore staff who become dysfunctional. Dysfunction frequently stems from burnout, cross-cultural adjustment struggles, pre-field problems, or moral failure. As one mission executive said, this often requires distinguishing between temporary versus long-term incapacitation.

One of the difficult decisions a mission must make is whether or not to bring a missionary home for help. One mission, for instance, made counseling help available to a couple on furlough who were experiencing marital difficulty. The problem seemed to have abated and so the couple was permitted to return to their overseas assignment. Within a few short months following furlough, however, the couple was once more struggling in their relationship with one another. The stresses of living in another culture, separated from normal support structures available in the homeland, had merely compounded the couple's marital distress. If adequate member care services were available overseas, the mission and/or couple would probably not face the dilemma of whether or not to "tough it out" or to return home.

Another form of member care has developed in response to the disruption missionaries experience in their ministries and personal lives due to international terrorism, national political chaos, and crime inflicted on them personally. Crisis response teams have emerged as a way of responding to these threats. Immediately upon release from their Muslim captors in the Philippines in 1992, for example, three missionary women and one child were flown to Manila where a crisis response team from Wycliffe (SIL) began attending to them in their trauma.

## Flexible Policies and Programs

Missions are developing more flexible ways of addressing the various needs of their people. Schooling for children is a good example. Parents frequently are presented with several educational options for their children, apprised of the pros and cons, and then encouraged to make informed choices based on their awareness of the possibilities, in contrast to earlier policies which often required that all children attend boarding school.

Other changes in policies have affected terms of service, furlough options, and retirement benefits. Furlough options typically range from a three-month leave every two years to a 12-month leave every four years, in contrast to previous 12-month leaves every six or seven years. One mission, for instance, grants three months of furlough time for every 12 months invested in direct service. Missionaries may then arrange the timing and length of their furloughs based on their family needs.

Improved health insurance policies and retirement plans are being made available. In the case of at least one mission, a cash bonus at retirement helps missionaries to make one-time big purchases, such as a home or automobile. Further, much more freedom is granted for missionaries to return home for additional training, furloughs, or in the event of a family emergency or death. While this practice potentially can complicate relationships with supporters who may not always understand why such frequent trips are required, it nevertheless enhances the missionary's sense of individualized care by the mission.

## Missionary Children's Care

Interest in the "missionary kid" (MK) grew rapidly in the 1980's. Earlier in the 1970's, the rise of the family and home schooling movements began to impact missions in important ways. Desiring to be faithful to their God-given responsibilities as parents, missionaries and candidates questioned the wisdom of sending their children away to boarding school. They tended to express their ambivalence in one of four ways: (1) choosing alternative forms of educating their children apart from boarding school; (2) switching missions; (3) returning to their home culture after their first term, or at the time their first child began school; or, (4) opting out of missions altogether.

Such pressure upon missions resulted in their taking a closer look at the needs of MKs. Few missions had structures within their organizations devoted to MK and family needs. Largely as a result of the International Conferences on Missionary Kids—held in Manila, 1984; Quito, 1987; and Nairobi, 1989—missions became more sensitized to the well-being of their MKs. Now missions provide a variety of support services to MKs such as transition seminars upon permanently re-entering their parents' home culture as well as the opportunity to return to the host culture in which the

MK grew up, along with his/her spouse, at the expense of the mission. In-house publications for MKs, such as "SIM Roots," "MK Communique," or "Catalyst" are now common ways to establish and maintain relationships among adult MKs.

## Performance Appraisals

There is a growing emphasis on improving accountability relationships for missionary personnel and mission organizations. Various missions have tried to implement evaluation processes at the end of a missionary's term of service and prior to departure for furlough. Sometimes this has worked well, other times not so well.

One mission, for instance, required that its field committees evaluate "problem families" one year prior to furlough. They were to evaluate all aspects of the ministry in order to determine whether or not the missionary family should be invited back. Field leaders found it difficult, however, to face up to and be the bearer of bad news and consequently would send a recommendation to the international office that "so-and-so needs counseling" with little more specificity.

Another problem, not yet resolved entirely, involves the apprehension to make use of counseling and assessment services on the part of missionaries themselves. At a time when mission leaders are becoming more and more open to psychological counseling, missionaries can be exceedingly reluctant to use psychological services due to negative connotations associated with seeking such help. Counseling can be perceived as "punishment," or a subtle type of performance appraisal, or even a sign of weakness rather than as an opportunity to grow.

A sub-set of the missionary community, single women, poses a particular challenge for field leaders who often are inadequately prepared for overseeing and working with these missionaries. Single women have often been discriminated against in ways such as living and housing allowances and leadership opportunities. While the typical trajectory for fulfillment in use of one's gifts remains open to men, at certain levels it is closed to women. Very few missions have women in field leadership roles or executive positions at the international level. In this case, the need is to hold the organization accountable in the way it uses or does not use its people—in this instance, its single women.

## Local Church Involvement

Increasingly individual local churches have assumed greater responsibility to provide long-term member care for the missionaries they send out. Consider the following example.

Whittier Area Baptist Church in California (described in chapter 22) trains missionary candidates from its congregation in the areas of self-awareness, marital relationships, and financial management. This church encourages the formation of support teams who develop personal relationships with these missionaries and maintain them through regular phone and fax contacts. Adult Sunday School classes adopt families of missionaries, while a Care Committee provides money for counseling, care, housing, and new clothes when missionaries return on furlough. The church even has a Training and Review Committee which functions specifically to do interventions in troubled situations. During the annual missions conference, a special service is held which is directed specifically to the healing of broken missionaries.

This church is but one example of many that, in conjunction with mission agencies, are actively caring for their missionaries.

## Para-Mission Service Agencies

Finally, a number of para-mission service agencies have been organized since the 1970's in order to serve the member care needs of mission agencies. *Mental Health and Missions* (MHM) is one such informal organization. MHM meets annually to bring together psychologists and others interested in issues like member care. The founders, Dr. John Powell and Dr. David Wickstrom, both consulting psychologists to missions, identified the need for mental health professionals who work in missions to have a forum for networking, sharing, and relating more knowledgeably with each other and with mission agencies. Since its founding in 1980, MHM has attracted approximately 240-250 people to its conference.

*Link Care* is one of the earliest para-mission agencies to be established. It is an outgrowth of an academic sabbatical in the early 1960's when Dr. Stanley Lindquist travelled around Europe visiting therapeutic centers and missionaries. As a result of affirmation received for his services, he began to provide counseling to missionaries back in the United States on an ad hoc basis. In the last 4-5 years, nearly 30 full-time staff at Link Care have served approximately 100 mission agencies in different ways, including candidate assessment, pre-field and on-field training, and short-term and long-term counseling services for missionaries.

Following World War II, *Missionary Internship* (MI) began as an effort to prepare former GIs for returning overseas as missionaries. Now MI serves approximately 60 agencies each year through its educational opportunities, including pre-field orientation, furlough missionary program, and special missions conferences.

*Interaction* was formed in the early 1970's under the leadership of David Pollock and services missions widely in providing transition seminars for returning MKs as well as missionaries. In addition, *MK-CART/CORE* emerged in the mid-1980's as an MK research agency working on behalf of member missions to identify, plan, implement, and evaluate research requested by these missions. Already two multi-mission research projects are nearing completion while a third longitudinal study is in development.

# Summary

Member care in earlier years was largely informal and unorganized; that is, when it even existed. If the mission or field leader were a caring person, then some type of member care may have happened. Significant shifts have been occurring, however, especially in the last 20 years, as reflected in the eight trends previously described.

Member care will play an increasing role in missions, serving the cause of Christ by preventing problems, supporting and developing missionary personnel, and restoring those who have become incapacitated. It will be a key to keeping the worldwide missionary force resilient and effective. Member care is more than just a trend. It is a crucial and practical mission strategy which is here to stay.

### Questions for Discussion

1. What can mission organizations learn from some of the member care practices of earlier Protestant missionary societies?

2. What other models may have been in operation over the years besides the "warrior model" described in this article?

3. Which of the eight recent trends described in this article have impacted your mission organization the most?

4. How can these two aspects of missionary life be balanced together: the reality of sacrifice and suffering in missions and the need for personal fulfillment and growth?

5. What might some of the future trends look like in the practice of member care?

# References

Anderson, C. (1972). *To the golden shore: The life of Adoniram Judson.* Grand Rapids: Zondervan.

Broomhall, M. (1924). *Robert Morrison: A master-builder.* New York: Doran.

Gunson, N. (1978). *Messengers of grace: Evangelical missionaries in the South Seas, 1797-1860.* New York: Oxford.

Kruger, B. (1967). *The pear tree blossoms: A history of the Moravian mission stations in South Africa, 1737-1869*. Cape Town, Republic of South Africa: Genedendal Printing.

Pollock, J. (1962). *Hudson Taylor and Maria: Pioneers in China*. Grand Rapids: Zondervan.

Tozer, A. (1943). *Wingspread: A. B. Simpson, a study in spiritual altitude*. Harrisburg: Christian Publications.

Wynbeek, D. (1961). *David Brainerd: Beloved yankee*. Grand Rapids: Eerdmans.

# 3

*LeRoy Johnston, Jr.*

# Core Issues in Missionary Life

My first real involvement in missions began in 1967. I was applying to a major missionary society for candidacy into their organization. Interviews, psychological testing, physical exams and various other evaluations transpired during this time. I was impressed with the procedures, especially the psychological evaluation process. I wondered if all this attention during the time of missionary candidacy would continue once stationed overseas.

Many good questions were asked by the personnel director. But with my limited missions background it was hard to appreciate the seriousness and implications of the questions. My answers came too easily.

I remember being asked about sending my children to boarding school. "No problem," I answered. It should be noted I was single at the time, and had not given much thought to children. Location was not an issue. I'd go anywhere, do anything. It all sounded adventuresome and spiritual. Anyway, I was not sure what I wanted to do or could do. I once heard a missions speaker say, "It is not ability but availability." That being the case, I certainly was available.

Disappointments frequently result from unrealistic expectations. This was definitely true in my early missions experience. Most candidates believe, as I did, that they will receive care and support from the people and the organization with which they associate. In most cases the missionary organization tries to do just that. There are pre-field and on-field orientation programs, regular formal evaluations during the term, field conferences and special retreats to provide times of renewal. Unfortunately, though, there will also be gaps—sometimes significant ones—in the supportive services that mission agencies provide their people. Disappointment, frustration, and even a sense of abandonment can result.

Agencies, like all people, have weaknesses and make mistakes. This must be clearly understood by candidates from the start. Expectations need to be adjusted.

It must not be assumed that candidates and missionaries, no matter how resilient they seem, are self-sufficient people. Adequate doses of member care are needed to keep them healthy and effective throughout their entire involvement with the agency.

All of this is to say that one initial issue for missionaries is to clearly understand any implicit or explicit expectations concerning the nature of their work and the types of supportive services that will be realistically available to them. Clarifying such mutual expectations through frank discussions with mission personnel is a must (Reapsome 1988).

## Cross-Sectional Issues

It is helpful to remember that missionary personnel come from various geographical, social, cultural, educational, and political backgrounds. Added to these different background influences are specific family of origin issues, inborn and developed capabilities, and life experiences. Each missionary then, is comprised of a unique "cross-section" of various elements in his or her background.

The selection process has a tendency to eliminate candidates who do not fit into specific criteria. Nevertheless, there are still major differences between missionaries, suggesting these different "cross-sectional slices" will experience the same issues in different ways. It is thus necessary to delineate and address the various issues of missionary life in terms of how they affect different types of missionaries.

One obvious category of difference involves the different roles that women and men usually have. Role ambiguity and role overload is a common occurrence for married women (Bowers, 1985). This is especially true for the wife/mother who struggles to balance the demands of work, marriage, children, and hospitality.

Then there is the category of the single person versus the married couple—one's marital status. The single female missionary, for example, has different issues compared to the missionary wife. One is the living situation. With whom does she live, especially if she is in a Muslim culture or the only single missionary in the area? The second is ministry assignment. What is she allowed to do in light of church and mission expectations? Sometimes work expectations can be poorly defined or else inappropriate. One single woman said, "I must think like a man, work like a horse, and act like a married woman." A third issue involves social relationships. The issue of singleness in some cultures can be problematic; certainly when it is perceived as being "abnormal." In addition, trying to conform to cultural expectations for dating, marriage expectations, and social companionship can be especially frustrating.

Another category that missionary issues cut across is term of service. The first term missionary wrestles with different issues from those of the fifth term person. Cultural adjustment and children's education are prominent with the first term folks while retirement becomes a focus of the missionary in advancing years. Sometimes the spread of years is great enough that the older missionary does not understand the "modern" concerns of the new missionary, and vice versa. The older missionary was raised on "Dr. Spock" while the new missionary is raising his family on "Dr.Dobson."

A fourth major generator of issues is the cultural and family backgrounds of missionary personnel. Missionaries often report their greatest struggle is getting along with other missionaries (Johnson & Penner, 1981; Gish, 1983). This has some bearing on personality differences but also relates to differences stemming from individuals' previous cultural/family norms for relating and resolving conflicts.

As a personnel director with the Christian and Missionary Alliance, I noticed that some of the best city church planters were people reared on farms. I often wondered how a person from the Prairies of Canada could go to a third world city and start a church. It seemed like a wrong match. My recent move to a farm community, though, has cleared up any misconceptions. Farmers have to take many risks. They must persevere, work very hard, and go against the elements and many unknowns, year after year, in order to produce a successful crop. Could it be that "farm culture" produces an inner strength and qualities in candidates that will allow them to deal successfully in cross-culture church planting situations? Maybe the issue here is learning transferable principles that can help people adjust and succeed in different settings. Working on an urban ministry team may expose a person to inner city needs and realities, but it does not necessarily develop the inner qualities that are necessary to minister in this type of situation.

## Primary and Secondary Issues

I find it helpful to differentiate between primary and secondary issues that affect the adjustment and care of staff. Primary issues are core concerns that are central to all the missionary is or does. They transcend things like culture, gender, and age, affecting the missionary during the entire period of service. Examples would be one's level of obedience, perseverance, trust, and faith in God. Further, primary issues are like guides which direct the way secondary issues are expressed. If the primary issues are unsettled, there will always be discontent within the secondary issues.

Secondary issues are not less important, yet are more idiosyncratic to age, gender, and culture. These seem to be the issues which gain the most attention from mission boards and missionaries. They are more tangible and visible. Secondary issues have been delineated in different journal articles and research projects and have to do with concerns such as:

- Selection process and psychological screening
- Education preparation and educational needs
- Women in ministry
- Single missionary concerns, male and female
- National church leadership concerns
- Short-term versus the career person
- Language learning and study
- Political and social unrest
- Health and physical needs
- MK education and opportunities
- Care for older family members in home country
- Spiritual nurture and growth
- Multinational team relationships
- Financial support concerns and concepts
- Administrative organization and design
- Dealing with social injustices
- Reentry problems for the family
- Pluralism of mission groups
- Vocational change and redirection

This brief list could be easily doubled. These are concerns that directly effect the life and ministry of the missionary. Again, this secondary position does not mean these issues are of lesser importance. I suggest they are better understood and considered in relationship to primary issues, five of which I will now discuss.

## Five Core Issues for Missionaries

Abraham is one of the great missionary figures in Scripture. Here was a man who by faith covenanted with God to be a channel of blessing that ultimately would effect all the families of the earth (Genesis 12:1-3). The book of Hebrews suggests five pivotal dimensions, or primary issues, in Abraham's life that are highly relevant to the life and ministry of missionary personnel: obedience, perseverance, trust, perspective, and testing. Let's take a look at this man's life.

## 1. Obeying God's Call

In Hebrews 11:8 we read that God called Abraham to go to an unknown land. Abraham packed up, left the familiar, and went to the place where God wanted him to be. Although Abraham knew how to care for himself, he would be exposed to many dangers and uncertainties as a result of his following the call of God. Here we see high trust and high risk at work. He believed God and believed this was His will.

Missionaries, likewise, must have an unwavering trust in God and obedience to His call. Understanding and obeying one's calling is a central issue in the missionary's life. The experiences of veteran missionaries testify to the importance of maintaining one's sense of call given by the Holy Spirit (Johnston, 1983). There is a need to maintain a delicate balance between the individual missionary's intrinsic sense of call and the mission assignment suggested or required by the mission agency.

Faithfulness to one's call can be tested, especially when the actions of mission leadership or colleagues have generated dissatisfaction. But the missionary whose call from God is strong and who is committed to working through such secondary issues as relationship struggles will remain stable in the difficult time.

A missionary call is to be nurtured and never presumed to be something that will not fade. It is spiritual in nature and affects all a missionary is and does. If a missionary becomes dysfunctional or struggles excessively with ministry issues, it may be wise to review his/her present walk with God and the original call from God concerning missionary work.

## 2. Persevering with God

The second primary issue, as seen in Hebrews 11:9, is persevering while one is living as a stranger. Abraham and his descendants lived as aliens for over four hundred years. They could never count on stability or acceptance by the people of the land. They were pilgrims, strangers. Security and survival were always concerns to be faced.

Abraham appears to have dealt successfully with these issues. He was prosperous, moved around the land, and knew the local leaders.

His trust in God's promise to him helped him to endure and successfully negotiate uncertainty and insecurity.

A missionary needs to feel an adequate degree of security so that survival does not become a major daily question. Having to fight for survival takes away the energy and concentration necessary for ministry.

Take financial matters. One of the never-ending challenges of missionary life is trusting God that the monthly support or allowance come on time and be adequate to cover the expenses. Most of us have known missionaries who have left the field due to inadequate support.

Physical survival in the face of life-threatening events are also a reality for many. I have worked with missionaries who minister in the border camps in Thailand. Every day there is the possibility of death through shelling. The stress level is high and the attrition rate reflects this constant threat to survival. Some situations are beyond the control of the missionary or the organization. But all threats to survival must be taken seriously and managed. Perseverance, supportive care, and wise mission policies are all needed.

## 3. Trusting in God

Abraham and Sarah had to deal with the impossible (Hebrews 11:11). It appeared to them that God's promise of a child was based on their being able to do something that they were not humanly capable of doing. This sounds a lot like the nature of missionary work. Both of them realized they did not possess the capacity to bring forth life, as Abraham, because of his age, saw himself "as good as dead" (Hebrews 11:12). Abraham, though, did not loose faith in his call and the promise. God did enable them to have a son and the promise was fulfilled.

Any missionary who questions the power of the gospel to change lives, the desire of God to save people, or the ability of the Holy Spirit to impart new life will become a discouraged or non-functional missionary. Missionaries survive on power—not their own power but God's power.

During my first month as a missionary in Thailand, a full-page spread appeared in the newspaper. It was very negative and questioned why missionaries would still be in Thailand in light of the poor response of the Thai people during the past 250 years. Less than one percent of the people have become Christians of any kind, Catholic or Protestant. It is easy to give up before one even starts!

In other countries as well, and among many people groups, the church growth and baptism statistics are low, and nonexistent! It can be discouraging: why preach or evangelize? Once God's power is questioned the doubt settles in and the missionary begins to major on the minors.

I conducted an informal study of mission groups working in Thailand during the late 1980's. The results indicated that the majority of cross-cultural missionaries were not involved in direct evangelism and outreach ministry. This aspect of ministry is possibly the toughest part of missions work to sustain. Most often the response is not there as expected. We may be able to plough the ground and plant the seed. But if we do not truly believe there will be a harvest the work can become a discipline of going through the motions. Soon discouragement sets in.

The missionary needs to know and believe he or she is not powerless. The task to which one has been called by God is achievable according to God's power and promise. This kind of faith needs to be nurtured and maintained in the life of the missionary.

## 4. Maintaining God's Perspective

The fourth primary issue has to do with seeing the short-term and the long-term picture for ministry. Abraham never did settle in to the land God had promised (Hebrews 11:13). He lived in the land and died in the land, always a stranger. He knew that someday it would belong to his family. But he also knew that his work here on earth was directly related to the home reserved for him in heaven (Hebrews 11:15,16). This home was already built and it was always his targeted location. He really was a person of two worlds, but his eyes were able to rise above the dust of the earth to the heavens. From this he gained and maintained an accurate, healthy perspective on life. His disappointments were measured in terms of future inheritance.

Abraham could have returned to his old country. He and Sarah had plenty of reason and opportunity to remember the "good life" back home. God never put them in a box and sealed it. They could still *choose* a different lifestyle, a different location, a simpler life. Yet they endured in their obedience, choosing to maintain God's perspective on their lives.

The missionary who loses perspective is easily caught up in immediate concerns and the "cares of this life" (Luke 21:34). He/she may even feel somehow forced into a job and lifestyle, eventually becoming resentful and frustrated. Being in accountable relationships and cultivating one's relationship with the Lord are the two keys to maintaining one's perspective in the midst of the challenges of missionary life. As Paul says in Philippians 3:20: "For our citizenship is in heaven, from which also we eagerly wait for a Savior, the Lord Jesus Christ."

## 5. Growing Through Testing

The fifth and final primary concern in the life of missionaries involves trials and testing. Testing is really a means of self-evaluation. It helps a person look deep into his/her soul, to see who he/she really is. Testing is like stepping onto a scale, although in this case you receive feedback on your spiritual and character weight.

Abraham was tested by God for Abraham's sake. How committed was he to the call, and how faithful was he to God's way of fulfilling the promise? It required Abraham to relinquish his plans. He understood his son to be part of the process of fulfillment. Now God said his son must go. But note, Abraham never surrendered his dream. The promise remained but means and methods changed. Abraham surrendered the temporal plan to retain the eternal promise (Hebrews 11:17-19).

Every Christian will encounter God's times of testing in his/her life. I do not believe God does this for His benefit but for ours. These tests ferret out the self-deception. God may not want to change direction or change anything about the work. He wants us to be honest about our call, purpose, goals, and ambitions. We never know how much something means to us until we lose it or have the potential to lose it. That is the test. Choose to let it go.

Every missionary is going to have his/her plans rearranged. National government, mission leadership, church leaders, family members, or even the weather, can generate opposition. Again, these are important, although secondary issues. And they do not only happen to the proverbial "guy over there." The missionary must be able to trust God in His sovereignty to control all. God does not abandon or hinder His work; but He does bring unexpected change to test us—to demonstrate His faithfulness and encourage our growth.

## Conclusion

The missionary's relationship with God is the preeminent issue. It is important to be aware of the numerous challenges of missionary life and to make sure that missionaries are supported as they face these. But ultimately, these are secondary issues, which must be understood in light of the missionary's need for obedience, perseverance, trust, perspective, and testing. This makes strengthening and encouraging a person's relationship with God the central component of any member care program.

Abraham and Sarah embraced God's call to pilgrimage and to receive the promise. May their examples encourage us in our journeys as we serve the Lord through missions.

### Questions for Discussion

1. With whom do you feel comfortable to discuss some of the "primary issues" in your life?

2. In what ways has your unique background influenced the way you respond to pressure and life's demands?

3. How did Abraham and Sarah struggle in their obedience, faith, and perseverance?

4. How might a missionary's sense of call encourage or frustrate him/her during times of transition?

5. What types of supportive experiences would help you and your department/team continue to stay close to the Lord?

## References

Bowers, J. (1985). Women's role in mission: Where are we now? *Evangelical Missions Quarterly, 21*, 352-362.

Foyle, M. (1985). Overcoming stress in singleness. *Evangelical Missions Quarterly, 21,* 134-145.

Gish, D. (1983). Sources of missionary stress. *Journal of Psychology and Theology, 11,* 238-242.

Johnson, C., & Penner, D. (1981). The current status of the provision of psychological services to missionary agencies in North America. *The Bulletin of the Christian Association for Psychological Studies, 7,* 25-27.

Johnston, L. (1983). Should I be a missionary? *Journal of Psychology and Christianity, 2,* 5-9.

Reapsome, J. (1988). Choosing a mission board. *Evangelical Missions Quarterly, 24,* 6-13.

# 4

*Kenneth Williams*

# A Model for Mutual Care in Missions

The Apostle Paul not only provides an excellent model of an effective missionary, he also sets a powerful example of one who needed others to care for him. In his letters Paul mentioned by name at least 75 specific friends and colleagues. These were significant people in his life and ministry, many of whom ministered to him. Except for Luke, we have no evidence that any of them were "professional" care-givers. Here are a few examples: Aristarchus, Mark, and Justus were a comfort to him (Col. 4:10,11). Onesiphorus often refreshed Paul and helped him in many ways (2 Tim. 1:16). Phoebe was a great help to him and to many others (Rom. 16:1,2). Stephanas, Fortunatus, and Achaicus refreshed his spirit (1 Cor. 16:17).

Like Paul, missionaries today need ongoing care right where they live and work, and this is most effectively provided by one's colleagues. We in missions do well to apply the biblical model of the body caring for its members (1 Cor. 12:21-26). This model calls for specific responses such as listening (Jas. 1:19), restoring those who fall (Gal. 6:1), bearing each other's burdens (Gal. 6:2), encouraging and building up one another (1 Thes. 5:11), helping the weak (1 Thes. 5:14), confessing our sins to each other and praying for each other (Jas. 5:16), along with a host of other activities. When a missionary fails, we tend to see it as his or her failure alone. Might it not also be a failure of the body of Christ on the field?

Current social realities, especially the rising numbers of dysfunctional families, have left many candidates and young missionaries vulnerable to personal problems and struggles on the field. Rather than decry this trend, we need to face the current situation squarely and allocate a higher percentage of missionary resources to maintaining our personnel. But this cannot and should not be borne only by professionals, or even by mission leaders. All field personnel need to see this as part of their ministry. Ministering to colleagues must come to be regarded as an integral part of the missionary call. If even Paul needed to be often refreshed by his colleagues, how can we expect today's missionaries to survive with less?

Missionaries can provide care for their colleagues in a variety of ways. Perhaps these are best illustrated by relating them to a modified version of a member care model proposed by Dave Wickstrom (1991). Based on this model, mission personnel can provide four types of service to each other: support, development, prevention, and restoration. Generally speaking, as care moves from support to restoration, greater skill is required. Further, each of these services can be provided in three separate contexts: pre-field, on-field, and back home. Services are expected to occur throughout the entire missionary life cycle, which means that everyone from missionary children to those who are retiring will be affected.

My purpose in this article is to describe the many practical ways that mutual support among missionaries can occur. I use the above model as a framework to organize the article, and conclude with a discussion on training approaches to prepare mission personnel to counsel and minister to each other.

While the primary focus of this chapter is on the contributions to care that fellow missionaries can make, I do not want to discount the important roles played by member care specialists such as personnel directors, psychologists, and pastoral counselors. Member care is a multifaceted, team effort, requiring the participation of everyone. Nonetheless, it is my belief that the backbone of any effective member care program is found in the ongoing mutual care that occurs among mission staff.

## Support

From the day one enters the process of becoming a missionary, spiritual, emotional, interpersonal, and physical stresses begin to multiply, and these stresses usually continue unabated throughout one's career. Thus, more than normal support is required by most persons. O'Donnell and O'Donnell (1990) stress the need for a commitment to the long-term care of missionaries over the entire course of their lives. As a missions community, we need a growing willingness to provide needed support at every stage of service, given the growing complexities of missionary life. Mission personnel themselves form the front line of support for each other. No one knows what support is needed in a given situation better than those who live and work there. And no one is more available than a neighbor.

### Pre-Field

New missionaries preparing for field service need all the support they can get. Experienced missionaries who are in the home country for various reasons can be mobilized to help provide this support. Some missionaries who are retired, on sick leave, or home because of family needs would welcome opportunities to come alongside new members and offer much needed emotional, spiritual, and practical support.

Many kinds of support may be supplied, including just being there as a caring listener, providing help with visa requirements, offering advice on developing financial and prayer resources, being a prayer partner, and giving insights into dealing with family members who are unhappy about the person's mission plans. Just knowing that someone who has "been there" is available to "be there" when times get tough can be extremely supportive for a struggling candidate or trainee.

## On-Field

Leaving one's home country means giving up the majority of significant support systems provided by family, society, church, work or school, and social contacts. Other missionaries become much more than co-workers. They must supply critically needed support as friends, co-servants of God, fellow-worshippers, confidants, allies against spiritual foes, and assume many other roles. Increasingly, missionaries must come to see that caring for one another, and especially for newcomers to the field, is a vital facet of being effective for Christ.

Friendship is the foundation for mutual support on the field. Robust, healthy friendships must be valued so highly that old and young, women and men alike will be willing to take the necessary risks to develop them. Healthy intimacy with a few good friends can make the difference between making it on the field and going home emotionally broken. But it is axiomatic that field friendships cannot last, with furloughs, changes in assignment, and attrition. So a painful cost of friendship is the inevitable grief of having to say goodbye, over and over. Missionaries need help to learn how to cope effectively with this recurring grief, so that they will not give up on making close friends after a few years of painful separations.

Mutual support on an individual basis comes in a myriad of ways. Some ways require more skill than others, but all demand a caring heart. Practical, down-to-earth help for problems is often needed. We will never forget moving into an old house in Papua New Guinea, to be greeted our first night by hundreds of huge cockroaches swarming over the kitchen. The local pesticide service had drenched the place with insecticide, yet in retrospect, I think those little critters actually liked it! When a new friend caught my wife in tears over it, she immediately brought two other friends with buckets, rags, and three hours of hard work. They helped clean up the mess, and carefully sprayed with something effective. That was many years ago, but we will never forget that loving support.

Loneliness is a major stress for many missionaries. Just sitting down over a cup of coffee and saying, "Tell me about what's been happening" can be an emotional lift that will last for days or weeks. Married people can invite one or two single people to become as much a part of the family as is appropriate. Singles can minister significantly to married people by entering into family life, being "aunt" or "uncle" to children, and a sister or brother to husband and wife.

Care groups, prayer groups, and small group Bible studies are vital support mechanisms contributing to emotional and spiritual well-being on the field. "Heart-level Bible study" groups provide unique opportunities for missionaries to share and care at a deep level, centered around relevant biblical themes. Leaders of most small groups must continually work at bringing the level of sharing from the head down to the heart, if members are going to be able to support each other in the important issues of their lives.

Leaders on the field must be thoroughly committed to the concept of mutual support and encouragement. Gardner (1987, p. 313) states that "substantial attention must be given throughout a mission to the practice of encouraging one another....All too frequently missionary work is done without either explicit or implicit reward; encouragement from colleagues or administrators may be their only tangible reward." Leaders who both value and model providing support for others will tend to have followers who do the same. One very effective way leaders can facilitate mutual support is to set aside a short time at the beginning of each work day for colleagues in each working group to share personal concerns and pray for each other. Everything shared should be kept strictly confidential, and leaders can set the tone by sharing their own joys and struggles.

## Back Home

It is a mistake to think that missionaries and their children no longer need support when they come back home. Coming home is rarely the unmixed joy one anticipates. Recently, a single woman on furlough who was extremely lonely said to me, "I could die here and no one would know or care." Too often, friends, family and church members are unable to truly enter into missionaries' field experiences and share their lives in significant ways. For this and other reasons many missionaries feel lonely, "different," and even alienated when they come back home. Fellow missionaries who have been on the field and have also gone through or are going through the coming home blues are uniquely equipped to give needed support.

However, structures or thoughtfully arranged opportunities to get people together are usually needed. For example, Wycliffe personnel leaders in Germany provide day-long meetings on a monthly basis for furloughing missionaries. Various activities are planned, including fun activities and seminars. But a major part of each day is devoted to sharing joys and struggles, and praying for each other. Participants express heartfelt appreciation for these opportunities to care for one another in ways that others cannot.

Mission personnel leaders might give thought to creative ways to involve home staff, retired missionaries, and other furloughing missionaries in a supportive ministry to those who come home, especially for their first furlough. Those who have served for years on the field and must return for extended periods, to work in the home office, care for family, retire, or leave the mission often go through great stress, including reverse culture shock and grief over the loss of ministry and friends on the field (Austin, 1983). These people may require special support and encouragement for a few months to a year. Other mission personnel may be the most effective providers of this kind of support.

Missionary children often need special support when they return home. Whenever possible support groups should be made available to them. In Dallas, Wycliffe members have facilitated small groups for teens and pre-teens during their first year or two back home, with some very positive results. Similar supportive services are provided by a host of other organizations, such as MuKappa, Interact, Missionary Internship, Link Care, Narramore Foundation, and of course sending churches.

## Development

A few decades ago the average missionary candidate seemed to be better prepared to face the demands of cross-cultural service, in terms of spiritual, emotional, and interpersonal issues. The gap between what is required of missionaries *as persons*, and the skills they bring to the challenge, seems to be growing. Widespread spiritual, emotional, and family deterioration in Western societies contributes substantially to this lack of personal preparedness. Sometimes missions respond to this by requiring more academic and/or technical training, hoping that this might bridge the gap. But the need is for a greater focus on the missionary's personal growth, with emphasis on spiritual, emotional, and interpersonal issues. Mission organizations can no longer assume that this is being adequately addressed in homes, churches, Bible colleges, and seminaries. Thus the "growing cost for world evangelization" must include mission resources devoted to developing and maintaining personal growth in members beginning at the candidate stage, and continuing throughout missionaries' careers.

Psychologists, counselors, and other professionals may have insights and skills to better develop personal growth in missionaries, and their help is urgently needed. At the same time, they cannot possibly bear this burden alone. Missionaries must take responsibility for facilitating growth in each other. The Apostle Paul, in discussing such growth in Ephesians 4:16, says that the "…body, joined and held together by every supporting ligament, grows and builds itself up in love, as each part does its work" (NIV).

Gardner (1984) has emphasized the importance of ongoing personal growth of missionaries, and points out that Scripture calls upon members of the body to exhort, animate, and encourage one another to further growth. Each of us must do our part in building others up, and this includes missionaries.

### Pre-Field

Candidates and trainees generally respond very well to programs designed to facilitate their personal growth. Ideally, issues of spiritual, emotional, and interpersonal growth should pervade every facet of pre-field training. Personal growth and development are best addressed in relation to the realities of life on the field. For this reason, personnel workers with field experience and other missionaries who have gifts and skills for providing training in this area are usually best qualified. In addition to formal training, efforts should be made to provide opportunities for experienced missionaries to mentor trainees during their pre-field experience, on a one-to-one or couple-to-couple basis.

### On-Field

Personal development must not cease after initial training. Williams (1973) stresses the need for field leaders to spend time with members for the purpose of discussing personal goals and personal development. Leaders can help develop a mission culture which values ongoing personal growth in each area of life. Seminars, devotional conferences, and other formal means may be utilized. While outside experts can be very effective in these formal structures, field leaders and other missionaries themselves need to assume responsibility for an ongoing ministry of building one another up. Mentoring by more experienced missionaries may be the most effective method for personal development on the field. Nearly thirty-five years ago, as a young newcomer to the field, a missionary took many hours to mentor me, and his influence still pervades much of my life.

### Back Home

Furlough times offer special opportunities to enhance personal development. Very often, personal issues for growth come up on the field which are not easily dealt with in the context of pressures there. Mission organizations have tended to perceive personal development of personnel as a very private matter, so this issue is seldom addressed as a furlough priority. Personnel workers can facilitate growth during furlough by broaching this subject with missionaries when they arrive home, or before they leave the field. A personal growth plan during furlough can be drawn up as a contract between the missionary and his personnel administrator. Such a plan should include accountability to the administrator, or to someone agreed upon by both parties.

Home staff need to be committed both to be growing as persons, and to be growth facilitators in each other. Opportunities may be sought to develop accountability relationships with each other, and with those on furlough.

I remember struggling for a few months upon returning home after twelve years on the field. Much of this was due to reverse culture shock. Fortunately, I was able to receive much encouragement and experienced significant personal growth through an accountability relationship with two missionary colleagues. We met each week for two hours to talk about critical growth issues in our lives, to commit to growing in these issues, and to pray for each other.

# Prevention

Prevention goes beyond development to address specific potential pitfalls facing the candidate, trainee, and missionary. Formal and informal research into why missionaries flounder in various situations should provide the empirical data needed to guide preventive efforts. For example, the stress factors on a given field need to be clearly identified, and workers must be prepared not only in general strategies for handling stress, but also in how to deal with the particular stresses in that situation.

## Pre-Field

During training programs, panels with experienced field members can be a very effective mechanism for prevention. Trainees have opportunity to learn from those who have struggled on the field, as they listen and ask questions. A variety of relevant field issues can be effectively addressed in this way, such as how to handle major field stress, maintaining spiritual vitality in isolation, various marriage and single issues, sustaining sexual purity, and avoiding destructive emotional patterns.

## On-Field

Prevention on the field should be the task of everyone involved in missions, not only professionals, but leaders at all levels, as well as the missionaries they lead. For example, in fields where loneliness is a major issue, missions can facilitate the provision of prayer groups, sharing groups, and social functions to help prevent its destructive effects. Where spiritual warfare is obviously difficult, special prayer meetings might be encouraged. In some settings immorality is a critical field issue. The incidence of immorality can be greatly reduced by encouraging and developing an accountable relationship with at least one other person. Actually, all healthy interpersonal and group interaction serves to help prevent emotional and spiritual difficulties.

### Back Home

Mission agencies need to be aware of the potentially serious struggles their personnel may have when returning home, and make efforts to help prevent these. Some efforts may be taken before people leave the field, in the form of seminars, furlough workshops, and personal interviews. These may be done by missionaries who have received special training for this purpose.

Whenever possible, time should be spent with returning missionaries and their families upon their arrival, and periodically during their time at home. Opportunities should be given for them to express apprehensions, personal struggles, family problems, and any other issues in a safe, caring, and confidential relationship. This process can be extremely useful in helping prevent serious problems later. Very often the best person to spend time with them is another missionary who perhaps has had some training in this kind of help.

## Restoration

Even with the best possible care in the forms of support, development, and prevention, some missionaries and even trainees will suffer spiritual, emotional and/or interpersonal difficulties to the point of no longer being able to function effectively. Restoration is the process of providing resources for missionaries and their families who are suffering or are unable to function adequately.

Today, resources for restoration in mission contexts are beginning to flower, providing better options in some cases. But the mission community still has a long way to go before hurting missionaries and their families will be able to consistently receive urgently needed services, especially in field situations.

One of the most practical and effective resources for immediate help is that of fellow missionaries who have received training in ministering to those who hurt. A second level of restoration may be provided by mission specialists, especially members who work well with people and who have had at least some training. These include administrators at various levels, personnel workers, consultants, and trainers. Mission specialists can significantly enhance their people-helping skills through seminars and workshops, and through courses such as those offered on various mission fields by Azusa Pacific University in its Operation Impact program, where an M.A. is offered in human resource development.

## Pre-Field

Trainers and other mission personnel play a vital role in intervention with candidates and trainees. Dealing with problems when they are first observed during training is often much more effective than waiting until patterns have become well entrenched after years on the field. At times, just confronting problems and giving specific ideas for change can bring about long-term change. At other times, trainers function best by accurately observing personal or family difficulties and helping trainees obtain professional help before going to the field.

## On-Field

Those in smaller missions may be tempted to think that they have very few human resources for restoration for their members on the field. But one resource is so near and obvious that it is easy to miss, and it provides the first level of member care: one's colleagues. Actually, in many cases, friends and colleagues do provide the backbone of restoration, spending a lot of time with struggling staff behind the scenes.

Leaders and colleagues are often surprisingly effective in intervening on the field, even in very difficult situations. Such interventions are particularly helpful with issues such as culture shock, interpersonal conflicts, emotional reactions to situations, spiritual difficulties, and struggles with handling stress. Even in cases as serious as psychotic breakbown or suicidal depression, fellow missionaries can serve to provide crisis care, until professional help can be obtained.

## Back Home

Professional help is usually more available in the home country than on the field. But even at home, experienced field members should be called upon first when missionaries and their families at home experience difficulties which do not require immediate professional intervention.

For example, most returning missionaries and their children suffer from some level of reverse culture shock, often without realizing what the problem is. The struggle can go on for months and even years, and can create additional problems, especially with children and teenagers. Fellow missionaries and MKs who have gone through the experience of readjustment are frequently the most effective resource for help in this area. Small groups comprised of newly arrived missionaries or MKs, along with those who have been home a little longer, can be very effective in dealing not only with reverse culture shock, but a variety of problems which began on the field and continue on at home.

## Training Missionary Personnel to Minister to Colleagues

Ideally, every new missionary should be given at least a few hours of training in interpersonal and ministry skills, with mission situations in focus. During this time those who demonstrate gifts in these areas can be identified and encouraged to avail themselves of additional, helpful seminars before going to the field. Azusa Pacific University's Operation Impact program and the counseling courses taught through Youth With A Mission's University of the Nations are examples of avenues for additional training while on the field. This suggestion is in line with Tan's (1990) emphasis that Christian lay counselors, in order to be effective, require systematic and disciplined training in counseling skills.

In orientation courses, emphasis can be given to the importance of caring for one another on the field. New workers need to see this not as an optional activity or for the gifted few, but as part of every missionary's call. This should be backed up with at least a minimum of basic training. For example, in Wycliffe's QUEST Personal Growth course, trainees receive approximately eight 90 minute sessions on interpersonal and ministry skills, with time to practice in small groups or triads. The implied message is, "We see this as important for every missionary."

Operation Mobilization's OASIS ministry provides another example of interpersonal and counseling skills training. These skills are used in the context of brief ministry endeavors. Before many of their evangelistic campaigns, people who have been identified as having gifts of ministry are trained in very basic counseling skills in an intensive three-day workshop. Then during the campaign, these nonprofessionals serve alongside professionals who provide close supervision, including sitting in on difficult situations. During Love Europe 1991 I had opportunity to participate in this training and help provide supervision during the week of orientation. It was encouraging to see the effectiveness of those young people working under supervision.

Experienced field personnel and especially leaders need to be oriented to the relevance of ministry within the missionary body. It is important that they agree on its priority in terms of allocating and developing personnel resources for this task.

A key factor in effectively caring for colleagues is the availability of on-field workshops for leaders and others. The goal of these workshops is to further develop appropriate attitudes and skills needed for ministry. These can be provided by mental health care professionals (mission and non-mission), as well as ministers trained in pastoral counseling. Inter-mission cooperation makes the best use of such resource persons. Field workshops in which more than one mission participates provide excellent opportunities for sharing of resources, as well as healthy interaction.

Recently, Operation Mobilization organized a workshop in Vienna on providing pastoral care for workers in Eastern Europe. They brought in a professional counselor and invited four other mission groups. Twenty-five leaders and various missionaries participated, with some receiving individual consultations on difficult issues. By cooperating together these missions were able to share the cost and provide enough participants for an effective workshop. One of the most helpful ministries which visiting mental health professionals and pastors can have is that of providing these kinds of workshops for field personnel.

Some missionaries demonstrate gifts of caring for colleagues during their time on the field. These workers also need to be identified by mission leadership, and encouraged to take courses and workshops while on furlough to increase their skills in ministering to others. Seminars and workshops for furloughing missionaries should be specifically designed to train missionaries to care for one another in field contexts. In most cases, a cooperative effort between mission leaders and non-mission professionals is necessary to develop and provide such workshops.

## An Example of Training Missionaries in Counseling Skills

Wycliffe's Interpersonal Skills Workshop for Administrators is one example of how missionaries can be trained to provide care for one another. The first seminar was given in 1968, born out of the vision of Dr. Phil Grossman and his wife Barbara, Wycliffe's first counselors. Subsequent seminars have been given in various locations around the world, both in home countries and on fields. Individuals from all levels of administration are encouraged to participate. Administrators from other missions are normally invited. Well over 1,000 mission personnel have received training through these seminars.

Wycliffe's seminars are usually five days long, with four 90 minute sessions each day. Training methods include lecture, demonstrations of skills—ideally with real situations—discussion, and practice of skills. Small groups, diads and triads are utilized. Professional counselors are available in the evenings for personal consultations and counseling.

Topics may include biblical bases for counseling, listening, encouraging, confronting, conflict resolution, problem solving skills, spiritual warfare, maintaining spiritual vitality, married and singles issues on the field, and group dynamics. Specific problem issues are covered, with emphasis both on understanding the dynamics involved, and how to help others handle them. Some of these issues include stress, anger, low self-esteem, guilt, depression, grief, moral problems, and co-dependency. Practical, legal, and ethical issues are dealt with, along with knowing one's limitations and referring to professionals. Deliberate efforts are made to integrate Scriptural principles into the curriculum.

Perhaps the greatest limitation of these seminars is their length. Looking over the above topics, one can immediately realize that five days is not very realistic. This becomes even more evident when one considers the great amount of discussion these topics generate. But realities in Wycliffe seem to dictate five days as a maximum.

Materials used in these workshops, information on heart-level Bible studies, as well as videos on stress, crisis intervention, and moral purity are available to other organizations and individuals involved in training missionaries. For information, write to the Wycliffe Counseling Department, 7500 W. Camp Wisdom Road, Dallas, TX 75236.

### Special Considerations in Providing Mutual Care/Peer Counseling

There are several basic issues to consider as mission personnel seek to provide effective care for each other. Here are four of the more salient ones.

1. *Supervision*. Adequate supervision for those involved in peer counseling is as important as it is difficult, especially in field situations. This points to a growing need for professionals and staff who are experienced in counseling to work on location in different fields. These people would not only provide counseling services, but would also give priority to training and supervising missionaries who provide care for others.

2. *Referrals*. Those who receive training in peer counseling skills also need to be prepared adequately to make appropriate referrals. Those who counsel need to be able to understand their strengths and limitations, recognize symptoms of serious emotional difficulty, motivate people to seek professional help, and locate specific referral resources in the area, if any.

A practical issue in many mission situations is the need to interface with administrators when someone needs professional care. This is especially true if a member needs to return home or go to another location. A clear protocol needs to be established to help peer counselors interact with leaders in such situations.

3. *Confidentiality*. It is very important to draw up guidelines for maintaining confidentiality. Usually nothing may be shared with one's family, friends, or colleagues, without specific, verbal or preferably written permission from the person receiving help. Only when one is required by law or ethical standards should information be reported to others. This would include any form of child abuse, physical abuse or violence toward other adults, and immediate danger to one's self or others.

If the care giver is convinced that an administrator or other person should be aware of the problem, it is appropriate to encourage the one receiving help to go and talk about it. For example, work pressures may be causing severe emotional stress, and the person's supervisor needs to know about it so he or she can help reduce the pressures. If the person is fearful or reluctant to talk with a supervisor, the helper may offer to go with him or her.

4. *Cross-Cultural Issues.* The intricate issues involved in cross-cultural counseling go beyond the limitations of this chapter. But those issues certainly apply in peer counseling as well. When training peer counselors, nearly every topic should be presented in light of how it applies to missionaries from other cultures. For example, cultures differ significantly in their ways to confront, encourage, resolve conflicts, express feelings, and show affection. The way problems are identified and the type of help that is seen to be appropriate also vary greatly.

## Conclusion

The stresses and personal problems that surface in mission settings are inevitable. To succeed and even survive in missions requires that missionaries place a high priority on caring for one another. This cannot be legislated, as it must come from the heart. Mutual support involves everyone connected to the mission enterprise—administrators, the sending church, home office staff, supporters, and missionaries themselves. Everyone plays an important part in keeping mission personnel healthy and effective.

### Questions for Discussion

1. Are there other types of mutual care that the author has not discussed? If so which ones?

2. How could a peer counseling program be set up within a mission agency?

3. What special considerations do agencies need to keep in mind when training and using nonprofessional counselors?

4. In what ways can mental health professionals be involved in training and encouraging mission personnel in mutual support?

5. What are some practical strategies mission personnel can employ in their organizations to increase an emphasis on mutual care?

## References

Austin, C. (1983). Reentry stress: The pain of coming home. *Evangelical Missions Quarterly, 19,* 278-287.

Gardner, L. (1984). *A case study examination of missionary terminations.* Unpublished doctoral dissertation. Conservative Baptist Seminary, Denver, CO.

Gardner, L. (1987). Proactive care of missionary personnel. *Journal of Psychology and Theology, 15,* 308-314.

O'Donnell, K, & O'Donnell, M. (1990). The increasing scope of member care. *Evangelical Missions Quarterly, 26,* 419-428.

Tan, S. (1990). Lay christian counseling: The next decade. *Journal of Psychology and Christianity, 9,* 59-65.

Wickstrom, D. (1991). A proposal for a pastoral care program for missions. *Proceedings of the Twelfth Annual Mental Health and Missions Conference,* Angola, Indiana.

Williams, K. (1973). *Characteristics of the more successful and less successful missionaries.* Unpublished doctoral dissertation, United States International University, San Diego, CA.

# 5

*Barry Austin*

# Supporting Missions Through Pastoral Care

We are living in a time when relationships in the world are breaking down. Family turmoil, community violence, and ethnic strife are rampant. We in missions have an opportunity to shine in such areas of darkness through both our ministry and lifestyle. Jesus said people would know we are His disciples when we show love for one another (John 13:35). This means that caring for one another is not just our biblical responsibility, but also a vital part of our evangelistic witness.

Pastoral care seeks to encourage healthy relationships and draw people closer to Christ. It involves setting up structures and providing oversight to promote the flow of love and care between us, and to stimulate spiritual growth. When our people feel cared for and are growing, they will be more fruitful in their service for the Lord.

This chapter looks at some of the ways in which pastoral care can be facilitated in mission settings. It overviews several avenues and structures for staff growth: leadership roles, support from fellow workers, personnel departments, pastoral coordinators, small groups, prayer partnerships, and the local church. This list is certainly not exhaustive, yet forms the core of a solid pastoral program that is relevant for many settings.

## Pastoral Responsibility

Pastoral care is committed to the well-being of people the way a shepherd is to his flock—nurturing, leading, protecting, healing. It is more than just caring for missionaries when they are in desperate need, as in crisis counseling. It is also more than just a few people providing staff with services. Scripture encourages us to have ongoing, interdependent relationships where we are mutually building into one another's lives (Eph. 4:16, I Thes. 5:14-15). In this way we are discipling one another for the Lord. As missionaries we are committed to making disciples—and this must include ourselves.

### Leaders as Shepherds

Chapter 34 of Ezekiel pronounces strong words against the Jewish leaders who were not being shepherds to their people. This chapter is of much relevance for us today. Even though as mission leaders we may feel that we do not have pastoral gifts, God still expects us to care for the people that He has placed within our oversight. This does not mean we should have a counseling relationship with everyone in our mission community, team, or work area; but it does mean that we are responsible to see that the necessary pastoral care is done. Work structures are not usually suitable as pastoral structures. This means that clear delegation of pastoral responsibilities is needed.

While some leaders neglect their responsibility to care for their people, others can tend to go to the other extreme. The problem is that of exercising too much control or influence over those they are leading or supervising. We need to be alert to this and recognize that there are limitations to the input that we can have into other people's lives. As leaders it is valid for us to give advice and counsel to people about personal areas of their lives, but it is inappropriate to dictate what they should do. Jesus calls us to serve and enable others through our leadership style, not to run their lives.

When helping people with guidance for the future, our first responsibility is to point them to the Lord that they might hear from Him. Recently a couple approached the leadership team at our base to discuss their desire to attend a three month training course. As a team we were unanimous in feeling that they should attend the course, but we did not communicate this with them. Rather we prayed with them and encouraged them to pray by themselves until they had an assurance of the Lord's will. Eventually they came to a place of peace and felt they were to attend the course; we then confirmed their guidance. It was important that they learned that God would guide them personally rather than just through their leadership.

### Mutual Care in Isolated Settings

The pastoral care of staff can be especially difficult in mission settings where there are no churches, where workers are isolated, or where opposition is common. We need to find some creative ways to support our people in such situations. Periodic field visits from pastoral people are useful, as are times away from the field for rest and renewal. But ultimately, the primary resource for care rests with those who are actually working together—be they missionaries on the field or staff in the home office. Relying on each other for support and encouragement is vital, although my experience has shown that many people in missions need additional relationship skills to do this effectively.

Mutual care among missionary personnel can be awkward at times. For instance, perhaps the person you want to approach for some help or advice is struggling just as much as you. Or you may feel hesitant to share your real thoughts and feelings with someone because your work relationship together might in some way be adversely affected. Maybe you are in a multinational setting and it is hard to communicate deeply in a second language and feel understood by others from a different culture. Or in the case where a pastoral care-giver is designated, you might just find it hard to relate together for whatever reason. Discussing the possible hindrances to pastoral support—and specifically mutual care—is an important consideration when setting up and reviewing plans for staff care.

Missionaries are not to be rugged individualists, committed solely to tasks, devoid of personal needs. Neither are they to be emotionally dependent people who are a drain on others. Needed are people who are willing to be both strong and vulnerable, capable of developing interdependent relationships that provide mutual support. By such relationships shall people know we are His disciples!

## Facilitating Pastoral Care

Let's look at several pastoral structures that can be used to care for and encourage staff. These structures can be experimented with and modified in order to fit the needs of most mission settings.

### 1. Administrative Help

Part of caring for people is helping them with administrative matters. Many new missionaries, for example, are not familiar with the legal requirements and the myriad of logistical details related to their work overseas. One effective way to accomplish the administrative care of our staff is to draw upon and develop the resources of a personnel department.

The personnel department typically sees people from their first contact with the agency through to their debriefing when they return to their home country. It can provide practical help through a variety of services, including insurance, visas, holiday planning, travel arrangements, support development, information for families on schooling, job placement, staff training, orientation, and hosting staff upon their arrival. Personnel departments are set up to serve, which means staff can spend more time actually working within their areas of calling.

One young man came to us to join us on staff, feeling sure that God had called him to work at our base in England. Unfortunately, he had no idea of how to raise the necessary financial support, as his local church was unable to help. Our personnel department helped him write to a number of his friends, inviting them to seek the Lord as to whether they could contribute to his support. He was amazed to find such a warm response, to the extent that all his monthly support needs were met. He would never have been able to do this without calling on the experience and counsel of the personnel department.

## 2. Pastoral Coordinators

It is helpful to appoint a pastoral coordinator for regions, and large mission communities and teams. The coordinator's job is to oversee and stimulate the functions of pastoral care, which is typically a full-time ministry. It is wise for the coordinator to set up and work with a pastoral committee that could give input and take on some of the responsibilities.

Coordinators and pastoral committees do not take care of all the needs in the mission community; neither should they be expected to do so. It is more accurate to see them as a type of resource broker, channeling staff and services to meet people's needs.

Work responsibilities for the pastoral coordinator are broad. Here is a job description for a pastoral coordinator which can be modified to fit into different mission settings.

### Qualifications
a. Is a mature individual or married couple who is respected and trusted by others, and whose pastoral gifts are recognized.

b. Possesses relationship skills, is sensitive to people, and is able to listen to and encourage others.

c. Has some organizational skills, and is able to delegate so that others are released into pastoral ministry.

d. Has a good relationship with the leadership of the agency and mission setting.

e. Is clearly committed to the agency's vision for ministry so that pastoral care and evangelism are not polarized.

f. Has a broad range of gifts and skills in order to fit the responsibilities listed below.

### Responsibilities
a. Facilitates the orientation and bonding of new staff to the people, vision, and ministry of the mission. Ensures that all new staff are met and welcomed by leadership. Works with others to help new staff have a positive experience as much as possible with the new culture.

b. Is available to staff for basic counseling and/or for referring them to other counselors.

c. Periodically updates leaders on the overall level of staff health, inclding spiritual, social, emotional, physical, and practical needs.

d. Makes sure that adequate time is set aside for social activities, like tea/coffee breaks, lunch times, free evenings, recreation, and days off.

e. Establishes and oversees a system of small groups. Meets regularly with small group leaders for training and encouragement.

f. Encourages the spiritual growth of staff by suggesting and organizing Bible studies, prayer partnerships, fellowship groups, audio or video tape studies, and seminars with guest speakers.

g. Facilitates the setting up of teaching times and retreats for couples, singles, families, departments, and teams.

h. Networks with local church leaders and encourages staff to participate in local church life as their mission responsibilities allow.

i. Oversees and meets regularly with the pastoral committee.

### Scope of Authority

The pastoral coordinator is responsible to the regional/base director or leadership team. As a staff or advisory position, the coordinator and pastoral committee work by influence and through communication. Therefore they cannot make decisions that would affect the line responsibilities of staff—for example, established policies, leave of absence, schedules, and staff discipline. In difficult counseling situations (moral failure, severe marital problems, incapacitating emotional struggles), the coordinator should usually consult with a designated leader, and consider working with a counseling team until the situation is resolved.

## 3. Small Groups

Another useful method of pastoral care is to establish a system of small groups throughout the mission community. These groups are voluntary, consisting of from five to ten members. Small groups provide forums where people develop closer, committed relationships by regularly sharing their needs and praying for one another. In this way staff bear one another's burdens in love (Galatians 6:2). The groups also provide a stimulus for relating to each other in contexts outside of the group.

It is important to encourage staff—especially candidates and new staff—to regularly share their lives together as openly as possible. Not only is this foundational for adequate pastoral care, but it is a vital learning experience for those people who form teams and are sent out into settings where there are minimal external supports.

If small groups are to be effective, their leaders need to be chosen carefully. The leader should be able to provide some direction without dominating the group. The emphasis is on the leader coordinating a group of people who minister to one another. Small group leaders are encouraged to meet together regularly with the pastoral coordinator and a mission leader for training, support, prayer, and planning activities for the groups.

Here are some suggestions for running small groups.

### Guidelines for Small Groups

a. Select group leaders who will encourage the participation and development of all group members, even those who are timid or more reserved. Leaders must be able to build trust by creating an atmosphere of acceptance and openness.

b. Be flexible when allocating people to groups. Some prefer to meet with those they already know; others are happy to get together with anyone. However, it is important for specialist ministry groups and departments to be integrated with others, where possible.

c. Have a clear understanding of the purpose for the group that is accepted by all members. Set some goals as a group and discuss what each person wants to see happen through the group. Be sure to discuss expectations for the frequency of meetings, how long the group will meet, and the responsibilities of each member.

d. Encourage the discovery and use of personal gifts in the group context, such as leading worship, intercession, teaching, and communication skills.

e. Study Scripture and discuss how to practically apply it to one's life. Do not insist on conformity of opinion on non-essentials of belief and behavior. No one should dominate the group or force his/her interpretations of doctrine or standards on the group.

f. Pray for people and situations outside the immediate concerns of the group. Do not permit groups to become cliques or overly introspective.

g. Be aware of potential small group leaders within the group. This is an ideal setting for training by example.

h. Assess the needs and status of the group regularly and be prepared to end, divide, or restructure as necessary. If the group gets too large it will lose its sense of intimacy. Plan to divide if the group gets larger than about ten people.

## 4. Prayer Partnerships

Organizing prayer partnerships can contribute significantly to the overall health of a mission setting. This is a regular meeting of two or three people of the same gender for the purpose of mutually encouraging each other's relationship with the Lord. Jesus promised to be with us in a special way when two or three gather in His name (Matthew 18:20). In Hebrews 10:24,25 we are told to stimulate one another to love and good deeds and to encourage each other. Prayer partnerships are one way of doing this.

One advantage of prayer partnerships is its practicality. At certain times of the year or in certain locations, for example, pastoral care may not be possible through leaders; yet it is possible for a few people to commit themselves to meet regularly and support each other through prayer. Prayer partnerships provide ongoing contact, care, and accountability among peers. Personal friendships usually develop naturally through this time together. Prayer partnerships can also reduce the counseling loads of leaders, and are particularly useful on short-term outreach teams.

Some important questions to explore and pray through with each other are: (a) What is your relationship with the Lord like? (b) How fulfilling are prayer and Bible reading? (c) Do you have any relationship or work-related struggles? and (d) In what areas are you wanting to grow?

Prayer partnerships are not the place to resolve major personal problems; in this case the skills of an experienced counselor may be required. However, by sharing together in a partnership like this, encouraging one another's spiritual growth, and supporting each other during difficult times, many major problems can be prevented.

## 5. The Local Church

We must not overlook the crucial contribution of churches to the care and growth of missionary personnel. Staff are encouraged to attend local churches, where possible. Relationships need to be built with local church leaders so that we can cooperate together in caring for our people. It is especially important to build and maintain a relationship with the home churches that have sent out and financially support our staff.

Church attendance alone, of course, is unlikely to be adequate to meet the pastoral needs of staff. This may be because staff's commitment to missions usually does not allow time to fully participate in church activities, or else they may be pioneering a new church where they themselves are expected to be the primary care-givers. Additional supportive structures and services are needed, most of which are provided through the mission agency itself.

# Leadership and Pastoral Care

Mission leaders play a key role in setting up and developing appropriate pastoral care structures. They need to be seen as giving a clear lead. Their involvement communicates the importance being placed on the care and development of staff.

Regular times of prayer and interaction with staff are needed to determine the best ways to provide pastoral care. Involving staff in this way assures that their needs are accurately identified and that they feel a sense of ownership in the ensuing pastoral care. This can best be done by inviting their opinions and ideas about pastoral care through discussions and informal surveys.

### Leaders Are Examples

Leaders need to model pastoral care to their people. They too are by no means immune to problems that require pastoral care; the leadership role itself creates many stresses which can lead to burnout. How does the leader go about receiving pastoral care? There are two primary ways. The first is by sharing responsibilities and the work load with other leaders, and the second is by building relationships with other leaders.

Leadership, as presented in the New Testament, is a plural function. It is not meant to be the lonely task that it often is. When the Apostle Paul started churches, he appointed groups of elders to oversee them. Paul also sought to minister in a team context, except when his time in prison did not make this possible. The New Testament leadership model emphasizes a team approach!

### A Case Study of Mutual Support

Leadership teams are a great place to cultivate mutual pastoral care. Several years ago I observed a mission agency going through a major crisis. Relationships between the leaders broke down and two of the leaders left taking half of the staff with them to start another work. After an extended time of prayer, the remaining leaders decided to decrease their emphasis on accomplishing tasks and spend more time developing closer friendships with each other. The format of their leadership meetings changed to reflect this new emphasis. Business matters were still discussed, but there were added times to intercede for the work and to provide pastoral care for one another. It took a major change in priorities to make adequate time to pray and care for each other.

The leaders were not accustomed to sharing their lives together at any great depth. This of course made it hard to really minister to one another. With some practice, though, and through "walking in the light" with one another (I John 1:7), a new depth of fellowship ensued. Their experience together also began to have a powerful effect on the rest of the staff, who started to follow their lead by developing stronger supportive relationships.

This new emphasis brought God's blessing on the whole work. Over the next four years the number of staff multiplied six times and many new areas of ministry were pioneered. It was the leaders' time of intercession and their caring for one another that were keys to bringing God's blessing. God promises that unity in relationships brings His blessing (Psalm 133).

## The Challenge of Pastoral Care

Pastoral care in missions today is as important as it is challenging. Our people and teams are often scattered over large areas and it is hard to get them together frequently. Some missionaries are mobile making it difficult to maintain consistent relationships over time. People come from different backgrounds with different expectations for receiving and contributing to the care of one another.

Because of these realities it is necessary to experiment with a variety of pastoral structures. Any of the structures previously discussed—personnel departments, pastoral coordinators, small groups, prayer partnerships, and the local church—may be more appropriate in one situation than another. The structure is not so important as long as we are achieving our objective to care for our people and see that they are growing in the Lord. And when our people are cared for, they will be more fruitful in their work.

## Suggested Readings

Collins, M. (1986). *Manual for today's missionary: From recruitment through retirement*. Pasadena, CA: William Carey Library.

Dennett, J. (1990). *Personal encouragement and growth for every missionary: A practical approach to biblical caring and counseling*. Pymble, NSW, Australia: Gospel and Missionary Society.

O'Donnell, K. & O'Donnell, M. (1990). The increasing scope of member care. *Evangelical Missions Quarterly, 26,* 418-428.

Welch, R. (nd). *We really do need each other*. Nashville: Impact Books.

White, G. (1989). Pastoral counseling—The key to a healthy mission force. *Evangelical Missions Quarterly, 25,* 304-309.

# PART TWO
## COUNSELING AND CLINICAL CARE

# Part Two
# Counseling and
# Clinical Care

*Brent Lindquist*

Consulting Editor

Part Two takes on the task of distilling some of the major issues in the clinical care of missionary personnel. The authors address five of these issues: candidate screening, psychopathology, stress management, counseling, and crisis intervention.

Traditionally, member care in mission agencies has focused on remedial care or restoration—that is, emphasis was placed on getting help for people once illness or dysfunction was observed. Perhaps this could be summarized in the old adage, "If it works, don't fix it." Fortunately, there is a growing recognition that caring for missionary personnel only after they fall apart is probably not the best stewardship of resources, both economic and human. A balanced approach to member care is thus needed which also includes prevention, personal development, and ongoing supportive services. Part Two, due to its clinical emphasis, focuses largely on remedial care issues. Nonetheless, several authors have also included relevant material on preventing problems and providing supportive care.

Chapter six, by Dr. Esther Schubert, looks at some of the dysfunctional types of backgrounds found in the current pool of missionary candidates. These include alcoholism, sexual abuse, general family dysfunction, and "bruising." These background experiences need to be carefully reviewed in determining a missionary's fitness for service. Esther also includes a helpful section on personality disorders and describes what they can look like in a missionary population. The final section considers the role of testing and other procedures that can facilitate the screening process.

"Psychopathology in Missionary Personnel," by Dr. Jarrett Richardson, reviews the classification system for psychological disorders found in the *Diagnostic and Statistical Manual III—Revised*, published by the American Psychiatric Association. Prior to discussing these diagnostic categories, Jarrett distinguishes between health and pathology and highlights research on missionary psychopathology. He presents numerous case studies and treatment examples throughout the article which help to clarify the often esoteric nature of psychiatric terminology and descriptions.

Chapter eight is written by Drs. Kelly and Michele O'Donnell. This article takes a fresh look at stress management in the missions context. While we have all known what stress is and what it does, their article makes a new contribution by going beyond an individual approach in assessing and managing stress. Kelly and Michele describe a practical model to identify stressors and resources (CHOPPSS) which can be applied to various levels of the mission organization—individuals, families, departments, and so on. The article concludes with a case study that raises several issues regarding missionary care and missionary stress.

Dr. John Powell's article, "Short-Term Missionary Counseling," addresses the use of brief counseling for missionaries. In most mission settings, long-term counseling by mental health professionals is not an option. John discusses how short-term approaches are usually the treatment of choice, given the time constraints and realities of missionary life. A major portion of the chapter focuses on problem areas that are amenable to short-term treatment along with some guidelines for providing this treatment.

The final chapter, by Dr. Laura Mae Gardner, explores the many facets of crisis intervention in mission settings. Her comments are primarily oriented towards mission administrators and others providing crisis care. Laura Mae's article is timely, given the reality of our rapidly changing, crisis-filled world, the effects of which frequently spill over onto missionary personnel. She draws heavily from the current literature on crisis and disaster management as well as from her experience in helping missionaries in crisis. Her article is especially important to counter the tendency only to pray over a crisis or experience, and rather superficially in terms of a developmental model, dismiss the continuing effects of crisis. The many practical suggestions for dealing with the immediate and the long-term effects of crisis will be of much service to the mission community.

The clinical content of these chapters may be quite different from the standard fare of many administrators working in a member care and missions context. This being the case, let me make three suggestions as to how administrators as well as non-clinical member care workers can best make use of this material.

First of all, it is an ethical responsibility for trained professionals to be the primary diagnosticians in any sort of medical, psychological, or psychiatric matter. Part Two, then, is by no means intended to equip administrators and others to function as a psychologist or psychiatrist—indeed, that is one of the great dangers of disseminating such materials. Rather, these chapters are presented in an effort to provide administrators, member care specialists, and missionaries themselves with a deeper grounding in some of the specific diagnostic and treatment issues involved in member care.

Second, discretion must always be used regarding diagnostic labels, no matter how accurate they are. To casually place a diagnostic label on someone is inappropriate, and can actually do great harm to that person. Diagnostic categories can also be erroneously applied to what are better understood as *cultural variations*. An example is the fact that many personality characteristics and ways of behavior that Americans tend to rate as very healthy and normal are seen as abnormal and unhealthy in wide parts of the world. The overt expression of feelings of anger and conflict resolution are only a smattering of issues that have greatly different viewpoints around the world. In brief: exercise caution, both as administrators and as member care practitioners.

Third, take note that psychology and psychiatry's diagnostic and prescriptive skills are not perfect. There still are margins of error. While there is general agreement that there are some dysfunctional people who probably should not be on the field, we must be careful when making judgements concerning someone's suitability for service. We must also seek God and His will for people, not merely consult our psychological tools and screening devices. Further, in order to make the best use of one's clinical skills, the member care consultant must also have a very clear view of the mission setting and the characteristics needed to be effective in that setting.

Taken together, the five articles of this section provide a wealth of information to help mission agencies in their selection process, supportive services, remedial care, and prevention approaches. One key to using much of the material presented is to utilize and consult with mental health professionals who are familiar with missions and missionary personnel. Such professionals can be real assets to an agency's overall member care program.

# 6

*Esther Schubert*

# Current Issues in Screening and Selection

The Christian psychological literature contains a number of excellent articles on overseas missionary selection (Britt, 1983; Foyle, 1986; S. Lindquist, 1983; Williams, 1983). The purpose of this chapter is to be an update, continuing where the previous articles have left off.

Included in this chapter will be a discussion of the changing missionary recruitment pool and the impact of emotional bruising on missionary candidates. Also addressed in this section will be the issues of dysfunctional families, missionary candidates from alcoholic families, and sexual abuse as it impacts future missionaries. Personality disorders are described in terms of how they might be manifested in a missions setting. Finally, the chapter will discuss the use of psychological testing and the Minnesota Multiphasic Personality Inventory (MMPI) in pre-field selection.

## The Changing Missionary Recruitment Pool

In late 1987, EFMA-IFMA sponsored a conference in Detroit for mission personnel departments on the subject of "bruising." This conference, led by Drs. Ken Williams and John Powell, opened the door to a concept that many of us understood intuitively but had not seen addressed in such a concise and specific fashion; namely, that many missionary candidates are coming to the selection process from difficult and damaged backgrounds. This appears to be a growing trend, although research is needed to explore this impression.

There are several fairly common sources for past emotional "bruising" among missionary candidates. Many of these individuals come from dysfunctional families and involve: (a) adults who were victims of child abuse or neglect; (b) adult children of alcoholics; (c) adult survivors of sexual abuse; (d) unresolved grief, guilt, anger or fear; (3) issues of adoption and divorce; (f) sexual identity problems; (g) previous sexual behavior on the part of the candidate, including past abortions; and (h) vulnerability or previous exposure to demonic involvement.

I would like to address the three most common sources of bruising in missionary candidates that I am currently seeing in the selection process and also the sources of bruising that most often have to be dealt with in crisis intervention with missionaries. These are, specifically, dysfunctional families, adult children of alcoholics, and sexual abuse.

## Dysfunctional Families

Most family systems that work effectively provide maintenance (food, clothing, shelter), nurture (emotional care and support), and guidance (guidelines for behavior, goals, choices). Healthy families provide safety, security, and stability. In contrast, dysfunctional families are ruled by rigidity, isolation, denial, and shame. They are unstable, and produce insecurity and pathology in their members. When children of dysfunctional families become adults they continue to see their world through the filter of dysfunction.

I believe that the deterioration of the family in Western society, the erosion of stable traditions, and the frequency of poorly functioning families contribute to the changing face of the pool of missionary candidates. Children in a dysfunctional family grow up in a closed system, one that teaches rigidity of roles and rules that must be played out in order for the family to survive. Beliefs about people and the outside world are distorted. The outside is viewed as an unsafe place. The child learns "don't talk, don't feel, don't trust" (Friel & Friel, 1988, pp. 75-90).

The boundaries that form structure, certainty, and consistency within functional families are distorted or non-existent in dysfunctional families. These boundaries are of three kinds: individual boundaries, inter-generational boundaries, and family boundaries (Friel & Friel, 1988, p. 57).

*Individual boundaries* are crossed when children do not have privacy, when they are abused, or when they feel their only worth is based on what they can produce, not who they are. *Inter-generation boundaries* are crossed when a child has to take adult responsibilities for whatever reasons or when sexual incest occurs. A child is robbed of his/her childhood. Functional families have communication between generations but it is understood that the parental generation is different from the childhood sibling generation.

*Family boundaries* can be extremely rigid in which no one in the family is allowed to communicate with anyone outside the family for fear that family secrets and myths will be discovered. They can also be very diffuse where there is no clear sense of uniqueness to the family unit. Dysfunction results from either extreme.

Boundary violations in dysfunctional families damage children, create a high tolerance for abnormal behavior among the victims, and decrease the inability to distinguish between healthy and dysfunctional behavior. Often the background of a dysfunctional family produces children who grow up without having traversed the normal healthy developmental stages. They become adults by age but retain significant childhood characteristics and are sometimes referred to as "adult children."

Unfortunately the victimization of childhood creates an inability to make good judgements in adult relationships. Often when these children grow up they do not know how to get out of the role they have played. For instance, the missionary who as a child was the rescuer or the hero in the dysfunctional childhood family may grow up feeling he/she has to be a rescuer as an adult. They may misperceive this "psychological agenda" to rescue as being a spiritual "call" to the mission field rather than understanding that it is an unhealthy pattern of thinking and behavior. If these individuals get to the mission field before obtaining psychological insight and healing, they often burn out quickly when they discover that the nationals or colleagues in their place of service do not want to be rescued.

### Adult Children of Alcoholics

There are an estimated 22 million adult children of alcoholics (ACOA's) in the United States, comprising 13% of the adult population (Sell, 1990). A significant number of the mission applicants are likely to be ACOA's. Often the scars of that background are denied or incorporated into a "Christ took care of it all" philosophy. Once the candidate is overseas, psychological problems can develop in that stressful setting. Depression, burnout, and personnel conflicts are the most common problem areas.

Secular psychological literature is replete with good studies on the effect of an alcoholic family on a child's eventual development into adulthood. Although the alcoholic or alcoholics in the family of origin may be considered the "dependent" individuals within the family unit, it is now understood that other members of the family frequently become "co-dependents." Often these co-dependents become enmeshed in the family structure, unintentionally becoming a part of the process that reinforces the alcoholic's behavior (referred to as *enabling*). The effects of this chaotic childhood are often felt into adult life.

ACOA's often have a common set of personality characteristics (Black, 1981). They may be very hard on themselves, take themselves and life very seriously, and have difficulty having fun. Many of these individuals feel estranged and different from other people. Often they struggle with low self-esteem and depression. Intimacy is particularly difficult for them because they have difficulty trusting others. They have a great need to maintain control in most situations in which they find themselves. They are constantly seeking approval and affirmation from others, but have difficulty accepting it when they receive it.

ACOA's tend to be extremely responsible and find it easier to be concerned about others than about themselves. They may be loyal even though their loyalty may be undeserved. They have a great deal of false guilt, much like children of divorce. Authority figures may create fear in them, and they are frightened by angry people and any personal criticism. They may have grown up needing to keep peace at any cost. They may sense they have few rights. They confuse love with pity and tend to love those who can be pitied or rescued.

The female adult child of an alcoholic may marry an alcoholic or a man who is addicted in some other fashion. These women are afraid of abandonment and will hold on to any relationship, even a bad relationship, rather than taking the chance of being without one. They have repressed their feelings from a traumatic childhood and have difficulty feeling and expressing feelings. They seem to deal with stress with a great deal of denial and repression.

Many adult children of alcoholics feel powerless, helpless and victimized. Unfortunately, they transfer the negative experiences of authority figures from their childhood to God and may have difficulty experiencing Him as loving, caring, forgiving, patient, accepting, and trustworthy. ACOA's often think in very black and white perceptions. They have difficulty tolerating ambivalence and may be very comfortable in a legalistic setting. They have deep-seated anger which is often unconscious. This anger may show itself in depression, but these individuals may not be able to make the connection between the anger and the depression. At times they may have difficulty following a project from beginning to end. Since they seldom felt safe as a child, they have difficulty establishing trust in adult relationships.

Often adult children of alcoholics can be helped to be more effective adults with prolonged intensive skilled counseling. A number of groups for ACOA's have been established throughout the country and one of the best functions of these groups is to provide them with a sense that they are not alone and that others have experienced these same traumas and struggles.

As significant numbers of ACOA's become Christians and some of these individuals go into missionary service, they may bring with them the misperceptions that were a part of their growing up process. It is important for mission organizations to investigate these potential issues and request candidates to obtain adequate therapy prior to overseas placement. If this is not accomplished, these individuals may continue to have difficulty with denial, repression, authority issues, misperceptions of God, and black and white perceptions. The inevitable stress of missionary living—especially for those who feel a strong need to control their environment but do not know enough about the culture to exhibit control—can quickly result in depression, burnout, and impaired interpersonal relationships.

### Sexual Abuse

By definition, sexual abuse is sexual contact between an adult and a child, or between an older teenager and a child at least five years younger, or an older child placed in a position of authority. Sexual abuse is not limited to intercourse or violence and may include fondling, touching, oral sex, or exposing the child to pornography. Unfortunately, this sexually intended behavior may not be remembered consciously by the victim and if remembered, may not be acknowledged as important or even as abuse. One professional woman shared with me that she had not been aware of sexual abuse that had occurred in her childhood until at the age of 39 while listening to an educational tape on sexual abuse she suddenly realized that some of her memories of her childhood constituted memories of sexual abuse.

Tragically, women who are victims of sexual abuse in childhood may have difficulty experiencing the freedom to be or become women. Men who are sexually abused may feel terribly degraded because culturally they are not supposed to be victimized, as it is not "masculine."

It has been estimated that at least 25% of females in the United States are subjected to sexual abuse before the age of eighteen (Harrop-Griffiths, 1988). There are significant numbers of men who have been sexually abused, but the percentages are thought to be less than for women sexual abuse survivors. Ken Williams has referred to this problem as "a ticking time bomb in missions"(Powell & Williams, 1987).

As I talk with other mental health care professionals involved in pre-field testing and crisis intervention for missionaries, the consensus of opinion is that approximately one-third of the female missionary candidates have been victims of sexual abuse in the past. This tends to mirror the percentages that we see in the general population in the United States. Certainly, mission organizations that are asking the right questions are coming up with these kinds of percentages.

Harrop-Griffiths (1988) found that women with chronic pelvic pain, depression, anxiety, premenstrual syndrome, and sexual dysfunctions were 2.5 times more likely than controls to have been sexually abused as children. Many of these women have common sexual problems including fear of intimate relationships, pain during intercourse, feelings of repulsion or lack of sexual enjoyment, and primary and secondary anorgasmia. Other common problems included marked interpersonal difficulties, multiple somatic complaints without clear physical disease, notable anxiety or depression, self-destructive behavior, and anti-social behavior.

In many cases, sexual abuse occurs because a child is not having his or her emotional intimacy needs met within the family. The child's craving for relationships may make him or her vulnerable for molestation by family members or outsiders. The initial contact may be pleasurable for the child, both relationally and emotionally, but over a period of time this relationship may develop from non-sexual secrets, special names, fantasies, into physical contact and eventually into sexual contact. In some instances, the process may take months or years. The child may be sworn to secrecy or threatened into secrecy which often creates a great deal of false guilt.

Once the relationship has become sexual there may be emotional discomfort, guilt and fear. At the same time, the child may feel a great deal of relational and even physical or sexual pleasure. The different feelings in this situation creates ambivalence (Allender, 1990). Eventually, the victim feels empty and used and may eventually develop hatred toward the molester. Further, contempt for others, for men, and especially if the abuser was a father or a father figure, may extend to God.

The impact of a sexual abuse history in a missionary who goes overseas is frequently augmented by the new stressors and challenges to adjustment. The personal pain and discomfort of these survivors varies according to their personalities and mission settings. Women survivors may manifest self-contempt by being a doormat to other missionaries. A lack of self-esteem may lead to depression and some of these women exhibit dependent or passive/aggressive traits. They are likely to be hypersensitive and have very low inner strength.

Other women may be very competent, but their contempt for men often creates conflicts within the mission team. They may have difficulties with authority issues especially since the leadership in many overseas fields is predominately male.

Sexual abuse survivors who become very promiscuous do not often reach the mission field; however, if they do, subtle tendencies in this direction may surface with histrionic and seductive behavior.

### Screening and Treatment

Those of us involved in pre-field evaluations for missionaries believe that candidates coming from bruised backgrounds, regardless of the source, must be thoroughly evaluated prior to overseas placement. In some cases, in-depth counseling needs to take place prior to being sent to the field. Homeland missionary staff should also be thoroughly screened prior to hiring, although the stresses of living in one's own country are usually significantly less than overseas living.

## Personality Disorders

Unfortunately there are some bruised individuals whose damage is so intense that I question whether they will ever be healthy or strong enough to withstand the rigor of missionary service. This could be represented by drawing a continuum as follows:

Healthy——————Bruised—————Personality Disorders

There have been very few articles written on the concept of personality disorders in missionary work. Two recent articles however, suggest the reality of this problem among missionaries (Schubert, 1991 and in press). Unfortunately these articles seem to be the sum total of the treatment of this topic within missionary or professional literature.

When people with personality disorders slip through selection without adequate evaluation, their presence on the field is usually surrounded by contention, dissension, disagreements, and exhaustion on the part of other missionaries and field executives who try to support them emotionally and spiritually. In addition, the mission organization can unintentionally set these people up for failure by expecting more than they can realistically provide.

By definition, a personality disorder involves life-long patterns of maladaptive behavior which cause impairment in interpersonal or occupational functioning and/or subjective distress. These patterns tend to be pervasive, inflexible, and very resistant to any kind of treatment. People with these disorders are not psychotic nor are they truly crazy, but their inter-relationships, sense of responsibility, ability to be a part of a team, and problems with authority tend to preclude successful missionary endeavors.

The nature of personality disorders among missionary personnel and candidates is often misunderstood. There are several reasons for this. First, personnel directors are usually pastoral people, not psychologists. They tend to think of people along a continuum of normal to neurotic to psychotic. The concept of a personality disorder which does not fall within this continuum is a foreign concept to many mission executives. Secondly, evangelicals can be reluctant to admit that committed Christians can have psychological problems that are not solved by spiritual modalities. Third, we would like to think that anyone with a willing spirit can serve. Fourth, it is hard for us to acknowledge the poor prognosis of severe personality disorders given the hope we have from the Gospel. Fifth, at times we have difficulty distinguishing between a "spiritual call" and what I have earlier referred to as a "psychological agenda." And finally, there is some expense involved in quality psychological testing and selection and this expense may create some controversy regarding the need for such tests.

There are several reasons why people with personality disorders should not be placed in cross-cultural situations. First, adjustment in cross-cultural situations is difficult, and most personality disordered individuals cannot handle their stress levels.

Secondly, mission organizations are using their resources for mission work, not for the delivery of mental health care. When a person with a personality disorder inadvertently gets to the field, other missionaries, field leaders, and the national church simply do not have the time, energy, or expertise to deal with these folks.

Third, a particular problem with personality disorders overseas is that these individuals tend to have difficulty in boundary issues. They may struggle to understand cultural boundaries since they have not adjusted to the boundaries in their own cultures. Sexual boundaries may be compromised by some of these people and psychological boundaries are seldom observed as many of these are quite intrusive and make others on the field feel trapped. Social boundaries are often inconsistent, and executives, field leaders, and health care professionals on the field have limited protection from the intrusive tendencies of personality disordered fellow missionaries. People with personality disorders can consume hours of time every week, exhausting fellow team members, causing divisions, and monopolizing time of vulnerable fellow missionaries.

Fourth, many people with personality disorders have very primitive defense mechanisms. These defense mechanisms play havoc with the missionary team, fellow missionaries, and national church members. One particular defense mechanism is *splitting*. Splitting is a healthy mechanism in infants and helps them to separate good from bad; that is, to preserve good experiences, feelings, and relationships in safely isolated mental compartments. However, what is healthy in infants is maladaptive in adults.

People with personality disorders, some of whom manifest "splitting" behaviors (especially the borderline disorder), have contradictory actions or beliefs, lack of impulse control, black and white relationships in which a fellow missionary may be the greatest fellow in the world one day and be the worst person in the world the next day, and contradictory self-concepts whereby one day a person feels very grandiose and the next day feels worthless. The inability to see things in shades of gray can be disruptive to the team. This person will often split the team, split individual relationships, and even split regarding his/her own self-concept from day to day. People with personality disorders also utilize a great deal of denial and projection defenses.

Mission personnel are sometimes uncomfortable with the fact that many personality disorders have some characteristics that remind us of ourselves. The key to overcome this discomfort is to remember that to diagnose a personality disorder, the patterns must be life-long, pervasive, inflexible, and maladaptive enough to cause either impairment in interpersonal or occupational functioning, or subjective distress.

## Types of Personality Disorders

I now describe the various disorders that occur in the general population, and what they might look like in a mission setting. Keep in mind that not everyone will display the full range of symptoms and that symptoms vary between individuals diagnosed with the same disorder. Qualifiers of "mild, moderate, or severe" are frequently used to identify the intensity of the symptoms. These disorders can also overlap with each other to form "mixed personality disorders." Care must also be taken to make sure that someone who is a bit "unique" or otherwise "different" is not inappropriately labeled as having a personality disorder.

People with *paranoid disorders* may be rigid, dogmatic, and suspicious. In mission settings a person with this pathology may be focused on legalisms, divisive doctrines, and theological deficiencies of others.

People with *schizoid disorders* may be extremely shy, aloof, and insensitive to other's feelings. If this individual gets through the selection process, he or she may be reclusive, a loner, and have few if any friends among the mission group.

People with *schizotypal disorders* have a tenuous hold on reality and may have eccentric convictions and beliefs. He or she may have psychotic "religious" experiences that mimic the real thing.

Often these first three personality disorders appear odd or eccentric enough that they are eliminated from selection by interview and close scrutiny of letters of recommendation and telephone calls to the writers of the letters.

People with *avoidant disorders* can slip through the selection process and may occasionally be seen in missionary settings as "loners" who function to some degree in a solo placement as independents or "pioneers." Oates (1987, pp. 102,103) describes Christians with this disorder as "actively detached adults" with histories of rejection and a deep fear of being hurt. Such individuals must be distinguished from missionaries who have characteristics of autonomy and self-sufficiency which are essential for effectiveness in many mission settings.

*People with dependent disorders* place responsibility for life decisions on others, support their personal needs through others, have markedly low self-esteem, and cannot tolerate being alone. They drain fellow missionaries dry in the overseas community where boundary setting is so difficult. They may be particularly unable to deal with the separations that are an inherent part of missionary living.

People with *obsessive-compulsive disorders* may appear to be overly conscientious and scrupulous, but are so exacting that conflict arises over criticism of other missionaries. Occasionally these people can function in a book work, a laboratory, or isolated setting; however, their rigid need for control and poor capacity for relationships interferes with the missionary team cohesion.

People with *passive-aggressive disorders* may appear to be fine Christians who never get angry. However, in the overseas situation which is already fraught with frustrations, this person's obstinacy and anger will be expressed indirectly with procrastination, delay and discreet refusal to follow orders. Other missionaries are puzzled by their own angry reactions to such a "nice" person. This disorder must be distinguished from personal characteristics which are largely culturally derived, such as indirectness in expressing desires and anger or a variety of "saving face" behaviors.

People with *antisocial disorders* were formerly referred to as suffering from *sociopathy* or *psychopathy*. The newer title is deceptive in that these people are often smooth, good talkers, and sociable on a superficial level. They may make wonderful deputation speakers, but they are often manipulators and exploiters lacking real empathy and compassion. They seem to be born with a social-moral learning disability. Boundary violations for these individuals revolve around deficiencies in their conscience. They may be indiscreet sexually, ethically, in business, in money management, in parenting, and in work behavior.

*Borderline disorder* has been more clearly defined during the past two decades. It is characterized by instabilities in mood, interpersonal relationships, and self-image. Identity disturbance is almost always present, especially in self view, sexual identity, long-term goals, career, types of friends and values. Many of these people have feelings of emptiness and boredom. They often alternate in their relationships between the extremes of over idealization and devaluation. They may have frequent outbursts of anger for which they are later sorry or they may deny that they were angry. Self-mutilation and suicide gestures may occur. These people are particularly effective at splitting both in the group setting, in one-to-one relationships, and in their self-image.

People with this disorder seem to have lost out on important developmental milestones, some of which may never be reclaimed. Fear of abandonment is intense and may persist in spite of therapy. This may be exacerbated by the frequent separations that constitute missionary living. Many borderlines were sexually abused as children.

Identity establishment can be so incomplete in these people that they find it almost impossible to successfully integrate into a new culture, hence the basic incompatibility of this personality disorder with overseas missionary service. Their identity is diffuse enough that they often do not know what boundaries are and their limited capacity for empathy precludes others' need for privacy and time alone. Their inability to "self soothe" creates inordinate demands on others missionaries to provide them with comfort and care.

*Narcissistic disorder* is a pervasive pattern of grandiosity, hypersensitivity to the evaluation of others, and lack of empathy. People with this disorder think of themselves as "special," but when faced with normal disappointments of life, they may "decompensate"—that is, fall apart emotionally. They often feel that they are unique and entitled to special treatment. Unfortunately, their sense of entitlement seldom has a corresponding feeling of reciprocal responsibility.

People with this disorder have a very fragile self-esteem. They have the exaggerated sense of self-importance of a small child. Becoming a missionary "star" may further feed the pathology though the stardom is usually short-lived. Most of these people in childhood did not have the opportunity to learn to face gradual limited disappointments with parental support. Consequently, they do not develop the mature ability to withstand disappointment and failure that are a part of life and are particularly a part of mission life. They then alternate between feelings of grandiosity and inferiority.

They have difficulty accepting criticism, disappointment, or suggestion. They seem unable to love, they are poor team players, and in the face of disappointment they may respond with a brief reactive psychosis which can be very disruptive to the work of the mission.

*Histrionic disorder* manifests itself with excessive emotionality and attention seeking. These people constantly demand and look for reassurance, praise, approval, and affirmation. They need to be the center of attention. Their emotions seem shallow and rapidly shifting. Loss and rejection, perceived or real, create severe distress. They may be creative and imaginative but they lack analytical decision-making skills.

Causes of the disorder may be early life separations and disturbance in attachments as well as poor bonding and limited role modeling. Self-esteem for the adult histrionic is centered on physical attractiveness, often to the point of seductiveness. This person has a limited capacity to tolerate delayed gratification and does not wear well on the field. The constant need for reassurance and affirmation wears down other missionaries and nationals creating a level of exhaustion in the entire team. These people are so desperate for attention that they may cross any boundary to get it. Their seductiveness may be either social, sexual, or both.

## On-Field Intervention

One of the most difficult issues any mission has to face is what to do when a person with one of these personality disorders slips through the selection process, arriving overseas with all of his or her emotional baggage. The individual's behavior quickly results in credibility gaps with the nationals, exhaustion on the part of the field executives, frustration, and sometimes resignations from other missionaries.

Compassion would suggest an extended effort at working with the person in the field environment. Unfortunately the statistical probability of rapid significant change anywhere, much less in the heat of the battle overseas, is negligible. Meanwhile the work, the nationals, the other missionaries, and the field leaders suffer.

It is possible for a Christian to have a personality disorder. Emotional damage is not necessarily solved by a committed Christian experience. We understand that a person with physical crippling such as polio is not necessarily made physically whole by salvation and spiritual growth. We must communicate that psychological crippling is not automatically healed with Christian commitment. In talking with mission executives, the analogy I draw is that we would not send our psychological wheelchair cases to the spiritual battlefront overseas. When we do, we compromise the work and expose the individual to unnecessary failure. We also add frustration, anger, and decreased effectiveness and efficiency to the stresses with which co-workers are already dealing. We can use past mistakes to educate our missions to the need for quality prevention.

In many cases, people with personality disorders are educated and intelligent. They may appear to be very spiritual and their skills may seem to be just what a particular overseas field needs. Too often though, the mission has chosen people to fill the immediate needs overseas without selecting according to emotional qualifications.

It is important to remember that a mission that accepts a candidate with a personality disorder who decompensates while in their employ may be responsible to provide hospitalization. In the United States, for example, the "Workers Compensation" matters involved in these cases can bankrupt the uninsured mission board since the costs to the organization may reach as high as eight hundred to one thousand U.S. dollars per day for extended periods of time.

## Testing and Pre-Field Evaluation

A well-honed selection process is key to identify the best candidates for long-term work. Consulting professionals may help avoid inadvertent recruitment of personality disordered individuals or profoundly bruised individuals by making wise recommendations in the pre-field evaluation and testing process.

1. I suggest that all candidates and spouses should receive the Minnesota Multiphasic Personality Inventory (MMPI) early in the selection process. The MMPI is the "gold standard" for detection of personality disorders. It also detects personality traits resulting from bruised backgrounds. Mission groups need to understand that this and other tests must be interpreted by a seasoned professional who should also require a personal interview (B. Lindquist, 1983). Missions also need to be aware of the limitations of the MMPI; for instance, it will not detect sexual deviancy. (The Rorschach may be a valuable tool in the right hands, to detect sexual problems such as pedophilia, sexual identity problems, and so forth.)

The three mistakes I see regarding the use of the MMPI in mission selection and personality disorders are (a) not doing it, (b) not doing it well, and (c) not following the advice of mental health professionals familiar with missions.

2. In-depth personal interviews must be conducted on all candidates. This should include separate interviews with each spouse and any older children. Delicate matters such as childhood sexual abuse, dysfunctional families or origin, alcoholic backgrounds, and other sources of bruising must be thoroughly addressed.

3. Each letter of recommendation should be followed up by a personal telephone call. Letter writers will often be more candid regarding problems if their opinions do not appear in writing.

4. All candidates should submit a detailed occupational and social history which has been verified by outside sources. My experience has been that many people with personality disorders have frequent job changes, though short-term jobs related to schooling may cloud the picture.

5. If any questions surface, the candidate should be interviewed by an experienced mental health professional with experience in diagnosing bruising and personality disorders, and with the awareness of the unique stresses of overseas living.

## Testing Issues

There has been a good deal of discussion over the years concerning the use of psychological tests in the selection process. Several other tests apart from the MMPI are routinely used by mission boards (Ferguson, Kleiwer, B. Lindquist, & S. Lindquist, 1988) and are useful to identify a variety of personal strengths and weaknesses.

First, the Millon Clinical Multiaxial Inventory (MCMI) can be utilized to identify the type of personality disorder an individual has. It is more effective in the clinical setting for a person already generally diagnosed as personality disordered. Other tests, such as the Myers-Briggs (MBTI), the Sixteen Personality Factor (16PF), the Taylor-Johnson, and the California Psychological Inventory (CPI), provide general personality descriptions which can be very helpful, but they may not detect the presence of personality disorders or personality traits due to severe bruising. At this time, my impression is that the MMPI is indispensable for those purposes.

Using the MMPI and other tests early in the selection process can help group candidates into three main categories. First, those who can be accepted unconditionally at the start. Second, those with great potential and promise, but who have issues that need to be addressed prior to overseas placement. Third, those with personality disorders who should not be sent overseas. It is important for mission leaders and the mental health professionals administering the tests to discuss the nature and limits of the testing process, test validity, the data upon which interpretations and recommendations are based, the type of feedback to give to candidates, how test results will be used, and confidentiality.

There has also been some discussion regarding the use of the newer MMPI-II in mission selection. At this point, the MMPI-II is still experimental and has not been normed for the missionary population. However, it does decrease some ethnic bias and may be useful in black candidates, American Indians, and eventually (when it is translated and normed) in missions whose members come from various nations (Schubert, in press).

## Summary

With recent changes in the missionary recruiting pool, mission sending agencies are needing wise professional people to help in the selection process. The increased incidence of dysfunctional family backgrounds, adult children of alcoholic candidates, and survivors of sexual abuse, has correspondingly increased the number of bruised individuals applying to sending organizations. In addition, some candidates are so bruised and damaged that they could be categorized as personality disordered. The inadvertent placement of these individuals overseas is a disaster for the missionary, the team, the field leader, and the national church. The key to wise selection is in the testing and pre-field evaluation process. The use of sophisticated testing (especially the MMPI) and professional evaluation prior to overseas placement should maintain the original purpose of mission agencies and insure that the most qualified missionary candidates actually arrive on overseas fields. In addition, candidates with limited emotional capacities will be spared the tragedy of unnecessary failure.

### Questions for Discussion

1. Under what conditions would it be appropriate to accept a candidate who comes from a severely "bruised" background?

2. What types of dysfunctional family backgrounds do missionaries have who come from the Two-Thirds World?

3. What steps could mission leaders take to help members of the mission who are struggling with a personality disorder? At what point should such a person be sent home for help?

4. How does your mission organization screen its candidates? What procedures and tests does it use?

5. Who is responsible to care for individuals whose personal problems began prior to their involvement in the mission agency?

## References

Allender, D. (1990). *The wounded heart*. Colorado Springs: Navigator Press.

Black, C. (1981). *It will never happen to me*. Denver: MAC Publishing.

Britt, W. (1983). Pretraining variables in the prediction of missionary success overseas. *Journal of Psychology and Theology, 11*, 203-212.

Ferguson, L., Kliewer, D., Lindquist, B., & Lindquist, S. (1988). Essentials and tools of psychological assessment. In O'Donnell, K., and O'Donnell, M. (Eds.). *Helping missionaries grow: Readings in mental health and missions* (pp. 62-69). Pasadena, CA: William Carey Library.

Foyle, M. (1986). How to choose the right missionary. *Evangelical Missions Quarterly, 22*, 196-204.

Friel, J., & Friel, L. (1988). *Adult children: The secrets of dysfunctional families.* Deerfield Beach, FL: Health Communications.

Harrop-Griffiths, J. (1988). The association between pelvic pain, psychiatric diagnosis, and childhood sexual abuse. *Journal of Obstetrics and Gynecology, 71*, 589-594.

Lindquist, B. (1983). Misuses of psychological assessment with missionaries. *Journal of Psychology and Christianity, 2*, 15-17.

Lindquist, S. (1983). A rationale for psychological assessment of missionary candidates. *Journal of Psychology and Christianity, 2*, 10-14.

Oates, W. (1987). *Behind the masks.* Philadelphia: Westminister.

Powell, J., & Williams, K. (1987). *Missionary bruising.* Presentation given at EFMA-IFMA Conference. Detroit, MI.

Schubert, E. (1991). Personality disorder and the overseas missions selection process. *International Bulletin of Missionary Research, 15*, 33-36.

Schubert, E. (in press). Personality disorders and overseas missions: Guidelines for the mental health professional. *Journal of Psychology and Theology.*

Schubert, E. (in press). Use of the MMPI-I and MMPI-II for selection and crisis intervention in overseas personnel. In Duckworth, J., & Anderson, W. (Eds.). *MMPI-I and MMPI-II Interpretation Manual (4th ed.).* Muncie, IN: Accelerated Development.

Sell, C. (1990, September 10). Sins of the fathers (and mothers). *Christianity Today*, 21-23.

Williams, D. (1983). Assessment of cross-cultural adjustability in missionary candidates: Theoretical, biblical, and practical perspectives. *Journal of Psychology and Christianity, 2*, 18-24.

# 7

*Jarrett Richardson*

# Psychopathology in Missionary Personnel

In this chapter I review a number of psychological problems that can affect missionaries and missionary support staff. I describe the most common disorders and emphasize those which may not be identified by the usual psychological interviews and screening prior to missionary appointment. My review is based largely upon my clinical experience and that of my colleagues, and follows the classification system found in the *Diagnostic and Statistical Manual III—Revised* (DSM III-R), published by the American Psychiatric Association (1987).

I use several clinical examples that have been disguised to assure confidentiality. Professionally accepted strategies for dealing with several of these problems will also be briefly described. I approach my examples largely from the perspective of clinical psychiatry and psychology. In many cases spiritual struggles, such as finding it hard to trust God, accompanied the psychological and relational problems. Spiritual issues are also an important focus of treatment. It is my hope that this chapter will equip the reader to better understand the various types of brokenness in our human experience and help insure that accurate assessment and effective intervention are provided for the individuals and families who are the primary resource for the world mission endeavor.

I wish to acknowledge the able assistance of my secretary, Kathy Pike, in preparing this chapter, as well as the helpful suggestions of my good friend and colleague, Dr. Don Kvernen.

## Health and Pathology

Psychopathology refers to the study of human behaviors, thoughts, and emotions that are viewed to be abnormal and unhealthy. Obviously one's view of health and normalcy will have a lot to do with what is considered to be "pathological" (Wakefield, 1992). One perspective I have found useful in my professional work is that of Kolb (1977), who describes both healthy and unhealthy human functioning in this way.

> The healthy adult shows behavior that confirms an awareness of self or personal identity coupled with a life purpose, a sense of personal autonomy and willing-ness to perceive reality and cope with its vicissitudes. The healthy adult has a capacity to invest in others, to understand their needs, to achieve a mutually satisfying heterosexual relationship, to be active and productive with evidence of persistence and endurance in pursuing tasks to their accomplishment, to re-spond flexibly in the face of stress, to receive pleasure from a variety of sources, and to accept [one's] limitations realistically….(p.120)

> It seems most fruitful to look upon most manifestations of psychopathology not as the result of expression of some "disease" but as a mode of behavior or of liv-ing which is the logical, although maladjusted, outcome of the particular individual's original endowment, of the molding influence of the home, of trau-matic experiences that modified personality development, of the stresses and problems springing from within…of [one's] inability to meet these strains, of the type of self-defense reactions habitually utilized for minimizing anxiety, and of any bodily ailments that impair the integrity or efficiency of [one's] bio-logical organism. Mental disorders should therefore be regarded as patterns of human reactions set in motion by stress. (p. 119)

The more we learn about psychiatric disorders, the more evidence there is that many of them do in fact meet the criteria to be called a "disease", having significant genetic and biological components, a relatively predict-able course and prognosis, and significant response to biological treat-ments. However, as is true of most "medical diseases", psychiatric disorders almost always involve biological, psychological, social, and spir-itual factors, and often all of these areas need to be addressed in treatment.

Lest we consider psychopathology to be something that only psychi-atrists, psychologists, and personnel directors need to be aware of, we should all be reminded about the ubiquity of individual and family strug-gles and difficulties in a world which is pervasively fallen. None of us have inherited a perfect biology, had perfect parenting, or been raised in perfect churches or communities. All of us then are subject to different degrees of pathology—personal struggles, inner conflicts, and sometimes actual dis-orders—and this of course goes for the missionary population as well.

Because of the high personal and economic cost of attrition among missionary personnel, it is particularly important not only to thoroughly "screen" for significant psychopathology early in the appointment and training process, but to utilize all information available to undertake thorough discussions with missionary candidates about those traits which may be helpful in facilitating their success overseas or in the home office. Understanding the weaknesses and strengths of missionary personnel is an important, ongoing process, and is part of the organization's responsibility to nurture and develop its people.

## Research on Missionary Psychopathology

One of the first descriptions of missionary psychopathology leading to attrition was published in the *British Journal of Medicine* in 1913 entitled, "Discussion on the Causes of Invaliding from the Tropics." The author reviewed 1051 missionaries from the Church Missionary Society between 1890 and 1908. Forty percent (428 persons) did not persevere in their assignments. Overall, 20.6% were "invalid" (returned home prematurely) because of nervous conditions of a neurasthenia type (this is similar to our modern chronic fatigue syndromes), and 4.8% because of mental disorder of an acute type. In Japan 81% of the "invaliding" was because of neurasthenia; in Africa 20%; in China 25%; and in India 20%. The leading cause of permanent invaliding through non-tropical disease was nervous and mental disorder with 21% being from melancholia (depression) and 17.5% from delusional insanity. This study also found that 39% of missionaries who returned prematurely and permanently from the tropics did so because of a nervous or mental disorder.

Palaszny (1971) examined the cases of 50 missionary candidates and described what he called the "missionary syndrome" in which six of the 50 candidates he interviewed as part of a pre-field screening process had chosen the mission field in an effort to resolve major underlying psychological conflicts. King (1975) identified the depressive syndrome as the most common diagnosable psychiatric disorder in a sample of missionary personnel working overseas. He found depression to be present in 10% of these workers. Dillon (1983) found that non-persevering missionaries demonstrated higher scores on the depression scale of the MMPI than did persevering missionaries.

These few articles are some of the more thorough published accounts of psychopathology in missionary personnel. The paucity of solid empirical research thus affects our ability to make reliable conclusions about the incidence and nature of missionary psychopathology. Missionary stress, however, along with the characteristics of successful and unsuccessful missionaries, have been studied and discussed at some length in the literature (Britt, 1983; Gish, 1983; Parshall, 1987; Williams, 1973); yet these areas are quite different from psychopathology per se. Clearly additional research is called for which focuses on psychological disorders among missionary personnel.

## DSM III-R Categories of Psychopathology

Although almost any psychological disorder or symptom may be found at one time or another in missionary personnel, the disorders which I now describe are common enough so that a mental health professional or administrative person is likely to encounter them in a general missionary population. There are many other types of disorders, of course, that I do not cover, including disorders that manifest in childhood. A discussion of all possible disorders is well beyond the scope of this chapter. For further discussion of disorders and descriptions of actual cases, refer to the *DSM III-R: Case Book* (1989) by Spitzer et al.

My descriptions of the typical disorders that affect missionaries highlight only the essential features of these disorders. The descriptions are based upon criteria taken from the *DSM III-R*, which defines a disorder as being:

> ...*a clinically significant behavioral or psychological syndrome or pattern that occurs in a person and that is associated with present distress (a painful symptom) or disability (impairment in one or more important areas of functioning), or with a significantly increased risk of suffering death, pain, disability, or an important loss of freedom (p. xxii).*

The application of these disorders to missionary personnel, as well as the case studies I discuss, are not intended to categorize people; rather my intent is to classify the various disorders that can affect people.

### *Organic Mental Disorder*

*Dementia* is a very common phenomenon, particularly in the older population, and it is *presenile dementia* which from time to time may be present in the missionary population in late middle age, manifested primarily as memory and learning problems. Impairment of a wide variety of brain functions, including attention, concentration, learning, language, speech, problem-solving, motor skills, relational skills, and emotional stability may be the presenting symptoms of a presenile dementia. Careful medical and neurological evaluation are indicated since there are a number of medical problems that can produce a dementia-like syndrome.

*Example: Presenile Dementia.* A very effective and competent missionary physician was noted by colleagues to deteriorate gradually in his punctuality, attention to clinical details of patient care, and clinical judgement, particularly in urgent care situations. An evaluation while on furlough revealed the emergence of significant learning and memory problems, and presenile dementia, Alzheimer's type, was diagnosed. Because of the progressive nature of this problem and the pervasive loss of function, the decision was made to recommend early retirement. The physician and his family had adequate time to re-establish a home and support system in the United States before any additional loss of functioning occurred. With education and support (e.g., Alzheimer's support groups), this man and his family were able to deal with this problem with grace and dignity.

## Psychoactive Substance-Related Problem

Although there is a wide variety of sensitivity and vulnerability to its use, caffeine is a relatively ubiquitous active chemical substance used by the missionary population, and symptoms such as chronic headaches, insomnia, anxiety, irritability, and fatigue may be the result of prolonged excessive caffeine use or withdrawal.

*Example: Caffeine Intoxication.* A middle-aged missionary teaching a number of courses and serving as administrator at a seminary developed progressively severe insomnia, headaches, indigestion, and urinary frequency. Severe lethargy and headaches, particularly, emerged on Sunday morning. Medical history revealed that this individual had been consuming increasing amounts of caffeine over a period of several months in order to sustain a very high level of output and long hours of work that he thought his position required. The workday symptoms of excessive caffeine intake contrasted with Sunday morning headaches and lethargy which characterized caffeine withdrawal. A gradual reduction in caffeine intake and reorganization of this individual's workload as well as attention to obtaining adequate rest and personal relaxation led to resolution of his symptoms.

Perhaps the most common prescription psychoactive substance involving missionary personnel is the chronic use of sedative and hypnotic (sleeping pill) drugs such as Valium (diazepam) and related substances. In one study involving 390 missionaries, 20% reported having used some type of tranquilizer during the course of their mission service (Parshall, 1987).

Chronic stress may lead to a persistent sense of subjective anxiety often accompanied by physical symptoms such as headaches, dizziness, vague aches and pains (particularly back pain and neck pain), gastrointestinal upset (such as chronic diarrhea or alternating diarrhea and constipation), or even urinary symptoms (such as frequent urination without the presence of anatomic or infectious disease). A sedative or hypnotic is often prescribed for symptomatic relief with the rationale that this will enable the missionary to keep functioning in the Lord's work in a distressing environment.

Although the use of these medications from time to time under crisis circumstances is appropriate, chronic use for symptomatic treatment, instead of developing appropriate alternatives for dealing with the stress, is not medically or psychologically healthy. Almost all sedative drugs produce tolerance and dependence when taken chronically, and many individuals actually experience greater anxiety as the medication becomes less and less effective and the duration of drug action becomes shorter and shorter. A common result is a roller coaster experience of temporary relief alternating with exacerbation of symptoms, and a consequent escalation of dose, only to have the same stress symptoms re-emerge a few weeks or months later as further tolerance develops.

It is wisest to view anxiety as a warning sign, just as we use fever as a warning sign for some underlying infection. (A notable exception to this is panic disorder which will be reviewed later in this chapter.) Although temporary treatment of warning signs may be appropriate and of some subjective benefit, if the warning signs are ignored, serious and progressive illness may result. Many assumptions about missionaries' work and God's calling may need to be reassessed and at times dealt with professionally in order to reduce short-term symptomatology as well as the longer-term risk of burnout and other major psychiatric symptoms.

*Example: Psychoactive Substance-Induced Organic Mental Disorder.* A middle-aged, single missionary developed increasingly severe restlessness, anxiety, agitation, insomnia, and hypertension in the week following an uncomplicated appendectomy. A prescription of Valium led to resolution of all of these symptoms. The physician subsequently obtained a history indicating that this patient had been taking Valium on a daily basis for a number of years for chronic tension headaches. The patient's post-operative symptoms indicated Valium dependence and withdrawal, and a very gradual reduction of the medication along with cognitive/behavioral treatment for his tension headaches was undertaken during the next furlough.

### Organic Mental Disorder Caused by a Known Medical Problem

A wide variety of toxic, metabolic, and infectious processes can produce gradual or sudden changes in cognitive or emotional functioning. An example is chloroquine, used for malaria prophylaxis, which may have psychiatric side effects, the more extreme of which are major psychotic episodes with paranoid delusions and hallucinations. Evaluation by a physician knowledgeable about infectious diseases unique to a particular missionary work environment, and the side effects of medications most frequently used in that setting, is the most important first step in evaluating and treating these problems. This group of difficulties usually responds very quickly to appropriate medical treatment and does not require ongoing psychiatric care.

*Example: Substance-Induced Organic Mental Disorder.* A missionary in a remote village became very agitated and paranoid during recovery from a febrile illness and had to be evacuated by helicopter. Further history revealed that he had taken a number of large doses of chloroquin over a

10-day period to treat his "malaria." Withholding the chloroquin, providing a supportive, safe environment, and administering a few days of an antipsychotic drug with sedative effects (chlorpromazine) led to complete resolution of symptomatology. An alternative treatment for the presumed malaria was provided prior to his return to the village, along with an exhortation to consult with medical personnel more quickly should he become ill.

## Psychotic Disorders

*Brief reactive psychosis* may be the most common non-organic psychotic disorder among missionaries, particularly since pre-field candidate screening can identify the vast majority of individuals with chronic psychotic disorders, such as schizophrenia. Brief reactive psychoses are usually characterized by the sudden and rapid onset of a delusional or hallucinatory state that is triggered by an overwhelming crisis or stress in a vulnerable individual. Because even the best of screening and pre-field training efforts cannot entirely prepare a missionary for what is to be faced on the field, some cases of brief reactive psychosis can be expected.

In general, individuals with this disorder respond very quickly to a supportive environment and antipsychotic medication, and the prognosis is good. Following recovery, specific attention must be given to an attempt to identify one's vulnerabilities and deal in a realistic way with the likelihood of recurrence of the particular stressors that led to this reaction. Professional consultation is usually indicated.

*Schizophrenia* may emerge in missionary personnel and require professional diagnosis and treatment. Delusions, hallucinations, and bizarre beliefs and behavior that interfere with functioning and last at least six months define schizophrenia. Schizophrenia usually surfaces in the second and third decade of life but does occasionally emerge for the first time in later adulthood. There is a wide variability of individual symptomatology, and response to treatment and continuation of service as a missionary may be possible for some individuals who achieve and maintain good remission of symptoms.

*Example: Schizophrenia.* A young, single missionary in his twenties who had a reputation for being an "independent thinker" was frequently in conflict with missionary authorities. He insisted on isolating himself from other missionary personnel and identified very closely with the nationals, including living in town away from the missionary compound and becoming very socially friendly with young single national women. After he very reluctantly moved back to live among the missionaries, he became romantically preoccupied with one of the more mature girls in a nearby MK school dorm and ignored advice from house parents and administrative personnel to discontinue his flirtatious behavior. He became increasingly seclusive and uncooperative, and developed delusions about himself and others. His behavioral and verbal resistance escalated to the point at which he had to be forcibly evacuated back to the United States for a prolonged period of hospitalization and treatment for what was diagnosed as an emerging schizophrenic disorder.

Another chronic psychotic disorder in adulthood that may develop in the missionary population is *delusional* or *paranoid disorder*. This may manifest itself in paranoid jealousy, progressive grandiosity, unremitting persecutory delusions, and at times somatic (physical) delusions. Because individuals developing this disorder may do so gradually and without dramatic external manifestations, their symptoms may be well advanced before family or colleagues come to the realization that something is seriously wrong. Diagnosis and intervention are frequently problematic in cases where the individual may have served a period of time on the field and achieved a significant degree of seniority.

People with delusional disorder are usually unaware of or have limited insight into their problems, and attribute their problems to other people. They do not usually respond to rational persuasion. This means that administrative personnel may have to deal with this problem in a very authoritarian manner and insist that professional evaluation and treatment be obtained. This group of disorders is among the least responsive to currently available psychiatric treatment, and the prognosis is often guarded for such individuals.

*Example: Delusional Disorder.* A middle-aged missionary wife gradually became convinced that her missionary executive husband was romantically involved with a number of younger, single missionary women. The intensity of her convictions became progressively more severe to the point at which she insisted on personally accompanying him everywhere he went and became increasingly accusatory anytime he had any interaction with other women. The best efforts of close missionary friends were not able to dissuade her from her intense jealous preoccupations, and the couple eventually resigned and were later divorced. She never accepted professional evaluation or assistance and continued to maintain her jealous convictions in spite of overwhelming evidence to the contrary.

There is also a group of psychiatric syndromes that has many characteristics of psychotic disorders combined with major mood disorders. The most likely to occur in missionary personnel following adequate pre-field screening and preparation is *schizoaffective disorder*. Individuals with this disorder have repeated episodes of rapidly emerging psychotic symptoms simultaneous with signs of major mood disturbance. These are not usually subtle symptoms, and they require professional intervention. Individuals with these problems can often achieve adequate and sustained remission of symptoms, though recent evidence suggests that the prognosis is less favorable than for individuals who have mood disorders (such as manic-depressive illness or recurrent depression) without accompanying psychotic features.

## Mood Disorders

*Depression* is probably the most common psychopathology present in missionary personnel. A wide variety of stressors express themselves through the final common pathway of the depressive syndrome and its variants. Depression is often camouflaged in a variety of other symptoms and not directly expressed as a depressed affect or mood. Chronic fatigue, persistent insomnia, loss of appetite and weight, loss of energy, inability to concentrate, loss of pleasure in activities one usually enjoys, excessive and inappropriate guilt, and social withdrawal are among the most common manifestations of depression.

In the workplace, depression may show up as decreased work performance, decreased social interaction, impatience and irritability, or even unexpected hostility. Among the missionary population a variety of medical complaints may be the socially acceptable manifestations of depression. These often include headaches, back pain, fatigue, and gastrointestinal and neurologic symptoms.

Because depression is common and has many causes, it may easily be overlooked or misunderstood until it reaches the more advanced and obvious stages. Most depression responds to treatment with practical and supportive care augmented by antidepressant medication. Often basic health hygiene such as obtaining enough sleep, eating properly, reserving time for recreation and family, more realistically addressing over-commitment and inability to accomplish all that needs to be done, and attention to pastoral care and spiritual welfare will reduce the likelihood of clinical depression and the related syndrome commonly referred to as burnout. Several types of psychotherapy have been shown to be successful in the treatment of depression.

*Burnout.* Although burnout is not an official DSM-III-R term, it is a phenomenon frequently experienced by missionary personnel. It develops from exposure to chronic stress that gradually exceeds the individual's physical, emotional, and spiritual coping mechanisms. The results are a wide variety of symptoms that vary depending on individual personality variables and circumstances. Sometimes burnout is not perceived by the individual while on the field because of the relentless demands of the work as well as the gradual onset of symptoms. It may manifest itself in symptoms as mild as fatigue and loss of enthusiasm for work or more extreme symptoms such as severe exhaustion, escalation of interpersonal conflict, major depressive or anxiety symptoms, and at times spiritual crisis or suicidal thoughts.

According to Rush (1987), burnout can be brought on by a number of factors: feeling "driven" to work, not pacing oneself, trying to "do it all yourself," having unrealistic self-expectations, being stuck in too many routines, persisting in a life of unbalanced priorities, being in poor physical condition, and maintaining ongoing and unrelenting contact with other people's problems. Almost all of these factors relate to the way a person approaches work—that is, one's work style. The type of work one does can also push a person towards burnout, especially for those who are work long hours with minimal rest or those who work full-time in a people-helping profession.

Many missionaries do not see burnout coming or do not identify it in themselves readily. It is therefore important to be in accountable relationships as well as have access to a pastoral or other professional counselor to help prevent and work through burnout. Effective restoration may require many months or even several years, and although the time taken to do this may seem to be a major disruption in missionary career plans and goals, long-term individual, family, and organizational health are often at stake.

*Example: Burnout and Depression.* A couple returned to the United States following their second tour as station manager and hostess at a port of entry into a country with a large number of missionaries. Although they were both aware that they were not functioning at an optimal level or feeling much emotional resilience during the last year of service, they were both surprised by the intense degree of exhaustion they experienced as soon as they arrived in the United States. An initial period of rest and supportive counseling led to some insight but minimal improvement in symptomatology. Further clinical evaluation revealed that the wife was suffering from symptoms of a major depression, and that the husband was experiencing persistent symptoms of exhaustion, weakness, irritability, and inactivity.

Upon reflection it became apparent that both he and the mission organization expected him to perform at "super normal levels." As the number of missionaries in transit increased, a significant conflict emerged between this couple's commitment to serve the individuals involved and the mission organization's need for them to attend to the many bureaucratic details. The couple scrupulously attempted to attend to both sets of priorities while experiencing increasing frustration and anger toward the organization for not providing more personnel to assist in this responsibility. The wife became more and more depressed and guilty about her inability to be all things to all people, and the husband became more overtly angry and at times seemed to be passive-aggressive toward mission administrators.

Treatment occurred over a period of several months. The wife received antidepressant medication and supportive counseling services. The husband also received counseling. She was eventually able to taper and discontinue her antidepressant medication, and he regained his sense of well-being. The impasse with the mission administration, however, was not satisfactorily resolved, and they requested assignment to a different area of work.

*Bipolar Disorder.* Formerly called *manic-depressive disorder*, this disorder is characterized by cycles of noticeable changes in mood, sleep, energy, appetite, sexual interest, self-esteem, physical activity, and degree of interpersonal or social engagement. The *manic episode* generally includes symptoms at the opposite end of the spectrum from the depression phase in each of these symptom categories. For both bipolar disorder and recurrent major depressive disorder there is frequently a family history of a mood disorder in siblings or previous generations.

The major mood disorders are among those most responsive to active treatment which almost always includes a combination of medication and one of a variety of psychotherapies. Once the diagnosis is accurately made and medical causes excluded, most individuals with major mood disorders can return to full and productive life and service, although about one-third of these individuals will need some kind of ongoing medication and may need intermittent psychological intervention and medication adjustment when the underlying disorder flares up.

*Dysthymia.* This mood disorder, which, in the past, was called *depressive neurosis*, is the persistent experience of depressive symptoms that are not of adequate severity to meet the diagnostic criteria for major depression, and are not usually as episodic as the major mood disorders. It is often described as a lifelong experience of depressive feelings that lend an unhappy or negative emotional tone to almost all aspects of life. Individuals with *dysthymia* are not as "obviously" depressed as are those with major mood disorders and do have some ability to respond to positive external events with elevation in mood. These individuals may seem to be mildly though chronically unhappy, mostly with themselves, yet for the most part are able to carry on normal functioning. Recent evidence suggests that some people with dysthymia respond to antidepressant medication better than to psychotherapy; however, many individuals with dysthymia can benefit from assistance in identifying and dealing with those experiences in life that have influenced their condition.

*Example: Dysthymia.* A married missionary woman in her early forties had struggled since adolescence with feelings of depression and over-dependency. She was an MK who at age 16 was sent home to the United States for the last two years of high school while her family remained overseas. During this time there was no support system for her, and she felt very abandoned. She seldom talked much to anyone about her feelings, especially as they related to her deep sense of abandonment, emotional pain, and need for others to take care of her. Her feelings of depression and dependency continued into her marriage and started to escalate around the time her children began going away to college. At this point she sought professional help.

About two years of weekly psychotherapy helped heal some of the past hurts, especially her negative feelings about her parents and their having sent her away. She also worked on her self-defeating personality patterns, although her dependent personality traits were not significantly modified. (Note: Individual vulnerability to separation and its effects and significance are difficult to predict.)

## Bereavement

Bereavement refers to the normal reaction of grief to the death of loved ones. It takes time to work through and resolve one's sense of loss and related feelings. Geographic distance from the deceased can also complicate the resolution of grief.

Many people experience symptoms of major depression during the first year of bereavement. Some may minimize their feelings or delay the process of mourning by becoming more involved with their work. Others may manifest grief in indirect ways through irritability, lowered self-esteem, or anxiety. *Complicated bereavement* can thus occur when one's grief response is covered up, postponed, or "masked" by other symptoms. Certain vulnerabilities of a psychological or biological nature can place an individual at greater risk for prolonged depression and grief that may need professional evaluation and intervention.

Variations of bereavement and grief may emerge in response to the cumulative losses that missionaries experience. Beginning with separation from family and friends at the initial departure to the foreign field, the missionary faces frequent and continuous separation and loss. Further losses include separation from children who leave for boarding school or college and eventually the loss of parents and colleagues as the missionary lives through the life cycle. Some individuals are especially vulnerable to separations due to traumatic separations early in life. In these individuals, cumulative separations can lead to clinical symptoms such as depression, somatization, anxiety, and even compulsive syndromes.

## Anxiety Disorders

Some of the most common *anxiety disorders* that affect missionary personnel include *panic disorder, obsessive-compulsive disorder, post-traumatic stress disorder*, and *generalized anxiety disorder*. Recent research and clinical experience provide convincing evidence that panic and obsessive compulsive disorders have significant biological components. As is true in individuals with a mood disorder, patients suffering from panic or obsessive-compulsive disorders often have close relatives who have had similar problems. Pastoral, professional, and medical care may all be important parts of helping these individuals.

*Generalized Anxiety Disorder.* Some individuals develop persistent, unrealistic, or excessive anxiety and a worried, apprehensive expectation about life's circumstances. These mental symptoms are often accompanied by signs of physical tension such as trembling, fatigue, nervous system hyperactivity (such as shortness of breath, palpitations, and neurologic or gastrointestinal symptoms), and emotional and cognitive symptoms such as irritability and difficulty concentrating. It is important to be sure that there is no underlying medical disorder such as excessive caffeine use or hyperthyroidism in people who experience anxiety.

Symptomatic treatment with minor tranquilizers is appropriate in the short-term, but because of the potential for physical and psychological dependence on these drugs, cognitive and behavioral therapy is very important. Many Christian people have difficulty reporting these anxiety symptoms because of a sense of guilt that their faith is not adequate to override their anxiety. Just as fever is often the first indication of a serious underlying infection, anxiety can best be understood as an indication that something is seriously the matter in a person's life. Aside from those patients with agoraphobia, panic disorder, and obsessive-compulsive disorder who do seem to have some physiological vulnerability and may need longer-term medication treatment, most individuals with generalized anxiety disorder are better served by addressing the source of unrealistic anxiety and symptoms that result.

*Example: Anxiety Disorder.* A young mother on her first term in Africa was so preoccupied with her own fear of snakes that she was constantly vigilant, anxious, and restrictive of her two-year-old's outdoor play. She became ill with abdominal cramps, episodic diarrhea, shortness of breath, chest heaviness, rapid heartbeat, and severe insomnia. The counsel of more experienced missionary women, realistic precautions, and the temporary use of diazepam (Valium) for the anxiety symptoms led to transient relief, but she was unable to tolerate the constant worry and had to return to the United States for early home assignment. After intensive cognitive/behavioral therapy and adjunctive treatment with fluoxetine (Prozac), she was able to come to terms with the sources of her fears and to achieve enough peace and reassurance about her calling to return to Africa and later begin an effective ministry with MKs.

*Panic disorder* often emerges after the second decade of life and is characterized by increasingly frequent episodes of symptoms including: sudden onset of severe anxiety, fast heartbeat, fast breathing with a sense of being short of breath, trembling, an upset feeling in the stomach that may be accompanied by diarrhea, and an associated sense of impending doom. If these panic attacks occur with adequate severity and frequency, many individuals develop *agoraphobia*, which is a fear of being in public or open spaces. Partly because of the fear of being emotionally out of control while in a public environment, some people with agoraphobia become confined to their homes and are severely disabled by this syndrome. The majority of people with panic disorder respond very well to certain types of antidepressants augmented for a brief period of time with antianxiety drugs. Cognitive and behavioral treatments often help accelerate recovery from anxiety and agoraphobic symptoms.

*Obsessive-compulsive disorder* is characterized by the repeated intrusion of unwanted and troublesome thoughts in the mind of an individual who recognizes that these fearful thoughts are irrational or not well-founded. More severely affected individuals develop a pattern of repetitive and ritualized behavior which they feel compelled to carry out. The attempt to resist such compulsions—for example, repeatedly rechecking doors to see if they are locked, or washing one's hands so much that they become chapped and sore—leads to an intolerable increase in inner tension that is only relieved by carrying out the compulsive act. Although some benefit may be derived from psychological exploration of the underlying causes of the fears that lead to obsessions and compulsions, the most effective treatment is a combination of certain medications (imipramine, clomipramine, or fluoxetine) with cognitive/behavioral therapy.

*Example: Obsessive-Compulsive Disorder.* A missionary in the middle of his career began to experience constant preoccupation with thoughts about the theological struggles that he had "dealt with" in seminary. He found himself unable to tolerate the thought of those that he knew who had not accepted Christ being condemned to eternal punishment. He also became convinced that his obsessions were the result of and the cause of having committed the "unpardonable sin" of thinking that Jesus was not who He said He was. Soon he was miserably distraught and depressed with uncontrollable thoughts of the problems of grace and works, free will and predestination, the humanity and deity of Jesus, and "the suffering of the innocent." He sought pastoral care, intensified his personal devotional life and Bible study, and even sought exorcism, all to no avail. While on home assignment he was able to find a Christian psychiatrist and gradually his obsessions remitted under treatment with clomipramine (Anafranil) and individual psychotherapy. Though he never felt the same as "before," he was able to experience relief and comfort for most of his working hours. The obsessions flared when he was under unusually high stress, but he learned to manage this well enough to return to the field and effectively serve out his career there.

*Post-Traumatic Stress Disorder.* If an individual experiences an event that is outside the range of usual human experience and that would be markedly distressing to almost anyone, they may develop *post-traumatic stress disorder*. In this disorder the traumatic event is persistently re-experienced; there is an avoidance of stimuli associated with the trauma and symptoms such as sleep disturbance, irritability, difficulty concentrating, hypervigilance, or exaggerated response to something that reminds the person of the traumatic event. At times these symptoms develop soon after a traumatic event such as kidnapping, rape, physical violence, terrorist activities, or major accidents or injuries. Early intervention by removal from the traumatic situation, provision of a secure and comforting environment, and permitting the individual to talk about the different aspects of the traumatic experience may help reduce subsequent episodes.

Other individuals seem to show few significant effects from major traumatic events until months, or at times years later. Sometimes "unexplained" symptoms such as irritability, moodiness, hypervigilance, emotional numbing, or sleep disturbances are somewhat mystifying until the individual is able to relate his/her disturbance to an earlier major trauma. Some eating disorders and personality disorders are associated with severe and repetitive childhood trauma.

Although antidepressants may provide some symptomatic benefit, most individuals with post-traumatic stress disorder will require extensive professional psychotherapy in order to achieve a satisfactory level of healing from the trauma they have suffered. It may not be until many hours of support and exploration have established a thorough level of trust with the therapist that the memories of remote trauma start to emerge and become available for healing work.

## Somataform Disorders

Many individuals develop physical symptoms for which there are no demonstrable or known organic causes. Even with the most sophisticated evaluation, many physical symptoms are unexplained. Although this does not prove that "nothing is there," it is frequently necessary to persuade an individual in this situation that exploration of the psychological, social, and spiritual aspects of life may well yield significant symptomatic improvement.

The most extreme forms of *somataform disorders* are non-neurologic limb paralysis (*conversion symptoms*). Much more common are symptoms of *hypochondriasis* in which an individual is preoccupied with the fear of having a serious disease. This fear is maintained in spite of thorough and adequate medical evaluation and reassurance. Even more common are the numerous physical symptoms that individuals develop as a result of fatigue, sleep deprivation, or stress (such as headaches, backaches, stomachaches), and most individuals with significant medical disorders are aware of the fact that emotional stress decreases their tolerance and at times significantly amplifies their experience of pain and discomfort. In environments in which acknowledging emotional distress is considered to be unacceptable, physical complaints serve as a primary means of communicating such distress.

## Dissociative Disorders

In some individuals a single overwhelming stressful event or accumulation of multiple stressful events may lead to an alteration in the normally integrative functions of identity, memory, or consciousness. The more dramatic form of this problem is manifest in *multiple personality disorder* (the existence of two or more "subpersonalities"), but *psychogenic fugue* (a state of unexpected travel from home with the assumption of a new personality), *psychogenic amnesia* (the sudden inability to recall important personal information too extensive to be explained by ordinary forgetfulness), and *depersonalization disorder* (the experience of feeling detached from one's mental processes or body) are equally distressing, though somewhat more uncommon forms of dissociation.

*Example: Dissociative Disorder.* A 30-year-old missionary, soon after the birth of her first child, began to demonstrate uncharacteristic fits of violent rage toward her husband when he made amorous advances. The next day she would act as if nothing had happened. Her husband became more and more bewildered and upset and eventually demanded that she seek professional counsel. Although she continued to deny any knowledge of these "fits," she did undergo a thorough medical evaluation to rule out seizure disorder and other physical disturbances. She also started to see a therapist. It was not until she had been in therapy for two years that she began to recall fragments of ritualistic sexual abuse that she had experienced as a child before she and an infant brother were adopted from a foster home where she had been placed after being abandoned by her biological parents. Eventually she was able to connect the trauma of early life with the experience of sexual advances, some of which occurred while their child was crying in the next room. Several years of individual therapy resulted in emotional healing of the early traumatic memories. Marital therapy renewed the trust that she and her husband had experienced early in their marriage.

## Sexual Disorders

Very few individuals reach adulthood without experiences that distort or impair certain aspects of their sexuality. For some, a sexual disorder can develop and is often among the most difficult problem areas for individuals to acknowledge and discuss with their spouse or their physician, primarily because of a sense of shame or guilt that one feels in having such a problem. Missionaries are not immune to such disorders.

Individuals with *paraphilias* are aroused by objects or situations that are not considered part of a normative pattern, and this type of arousal interferes with comfort and mutuality in sexual activity. *Sexual dysfunctions* involve disturbances in sexual desire or in the phases of the sexual response cycle (excitement, orgasm, and resolution). *Ego-dystonic homosexuality* also occurs among missionaries, in which one struggles with his or her sexual orientation, desiring instead to initiate and maintain heterosexual relationships.

Helping individuals and couples deal with this very sensitive area requires a great deal of wisdom, sensitivity, and knowledge on the part of the mission board and counselors. Sometimes the real issue may be poor marital communication or a lack of information on sexual functioning. At other times these areas can be so difficult to deal with that they require specialized professional expertise.

*Example: Inhibited Sexual Desire.* A middle-aged missionary sought counsel about the lack of sexual attraction he felt for his wife. This had become apparent to him just before they were married 25 years earlier, but he had not begun to feel hopeless about it until he was in the midst of facing many realities of middle adult life. Extensive psychotherapy addressed early life experiences that led to his separating sexual desire from personal relationships, his image of sexual attractiveness that had been influenced by the secular media, and the role that sexual fantasies played in his overall sexual satisfaction. Although there was not a complete resolution of the primary problem, he achieved enough improvement to establish a satisfying sexual relationship with his wife.

## Adjustment Disorders

Short-lived maladaptive reactions to psychological, social, or physical stressors are called *adjustment disorders*. There is usually a specific stressor that can be identified. Symptoms may include anxiety, depression, disturbance of conduct, physical complaints, social withdrawal, or work or academic impairment. The symptoms usually resolve either when the stressors end or when a new equilibrium is established—for example, adjusting to the effects of a stroke. Adjustment disorder symptoms are greater than would be expected in a usual reaction to a particular stressor but do not persist long enough to become one of the major psychiatric disorders previously mentioned. Individual vulnerability and circumstances are important factors in the development of adjustment disorders since the intensity of the stressor itself may not explain the emergence of the symptoms.

Very practical, supportive, and directive counseling may shorten the duration of an adjustment disorder and/or accelerate progress toward adaptation to a chronic situation. Occasionally, symptoms that emerge during the experience of an adjustment disorder may point to the need for more extensive counseling or psychotherapy to deal with those things that have made the individual vulnerable to the particular kind of stress he/she experiences. Symptomatic treatment with medication may also help accelerate recovery, but medication is usually adjunctive to psychotherapy for adjustment disorders.

*Example: Adjustment Disorder with Anxious Mood.* A missionary in his late thirties returned home to obtain further medical treatment for a slow-healing, painful, and somewhat disabling fractured hip. He experienced difficulty with the ongoing stress of the medical problem and was preoccupied with whether or not he would be able to "save his leg" and return to overseas service. His preoccupation was resolved rather quickly with supportive counseling.

His wife, however, who accompanied him home, was actually more distressed than he was. She had become very insecure, and when her husband became less strong and more dependent due to his illness, she became extremely distressed and anxious. She received some supportive help from an older friend and experienced a renewed sense of confidence about herself and her situation. As her husband regained strength and became less dependent on her, her anxiety also began to be resolved. The couple were able to use their time back home to regroup, and subsequently returned to the field.

## Personality Disorders

Every individual has personality traits that reflect his/her particular way of thinking, feeling, relating, and perceiving. These traits tend to persist over time and are consistent in a wide variety of settings. When an individual's personality has significantly interfered over an extensive period of time with his/her adaptation to life and relationships, his/her personality is considered to be clinically disordered. These *personality disorders* are generally recognizable in adolescence and in most cases persist throughout adulthood.

Except for the most dramatic presentations of personality disorders, identification of significant personality dysfunction usually requires a great deal of discernment on the part of the missions administrator as well as psychological testing and assessment by a mental health clinician (see chapter six for a fuller discussion). Personality disorders among missionary personnel can thus escape identification in the interview process but become apparent when exacerbated by stressors in specific mission settings. Consider the following examples.

People with a *paranoid personality disorder* may exacerbate their underlying tendency to misinterpret and mistrust others as they seek to relate to nationals and work with colleagues.

Individuals with a *borderline personality disorder* may not manifest the characteristic pattern of instability of mood, interpersonal relationships, and self-image until they leave the highly structured religious context of home and school for the much more stressful and unstructured setting of missionary work.

Personnel with a pervasive pattern of excessive emotionality and attention-seeking characteristic of *histrionic personality disorder* may not become dysfunctional until the demands of mission work on the spouse threaten to undermine the spouse's ability to meet his/her needs for attention. Similarly the pervasive pattern of submissive behavior of a person with *dependent personality disorder* may not become problematic until circumstances prevent one's partner from attending to his/her deep sense of insecurity.

Many individuals with *narcissistic personality disorder* manage to control their grandiose sense of self-importance while they are the center of attention and admiration during the first stages of becoming a missionary.

When the realities of the difficulties of missionary life begin to sink in, often during the first term of service, these individuals may not be able to tolerate feeling "ordinary."

The pervasive pattern of perfectionism and inflexibility characteristic of *obsessive-compulsive personality disorder* may not express itself fully until an individual with these traits is in a missionary role which has unattainable standards and expectations and the individual, perhaps for the first time, realizes that he/she will not be "good enough" for the task.

The ongoing pattern of passive resistance to demands for adequate social and occupational performance characteristic of *passive-aggressive personality disorder* is most likely to present when the individual faces situations that produce intense frustration and anger that they are unable to deal with directly. Procrastination, forgetfulness, tardiness, and excessive deliberateness that leads to incomplete or delayed work are common signs of this disorder in individuals who are not able to assertively deal with conflict, especially conflict with authority.

In general, traditional treatment approaches for personality disorders have not led to significant change in basic personality structure. However, many people can learn to adapt to the problems that their personality produces. Treatment on the field though, is usually not available nor desirable, as the likelihood of significant change while on the field is negligible (Schubert, 1991).

New psychotherapeutic approaches derived from an understanding of the interpersonal world of humans beginning in infancy have been helpful in the treatment of certain personality disorders, particularly narcissistic, borderline, and obsessive-compulsive personality disorders (Masterson & Klein, 1989). This form of treatment is intensive and expensive and seldom available on the foreign mission field. It is usually best for missionaries to find a situation in the home culture that will permit and support the treatment needed and to reconsider overseas service after achieving significant improvement in one's dysfunctional personality.

## Conclusion

One of my goals in writing this review of psychopathology in missionary personnel is to destigmatize the psychological difficulties that missionary personnel may face. I also hope that the reader will be able to better understand, empathize with, and help those who are on the front lines of the world mission endeavor.

Since all of us involved in missions are fallen human beings with various degrees of "brokenness" in our personalities, facing these realities together with the most accurate and effective assessment and interventions is a crucial part of our witness to the grace of our Lord Jesus Christ. As we learn from all that God has taught us through His word and our study of His creation, and apply this learning to His purposes, we are able to be part of His reconciling and healing activity within the mission community and the world.

## Questions for Discussion

1. How does Kolb's definition of psychological health at the beginning of this chapter match with your definition?

2. What is the place of prayer, deliverance, inner healing approaches, and spiritual warfare in the care and treatment of missionary personnel with clinical disorders?

3. What types of member care resources need to be made available for the evaluation and treatment of missionary personnel, both pre-field and on-field?

4. How realistic is it to assume that better screening and preparation procedures will decrease the incidence of psychological disorders among missionary personnel?

5. What are some of the problems and disorders common among missionary children and their families?

## References

American Psychiatric Association. (1987). *Diagnostic and Statistical Manual of Mental Disorders (Third Edition—Revised)*. Washington D.C.: Author.

Britt, W. (1983). Pretraining variables in the prediction of missionary success overseas. *Journal of Psychology and Theology, 11*, 203-212.

Dillon, D. (1983). Personality characteristics of evangelical missionaries as measured by the MMPI. *Journal of Psychology and Theology, 11*, 213-217.

Gish, D. (1983). Sources of missionary stress. *Journal of Psychology and Theology, 11*, 238-242.

King, L. (1975). The depressive syndrome: A follow-up study of 130 professionals working overseas. *American Journal of Psychiatry, 132*, 636-640.

Kolb, L. (1977). *Modern clinical psychiatry (9th ed.)*. Philadelphia: W. B. Saunders Company.

Masterson, J., & Klein, R. (1989). *Psychotherapy of the disorders of self: The Masterson approach*. New York: Brunner/Mazel.

Paluszny M., & Zrull, J. (1971). The new missionary. *Archives of General Psychiatry, 24*, April, 363-366.

Parshall, P. (1987). How spiritual are missionaries? *Evangelical Missions Quarterly, 23*, 8-19.

Price, G. (1913). Discussion on the causes of invaliding from the tropics. *British Medical Journal, 2*, 1290-1297.

Rush, M. (1987). *Burnout: Practical help for lives out of balance*. Wheaton, IL: Victor Books.

Schubert, E. (1991). Personality disorders and the selection process for overseas missionaries. *International Bulletin of Missionary Research, 14*, 33-36.

Spitzer, R., Gibbon, M., Skodol, A., Williams, J., & First, M. (1989). *Diagnostics and Statistics Manual of Mental Disorders III—Revised: Case Book*. Washington, D.C.: American Psychiatric Press.

Wakefield, J. (1992). The concept of mental disorder: On the boundary between biological facts and social values. *American Psychologist, 47*, 373-388.

Williams, K. (1973). Characteristics of the more successful and less successful missionaries (Doctoral dissertation, United States International University, 1973). *Dissertation Abstracts International, 34*, 1786B-1787B.

# 8

*Kelly O'Donnell*
*Michele Lewis O'Donnell*

# Understanding and Managing Stress

Stress affects us all. It is an inevitable and normal part of life. Too much accumulated stress, though, will sideline even the most robust of missionaries.

Several excellent materials are available on missionary stress. Marjory Foyle's (1987) book *Overcoming Missionary Stress*, the articles by Wayne Dye (1974) and Sally Dye (1974) on "Stress-Producing Factors in Cultural Adjustment" and "Decreasing Fatigue and Illness in Field Work," and Ken William's (1988) "Worksheet on Balanced Living" are but a few of the many examples.

The present chapter continues the discussion of this important subject by approaching missionary stress from the perspective of member care. Some practical tools are presented to help missionaries and mission agencies understand and assess different sources of stress. The chapter closes with a case study focusing on missionary adjustment and stress management.

Let's briefly review stress. Stress is the response of the entire person to various internal and external demands (stressors). This definition assumes that stress will affect one's spirit, emotions, mind, and body. For example, a person may be experiencing self-doubt, grief, or physical illness (internal stressors) in conjunction with work pressures, financial difficulties, or friction with colleagues (external stressors). Put them all together and the result is the subjective experience of "stress." This may then

This chapter is a revision of the authors' article, "Stress Can Be Managed" (1991, *Evangelical Missions Quarterly*, 27, 40-45). Used by permission.

manifest itself in physical problems such as insomnia, hypertension, and headaches, as well as irritability, depression, spiritual doubts, and apathy.

## Examples of Missionary Stress

The following accounts poignantly illustrate the realities of stress on the field. These excerpts are from letters written to us by mature, committed missionaries.

1. *A single medical missionary in Asia working with refugees.* During times of stress this year I find myself struggling to maintain a balanced eating pattern. It seems we are always on call, and it is hard to turn away such needy people. There are days when I go to the refrigerator and look for things to eat and yet I am aware that I am not even hungry. This really bothers me because I hate to see myself falling into the trap of eating to cope with stress. I wish our base had a person with a pastor's heart who was willing to listen to our concerns and offer advice and encouragement.

2. *A mission leader in India coaching first-term missionaries.* Culture shock is the biggest struggle as our new missionaries pursue learning a different language and culture. This usually is hard on their sense of identity and sifts through those who can stay on long-term from those who cannot. Loneliness and isolation are two words to describe the first year. Depression is frequently a part of the stress they feel as they try to cope with their new and demanding work.

3. *A missionary couple teaching in the Middle East.* As tentmakers, we must fight the fear of being unfairly labeled as politically subversive or as enemies of the established religion, and consequently be deported from the country. Paranoia is the tactic of the Enemy to keep God's representatives from sharing and being Good News. We often feel forced to lead divided and overly busy lives. Our "free time" is spent making visits, holding Bible studies, and housing visitors. Faith compels us to be people-oriented and compassionate, willing to "waste time" on individuals. The problem is there just isn't enough time!

4. *A middle-aged mission administrator in Europe.* What are the issues that led my wife and me to resign? First, I had labored here for over three years without having the slightest contact from other leaders from our mission in this country. No one asked how I was doing, what I was doing, or why. The isolation from full-time workers, from fellowship, and from avenues of dealing with the problems here, were the primary factors. Oddly, in discussing these issues with another leader, he seemed perplexed that they would even be issues. Such mentality prompted a letter to our international director in which I expressed my concern for more in-depth and comprehensive pastoral oversight of staff and leaders. It seems that too little is understood and too much is presumed.

## Research on Missionary Stress

What types of stress do missionaries go through? Many! Cedric Johnson and David Penner (1981) surveyed 55 North American Protestant mission agencies with over 100 staff overseas. Respondents included personnel directors, associate directors, and other home office staff, who were asked to rank order the most frequent missionary problems requiring counseling. By far the highest ranked problem was relationships with other missionaries, followed by cultural adjustment, managing stress, and raising children. Other problems included marriage difficulties, financial pressures, and loneliness.

Another study, by Dorothy Gish (1983), sought to identify specific stressors equally applicable to all missionaries regardless of age, sex, or marital status. A questionnaire consisting of sixty-five items (stressors) was completed by 549 missionaries from various mission boards and who were working around the world. The greatest stressors, in order, were confronting others when necessary (especially true for women), communicating across language and culture barriers (especially those involved in more "frontline" work), time and effort needed to maintain donor relationships (especially members of faith missions), managing the amount of work, and establishing work priorities. This researcher goes on to point out how each of these stressors can be either prevented or minimized through better training in conflict resolution and organizational management.

Phil Parshall (1987) explored different aspects of adjustment and spirituality for a sample of 390 missionaries serving in 32 countries with 37 mission boards. Some of the results reveal that the majority regularly face discouragement and frustration, with over 20 percent having taken tranquilizers at some time. The greatest spiritual struggles were listed as maintaining a successful devotional time, experiencing spiritual victory, and managing feelings of sexual lust.

Taken together, these studies reflect some of the common challenges facing missionaries: cross-cultural adjustment, work pressures, spiritual resiliency, family life, finances, and relationships with colleagues. Individual responses to these stressors will vary, of course, for different missionaries and across different mission settings.

## Clinical Impressions

Our experience in counseling primarily Western missionaries suggests that some do in fact experience stressors that can lead to more serious problems. Depression, anxiety, and separation grief, for example, are three problem areas that we frequently treat.

Depression can take a variety of forms ranging from a "biological or hormonal-based" depression which often responds well to medication, to the more "reactive" type which is usually related to recent situational stressors. Anxieties can involve anything from a phobic fear of air travel, a fear of intimacy, feeling overwhelmed by a strong emotion such as anger, apprehension in going outside one's neighborhood or house, panic disorders in which one feels temporarily out of control and close to dying, or a more "generalized" disorder marked by tension and nervousness about many aspects of life. Separation grief results from the sense of loss experienced when, for example, a close friend leaves, a loved one dies, or from the cumulative effect of multiple goodbyes over time. "Masked" grief is also possible, whereby a person is not aware they are grieving, but rather expresses their sadness through such things as poor work performance or irritability.

Some feelings of depression, anxiety, and grief are certainly normal. They are the natural consequences of being blessed with emotions and of living in a fallen world. However, the chronic experience of these feelings usually reflects a mood or personality disorder and the need for professional treatment (Schubert, 1991).

Some missionaries may find it hard admitting to emotional struggles, as this could cast them in a less favorable light and possibly result in negative consequences. Problems which are primarily emotional can be presented in terms of having sinned (pride, rebellion, lack of faith), physical ailments (headaches, fatigue, hypertension), and being "stressed out." We have noted that the term "stressed out" is frequently used as a safe way to communicate something which may be more serious—namely, the missionary is experiencing some inner struggles and is finding it difficult to negotiate some of the demands of missionary life.

In general, the types of problems we have dealt with on the field are quite similar to those we have dealt with among Christians in the United States. These include marital conflict, career change, sexual dysfunction, work frustrations, behavior problems in children, eating disorders, unwanted habits, feeling distant from God, guilt, and long-standing "bruises" stemming from one's childhood. We have often found that the added elements of cross-cultural adjustment and spiritual warfare can make life more stressful for missionaries as well as amplify unresolved problem areas.

All of the foregoing is not to say that missionaries are a maladjusted group of people. On the contrary, we are impressed with the overall quality of missionaries, their emotional stability, and their spiritual maturity. A small minority, however, do experience significant problems on the field requiring professional consultation and/or care. Missionaries are by no means emotionally weak. Yet they do need ongoing member care services—along with an organizational "ethos" that allows for openness and an acceptance of human weakness—in order to stay healthy and effective.

## Organizational Ethos and Adjustment

An agency's culture, or ethos, significantly influences the quality of life of its people. Ethos is a multifaceted, fluid entity that is both visible and invisible, developing over time. It influences the values and practices of a mission, such as leadership style, the pace of work, type of evangelistic outreach, and sense of community among the members. Schein (1990), describes it as:

> (a) a pattern of basic assumptions, (b) invented, discovered, or developed by a given group, (c) as it learns to cope with the problems of external adaptation and internal integration, (d) that has worked well enough to be considered valid and, therefore (e) is to be taught to new members as the (f) correct way to perceive, think, and feel in relation to those problems.

Compatibility with an agency's ethos is one of the key factors affecting staff adjustment. Personal satisfaction is more likely when there is a good match between the staff member, his/her job, and the organization. Fitting into an organization can be challenging, when you consider the diversity of personalities and backgrounds among staff. For some the greatest stressor in missionary life may be trying to blend their career, denominational, social, and family backgrounds into the ethos of the organization. In such instances, it takes a good measure of inner security and integrity to weather the process of blending together.

The following diagram highlights the parameters and consequences of blending into an agency's ethos.

```
|————————————————|————————————————|
Excessive           Desirable        Range Insufficient
```

*Dangers and Dichotomies*

| | |
|---|---|
| Overidentification | Underidentification |
| Etho-centrism | Alienation |
| Convergent thinking | Divergent thinking |
| Status quo | Instability |
| In-group cliques | Out-group cliques |

Having staff at either extreme on this continuum can lead to problems. For instance, taking on too much of the agency ethos to the exclusion of one's own values and ideas can lead to a subtle "etho-centrism"—the view that the agency's way of doing things is best. Taking on too little is also dangerous, and can result in contrasting feelings that one's way of doing things is superior. Factions and frustrations can result. Those who embrace the status quo may feel defensive, and challenge the level of loyalty and commitment of those who question or call for changes. They may form work or social groups (in-group cliques) which others find hard to penetrate unless they are like-minded. Those who are uncomfortable with basic aspects of the agency ethos may feel alienated and wonder about the level of open-mindedness and flexibility of others. They may also form work or social groups (out-group cliques) which share their divergent views.

So what helps staff avoid the extremes and work through differences? Needed is much grace, demonstrated through accepting one another and building each other up (Romans 15:1-7). Practically this means having a mutual respect for diversity, open discussions about personal and organizational values, conflict resolution skills, and a solid commitment to work together.

Mission agencies, like individuals, have many weaknesses. Remember that when you are examining your agency you may very well be looking into a mirror. Mercy triumphs over judgment (James 2:13).

### Self-Disclosure and Stress

Every missionary (including MKs, home office staff, and leaders) needs an acceptable and safe outlet to openly share personal and group concerns. Some ways of doing this include spending time with friends and confidants, getting staff feedback from anonymous questionnaires, planning meetings where ideas and perspectives can be exchanged, and providing opportunities for confidential counseling. These outlets are real safeguards to prevent poor morale, bitterness, and needless frustration.

An agency's ethos influences the types of outlets that are made available for its people. This in turn affects the way in which staff relate personal struggles and express feelings about departmental or organizational practices.

In consulting at different mission locations, we have observed various organizational styles for making self-disclosures. Agency ethos becomes a type of monitor, determining what and how comments can be made. This is especially true in group situations. Most agencies seem to gravitate towards one or possibly two styles in particular, although this can change over time.

*Style 1—Spiritualization of the past.* The organization is most comfortable focusing on past issues using spiritual terms. Problems are usually only talked about when they have already been overcome. An example is the statement, "I thank God for victory over my temptation last month to rebel against my supervisor."

*Style 2—Past focus.* Issues are discussed fairly openly, but usually not until they have already been resolved. They are not necessarily spiritualized, yet only shared when it is safe—that is, after the fact. Here is an example. "We were really upset about the decision to decrease furlough allowances, and were privately hoping that it would get overturned."

*Style 3—Spiritualization of the present*. Current issues and problems are discussed but referred to largely in spiritual terms. Spiritual concepts may be used as a metaphor to refer to other ideas and feelings. For instance, "This mission station needs to pray more", may mean "I am feeling really hurt that people around here seem to overlook me."

*Style 4—Present focus in vague terms*. Current problems are mentioned in indirect, general, roundabout ways. Potentially threatening material is kept at a distance. An illustration would be a team leader who states at an inter-departmental meeting, "Its interesting working around here these days" when the real feeling might be more "The Personnel Department's chronic shortage of staff is significantly undermining our team's ability to recruit needed members."

*Style 5—Present focus with contact*. This involves making genuine, usually direct comments, in which issues, feelings, and reactions are shared promptly. Feelings are seen as vital sources of information rather than stumbling blocks. The result is that everyone involved senses that real contact with each other has been made. "I so appreciate the quality of your work on this project" or "I am frustrated that this agency has an inner circle which makes all the decisions," would be examples.

By and large the healthiest style in which to operate is Style 5. Well, at least this is true for many missionaries from the Western world. We believe this reflects the Biblical admonition to "speak truth to one another" (Ephesians 4:25, Zechariah 8:16). The timing, attitude, and setting for such disclosures are, of course, crucial. It is easy to understand the inappropriateness of giving critical feedback at certain organizational or team meetings. The basic guideline is to edify, not simply express oneself candidly (Ephesians 4:29, Proverbs 12:18). Responsibility always takes precedence over spontaneity.

## Member Care Services

Mission agencies certainly play a key role in helping staff prepare for and deal with stress. It is their job to support their people by providing appropriate member care services. Here are four types of services that mission agencies can provide.

1. *Prevention approaches* seek to decrease the incidence of potential stressors. The goal is to eliminate problems before they even arise. Choosing missionary candidates who are healthy and thus less prone to problems on the field would be an example of prevention. Making sure that there is a reasonable person-job match to decrease work frustrations is another example.

2. *Development approaches* help missionaries acquire and improve important skills to better cope with the challenges of missionary life. For instance, training in conflict resolution will help team members work through the inevitable tensions that arise from working together. Or receiv-

ing pre-field instruction on language-learning techniques will help missionaries more readily master the new language and hopefully make them more effective.

3. *Supportive approaches* offer encouragement to missionaries experiencing stress. Having prayer together during a hectic work week, offering brief counseling, or sending field coaches to struggling team leaders are examples. Support is available through organizational services and the mutual care staff provide each other.

4. *Restoration approaches* reduce the effects of debilitating stress and significant problems. One example of this would be a mission agency with a crisis intervention team that can be sent to locations where missionaries need immediate care. Intervention in such cases may not undo any damage that has already occurred, but it will hopefully decrease the effects of any remaining problems.

## Stress Management: The CHOPPSS Model

How can missionaries manage stress more effectively and prevent the development of more serious problems? And how can mission agencies keep abreast of the needs of their personnel? One way is to do a periodic "stress assessment."

Stress assessment involves first identifying current stressors and then trying to anticipate future ones. The importance of this process is reflected in the Lord's warning to his disciples, "Behold I send you out as sheep in the midst of wolves; therefore be shrewd as serpents and innocent as doves" (Matthew 10:16, NASB). These are strong words of caution about the need to appraise and understand the various "wolves"—or for our purposes, stressors—that can jeopardize if not destroy one's service for the Lord.

We have found that for missionaries, stress assessment includes at least seven basic areas—referred to as the acronym "CHOPPSS." The thought behind this term is to be "shrewd as serpents and innocent as doves" in order not to become prey ("lamb chops") for the stress-producing "wolves" of missionary life. These seven areas, along with some of the typical stressors associated with them, include:

1. *Cultural stress*—language learning, adjusting to the new culture, getting needs met in new ways, repatriation

2. *Human stress*—conflicts with colleagues, opposition within the host culture, family responsibilities and strains

3. *Organizational stress*—job satisfaction, red tape, mission policies, leadership styles, work pressures

4. *Physical stress*—illness, aging, adjustment to a new climate and environment, tiredness

5. *Psychological stress*—unresolved past hurts, depression, sense of failure, boredom, midlife transitions

6. *Support stress*—raising finances, housing needs, retirement issues, limited clerical and secretarial help

7. *Spiritual stress*—maintaining one's devotional life, spiritual warfare, subtle temptations.

Adjusting to different cultures is frequently the most obvious stressor. It is but the tip of the iceberg, though. Other challenges lie beneath the surface, such as team conflicts, family separations, and visa restrictions. At the very foundation lurk spiritual stressors—that is, demonic pressures—which accentuate the other ones. Missionaries do not merely struggle against things like language frustrations or interpersonal friction, but ultimately against spiritual entities that seek to hinder the expression of Christ's life through them.

We think it is wise to include stress assessment as part of a regular (at least annual) ministry review process. This is not only intended for individuals, but for all levels of the mission system. Here are seven system levels, with some examples, that should also be assessed.

1. *Individual*—field workers, home office staff, leaders
2. *Family*—newlyweds, one-parent families, nuclear families
3. *Team*—field partners, evangelism teams, small ministries
4. *Department*—different ministries and support structures
5. *Base*—stations or offices coordinating several ministries
6. *Region*—geographic areas usually including many nations
7. *Agency*—the overall organization and its ministries.

No stress assessment is complete without also looking at the avenues available to reduce stress. We use a resource assessment inventory that relates the CHOPPSS stressors with the four member care approaches for stress management previously discussed (prevention, development, support, restoration). This results in an assessment tool that mission agencies can use to identify current and potential resources for managing stress. It too can be used for all levels of the mission system.

How problems are viewed largely influences the means chosen to deal with them. If problems are over-spiritualized, then spiritual solutions will be inappropriately devised for dealing with all sorts of problems. The same goes for overemphasizing the role of certain psychological and emotional factors. The challenge in member care is not just spiritual adjustment, or psychological adjustment, or even cross-cultural adjustment; the real challenge is to facilitate *missionary* adjustment and growth. This involves taking into account all seven of the CHOPPSS stressors.

Going through the stress assessment process can be a bit uncomfortable. It is not always easy taking a hard look at your life. It is also difficult to predict when threatening issues may surface, especially when organizational-related stress is addressed. Fortunately, the assessment process will

## TYPES OF MEMBER CARE SERVICES
### Prevention  Development  Support  Restoration

-------------------------------------------------------------------------

```
S                          |
T  Culture                 |
R  Human                   |
E  Organizational          |
S  Physical                |
S  Psychological           |
O  Support                 |
R  Spiritual               |
S                          |
```

### Mission Level Being Assessed:
Individual, Family, Team, Department, Base, Region, Agency

also help bring healing. Staff ventilate and share their hearts; practical resources are identified and drawn upon to reduce stress.

## Application

As an example of how the CHOPPSS tool could work, let's consider a 300 member mission agency which decides to randomly survey 20 percent of its overseas staff. A research team is formed which uses a modified version of the CHOPPSS model described above. The purpose is to identify sources of stress for individuals, and to ascertain which pre-field and on-field member care resources have been most helpful for them.

The survey results are revealing. Almost 25 percent of the respondents cannot adequately converse in the national language (cultural stressor), 40 percent do not feel they have enough access to leadership (organizational stressor), and 10 percent regularly struggle with a sense of apathy (psychological stressor). The three-week pre-field training seminar on culture and language acquisition techniques was appreciated but seen as quite inadequate. Opportunities for further development on the field are reported to be infrequent.

Based on this information, the mission agency takes action to improve its member care services. First, it extends the candidate training program so that staff are better prepared for overseas living (prevention and development). It also releases 30 of its leaders and middle managers to attend a two-week "Leadership Training" workshop held in conjunction with another mission agency (development). And finally the agency organizes a pastoral care team available for on-field visitation to encourage missionaries (support) and counsel with those who may be struggling (restoration).

Member care interventions such as those in the above example are most effective if a few conditions are met. First, there is an ongoing organizational commitment to assess staff needs and develop resources to meet these needs. Second, there is an organizational climate which encourages staff—including leaders—to openly share needs and provide mutual support. And third, staff can participate in the development of member care services and feel a sense of "ownership" for them.

## The Case of Juanita Bonita

The following fictitious account raises several issues regarding missionary care and missionary stress. As you read through this case, try to think in terms of the CHOPPSS model. Note any possible "red flags"—that is, indications of current or future problem areas. The case concludes with several questions to guide your study.

Like most mission families, the Bonita family is complex. It will take more information and exploration to adequately understand its strengths and needs.

## Carlos-Esther (parents)

## Eduardo, Juanita, Lupita (children)

Juanita is the five-year-old daughter of a middle-aged couple from Latin America. She is of average height, weight, and is in good physical health. Eduardo, her older brother (aged 7), sometimes teases her, but basically they get along well. She also has a younger sister named Lupita (18 months old).

Juanita is quite a sight to behold—and to touch—when she walks through the open market with Esther, her mother. The well-meaning nationals approach her and grasp her long braided hair, smile, and say "how cute". This happens time and time again. Juanita liked the novel attention at first, but now generally ignores the touches and smiles.

The Bonita Family is in its second term of service with an international mission agency in Southeast Asia. Carlos, the father, functions as the assistant field director for the region. He frequently travels to other offices of the mission throughout Asia, averaging two trips per month from three to ten days' duration each. Carlos tends to be introverted and emotionally reserved.

Carlos and Esther receive approximately $1,500 per month in support. Typically they need $1,700 to make ends meet each month. The additional money usually comes in "miraculously," although not always on time to pay the bills.

Family life is characterized by lots of time together on the weekends that Carlos is home. Most Sundays are spent at a local English-speaking church, attending Sunday school, the worship service, and then staying after for a potluck meal. It is a priority. They also have a live-in maid who spends time with the children and helps around the house, freeing Esther to do part-time work for the mission.

Carlos believes that God has called his family to live among the poor in the city. Towards this end they are renting a three-bedroom apartment in a low-income housing estate. Although the area is not too attractive, it is relatively safe for the family.

The two older children (Eduardo and Juanita) play outside in the street with the other children. Juanita is noticeably more active than Eduardo and sometimes becomes aggressive with her peers. She usually has some bruises on her arms and legs. Eduardo, though, is typically "shy" and prone to allergies. He says he sometimes plays with an "invisible friend."

Over the last twelve months since their return from furlough, Juanita has been impudent and begun to throw tantrums. She even refused to go to school during the first week of kindergarten at a national school, and would cry and intermittently scream until she was taken home. Her parents are concerned about her "unusual behavior". One option they are considering is to send her to a boarding school in a few years. Although the separation would be hard, the training would be excellent and Juanita would quickly learn to like the new school and make friends. In the meantime, Esther is homeschooling Juanita.

Two weeks ago Esther approached a male friend from church to discuss some of the pressures she was experiencing. She has put on weight, feels ineffective as a mother, and is especially concerned that Juanita is overdependent on her. Esther has started to drink a small glass of wine when her husband is not home to help relax before she goes to bed.

## Questions

1. What stresses are going on for the Bonita family? Consider this in terms of the seven CHOPPSS stressors.

2. Where is the locus of the problem? Keep in mind the various levels of the mission system—individual, family, team, department, base, region, and agency.

3. What recommendations would you make? Try to answer this in terms of the member care approaches of prevention, development, support, and restoration.

4. Further issues to probe:

a. Juanita—How do you understand Juanita's school tantrums, bruises, her relationship with her siblings, and aggressiveness with peers? Are these her main struggles or do they reflect more basic, underlying needs?

b. Eduardo—What do you think of Eduardo's shyness, invisible friend, and teasing Juanita? Are these signs of problems or normal developmental experiences?

c. Carlos—What about Carlos' travel schedule, family time, and relationship with his wife? Try to identify some of the things he might be feeling.

d. Esther—How do you see Esther's "dependency" concerns, use of wine, and work involvements? Is she experiencing normal levels of missionary stress?

e. Mission agency—Which member care services should the agency be responsible to provide this family? How might the overall agency ethos affect the family's life and adjustment?

f. List any additional information you would need to better understand this family.

5. How could you use the CHOPPSS model to identify stressors and resources for you and your mission organization?

# References

Dye, S. (1974). Decreasing fatigue and illness in field work. *Missiology, 2*, 79-109.

Dye, W. (1974). Stress-producing factors in cultural adjustment. *Missiology, 2*, 67-77.

Foyle, M. (1987). *Overcoming missionary stress.* Wheaton, IL: Evangelical Missions Information Service.

Gish, D. (1983). Sources of missionary stress. *Journal of Psychology and Theology, 11*, 238-242.

Johnson, C. & Penner, D. (1981). The current status of the provision of psychological services in missionary agencies in North America. *Bulletin of the Christian Association for Psychological Studies, 7*, (4), 25-27.

Parshall, P. (1987). How spiritual are missionaries? *Evangelical Missions Quarterly, 23*, 8-19.

Schein, E. (1990). Organizational culture. *American Psychologist, 45*, 109-119.

Schubert, E. (1991). Personality disorders and the selection process for overseas missionaries. *International Bulletin of Missionary Research, 12*, 33-36.

Williams, K. (1988). Worksheet for balanced living. In O'Donnell, K. and O'Donnell, M. (Eds.). *Helping missionaries grow: Readings in mental health and missions* (pp. 390-398). Pasadena, CA: William Carey Library.

# 9

*John Powell*

# Short-Term Missionary Counseling

To be heard is to be healed. A simple statement, perhaps, but often true. The Swiss physician Paul Tournier observed that each of us yearns deeply to be listened to, to be understood, to be taken seriously. Perhaps this is even more true for the missionary who labors overseas without the same emotional and relational support that his/her compatriots have, and who would welcome a listening and understanding ear. To be listened to and understood by a skillful and caring person would be not only welcomed and supportive, but also healing and freeing. The stresses and demands in mission service often create more than the usual needs for expression, discussion, and understanding. Short-term counseling is one means by which some of these needs can be addressed.

The past twenty-five years have witnessed remarkable growth in the recognition of missionary needs on the part of mission agencies, and in providing means for meeting them. Psychologists, psychiatrists, social workers, pastoral counselors, and others in the broad area of counseling are being increasingly utilized within missions. Teams and individuals with caring skills and hearts for missions have been invited to use their gifts in serving missionaries. The combination of professional competence, personal sensitivity, and Christian commitment in such persons is having positive effects. The missions community itself, and the individuals receiving such interventions, have made it not only acceptable but in some cases nearly indispensable.

Short-term counseling within missions is one type of intervention within a broad milieu of member care services. It is designed to assist in personal and spiritual development, in managing crisis and trauma, in helping with greater effectiveness and satisfaction, and as a step toward healing and/or restoration. It is relational and focused in nature and may be practiced effectively with home office staff or with field personnel. At times, however, brief counseling may be only a temporary measure (largely diagnostic or crisis oriented) until more adequate resources are available. But in many situations it is the intervention of choice. As in any counseling situation it is of utmost importance that the specific intervention be determined on the basis of an understanding of the person(s) involved and their particular situation and/or need.

Short-term counseling encompasses several areas of concern. To begin, it involves appropriate training and skills, professional credentials, personal competence, and an understanding of missions. It also requires the capacity to understand and apply the truth of Scripture to the growth and development of others. Further, it implies the ability to be adaptable to a range of people and situations, and the willingness to tolerate often less than ideal settings in which to practice the sensitive and usually subtle processes of counseling.

In the discussion which follows I will elaborate upon many of these areas, identifying several principles of short-term counseling. My purpose is not to write a "how-to" chapter on counseling techniques or on conducting therapy, but rather to highlight some important guidelines for conceptualizing and setting up these types of counseling services.

## Definition and Description

Counseling, as used here, can be defined as: *a dynamic relationship between two or more persons in which one person (the counselor), utilizing various skills, understanding, and other appropriate means, assists the other(s) in living more wholly and effectively before God—in relationships, self-understanding, and vocation.* The term "counselor" is used throughout in a generic sense, including several types of mental health professionals, pastoral counselors, and others trained specifically in counseling at a graduate level.

Short-term counseling by its very nature implies a time limit. It is sometimes described as brief counseling or therapy (as compared to longer-term or open-ended approaches). Other designations such as time-defined counseling or therapy, time-limited therapy, short-term dynamic psychotherapy, and others have been given to this practice, each with variations in theory and application (e.g., Bauer and Kobos, 1987; Mann, 1973; Strupp and Binder, 1984). Considerable effort has been put forth to understand the most effective means for working within time limits and utilizing the counseling/therapeutic relationship toward effective ends.

Counseling on the mission field is usually short-term, whether intentionally designed or not, and especially if provided by someone outside the mission. Exceptions may be in missions which have a strong contingent of well-trained and experienced counselors available within the mission itself (such as Wycliffe Bible Translators). But even in those situations, long-term, open-ended therapy is usually unavailable to the on-field missionary. Therefore, short-term counseling becomes of considerable importance as a means of providing assistance to missionaries on the field.

There are several common features of short-term counseling and therapy that are also relevant for mission settings. The following list is derived from my own experience as well as from some of the literature in this field (e.g., Bauer and Kobos, 1988; Mann, 1973).

1. The utilization of time as a variable in treatment.
2. A limited number of sessions.
3. Concentration on one issue or goal.
4. Rapid, early assessment.
5. High level of counselor activity.
6. Ventilation of emotional tension.
7. High therapist flexibility, pragmatism, and creativity.
8. Formation of a quick therapeutic alliance.
9. Careful attention to the selection of clients.
10. High client motivation for change.

Short-term counseling for missionary personnel is particularly useful in these areas: personal/spiritual growth and understanding; family life, work, and career issues; conflict resolution (intra- and interpersonal); stress management; crisis intervention; initial understanding and management of psychological trauma; and the identification, diagnosis, and temporary alleviation of a variety of psychological disorders and behavior patterns. The latter, for better resolution, may require more extensive treatment in a different setting. Short-term counseling may be applied to a number of other specific categories as well, and at times may be limited in effectiveness only by the creativity, skill, and faith of the counselor and missionary.

## Themes and Needs in Short-Term Counseling

While a variety of issues can be successfully addressed in short-term counseling, three areas of struggle in particular are a frequent focus of treatment. These involve what George Ensworth (1979, personal communication) has called "the destructive triangle"—guilt, anxiety, and depression.

### Guilt

Whatever its stimulus, guilt results in the individual feeling unacceptable in some measure, and usually unacceptable to God. The natural response, as with Adam and Eve following their violation of the relationship with God in the garden, is to hide—from God, from others, from self. Many times one's real or imagined failure in cross-cultural adaptation, language acquisition, ministry, relationships, or discipline are at issue and often painful to face. The layers of defense necessary to insure this hiding over time requires, through a counseling or other type of healing relationship, an unraveling of these layers and the experience of forgiveness for the person to feel free again.

A counseling relationship can go far in bringing about release and healing as specific thoughts and feelings and areas needing forgiveness are addressed. Sometimes deep shame, a dynamic different from but related to guilt, can also begin its course of reversal through an accepting, trusting relationship in which matters relating to its formation are surfaced and resolved.

### Anxiety

This frequent experience, often felt as pervasive uneasiness, a specific fear, or a dread associated with particular circumstances or events, is perhaps an area where we all stand on common ground but negotiate quite differently. The natural response is to flee from the source of anxiety. Sometimes the flight is as symbolic as real, but nevertheless results in blocked feelings, less than adequate work, and undue attention to oneself in relation to how others view him/her.

Several aspects of mission service can produce anxiety, ranging from having to negotiate the unfamiliar to very specific threats to health, family safety, and to life itself. Other areas involve unresolved interpersonal conflict and personal issues of acceptability, worth, and value. Being able through a counseling relationship to better understand oneself, practice improved ways of relating, and develop more effective means of managing anxiety and its triggers, are important goals for dealing with anxiety. Ultimately, effective counseling encourages people to cast their anxieties upon the Lord, and to know that He cares for them (1 Peter 5:7).

## Depression

Considerable attention has been given to the study and treatment of depression—a common and often debilitating human experience. It is a complex phenomenon and in its more serious manifestations usually requires extensive intervention, often including medication. However, it also has its milder to moderate forms which may be successfully helped in short-term counseling, especially when its precipitants can be identified and addressed. Precipitants may be internal conflicts or external stressors. The experience of depression itself usually results in a lower sense of self-esteem along with feelings of being unable to go forward, participate, or be productive.

Psalms is filled with descriptions of depressive feelings. In Psalm 42 the psalmist cries out in loneliness and with feelings of abandonment, saying that "tears have been my meat day and night" (KJV). Psalm 130 records, "Out of the depths have I cried unto thee, O Lord" (KJV). And in each instance God answers, causes the psalmist to remember and acknowledge His presence and love, and times of His joy, rescue, or restoration, and the despair lifts.

A similar process can take place in the intimacy of a counseling relationship. Confessing one's despair, feeling acceptance in the presence of another, and beginning to look realistically at future possibilities, not past failures, constitute important steps toward overcoming the effects of depression.

Ensworth (1979, personal communication) articulates the antidote to the destructive triangle of guilt, anxiety, and depression by suggesting the application and experience of the "redemptive triangle"—love, faith, and hope. Through the process of a human relationship (reflected in short-term counseling), one's relationship with God is deepened or restored, and redemptive healing occurs. Love overcomes guilt, and the person no longer needs to hide; faith replaces anxiety, and the person no longer fears nor needs to flee; and hope replaces depression as the person is able to move forward again in growth and mission.

Three other areas of need which are frequently a part of missionary life deserve mention, those being the experiences of grief, anger, and crisis.

### Grief

Missionary service frequently requires a continuing series of transitions, and transitions almost always stir up a sense of loss. They can be losses of relationship, meaningful activity, familiar and comfortable surroundings, or even of home, health, earthly goods, and friends, and loved ones by death. Sometimes the losses are immediate and very real; at other times they are cumulative and subtle. Nonetheless, unacknowledged and unexpressed, they leave their negative mark.

Some missionaries attempt to handle these by denial and sometimes develop well sounding but overly spiritualized phrases regarding God's presence and intervention in their grief. The opportunity for facing honestly and realistically the impact of losses, transitional and otherwise, can have a healing effect. The example of the Apostle Paul's farewell to the elders at Ephesus (Acts 20:17-35) and the response of Jesus to news of the death of his friend Lazarus (John 11) and his interaction with Mary and Martha show healthy responses to grief.

Missionary personnel can be helped within a short-term counseling relationship to come to a fuller understanding of their own losses and grief. Some of the therapeutic goals are to better understand one's manner of coping with grief, emotional ventilation, and finding comfort in the one who was Himself "a man of sorrows, acquainted with grief" (Isaiah 53:3).

### Anger

"Be not hasty in thy spirit to be angry; for anger rests in the bosom of fools," says the preacher (Ecclesiastes 7:9, KJV). "Be angry yet do not sin" writes the Apostle Paul (Ephesians 4:26, NASB). Anger, like grief, anxiety, guilt, and many other feelings, is patently human. In fact, properly handled, it is healthy and can actually build relationships. Yet, unrecognized, unacknowledged, and unexpressed it quickly becomes destructive. Held onto as a false (and often unconscious) sense of power or "righteous control," it can "rest in one's bosom" and greatly reduce satisfaction and effectiveness. The anger that builds through frustration in work, lack of recognition by others of one's work or person, being unsupported, neglected, or overlooked, and as a cover for deeper hurts, often becomes the subject for work in short term-counseling.

In many instances simply recognizing and owning anger as a feeling is a significant step toward resolution. In so doing, it is a step toward responding to God's grace and prevents "a bitter spirit which is not only bad in itself but can also poison the lives of many others" (Hebrews 12:15-16, Phillips). Counseling can often help the missionary become aware of anger, identify its sources, detail his/her ineffective patterns for managing it, and develop more constructive alternatives.

### Crises

Everyone experiences crises of one type or another, and missionaries in certain settings can have more than their share. Recent news accounts of missionaries serving overseas report a number of severe crises and tragedies (terrorism, kidnapping, murder, natural disasters, to name a few) which go well beyond the range of typical human experience. These experiences, by any measure, constitute crises. Fortunately, an increasing number of missions have teams and other resources in place which can be called into action to minimize the long-range effects of these crises. Crisis teams intervene through short-term counseling for individuals and groups. Increasing attention is being placed on how to treat victims of such events. Many Christian mental health professionals both within and from outside mission organizations are developing crisis management skills.

But less traumatic crises can also be helped through short-term counseling. It is helpful to remember that a crisis is not always defined as an objective event, but by the *interpretation* of that event by the person experiencing it. Interpretations vary almost as widely as individual personalities do, and must be understood in the context of that person's background and adaptive skills. Brief interventions can be very helpful in assisting the person to understand his/her responses to a given crisis, discover God's grace in the crisis, and begin to work through the crisis.

Each of the above areas of need have focused on general problems seen frequently in short-term counseling on the mission field. It is important to remember that much of short-term counseling is also focused on growth and development as well as problem resolution. Counseling is too good an experience to be available only for those who are hurting. It is also appropriate for those who want to pursue personal growth in the context of a special, confidential relationship. Some examples include: understanding parent/child relationships, developmental transitions, responsibilities to relatives in the home country, decisions about assignment shifts or pursuing new ministry opportunities; and developing time management skills, relationship skills; and more satisfying devotional and prayer experiences.

## The Use of Prayer

Just as missionaries need prayer for their protection, development, and work, so do counselors. This is especially true for those intense times involving heavy travel, emotional exposure, and the personal depletion sometimes experienced in brief visits to the field. The prayerful preparation of the counselor through his/her own devotional worship, openness and expression to the Lord, and the involvement of several others who will pray diligently during travels and ministry, are crucial. For the counselor continually on the field or within the mission, the need for continuous prayer support cannot be overemphasized. Many examples from my own life and the experiences of others could be cited in showing the efficacy of prayer and God's faithful answers. Sometimes the unusual and unexpected almost become, by His grace, the common.

The development of the discipline of prayer, like many of the Christian disciplines, must be a growing and emerging practice for counselors and missionaries alike. In many counseling situations, the intimacy of prayer together confirms the truth of His being "in their midst" when "two or three are gathered in His name."

# Counselor Characteristics

In this section I will overview several characteristics that are needed by those who counsel missionary personnel. These include the three broad areas of spiritual qualities, cross-cultural understanding, and professional competence.

## Spiritual Qualities

Galatians 6:2 instructs us to: "Bear one another's burdens, and thus fulfill the law of Christ" (NASB). Burden-bearing, which is one way to view counseling, involves the attentive hearing of hurts, frustration, disappointment, anger, and other feelings in another. In the first verse of Galatians 6, the one who would help restore another is seen as needing spiritual sensitivity, gentleness, and self-awareness: "...you who are spiritual, restore such a one in a spirit of gentleness, looking to yourself, lest you too be tempted" (NAS).   The Galatians passage seems to indicate that the one "who is spiritual" is one who shows fruits of the Spirit—love, joy, peace, patience, kindness, goodness, faithfulness, gentleness and self-control (Gal.5:22,23 NASB). These qualities, focusing upward, inward, and outward, witness to a relationship with Christ. This   relationship must be the first and most important attribute of the counselor who would provide services to missionaries.

The attitude of servanthood is a crucial characteristic as well.  The fruits of the Spirit combine well with a servant's heart to create a safe atmosphere for discussing difficult or painful concerns, clarifying decisions, and/or resolving conflicts.

## Cross-Cultural Experience and Understanding

Previous involvement with other cultures and an experiential knowledge of the challenges of cross-cultural transitions are crucial to understanding stresses common to missionaries. There is a growing body of literature on reentry, the adjustment of missionary children, and the organizational and structural aspects of missions and other non-profit organizations. Although studying the member care literature is important, the understanding which takes place when one has had the experience itself is unmistakably stronger than if that has not been a part of the counselor's experience. Some missions with internal counseling services require their counselors to have served on the mission field or to undergo specific missions experience in preparation for their roles as counselors. Those who serve frequently and effectively as "outside" counselors usually have had substantial cross-cultural experiences as well.

It should be noted, however, that one must have opportunities for experience to become experienced. Some missions and professional training programs are now providing cross-cultural and counseling experiences for those interested in serving missions. Many graduate students and young professionals alike, who are committed to missions, are taking advantage of these opportunities.

## *Professional Competence*

A person providing short-term counseling on the field may be called upon for a variety of tasks and interventions. Graduate level training is needed which includes supervised experience in providing counseling, assessment, and consultation services to various population groups. Basic competency calls for being well aware of one's own limits and not exceeding them in attempting to provide service. Dedication and commitment are qualities which, by the Lord's grace, sometimes override deficiencies of training or competence, and in mission service one often has occasion to witness such grace. However, it is important to remember that even dedicated incompetency is still incompetency, and that missionaries deserve a high quality of care from those providing short-term counseling.

Many mission organizations have within their membership persons with natural gifts and skills for counseling and helping. Mission agencies would do well to identify and further develop these individuals. Training in peer counseling is one way to this, and can increase the range of member care services and mutual care provided within a mission agency.

## A Context for Short-Term Counseling

Short-term counseling, especially within missions, seldom occurs in a vacuum. While its nature is highly personal and many of its processes subtle, its effectiveness depends in part upon the context within which it occurs.

Short-term counseling will have its best effect in a mission context which has in its very ethos an attitude of growth, care, and support for its personnel. A balance is necessary between realistic work assignments and time for family life and other relational enjoyments and responsibilities. Where this is lacking or is not yet very well developed, much of the time within counseling may have to be spent on issues generated by conflicts or deficiencies in the mission organization itself.

The availability of short-term counseling in the context of other activities such as seminars, groups, and workshops—where the counselor and his/her style are visible to members—can help missionaries resolve issues on their own as well as increase their willingness to request individual counseling. Workshop and seminar topics might focus on anger, interpersonal conflict, family communication, parent-child relationships, overcoming past hurts, effectively negotiating transitions, and handling personal crises, grief, or loss. Explicating a Biblical base for coping with such issues is essential, and in turn provides a good foundation for individual work which may need to be done.

Ethical guidelines for counseling are necessary and must be communicated to and understood by all members of an agency. Clarifying the relationship of the counselor to mission leadership is especially important. Expectations regarding feedback, confidentiality, and the release of information to outside parties should be established and missionaries assured of these bounds. Examples where permission is needed to utilize counseling-derived data for discussion with field leadership (following proper release of information procedures), could be possible reassignment options, recommendations regarding leaving the field for treatment, resolution of family conflicts, working through grief, or working with another counselor who will be providing continuing support after the counselor has left that location.

Logistical matters must also be considered. Responsibility for the cost of international and in-country travel, ticketing arrangements, accommodations, expected work load, and activity schedule, must be settled in advance. These matters may seem insignificant to the counseling ministry. However, if not handled properly, such details can create a number of unnecessary hassles that can preoccupy those who minister through counseling.

Finally, counselors must be careful to consider the match or *fit* between the person, the organization, and the mission setting, and not just assume that problems originate and reside within the individual. Caution is also needed to understand and anticipate some of the possible long-term effects—positive and negative—that can result from brief interventions.

## Final Comments

Cultural adjustment, interpersonal conflict, ministry pressures, and unresolved wounds from the past are but a few of the many issues that affect missionary personnel. Short-term counseling, done by professional counselors as well as on a peer level, can play an important part in alleviating the distress and struggles inherent in missionary service.

Because of the diversity of problems and cultures represented in the mission force, counselors are encouraged to develop a large armament of skills to work in mission settings. Counselors—who in mission contexts function much like general practitioners—must be flexible in their approach, practical, resourceful, sensitive to spiritual issues, and aware of their counselee's cultural background and organizational ethos.

Short-term counseling offers no panacea for the challenges of missionary life. Life is difficult, with or without supportive counseling services. Counseling is but one ingredient—albeit an important one—in an agency's total member care program. Mutual support, dependence upon God, personal resilience, and many other member care services are all needed to keep mission personnel healthy and effective.

### Questions for Discussion

1. Where do members of your mission organization go to receive help and counseling?

2. What types of struggles commonly affect members of your team, department, and/or organization?

3. How could your mission organization further develop and utilize the services of short-term counselors?

4. What are some cautions to consider when providing short-term counseling in multi-cultural mission settings?

5. What are some of the pros and cons of using in-house versus outside professional counselors?

# References

Bauer, G., & Kobos, J. (1988). *Brief therapy: Short-term psychodynamic intervention.* Northvale, NJ: Jason Aaronson.

Mann, J. (1973). *Time-limited psychotherapy.* Cambridge, MA: Harvard University Press.

Strupp, H., & Binder, J. *Psychotherapy in a new key.* New York: Basic Books.

# 10

*Laura Mae Gardner*

# Crisis Intervention in the Mission Community

The mission community is subjected to the full range of crisis situations, whether they be due to natural disasters (hurricanes, earthquakes, epidemics) or human-induced traumas (wars, accidents). Crises are virtually inevitable, and mission leaders are frequently unprepared to handle them. This chapter is oriented towards mission leaders and administrators who are called on to work through crisis situations. It explores the nature of crises, the various reactions of those affected, and how leaders, as nonprofessional care-givers, can provide appropriate help.

## Overview of Crises

A crisis is a time-limited event that demands a response or some sort of intervention. It is usually temporary, accompanied by mental or cognitive uncertainty, disequilibrium, perhaps even immobilizing some of the participants, causing paralysis of thought or will. Participants will not plan well or think well. The situation feels like it has no exit—yet emotions are at such a high level that something has to give. There are exaggerated defense mechanisms such as rationalization, blaming, and compensation. Fear is usually present, and may even begin to look like phobia if the crisis goes on for an extended period of time (Kennedy, 1984).

Here are some typical examples of crises that affect missionaries:

- Runaway or lost child or teenager
- Threatened, attempted, or completed suicide
- Bomb threat or explosion
- Violence within the family

- Violence to the family (rape, assault, burglary)
- Kidnapping; hostage situations
- Exposed immorality within the mission membership
- Epidemic; unexpected illness
- Sudden death by accident or natural causes
- Severe conflict erupting among members
- Bizarre behavior; unresolved past problems
- Political coup; war; revolution
- Threatened or actual expulsion from host country
- Natural disasters (typhoon, earthquake, fire, flood)

## Disasters

A disaster is different from a crisis in that it may encompass a longer period of time and be attended by calamitous consequences.

> *A disaster may be defined as an event, concentrated in time and space in which a society, or a relatively self-sufficient subdivision of a society, undergoes severe danger and incurs such losses to its members and physical appurtenances that the social structure is disrupted and the fulfillment of all or some of the essential functions of the society is prevented. Viewed in this way a disaster is an event that disturbs the vital functioning of a society. (Wilkinson, 1985, p. 135)*

Tyhurst (in Wilkinson and Vera, 1985, p. 175) suggests that during the initial impact of a disaster, approximately 75% of the survivors respond in a normal way—that is, they are stunned, bewildered, behave in a reflexive, automatic fashion and generally report a lack of feeling despite physiologically showing those bodily changes associated with fear. Tyhurst estimated that between 12% to 25% of victims remain calm during this period, maintain their awareness and are able to function quickly and appropriately. Some members of this group may even initiate helpful activities. The remaining survivors comprised of about 10% to 25% demonstrate obvious inappropriate responses including hysterical crying or screaming, marked confusion, anxiety, and sometimes a break with reality.

Horowitz (1985) agrees with the general distribution of these reactions:

> *...when events are progressing and demand immediate coping efforts, the majority of an exposed population will respond quite well, a significant small proportion will show creative leadership, and if coping is possible, only a small proportion will enter panic-stricken, dissociative, or severely disrupted states of mind (p. 161).*

### *Understanding Feelings During Crises*

Crises allow little time for preparation. They usually elicit an immediate emotional response from all persons involved regardless of whether an injury is suffered; it is a time of concern for the entire community. Wilkinson (1983, pp. 1134-1139) has shown that there is little difference in emotional reactions between victims, observers and rescuers.

Feelings expressed at such a time tend to be strong and often negative—fear, anger, frustration, grief, disillusionment, guilt, defensive reactions and panic. Some experience psychological numbing, widespread depression, irritability, and nervousness (Bromet and Schulberg, 1986, pp. 676, 677). A major issue for victims of violence is coping with feelings of vulnerability and helplessness which can, in turn, lead to feelings of humiliation and shame (Krupnick and Horowitz, 1980, pp. 42-46).

Reactions of children may include aggressive behavior, anxiety, depressive symptoms, belligerence, fearful reactions, sleep disturbances, regressive behavior, and crying (Bromet and Schulberg, 1986, p. 677). Figley (1989) suggests that reactions differ according to age of child, though fears, worries, and nightmares and sleep disturbances are characteristic of both preschool, school age, and adolescent children (p. 125).

Disasters provoke similar feelings as do crises. Prolonged disasters have led to elevations in affective conditions, such as reactive depression and anxiety states, and may result in post-traumatic stress disorders (Bromet and Schulberg, 1986, pp. 676-677). Researchers though, have not found a singular pattern of psychiatric consequences to natural and man-made disasters. This may reflect the fact that disasters vary in intensity and duration and thus are capable of producing quite diverse psychological reactions (Bromet and Schulberg, 1986, p. 677). Obviously the mission leader must be prepared for the expression of a variety of strong and largely negative feelings during times of crisis and disaster.

## Crisis Categories

Crises can be classified in terms of the types of situations which give rise to the crisis event. There are at least four kinds of situations. Each requires that the participants be treated differently as far as on-going attention is concerned, although the immediate crisis or expressions of reaction may be treated similarly.

1. *Crises from Ongoing Stress.* This describes the eruptive expression of prolonged stress, where the reaction is out of proportion to a seemingly small irritation. A worker has been functioning for a long time, perhaps in a state of exhaustion, and one final small event is one too many, and an explosion or breakdown occurs.

When the response seems out of proportion to the irritant, one needs to look at long-term factors in the life of the member. The situation is likely to stem from stress-related causes, and external intervention is necessary (Kennedy, 1984, pp. 14-15). A person in this situation could recoup health and equilibrium with a period of rest and support and may respond well to administrative intervention after appropriate crisis help. Spiritual resources presented in a non-condemning way may be effective with such a person as well as life-balancing techniques and appropriate assertive behaviors.

2. *Crises from Personal Problems.* Some crises are the manifestation of long-term dysfunctional behavior, an exacerbation of an intrinsic pattern (Pittman, 1897, pp. 13-16). This kind of crisis may be similar to those stemming from prolonged stress—threatened suicide, runaway child, violence within the family—but the behavior has longer roots and will necessitate different and on-going treatment. After the immediate crisis is met, the participant is likely to need serious professional, possibly psychological or psychiatric help of a long-term nature. Family counseling may also be necessary.

Obviously it becomes important to have clear and dependable criteria for the diagnostic assessment of crisis victims beyond the initial phase of intervention. The surface symptoms are likely to vary greatly from minimal to serious although their intensity does not correlate with long-term prognosis. The question of whether one is seeing mainly a response to the actual crisis situation or a decompensation from previously existing pathology is an important clinical concern and its clarification is relevant to the choice of a given method of psychotherapy as well as to the establishment of realistic treatment goals (Wilkinson and Vera, 1985, p. 177). Consultation with mental health professionals is useful in these situations.

3. *Crises from Hostile Sources.* These are crises from outside the family or group that spark sudden fear and tension, such as a bomb threat or explosion, kidnapping, coup or war, where the level of stress is high and the fearful situation is ongoing. For further discussion on consequences to victims of human-induced violence as compared to victims of natural disasters, see Beigel and Berren, 1985, p. 143 and Figley, 1985, pp. 19-20, 400-401.

Treatment of the immediate crisis is called for but also long-term help in the form of spiritual resources, stress management techniques, dealing with strong expressions of feelings and perhaps bizarre behavior. A non-professional person may or may not be able to deal with this kind of ongoing crisis situation.

4. *Crises from Sudden Jolts.* Some crises involve accidents, tragic life events, and things happening in the family or community which do not emanate from a hostile source (Pittman, 1987, pp. 66-67). Examples include a sudden death in the family, drowning of a child, major sudden illness of a member, discovery of a terminal illness, a suicide attempt following

retirement and loss of position and prestige. Participants may find that in such cases they cannot cope with the ordinary demands of life along with this bad news.

Such crises can be fairly temporary and participants often respond well to the emotional support given by family and friends. Emotional help from colleagues is likely to be more efficacious than either professional help or administrative intervention, though these may be beneficial.

## Crisis Helpers

Where does a mission leader begin? Since both adults and children use denial as an initial method of coping with major disaster (Benedek, 1985, p. 169), I propose that accurate self-knowledge should be characteristic of a crisis helper. This is also true of the mission administrator who wants to lead his/her people wisely in times of uncertainty and crisis or disaster. Therefore, he/she should begin with a personal assessment, and begin now.

1. What life experiences do you bring to this event? What are your fears? Taboos? Must you be liked?

2. How do you deal with hostility, rejection, and the expression of strong emotions in yourself and others? How much hurt, anger, criticism, rejection can you handle?

3. Are you inappropriately curious about other people? Are you respectful of their privacy?

4. Do you tend to panic in an emergency or overreact? Do you have a need to solve others' problems, to be the savior or rescuer?

5. How objective are you? How defensive?

6. Were you molested or raped or have memories of a family suicide, so an event like one of these could trigger strong memories for you?

The administrator who may not have an accurate awareness of his or her stance on the above questions could profitably discuss these issues with family and close associates, to get their input. If an administrator cannot answer such questions honestly and appropriately, he should identify another person to be the resource person in time of crisis. In other words, simply being the designated leader does not necessarily qualify one to lead and care for others in times of crisis.

### Characteristics of Effective Crisis Helpers

The following personal qualities are essential for individuals who do crisis management, or disaster control.

1. Common sense, knowing the simplest, easiest thing to do and how to get it done—this is not the time for the exotic and creative or most original interaction (Kennedy, 1984, p. 11).

2. Self-control, self-assurance, calmness; not overwhelmed by the urgency of the situation. He or she deals well with pressure, thinks clearly in spontaneous situations.

3. Understanding, empathetic, objective, and controlled, not minimizing others' feelings yet not overreacting either. Not so "righteous" or "religious" that the helper stifles the expression of strong feelings or strong language that may seem "unchristian." He or she likes fellow workers and is liked and respected by them.

4. Natural; neither phony nor trying to give responses which are cliches. The helper needs to be him/herself, but self-controlled. Jesus cried too in times of loss and grief while still continuing to lead His disciples.

5. Accuracy in assessing the situation and gathering information. One must not exaggerate and make things worse than they are, but not underestimate either. An accurate cognitive appraisal of the situation is needed which is based on facts rather than personal feelings or the feelings of those involved. The helper must be realistic yet give hope if possible. Things may be bad but they are seldom as bad as they could be (II Cor. 4:8-9). He or she knows how to listen, and avoids jumping to premature conclusions or solutions.

6. Self-confident. The helper does not need to apologize for not being a professional. One does not need to be a professional to bring a sense of calmness, control, and order to the situation. The helper will probably always feel he/she does not know enough to deal with this situation, or someone else could do it better, but this is not the time to give in to feelings of inadequacy.

7. The helper is not rigid or opinionated, defensive or touchy. Yet firmness and decisiveness are needed.

### Ascertaining Administrative Responsibility

Mission leaders and local administrators must clarify the extent of their responsibility for managing crises. Do you have an ethical or legal responsibility? The administrator needs to know the legal parameters of the situation. For example, gunshot wounds, sexual molestation or abuse of a minor must be reported to the police or child care authorities in the United States. What are the laws of the host country? Do they apply to an expatriate in this situation? What are your imputed responsibilities as leader or administrator of this group of people? Does your responsibility extend to the children of members? To whom are you obliged to report within the organization, and what needs to be reported? Remember that many missionaries come from litigious societies. Missionaries and relatives of missionaries are not exempt from the threat or reality of suit.

## Goals of Crisis Helpers

In Chinese the word *crisis* is a combination of two characters, together meaning "dangerous opportunity." Crisis, according to Webster, is "a state of things in which a decisive change one way or the other is impending." Crisis is the turning point at which things will either get better or get worse. During the resolution of the crisis, the affected person is generally ready to accept help. He or she is more available because his or her defenses may be down and previous patterns of coping may be disorganized. A little effort at this time can produce great improvement. In some cases, the crisis may result in a level of living higher than the pre-crisis state.

Just as there are three phases to a crisis—immediate impact, recoil, post-impact (Tyhurst, quoted by Wilkinson and Vera, 1985, p. 176), so there are three phases or goals of intervention. First, the short-term phase should be to lessen stress, keep panic down, get participants through this immediate event and get things functioning again. If possible one should aim to alleviate immediate cognitive disorganization and/or psychophysiologic reactions of the victims (Bromet and Schulberg, 1986, p. 685). Messick (1974) and Lipsitch (1973) suggest that a legitimate expectation in crisis intervention is to restore the individual to no less (if not more) than his/her pre-crisis level of functioning.

The secondary phase is to assess level of need. This would include determining which situations brought about this crisis as well as implementing crisis counseling and providing therapy as needed (Figley, 1989, pp. 43-57).

The third phase is longer-term, and should include assisting those with social and legal problems, as well as those with vulnerable defenses who are unable to cope with new stressors, or those who are exhausted. Part of this involves setting up a support network for those affected. It should also set processes in motion for long-term changes and healing and/or prevention of future occurrences (if possible). This means one will need to know the precipitating events that led to the crisis so he can suggest the right steps for this particular participant. Some crises can be helped by the entity support systems, and some crises call for long-term professional psychological or psychiatric help.

It is important that mission leaders and crisis workers be aware of "hidden victims" of crisis situations. These are the persons who consider a show of distress to be evidence of weakness or have no conception of the fact that talking about their feelings might be helpful (Wilkinson and Vera, 1985, p. 176). In a mission community the hidden victims would include those persons who minimize the psychological or emotional world, or who use spiritualizing as a defense mechanism.

### Help for Care-Givers

The most stressed people in time of crisis in a mission community may well be the leaders themselves. They may be called on to make decisions for which they feel completely inadequate, and in which they have had no experience, nor have their advisors. Their decisions, whatever they are, will have long-term ramifications. Whatever they decide to do is likely to be seen as wrong by certain participants. How is the crisis worker, or the mission leader, to care for himself/herself at such a time?

1. Maintain physical health—adequate rest, a balanced diet, enough exercise and relaxation to keep balanced and in perspective. No one can go from one crisis to another without coming back to baseline now and then, to keep matters in focus.

2. Have a grown-up God. Many times there is a type of spiritual hysteria surrounding a crisis that issues in fervent prayer that "demands that God act" and dictates just what He must do. God will not be manipulated by anyone, even His people. Someone needs to lead the group in trusting God whether He delivers or whether He does not (see Dan. 3:17, 18). Mission leaders need to be sure their spiritual insight is clear, and their focus is on Christ so as not to become disillusioned with colleagues...and maybe even with God.

3. Find a resource person, a professional care-giver, or supervisor/peer who can help them deal with the stresses that come in this line of work. They need someone who can help them improve their skills, see what went wrong with their intervention the last time, ascertain whether their emotional needs are being met apart from these crisis matters, and minister to them (Kennedy, 1984, p. 178). It is also helpful to share one's reactions and feelings in a formal or informal manner with colleagues. Participating in group sessions to help crisis helpers work through their experiences can also be beneficial (Figley, 1989, pp. 145-146).

## The Process of Helping

How do crisis workers go about the helping process? Here are several principles that are important to understand and employ.

1. Alleviate the immediate impact of the stressful event. This involves "being there," calmly giving comfort, taking charge without telling participants how they should act and feel. "The information provided victims must be presented as potentially helpful but not necessarily as absolute. Nothing is more detrimental for a traumatized person than to be told how he or she should be feeling or acting at this point" (Wilkinson and Vera, 1985, p. 176). Nevertheless, the person may be immobilized and may need someone to be directive, sequential, clear: "Let's do this first, then let's do that." These need to be manageable ideas, step-size coping responses.

2. Help the participants utilize their own resources to cope with or adapt to the situation. Don't do everything for them. Doing something often brings a measure or sense of control and restores some semblance of order.

3. Let them express their feelings—these strong feelings have to go somewhere. But do not let this develop into uncontrolled, prolonged expressions of emotion.

4. Gather information. You need to gain understanding of the situation—why did this happen now to this person? Crises seldom occur in a vacuum. What was the precipitating event? Go through the last 24 to 72 hours to learn what happened. The events which threw things off balance are those things which must be righted (if possible) in order for life to go on. Gain an accurate cognitive awareness of the situation. This will keep you from acting impulsively or without adequate options. Most likely some reporting will be necessary—this step helps you be sure to get the facts straight.

5. Give hope but do not belittle. The situation is not endless; it won't go on forever. Take it in manageable doses. Crises are often hopeful times for significant change to take place. However, if you, the intervener, are too hopeful, you may be minimizing the difficulty of the situation. This may be the time to help the participant discover new options, but this is not the time for long-term decisions.

6. Be clear about confidentiality. The participant may ask you to promise not to tell anyone. Be careful about making such promises. "I understand your desire for confidentiality, but I cannot promise you that I will keep all this information secret. I may have to share some of it in order to help you or help others who are also involved." However, you need not say anything to those who are merely curious. Others involved may need some pieces of information—the missions community, the biological family in the home country, the local Christian community in the host country, mission leadership at headquarters. I have observed that if members of the community are not given factual information, they will invent their own. Rumor control is an important part of managing a crisis. The best way to keep rumors at a minimum is to have a designated media-contact person to give out sufficient amounts of accurate information.

7. Gradually taper off. Set up a plan of action to help the person in crisis get through the next period of time. "This is what you should do; this is what I will do. I will get in touch with you tomorrow to see how it is going." Ask yourself if there is any risk of suicide. If so, someone should be present with the person in crisis for at least the first period of time following the crisis event.

8. Know when to let go. You have done all you can or should do, and need now to back out of the situation. You should have rallied the person's support system (friends, church, relatives) so you can let someone else carry this load. Do not let yourself get trapped into becoming indispensable.

9. Do some follow-up. Determine if additional care is needed, especially if severe disorders seem to be developing. The most frequent diagnoses in such populations would probably be post-traumatic stress disorder, adjustment disorder, brief reactive psychosis, phobic disorder, generalized anxiety disorder, and major depressive disorder (Horowitz, 1985, p. 167). Reactions of anger and guilt are often prominent features of the post-traumatic stress syndrome (Wilkinson and Vera, 1985, p. 175).

## Dealing with the Ripples

A crisis worker must always ask, "Who else is at risk?" This is especially important in times of family violence, or following a suicide. Who are other potential victims? Wilkinson and Vera (1985) state, "To know early after a disaster…what group of persons may have greater needs could allow a more precise targeting of treatment effort" (p. 175).

Children, for example, are frequently overlooked in times of crisis or disaster, their physical safety considered the only consideration. Benedek (1985, p. 168) suggests that there is a long tradition of denying the psychological and psychiatric impact on the child-victim of disaster. Where adults can be helped and comforted by information, this does little to comfort children. They need the assurance of knowing their big people are in charge—someone is at the helm of their boat, preferably their Mommy and Daddy, and they know how to get us out of this and make things right again.

A recurrent theme in the literature of children and disaster is the importance of parental reactions to the ultimate psychological sense of well-being experienced by children (Benedek, 1985, p. 169). The idea is that if parents exhibit symptoms, the symptomatology is transferred to the child and expressed in a similar fashion. The importance of maintaining family bonds and keeping families intact if at all possible during times of catastrophe is obviously an important element in helping the children involved (Benedek, 1985, p. 170).

In situations involving child abuse, the parent's concern for confidentiality or personal comfort can frequently keep him/her from adequate reporting or assertively maintaining that the child should not have been subjected to such physical, sexual, or emotional harm. Steps need to be taken to care for the child and deal with the perpetrator. Many times the desire for confidentiality to protect the perpetrator (on the part of either the perpetrator, his relatives, or the administration) keeps the child's needs from being addressed, hinders the search for further victims, and keeps the perpetrator from receiving adequate treatment.

## Identifying Resources

Spiritual resources are some of the most important in times of crises for all those involved, including the crisis workers themselves. Some of these spiritual resources are faith (this situation has not taken God by surprise), God's wisdom and strength, prayer, the Holy Spirit, and the Word of God. Jesus had many crises in His life. He met each one differently, but appropriately—taking charge, calming fears, withdrawing for a time of solitude, releasing His feelings (Matthew 8:23-27; 9:18-26; 14:1-13; 26:47; Mark 4:35; Luke 8:22; John 11:33-36).

1. What other resources do you have—life experiences, emotional optimism and stability, insight, wisdom, calmness?

2. What psychological network can you call on or refer to for longer-term care of participants, or for personal debriefing?

3. Do you know where to get legal advice and other specialized services? Take the initiative to identify and develop relationships with referral resources. Having a referral list on file can help speed up the care provided during crises and traumas.

## Beware of the Traps

Some of the traps or pitfalls for the mission leader or administrator in times of crisis include the following:

1. Over-responsibility. "I should have anticipated this and planned better. I was not caring for my people. I am a failure."

2. Disillusionment. "What kind of God would let this happen? What kind of people are missionaries anyway?" There is likely to be a sense of betrayal when a mission worker falls into sin, followed by cynicism, distrust and suspicion.

3. Feeling manipulated, shamed. The victim insists on confidentiality, and the leader agrees, then avoids sharing information because he or she has been manipulated into secrecy. 4. Denial. Refusal to report the news is a form of denial—"We can handle this ourselves." This keeps the matter hidden, and does not allow objectivity and the perspective of an outside person into the problem. When the crisis worker allows himself or herself to keep the matter hidden, it is seldom resolved adequately.

5. Overspiritualizing. "God will minister to us; we do not need human or psychological help—we're missionaries!" Help is thus not requested or forthcoming. Hurting people can try to cope through denial or hiding their pain.

6. Feeling threatened. "If you do that, I will resign." "If I discipline her, she may attempt suicide." A mission leader can be vulnerable to such threats and kept from doing what must be done to deal adequately with the crisis, which (in some cases of immorality) may have devastating ramifications for some participants.

7. Becoming the object of displaced anger. All the strong feelings experienced by the victim of a crisis need a target and the mission administrator may be it. Leaders must take the job of crisis managers knowing they cannot possibly please everyone, so they must be able to handle hostility and rejection. These are as true in the mission community as anywhere else.

8. Acting impulsively, hurriedly, without thinking through all the options, or without adequate information. A leader may be pressed into making a decision too soon.

9. Neglecting follow-up. A mission leader may erroneously believe that as soon as the crisis is over, participants no longer need help with their emotional reactions. Be sure to be available and to talk with them periodically during the months following the crisis.

## Who Copes Least Well with Crises?

Ahlem (1978, pp. 129-141) and Wright (1985, pp. 16-17) suggest that it is possible to predict those who will cope well with crisis and those who will not. Characteristics of those who cope poorly in times of crisis include the following:

1. Those who are already hurting emotionally, or are emotionally weak. They are nearly overwhelmed in a crisis and are likely to respond in such a way as to make matters worse. They have probably been unable to cope with previous crises and their emotional problems limit their coping ability.

2. People in poor physical condition. Chronic or acute physical illness may leave them with fewer resources to draw on during a crisis.

3. Individuals who tend to deny reality. They are already avoiding their anger and pain so they simply continue to deny this new painful reality.

4. Those who have an unrealistic approach to time. They demand instantaneous solutions or extend time limits unreasonably, which avoids the discomfort of reality, but enlarges the problem.

5. People who struggle with excessive guilt. Blaming themselves causes them to feel still more guilt and further immobilize themselves. This "victim posture" causes them to feel they deserve whatever bad situation life sends them or to assume unrealistic responsibility for the crisis.

6. Those who minimize their role in their problems. Having a cause and effect mindset,they look for someone to focus their anger on. Their approach is to find some enemies, either real or imagined, and project the blame onto them.

7. Individuals who have a tendency to be either very dependent or very independent. The dependent person may become a clinging vine while the independent person may not cry out for assistance.

8. People whose perceptions of God are too narrow. The individual who believes in the sovereignty of a magnificent God can trust Him even when things seem inexplicable. Those whose God is small must have a God who rescues them or else gives them a good explanation for the current disaster. When God fails to deliver either a solution or an explanation, their faith is shattered.

9. Super-responsible people who must be in control at all times, who are "owners of themselves" and therefore responsible to make things come out right. These folk have assumed the place of God to take care of themselves and their world.

10. From my experience I would add the person for whom the crisis event is a trigger. These are the people who experienced something similar in their past, and this new event brings sharply to the surface all the old feelings of pain, fear and anxiety. Even with testing and screening it can be hard to identify people like this. Mission leaders can only be aware that such people are there, and be prepared to minister to them after the fact.

### Who Copes Best with Crises?

Ahlem (1978) summarizes the characteristics of those people who cope well in crisis situations. These individuals honestly express grief and pain; they convert uncertainty to manageable-sized risks and tasks; they acknowledge increased dependency; they avoid impulsive action; they relieve tension constructively with work, play, diversion, exercise, entertainment; they recognize that there is guilt for both winners and losers in any great change; they have a minimal sense of shame; they will discuss the problem—see fear as normal, not as an illness; they stay close to people without clinging or withdrawing; they maintain psychological integrity; they have previously coped well in crisis and change; they have realistic information to work with; they are in good physical condition; they have adequately processed their own emotions and pain; they have genuine spiritual hope; they do not suffer from excessive responsibility (pp. 143-158).

## Conclusion

Crises will come. Mission leaders must be prepared by developing basic helping and crisis management skills. Self-understanding is essential as are understanding the needs of the people affected and the situations which cause crises. In most cases, there is the need for immediate intervention and support, frequently followed by long-term care and follow-up. Crises can be times of growth. If handled properly, they can result in the recovery and well-being of those involved, and promote the work of God in that location.

## Questions for Discussion

1. How can a mission identify its members who are vulnerable to responding poorly to crisis situations?

2. In what ways can mission personnel provide supportive care to one another during and after crises?

3. How was the last significant crisis handled within your team, region, or mission? What helped individuals adjust and what did not help?

4. What resources are accessible to your mission to help during crisis times?

5. What are some of the special concerns when doing crisis management in a cross-cultural setting?

# References

Ahlem, L. (1978). *How to cope with conflict, crisis and change.* Glendale, CA: Gospel Light Publications.

Beigel, A. & Berren, M. (1985). Human-induced disasters. *Psychiatric Annals, 15,* 143-150.

Belenky, G. (1987). Psychiatric casualties: The Israeli experience. *Psychiatric Annals, 17,* 528-531.

Benedek, E. (1985). Children and disaster. *Psychiatric Annals, 15,* 168-172.

Bromet, E. & Schulberg, H. (1986). Epidemiologic findings from disaster research. *Psychiatric Epidemiology, Annual Review, 6,* 677-685.

Figley, C. (1985). (Ed.). *Trauma and its wake: The study and treatment of post-traumatic stress disorder.* New York: Brunner/Mazel, Inc.

Figley, C. (1986). (Ed.). *Trauma and its wake: Traumatic stress theory, research, and intervention (vol. 2).* New York: Brunner/Mazel.

Figley, C. (1989). *Helping traumatized families.* San Francisco, CA: Jossey-Bass.

Horowitz, M. (1976). *Stress response syndromes.* New York: Aronson.

Horowitz, M. (1985). Disasters and psychological responses to stress. *Psychiatric Annals, 15,* 161-167.

Jones, F. & Hales, R. (1987). Military combat psychiatry: A historical review. *Psychiatric Annals, 17,* 525-527.

Kennedy, E. (1984). *Crisis counseling: The essential guide for non-professional counselors.* New York: Continuum.

Krupnick, J. & Horowitz, M. (1980). Victims of violence: Psychological responses, treatment implications. *Psychiatric Annals, 10,* 42-46.

Lipsitch, L. (1973). *The crisis team.* Hagerstown, MD: Harper & Row.

Messick, A. (1974). *Crisis intervention.* St. Louis, MO: CV, Mosby Company.

Pittman, F. (1987). *Turning points: Treating families in transition and crisis.* New York: W. W. Norton & Company.

Wilkinson, C. (1983). Aftermath of a disaster: The collapse of the Hyatt Regency Hotel skywalks. *American Journal of Psychiatry, 140,* 1134-1139.

Wilkinson C. (1985). Introduction: The psychological consequences of disasters. *Psychiatric Annals, 15,* 135-139.

Wilkinson, C. & Vera, E. (1985). The management and treatment of disaster victims. *Psychiatric Annals, 15,* 174-184.

Wright, H. (1985). *Crisis counseling: Helping people in crisis and stress.* San Bernadino, CA: Here's Life Publishers.

# PART THREE
## TEAM DEVELOPMENT

# Part Three
# Team Development

*Kenneth Harder*

Consulting Editor

Teams are a dominant feature of mission strategy today. Both long-term church planting teams and summer ministry teams are commonly used. Translation teams demanding 10-15 years of cooperative effort have been with us for several decades. Add to these the task groups, committees, councils, and strategy groups utilized in the everyday life of the mission and we find missionary personnel frequently engaged in team activity. In spite of the varieties of group involvement, mission staff are seldom deliberately trained to work in team contexts.

Part Three attempts to narrow the gap between team involvement and the minimal training in team life that team leaders and team members often receive. Missionary teams, of course, do not develop automatically. Like plants, they must be cultivated during their formation and subsequent stages. As the five articles in this section point out, teams require periodic, planned care and regularly scheduled times for coaching and team growth activities. Although most of the chapters are oriented towards teams in field settings, much of their content can be applied to teams and departments back in an agency's home office.

Chapter 11 analyzes a variety of relational issues that need to be understood and resolved on multinational teams. The author, Sandra Mackin, presents several biblical perspectives to help team members deal with differences while also preserving love and unity. Leadership style, decision making, conflict resolution, and male-female relationships are but a few of the topics that Sandra explores.

Tim and Becky Lewis author the next chapter, entitled, "Coaching Missionary Teams." They highlight the importance of itinerant coaches for guiding and supporting church planting teams. Tim and Becky describe the nature of coaching and profile the characteristics of an effective coach. They round out the article with ten brief examples of successful coaching trips that involved, among others, a linguistics specialist, an entry strategist, a mission executive, and a mental health professional.

Chapter 13, by Dr. Kelly O'Donnell, reviews over 40 practical tools to help build and develop teams. These tools consist of exercises and group experiences that teams can use to explore and improve the three dimensions of team life: relationships, task, and ethos. Kelly also includes a helpful section where he outlines principles for doing team development exercises and concludes with a case study of a team in North Africa.

"Field Leaders and Team Nurture," chapter 14, offers a specific strategy for developing effective teams: use field leaders to visit with teams at regular intervals. Dr. Ken Harder encourages teams, team leaders, and field leaders to meet consistently for what he calls "focus times." Focus times help team members review their personal life and ministry as well as plan for the future. Ken weaves a fascinating case study throughout the entire article (involving a fictitious but all-too-familiar team situation) to illustrate the positive influence that field leaders can have on the teams they oversee.

Dr. Frances White, in the final chapter, looks at eleven broad guidelines for doing field consultation. Some of these guidelines include becoming oriented to the field situation in advance, working with a partner, remaining flexible with the schedule, and clarifying financial arrangements. Fran advocates for the use of member care specialists who can contribute their skills on a mission field in a focused, well-planned, and time-limited manner. Her article will help both missionary personnel and consultants get the most from their time together.

Part Three is a good starting place for missionary teams desiring to survey and discuss substantive issues in team life. These five articles can be supplemented by the various materials that appear in their reference sections. Literature on team development in a missions context is still fairly sparse. Future articles and research are certainly needed. Relevant topics would include team formation, the use of multinational teams, the interaction between team stages and cross-cultural adjustment, and the impact of specific member care interventions on teams.

Teams, especially multinational teams, are part of our mission landscape today. The challenge before us is to invest the necessary time, effort, and personnel to properly form, maintain, and develop the growing numbers of teams that are being used by mission organizations around the world.

# 11

*Sandra Mackin*

# Multinational Teams

A Filipino missionary serving on a multinational team in Japan reports that her Dutch teammate is "against new ideas and insists on what she likes." Her German teammate is a "very negative lady who always complains and asks *why* a lot." Her Australian teammate finds it difficult to accept Filipino leaders.

A Pakistani missionary in the Philippines reports he was shocked by Filipino Christians having dates and was hurt by his American director's busyness and failure to spend time with him.

A missionary in the Philippines from Tonga was hurt by his Indian leader's bluntness, especially when correcting him, telling him, "It's very bad. You shouldn't do it like this. Do it again."

What do these missionaries have in common? What is at the root of their hurt feelings? Stress caused by cultural differences.

For over nine years I have worked on multinational teams in the Philippines and I have seen many conflicts like these. Further, I have conducted more than thirty interviews with a variety of people in Manila (e.g., Western and non-Western missionaries, seminary students, Christian workers in cross-cultural ministries) which reveal similar experiences.

Consider a team from the United States, Korea, and Britain working to reach an area of the Philippines. Typically, they will focus on adjusting to Filipino culture, not on their own cultural differences. Eventually, however, cultural conflicts will arise among them and cause such distress that the team's effectiveness may be seriously hampered.

It is axiomatic that cultural differences lead to misunderstandings and conflicts. On multinational teams, people think differently, use different

This article is reprinted from *Evangelical Missions Quarterly*, 28, April, 1992, pp. 134-140 (Box 794, Wheaton, Illinois  60189). It is based on the authro's master's thesis, "Resolving Conflicts on Multicultural Staff Teams." Used by permission.

body language, and speak different languages (there is considerable confusion among English speakers from different countries, too).

Whatever the cause, the results of such culturally induced conflicts are stress, frustration, and disappointment. Ultimately, the conflicts can preoccupy and distress team members to the point where they do not function effectively.

What can be done about it? Disband our multinational teams? Hardly. The worldwide trend is to establish more of them. Therefore, we must strive to reduce the cultural conflicts. But before trying to improve team conflicts, we need to acquire a biblical perspective on the problem.

## Biblical Perspectives

There are four ways to look at our cultural values and practices. First, some are clearly right when measured against Scripture, for example Filipino hospitality (I Peter 4:9). Second, some directly conflict with Scripture; e.g., child sacrifice in some cultures.

Third, some fall into a gray area. For instance, Christians from different countries differ on drinking alcoholic beverages. Fourth, many are neutral; e.g., the Bible does not address the issue of how much space is proper between two people conversing.

One of our problems on multinational teams is that people often confuse the four categories, insisting that a cultural practice is wrong, when it may fall into a neutral or gray area. On the other hand, some team members may take something in the neutral or gray category and insist that it is biblically mandated. When conflicts arise, we must carefully think through the issue and determine in which of these four categories it belongs.

Most of our cultural conflicts revolve around practices that are gray or neutral. In such cases, members need to study and apply Romans 14 and 15:1-3, where Paul teaches self-denial for the sake of other believers' values. In gray or neutral areas, the godly response is to defer to the cultural practice of one's brother.

The Bible also speaks to the positive side of team relations: love and unity (John 15:12; 13:35; 17:21). If we exhibit love and unity, the world will sit up and take notice that we are disciples of Jesus. What an even greater testimony it is when that love is practiced by people from different cultures and nations.

The Bible also gives us guidelines for practicing love and unity, but they are sometimes hard to apply across cultural lines. For example, the apostle Paul tells us to "speak the truth in love" (Ephesians 4:15). In some cultures, the truth is communicated bluntly. That is what the Indian team leader did to the Tongan: "It's very bad. You shouldn't do it like this."

However, in other cultures—Japanese and Filipino, for example—the truth is softened to save face or avoid confrontations. In some cases this may be a matter of tact, but in others the truth is compromised.

When missionaries work together without considering how to "speak the truth in love" in ways appropriate to members' various cultures, hurt feelings develop. We must learn how to communicate "love" to a teammate from another culture, and how to present "the truth" so they can receive it without feeling offended.

Another biblical guideline particularly appropriate to team relations is, "Let no unwholesome word proceed from your mouth, but only such a word as is good for edification according to the need of the moment, that it may give grace to those who hear" (Ephesians 4:29, NASB). *Unwholesome* in Greek means "rank, foul, putrid both in a literal and figurative sense...it carries the connotation of pernicious and offensive" (Simpson & Bruce, 1973, p. 110).

To obey this, we must learn what our teammates consider unwholesome and offensive. A Filipino pastor's wife, trying to compliment me, once told me I looked "sexy." To many Filipinos *sexy* means "nice," but I did not interpret it that way and was surprised to be given such an unwholesome label.

When such misunderstandings happen, we must "be kind to one another, tender-hearted, forgiving each other, just as God in Christ also has forgiven you" (Ephesians 4:32, NASB). Learning to resolve conflicts in ways appropriate to our teammates' cultures is crucial for healthy relationships.

## How to Improve Relations

Knowledge of our teammates' cultures is the key to expressing love, pursuing unity, and building healthy, biblical relations. There are many things we can do to foster such understanding.

### 1. Pre-field Orientation

Before joining a team, each member should be helped to analyze his or her own cultural values. "It is purely axiomatic to argue that the more we know about ourselves, the more effective and accurate our communication is likely to be" (Singer, 1987, p. 132). But apparently we are not doing too well at this.

> We go to the field, neither understanding who we are culturally, nor how we will affect our recipient cultures, nor what changes we need to make in ourselves....We must develop a set of methods, ideas, literature, and communications designed to ensure that before we leave for the field we understand the culture we will leave behind, but also carry with us. (Atkins, 1990, p. 27)

There are many excellent tools to help us fill this gap in our missionary training. Paul Hiebert's (1985) book, *Anthropological Insights for Missionaries*, contains a chapter, "Cultural Assumptions of Western Missionaries," which should be studied and discussed. L. Robert Cole's (1979) helpful book, *Survival Kit for Overseas Living*, is a gold mine of information on analyzing culture, with a pertinent section on American culture. By studying books such as these, each candidate should emerge with a list of his or her culture's values.

Of course, any such list is a generalization. It is also helpful to analyze one's own personal values, which may not be exactly the same as the prevailing culture's. For example, Americans generally are considered to be time-oriented, but that is not true for all Americans.

Then the candidates must think through each cultural and personal value in terms of the four categories mentioned above. Is it clearly right when measured against Scripture? Is it in direct conflict with the teaching of Scripture? Does it fall in a gray area? Or is it morally neutral? Such analysis will be invaluable later on when one of his or her values conflicts with a teammate's.

A particularly helpful tool for determining one's personal values is *Ministering Cross-Culturally: An Incarnational Model for Personal Relationships*, by Sherwood Lingenfelter and Marvin Mayers (1986). They provide a questionnaire to help find your basic values (mainly those that are neutral or fall into a gray area). It can be used by both Western and non-Western missionaries. After you answer the questions, you plot a profile to show where you stand on the following values:

1. Time orientation vs. event orientation
2. Dichotomistic thinking vs. holistic thinking
3. Crisis orientation vs. noncrisis orientation
4. Task orientation vs. person orientation
5. Status focus vs. achievement focus
6. Concealment of vulnerability vs. willingness to expose vulnerability.

The authors then discuss the six pairs of contrasting traits, pointing out the tensions that result when people at opposite poles interact.

## 2. Field Orientation

Once on the field, team members will analyze each other's cultures. They must keep in mind that some of their teammates' values will be clearly right biblically and some may be in conflict with Scripture, but the majority will fall into the gray or neutral categories. The purpose is to understand each other well enough to communicate in love, pursue unity, build healthy relations, and decrease misunderstandings. The result will be a decrease in conflicts and a reduction of stress.

Three ways to reduce cultural stress are to recognize it, accept the new culture, and improve communication (Dye, 1974). By analyzing each team member's culture, potential areas of stress will be recognized. Acceptance of another person's culture as a valid way of life is built as we learn more about each member's culture and the reasons for his/her customs. Communication reduces stress because it fills our need for interaction and reduces loneliness and isolation. By talking about their own cultures, in a context of love and acceptance, missionaries feel less lonely and better understood.

Therefore, when the multinational team gets together for the first time, it would be helpful for the team leader (who would have been previously trained) to conduct a seminar, to help each one get acquainted with the others' cultural and personal values. Each member would share what they have learned in pre-field orientation about their home cultures and about themselves. Each one would take careful notes on what is said. The team leader must be sure that all this is done in an atmosphere of love and acceptance.

### 3. Crucial Areas to Discuss as a Team

After team members have talked about themselves and their cultures, the leader should open the discussion about crucial matters that lead to cultural conflicts. Among them are: leadership style and decision making; male-female relations and the role of women; physical contact; and preferred means of conflict resolution.

*Leadership Styles and Decision Making.* Cultures differ in the way leaders conduct themselves and in the relationship staff have with their leaders. Some prefer authoritarian leaders, those who make their decisions with little counsel from their staff. Others prefer democratic leaders who encourage members to share their ideas. Westerners who are used to being led by democratic leaders find it difficult to adjust to being led by an authoritarian leader.

In the discussion, as members talk about this difference in their cultures, they will gain insights into why they respond differently to their team leader's leadership style.

How will the team arrive at decisions? Each culture has a favorite method. Missionary Ben Reed works with a team in Japan led by Hong Kong Chinese. This is what he learned:

> Being from the West, where submission of the minority to the will of the majority has been the norm, we struggle with the cumbersome process in the East [Japan] referred to as consensus taking, where all opinions are reconciled to reach a unanimous decision. So unnatural to Western thought patterns, consensus taking is easily overlooked in administrative habits of Westerners...We Westerners sometimes blunder ahead trying to streamline our schedules and

*eliminate what we consider excess work. Often we simply alienate those who might otherwise have valuable input into the decision to be made and its out working. (Reed, 1990, p. 3)*

On teams where discussion is permitted, difficulties often arise because of cultural differences in the way discussions are conducted. Lehtinen (1988) explains:

*Most Germans, when they discuss, have a dialectical approach. You say something and a German feels that he has to say the other side of the issue. The first two words are, "Ja, aber..." (Yes, but...). Germans tend to be frustrated when there is no such tension in discussion. They feel: "We are just wasting our time, it's small talk" (p. 7).*

With this understanding of German culture, it is easy to understand why the Filipino in my earlier example saw her German teammate as "a very negative lady who always complains and asks *why* a lot." The Filipino was reacting to significant cultural differences. The tragedy was that she did not recognize that the differences were cultural, but instead judged the personality and spirituality of her teammate.

Lehtinen also explains:

*People of different cultures come to conclusions in their thinking patterns and decision making in very different ways....When [Americans] need to make a decision, they gather the positive information about the topic and then they make a decision....The British try to see the problems, too, and the solution which includes the least problems is often the one they choose....[However] when an African talks about an issue, he paints a picture. Everything is included. He does not need to have a central point. Contextual logic is also very common in Southern Europe. People paint a picture with their words. When they discuss, it's a long discussion. They talk and talk and talk and talk. And a person who comes from a linear culture asks, "When will they get to the main point?"....The whole discussion is the answer to the question. At a certain time they start to agree, they reach a consensus, and then they all finally agree, "Yes, yes, now I see the whole picture" (p. 10).*

Because of cultural differences in leadership styles and decision making, team members must communicate how their cultures handle these issues. The leadership style the team adopts will depend on the structure of the mission and the attitude of the leader. By discussing these issues, mutual understanding will be fostered.

*Male-Female Relations and the Role of Women.* Many of the people I interviewed said that relations between men and women produced numerous misunderstandings and conflicts. Men who come from cultures where women are seen as inferior often have difficulties working with women from cultures where women are seen as equal partners in ministry.

Courtship and dating patterns should be discussed. This has been a serious point of tension between Filipinos and Americans. An American may think he is just casually dating a woman from the Philippines, but in her culture's courtship patterns his actions mean pre-engagement.

*Physical Contact.* The team should discuss what each culture considers appropriate physical contact between men and women. Many cultures do not allow unmarried persons to have any physical contact at all. Westerners can easily offend their teammates because of this. When Americans greet with a hug, people in some cultures view this as immoral.

Physical contact between people of the same sex should also be discussed. In the Philippines, it is acceptable for a man to take another man's hand as they walk down the street, but this makes Americans very uncomfortable. When I worked on a team with a Fijian, I discovered that touching a Fijian's hair is a grave insult.

The team should also be aware of how different cultures see the need for personal space. Americans need four or five feet for general conversations, less for personal matters; but Latin Americans tend to stand two or three feet apart in ordinary conversations and much closer for personal discussions. By talking over issues such as these, the team can avoid many misunderstandings and hasty judgments.

*Conflict Resolution.* The team needs to discuss how conflicts are resolved in their home cultures. For instance, Americans tend to go face-to-face, but Filipinos prefer using a third party to mediate. Beyond cultural differences, however, the team needs to grapple with biblical principles, working through such texts as Matthew 6:12-15; Mark 11:25,25; Colossians 3:12-14; and Ephesians 4:26,27,32.

*Follow-Up.* The usual result of discussing these four basic cultural issues is new efforts to communicate and behave so as to avoid giving offense. But there will still be some miscues and the leader needs to conduct periodic follow-up discussions to keep members sensitive and to increase their understanding of one another.

## Conclusion

I have discussed how cultural differences affect multinational teams and have given some ideas about how to train members to understand each other better and to function more harmoniously. Understanding cultural differences is crucial, but this understanding must be combined with love and a desire to pursue unity. When understanding is coupled with love and unity, teams develop healthy relations and effective ministries.

## Questions for Discussion

1. What are some of the advantages of working on a multinational team versus a team comprised of members from only one culture? What are some of the disadvantages?

2. What types of misunderstandings and tensions have you experienced as you have related to others from different cultures? Could any of these have been avoided?

3. How might team members from different cultures respond to the authors advice to "analyze and discuss" differences and issues? Are some cultures more willing to do this than others?

4. What are some additional issues that should be discussed by a multinational team?

5. What type of training do team leaders need to be able to facilitate discussions about differences and help teammates work through periods of friction?

# References

Atkins, A. (1990). Know your own culture: A neglected tool for cross-cultural ministry. *Evangelical Missions Quarterly, 26,* 266-271.

Dye, W. (1974). Stress-producing factors in cultural adjustment. *Missiology, 2,* 61-77.

Hiebert, P. (1985). *Anthropological insights for missionaries.* Grand Rapids, MI: Baker.

Kohl, L. (1979). *Survival kit for overseas living.* Yarmouth, Maine: Intercultural Press.

Lehtinen, K. (1988). *Through the prism.* Paper presented at Agape International Training, Campus Crusade for Christ—Europe, April, 1988.

Lingenfelter, S., & Mayers, M. (1986). *Ministering cross-culturally: An incarnational model for personal relationships.* Grand Rapids, MI: Baker.

Reed, B. (1990). Our team leader is an Asian. *East Asia's Millions.* November-December.

Simpson, E., & Bruce, F. (1973). *Commentary on the epistles to the Ephesians and the Colossians.* Grand Rapids, MI: Eerdmans.

Singer, M. (1987). *Intercultural communication: A perceptual approach.* Englewood Cliffs, NJ: Prentice-Hall.

# 12

*Tim Lewis*

*Becky Lewis*

# Coaching Missionary Teams

For the last ten years we have been working to establish long-term church planting teams in limited access situations. Along the way we have taken note of our mistakes as well as what we have done right. We have learned that relatively young and inexperienced teams can see breakthroughs in some very difficult circumstances if they are adequately coached by more experienced veterans.

In this article we will explore some of the approaches for coaching that we have found to be effective. We will define coaching, elaborate upon its important components, explain its application in a team context, discuss whom we use as coaches, profile an effective coach, and give some examples of coaching visits.

## Definition of Coaching

We would like to define the coaching of missionary teams quite narrowly in order to accentuate its distinctives from other forms of member care. Coaching is a term borrowed from the athletic world, which we use to designate the ongoing supervision, counseling, and support that occurs "in the thick of the action." We define coaching as: *the use of appropriately gifted individuals in a mobile ministry of support and development of missionaries and missionary teams in the field context in order to maximize the team's effectiveness in ministry*. Let's take a closer look at what is involved in coaching.

## Coaching Takes Place in the Field Context

Coaching involves the supportive direction that takes place "during the game." It is the personalized attention, encouragement, vision-building, mentoring, and yes, stimulating into action, of those who are on the field—whether they are making great strides or struggling to just survive. We have found that case-specific problem solving, training, counseling, and monitoring the effectiveness of each individual and team, is best accomplished "on the job" in the field context. It is impossible for pre-field and off-field training to anticipate or give personalized direction for the many unexpected problems that inevitably arise in any field situation.

## Coaching Is Committed to Ministry Effectiveness

The ultimate goal of "winning the game," not merely developing better athletes or keeping the team together, is crucial to the coaching perspective. Effective coaching is often the key to whether or not a team succeeds. Athletic coaches and mission coaches have similar tasks. Both must know the goals and the nature of the "game," understand the strengths and weaknesses of each team member, and learn how to best coordinate the team's efforts.

Coaching necessitates maintaining a balanced perspective: the "winning of the game" being as important as the safety and development of team members. Members that have become so weakened that they are dragging the whole team down may temporarily be removed, but for the most part, the coach attempts to keep the team functioning on the field at top capacity. We have found that the longevity and sense of fulfillment of workers on the field is directly proportional to their commitment to and effectiveness in their original calling and vision, even more than their relationship with fellow workers. By helping missionaries to become effective in their ministry, many problems that would otherwise seem intolerable can be kept in the proper perspective.

## Coaching Is Personalized and Interactive

Coaching involves a great deal of proactive training and development of individuals and teams; however, because of its field context, the training is not theoretical but is applied directly to the situation at hand. Coaching must therefore be done by a person or persons who can come into a situation, listen and observe, and give guidance and perspective to those involved. This kind of input requires that the coach be well-acquainted with both the field situation and the strengths and weaknesses of the individual missionaries. Coaching does not replace generalized training; rather it insures that knowledge is being applied and skills are developed to deal with the specific, current challenges facing a team.

Coaches are encouraged to maintain ongoing relationships with teams on the field by letter, phone calls, and future trips. Those on the field need regular, high-quality support if they are to survive, grow personally and spiritually, and be effective in their work.

### Coaching Provides Greater Networking

Coaches can be important channels to pass on news within the mission family and update teams as to events going on in other places. Missionaries in isolated circumstances, for example, can be encouraged as they hear accounts of what is happening on other teams and in other contexts. Those things that are proving to be helpful in one area, whether it be in church planting strategies, care of missionary children, or improving team life, can be recommended for use in other areas as well.

Coaching can also enhance networking between field personnel, home offices, and home churches. Coaches can keep each group in closer touch with the real needs and problems facing the others. As the coaches report back to the agency field office concerning the field situations, they can provide insights into the needs and effectiveness of the missionaries, personnel problems, inter-agency issues, and needs for follow-up.

Coaching can extend the resources of an agency by making use of specialists from other organizations: pastors, missiologists, health care specialists, educators, linguists, business consultants, and other professionals. Even small agencies can provide top quality input to their field personnel by developing a network of coaches.

## Understanding the Team Context

Our mission agency requires individuals to work together in teams. Many of our teams work in mission fields where high-quality support cannot be provided from a distance no matter how well-intentioned mission home offices and home churches are. In such fields the need for mutual support, transparency, and perseverance become essential for team survival and success.

We led a large team in North Africa which eventually consisted of 38 adults and 46 children. Each member signed a common document that clearly stated our goals and the nature of our relationship with one another (referred to as a "memo of understanding"). We actively cultivated a sense of responsibility for each other's welfare. Even though we were geographically spread about, there was a strong feeling that "we're all in this together." At one point we asked our team members to identify some of the factors that were keeping them on the field; almost all of them put "commitment to the team" as the main reason they were sticking it out. Strategies were discussed regularly as a team, and any approach that helped with adjustment or to effectively communicate the gospel was passed on to others.

Using a team approach in these more isolated situations facilitates the care and growth of each team member, in everything from language progress to relational struggles. A great deal of the supervision can occur on a regular basis for team members by their team leader.

### Coaching and Team Struggles

Any team, no matter how cohesive or highly committed, has the potential of becoming a relational nightmare. This certainly has been our experience from time to time. As in an extended family, a significant relational disturbance can throw the whole team into a tailspin. Occasionally one team member becomes so emotionally needy that the energies of the entire team can become focused on and drained by the ups and downs of the one member. Power plays, jealousies, judgmentalism, and gossip can also abound. Further, those with certain needs and gifts can virtually ignore or deny the appropriateness of the needs and gifts of other members.

Most teams will have either a recognized or a natural behind-the-scenes leader, who may become the focus of any frustrations, or be looked on as the one who should make the team successful somehow. Conflict between two or more natural leaders can shipwreck a team.

In situations like the ones just described, the role of a coach is especially important. The coach can help overcome some of the inherent struggles in the team. Each team will have some strengths and some weaknesses because of the combination of personalities and gifts of its members. Coaches can make sure that these characteristics are clearly understood, openly discussed, and prayed about in order to prevent the eruption of major problems.

In cases where there is significant conflict, the coach can act as an outside mediator to bring understanding and reconciliation in relational conflicts. Trying to isolate "the problem causing person" and removing that person from the field is seldom the answer because relational problems are rarely totally one-sided. We have often observed the personal growth that transpires through trials and conflicts that are brought full-circle to resolution on the field.

Sometimes resolution only requires accepting the fact that others are genuinely different and loving them anyway. Other times a coach may need to call in the field director if there is a situation that requires restructuring of a team or the discipline or removal of a team leader or member. Teams need help working through these rough periods in their development. Coaches with interpersonal skills can play a key role in providing the practical, on-the-job input that is needed to keep relationships healthy.

## Who Does the Coaching?

Both our General Director and our Field Director make frequent coaching trips, and together, visit more teams yearly than any other coach. Coaching is an important part of their respective job descriptions. The frequency of their visits to the fields and teams is necessary to adequately understand and administer the 30-35 teams that we have.

Team leaders can also provide valuable insights and encouragement to each other. We often call upon certain team leaders to visit other teams in a coaching capacity.

Most coaches, though, who work with our teams, are drawn from other organizations. They usually work on a part-time or emergency basis, and often on the request or suggestion of the team itself. Certain teams have developed ongoing relationships with specific coaches of their choice who make yearly visits of encouragement to their field. Some of these coaches are pastors from home churches; this has the added benefit of keeping the home church closely tied in with the vision and needs of field teams. Most coaching is done on a voluntary basis, with the churches, teams, and mission contributing as they are able to cover the travel expenses.

We are open to coaches from a broad range of backgrounds. Some are senior pastors or mission professionals, others are counselors or member care professionals, but many are simply Christians, mature in the Lord, who bring a certain expertise to bear on the situation. We desire to strengthen the coaching role of women, but the constraints of economics (e.g., travel costs for coaches' wives), as well as the difficulties for women traveling in the areas in which our teams live, have kept us from making as much progress in this area as we have desired.

Coaches often attend our annual International Council Meeting, where they develop relationships with team leaders and other mission personnel. Their involvement frequently results in invitations to visit teams on-site. Coaches are primary resources for conference workshops on strategy, interpersonal dynamics, family life, leadership development, spiritual growth, and other topics.

It is important to understand that with the exception of the General Director and the Field Director, our coaches are not in "line" authority with the teams or team leader. They have no power to act on behalf of the International Headquarters unless specifically given that mandate by the General Director or Field Director, and with prior arrangement with the team.

Coaches give written feedback to the Field Director on how the team is functioning in several important areas (e.g., language learning progress, social contacts), as well as on the personal adjustment of individuals and families. A "Coaching Report" form provides a framework for their written feedback.

## Profile of an Effective Coach

It is a rare individual who is capable of coaching a missionary team in every major area of need. Those who are effective in resolving interpersonal conflicts may not be able to give input into church planting strategies, for example. In our mission agency we have found it helpful to identify the different types of coaching that are needed by our field teams. Some of these are:

1. Strategic (experience in Muslim church planting)
2. Pastoral (counseling, biblical instruction)
3. Trouble-shooting (conflict resolution, team dynamics)
4. Counseling/therapy (individuals, couples, and families)
5. Socio-linguistics (language learning and analysis)
6. Entry strategist (to help with tent-making problems).

Some of our best coaches have been "discovered" by one of the teams and subsequently recommended to the other teams. We have also found that some coaches are appreciated more by some teams than by others, determined in part by the needs and "personality" of each team.

There are certain characteristics that we look for in selecting potential coaches for our field teams:

1. Coaches must be spiritually mature individuals, able to minister encouragement from a biblical perspective, and capable of withstanding the pressures of erratic travel, primitive living conditions, and team struggles.

2. Coaches with previous field experience are desired, as their experience increases their understanding for the team situations in which they work.

3. Coaches must have knowledge and experience in the area of need in which they are consulting.

4. Coaches must be committed to maintaining the confidentiality of all parties involved, not violating the confidences among people on the team, of the team leader, or with members of home churches, relatives, and friends.

5. Coaches must have a clear understanding of and commitment to the ministry of our mission. This vision includes a commitment to reaching Muslim peoples with the goal of planting self-propagating churches. A good understanding of and respect for Islamic religion and culture, and the restrictions and security constraints working in these countries is paramount.

6. Coaches also need to have a basic understanding of and commitment to upholding the authority structure of our mission agency, including the authority of the team leader. Without this understanding they will not be able to help a team work through problems in a way that will strengthen their relationship with their working partners and overseers.

7. Coaches need to be able to help teams think through and determine their own course of action, instead of merely giving an answer. The goal is to make the team stronger and more self-reliant instead of more dependent on outside help.

8. Coaches must ascribe to the "grace orientation" of our mission. This gives each team leeway to not only determine their strategic approach and team ethos, but also to pick which coaches they desire to use.

9. Coaches need to be available when needed, as much as possible, sometimes on an emergency basis.

In addition to the above points, we have observed that coaches are most effective when there is an ongoing relationship between the Field Director and the coach as well as between the coach and the team; when the coach is briefed before visiting a team; when the coach is debriefed after a trip; and when teams provide specific feedback on the effectiveness of a coach to both the coach and the Field Director.

## Examples of Coaching Visits

What does coaching really look like? Here are ten quick summaries of successful coaching trips.

1. Our General Director visited one team that was doing very well in team life matters but seemed to be making little headway in ministry. As a result of a concrete evaluation of the situation and some specific suggestions, that team is now experiencing unprecedented ministry opportunities and conversions.

2. Our coordinator of Team Development was able to visit a team in a very harsh, inaccessible environment and function as a mediator and sounding board, helping the members with conflict resolution and getting the team back on track.

3. A specialist in missiology gave a series of training talks at a regional gathering of five teams in order to explore ways to minister to the targeted people groups.

4. An expert in community development was able to visit a development project and give the team advice on gaining political and community approval of their project.

5. A pastor and his wife provided needed intervention in a team leader's marriage, and on specific instruction of the International Headquarters, helped the team to make a transition to new leadership from within the team.

6. One experienced team leader was able to visit another team and give them specific training in power encounters and spiritual warfare.

7. A coaching trip by a mental health professional helped one team leader see himself more objectively and make some needed adjustments in his leadership style.

8. A retired couple was able to move into a large city on the field where they could service the teams there by providing wisdom, stability, hospitality, and child care to the heavily stressed families.

9. A couple with many years of experience in teaching children with developmental disabilities visited some of our teams as consultants on children's educational needs and problems.

10. The Field Director, from his own church planting experience, was able to demonstrate a non-confrontive approach to evangelism to a team leader who had been seeing no success with his more confrontive approach, giving him a specific alternative to his previous training in Muslim evangelism.

## Final Comments

At its most basic level, coaching provides ongoing support to field personnel within the team context. Problems and persistent issues (relationship conflicts, spiritual vitality) are dealt with on the field to keep the missionary and the team progressing toward the goal (church planting in our case). Coaching should strengthen the commitment of the team members to each other and to the task before them. Coaches help missionaries clearly assess how they are doing and whether their plans need to be re-evaluated and upgraded.

The great preponderance of mission agency resources, research, and thought go into the pre-field and off-the-field preparation and counseling of missionaries. These are not enough, however. The particular challenges and realities of the "third era" of missions—unreached peoples and limited (or creative) access situations—requires that we focus on getting more help and resources to the missionary on the job. One strategic way to do this is to use qualified coaches who can encourage teams, foster personal growth, and guide members to greater ministry effectiveness.

### Questions for Discussion

1. What are some issues to consider when using coaches on multinational teams?

2. How often and for how long do you think coaches should visit a team on the field?

3. What types of supportive care might coaches need themselves?

4. Which personal and professional qualities are most important for coaches to have?

5. How could your mission organization develop or improve its coaching program?

# 13

*Kenneth Harder*

# Field Leaders and Team Nurture

Ministry teams have become a trend in missions since the 1980s. A major reason for the popularity of this approach is that teams are the preferred assignment pattern of missionaries and missionary candidates. Today it is hard to find people who will admit being the "lone ranger" of earlier missionary eras. Even those who desire significant autonomy prefer the team approach. For many missionary candidates the perceived security and care inherent in an excellent team is a major factor in their selection of a mission organization.

The results of this trend to use teams have been varied. One reason for the mixed results is that some missions joined the team "band wagon" without adequately examining and adjusting their current selection processes, pre-field training programs, and field care approaches in light of the new team emphasis. Teams require additional types of attention that build upon and go beyond approaches focusing on the individual.

Development of an effective team is a long-term process that begins with the careful selection of members. It involves significant time in group formation to forge a common vision and common expectations concerning work goals, ministry strategy, leader and member roles, personal responsibilities, and type of team. The molding of diverse personalities into a team also requires time for the members to appreciate their differences, build team synergy, and develop mutual trust.

Seldom do ministry teams function in life as designed on paper. Rare is the team where the chemistry seems "made in heaven." Even with successful selection and formation activities, the team will not reach its potential for several years. During those years, mission leadership must spend significant time in team development and team building as their teams deal with the challenges of ministry and the undeniable differences among team members. Even teams at peak performance need periodic and planned care, development, and training.

My purpose in this chapter is to discuss how field leaders can nurture the long-term ministry teams that they oversee. My primary focus on field leaders is intended to complement the important roles of team leaders, field coaches, and the mutual support provided by team members. I present several principles for team development, and discuss a nurturance model that relates team dimensions (relationships, task, strategy, and personal wholeness) to team levels (team leader, team members, the team as a unit). Central to my approach is the need for regularly scheduled times of personal and group reflection and an ongoing commitment to team development. Let us turn our attention now to a fictional team situation to highlight a variety of team issues.

## Case Study: Kola Team

George, the country field director, has responsibilities for several church planting teams in Matolia. Yesterday, during an unexpected visit, the newest members of the Kola Team, Bob and Sue, shared candidly about the team.

### Background

Bob and Sue accepted their first missionary assignment by joining the Kola Church Planting Team. They looked forward to the team approach because they had used the team strategy in two successful church planting assignments in their home country. They viewed this mission assignment as a natural extension of their calling and previous experience. Their two children, ages 13 and 10, accepted the challenge, including the need to live at a distant boarding school.

The Kola Team began eight years ago with two couples, Tom/Jane and Bill/Joyce, as its charter members. Jackie and Ruth, two single women, joined the team three years ago from other ministries in Matolia. Bob and Sue began working with the team ten months ago, after having successfully completed language school.

The team invited Bob and Sue to join the team for two reasons. First, the two couples were seminary classmates and friends of Bob and Sue. They had several opportunities to get to know each other during seminary and each couple enjoyed the others' company. Second, Bob and Sue's church planting success demonstrated their ability to match ministry with people concerns resulting in mature believers and strong churches. Even so the mission had reviewed the team's request with an outside consultant before approving the placement.

Initially, George had taken some deliberate steps in forming the Kola Team. The mission had interviewed and tested each team member to discover the areas of potential tension and synergy. Time was set aside, with a facilitator, for the original two couples to have team building and strategy sessions. Since then, however, George has given minimal time to the Kola Team, expecting the senior members to establish the ethos and team development activities.

To date, the team's ministry with the Kola church and local Christians has been exemplary. Their church planting strategy, mutually developed with the national Christians, has resulted in steady growth in numbers and believer maturity. In light of this George has felt little need to visit the Kola Team during the last three years.

The exceptional and complementary giftedness of each member, when combined with strong interpersonal ability and common training, created high expectations for the Kola Team within the mission and the team itself. Everyone was hoping that they would demonstrate the mission's new team approach. Until yesterday those expectations seemed to be on target.

### Bob and Sue's Story

From the outside it seems that all members are doing their part to accomplish the team goals. Yet, Bob and Sue do not see the team functioning as a unit. Rather they are a group of individuals "doing their own thing" within a general plan. Questions and new issues raised by church members or team members are not discussed. The team leader, Tom, has a busy schedule of administration, teaching, and other tasks, which consumes all his energy. New ideas seem to overload Tom. He prefers to talk about the team's general plan formulated six years ago. Tom also seems discouraged, slowly withdrawing.

In many ways Bill is the informal leader. With a quick mind and engaging personality he often dominates the meetings. When challenged about this behavior he becomes defensive. There seems to be a subtle competition for ideas and results between Bill and Tom. This has impacted their wives' relationship, according to Sue. Yet during school holidays, the two families collaborate to plan activities for their children (high school and upper elementary age).

Jackie and Ruth have their own successful ministry areas in youth and team administration respectively. Being newer team members without seminary education, they defer to Tom and Bill in most of the matters that come up on the team.

The regular team meetings focus on the administrative problems and routine reports. Creative tackling of new challenges is often replaced with the recalling of past successful events.

Bob and Sue are wondering if they can continue with the Kola Team. Did they mistake the call of friends for the call of God? An added concern is their low level of ministry, much lower than back home, "even after being a year beyond language school." They tried to set up a time to talk with Tom, although he was unavailable due to his preparation for a leadership training course and an upcoming evangelistic outreach.

## Reflections on the Case Study

Let's start off with three important questions that relate to the Kola Team and other teams that struggle.

1. What are the basic strengths and problems on this team—that is, what promotes team effectiveness and what hinders it?

2. If you were the field leader, what steps would you take to help this team?

3. What recommendations would you make to the organization concerning its use and care of teams?

Bob and Sue's story points out some common issues for teams: the need for supportive care and a systematic plan for long-term team development. George thought that team formation equals team development. He assumed that if sufficient time and energy were spent in group formation activities, he could shift his focus from the team—except in the "rare" cases of interpersonal conflict, ministry failure or inactivity, or personal problems—and concentrate on other ministry and administrative areas.

In addition, George, partly due to his busy schedule, did not feel a need to look below the "activity layer" of the Kola Team. He assumed that significant activity was a sign of team health. In both assumptions George followed the axiom, "If it isn't broken, don't fix it."

Bob and Sue, on the other hand, may have underestimated the amount of adjustment and learning required to become effective missionaries. In the midst of their adjustment struggles they, like other missionaries, may have longed for the success of the past and doubted their calling and/or capabilities (Smalley, 1966; Harder, 1990). If Tom, as team leader (or another mentor/coach), were more available to them, their adjustment to both the team and the new culture would surely have gone more smoothly.

There are several important long-term concerns in this case. These include the reported lack of Tom's leadership within the team, the unhealthy type of team communication, the seeming competition between Tom and Bill, and the uncoordinated, autonomous work within the team. If these reports are accurate, the team has regressed, needing gentle help to regain shared commitment, harmonize expectations, and establish healthier group norms.

As George explores the functioning of the Kola Team, he will probably hear of other issues which need resolution. A review by George and Tom of the team's covenant/memorandum of understanding (if one was written) and a list of characteristics of an effective team (Parker, 1990, p.33) might be a starting point for their reflection and planning. The type of relationship between George and Tom will dictate the first actions in discovering the road blocks and developing a team building strategy.

Clearly a long-term, developmental approach is needed to nurture this intercultural ministry team. This will probably be a difficult process, especially at first, as team members sort out expectations, disclose feelings, and try to work together in new ways. George, as field leader, needs to regularly interact with the Kola Team, overseeing team building exercises, and spend time with individual members. He must especially help Tom, the team leader, become a nurturing leader who equips and cares for other members. Practical ways to provide mutual support—such as through Bible studies, prayer, and fun times together—will also help this team become more cohesive and effective.

## Basic Issues in Developing Teams

Before responding to the team and individual issues raised by Bob and Sue, George would profit from a review of six basic issues related to effective missionary teams.

### Personal Adjustment

The added stress of living and ministering in a new culture can inevitably stir up frustrations, misunderstandings, and personal weaknesses that can affect other team members (Gradin, 1980; Grove & Torbiorn, 1985; Harder, 1990). Bob and Sue, in addition to entering the Kola culture, are also entering the Kola Team with its established group culture. Both of these "cultures" will require them to make personal adjustments. Like many mission teams, the Kola Team needs to pay attention to group formation each time new members enter because the entrance of even one new member changes team dynamics. Without such intentional activity a team can lose momentum, regress into earlier stages, and experience conflict. These fruits of benign neglect may not be visible immediately.

### Team Stages

Teams progress through different stages of development. Each stage has different concerns which need to be worked through and resolved (Tuckman & Jensen, 1977; Schein, 1985; Harder, 1990). Unresolved issues at any stage will impede the team's effectiveness at later stages. By understanding the present stage of Kola Team functioning, George can sort through ministry and relationship issues as they relate to the stage of team development, as well as anticipate upcoming issues.

Francis and Young (1979) identify four team stages that relate to most work teams: testing, infighting, getting organized, and mature closeness. *Testing* refers to the early process in which team members examine their team involvement in relation to vision, leadership, and interpersonal fit. The next stage, *infighting*, requires members to sort out issues of influence, power, control, decision-making, and tolerance. *Getting organized* involves a stage whereby members become committed to work effectively around a common vision with a growing sense of mutual respect. Finally, the *mature closeness* stage is experienced when members know their own role and contribution, and are willing to extend themselves for colleagues. There are, of course, many models of team stages, most of which have similar and overlapping features. An additional model of relevance to missionary teams is Reddy and Jamison's (1988) seven-stage "Team Performance" model.

## Team Models

Many conflicts arise within teams because of the different team models held by the members. Using sports teams as examples, Torres and Spiegel (1990) explore how various models result in different expectations, diverse work strategies, and degree of interpersonal activity. While the team's ultimate goal for baseball, football, basketball, volleyball, and tennis is winning, the way of functioning within each type of team is obviously different. Sport coaches employ extensive practice sessions to insure that each player understands the game and his/her role, not confusing the techniques of one sport with those of another.

Members of mission teams bring different "team models" to their mission team. This is true of the Kola Team as well. Bill's preferences for team life and ministry will likely be different from those of Jackie, Bob and Sue, and so on.

The team models for each member come from that member's personal history of home/family life, school activities, sports experience, and church life. Teams with an international composition include expectations based on each member's cultural experience. If not expressed, these expectations cause serious conflict and tension. Discussed, these expectations can be harnessed to fashion a mutual, common set of norms which produces group solidarity and stability.

## Team Building Versus Team Development

Understanding the difference between team building and team development will help field leaders and team leaders maximize the growth and ministry of their teams. "Team building focuses on deficits in team performance and its primary goal is remedial—to fix something. Team development does not assume that something is wrong and should be fixed but proceeds on the expectation that there are always positive opportunities for improvement" (Kinlaw, 1991, 24). Further, team building usually involves shorter-term, brief experiences whereas team development embraces a longer-term perspective in which a variety of growth experiences become a regular, ongoing part of team life.

Because of Bob and Sue's concerns, George will need to initially focus on team building activities. He might even need to bring in an outside facilitator or counselor to help the Kola Team address the group dynamics and personal issues. After the team is stabilized through such group and individual interventions, he will need to switch to long-term team development. While team development will not avert team building issues, it will provide a proactive foundation to acquire new skills and perspectives to help prevent and work through future problems on the team.

## Approaches to Team Nurture

The maturation of teams requires more than intermittent training or care. It necessitates an ongoing, nurturing approach which consists of three prongs. The Kola Team must integrate all three prongs into its team life in order to become and remain healthy.

One prong focuses on *personal and team development*. It is not training for training's sake or pursuing the latest intercultural trends. Rather it is proactively equipping the team in skills, understanding, perspectives, and behaviors for dealing with significant issues facing the team as a corporate unit and as individual members.

*Problem solving* is the second prong. Here the field leader and the team seek to resolve relationship or ministry problems which are hindering the service and functioning of the team. Kinlaw refers to this as team building.

A third prong is *responsive, supportive care*, to encourage team members as they experience cross-cultural and ministry challenges along with normal life issues. The care is not necessarily directed at fixing a problem or changing a negative event, but at helping a team or team member positively respond to an issue or creatively live with present realities.

## Team Levels and Team Dimensions

Missionary teams require nurturing by mission leadership at three levels: the team leader, the individual members, and the team unit as a group. Field leaders usually do not have direct responsibility for the nurture of individual team members, although they are responsible to help the team leader provide this. Field leaders have a special responsibility to coach and support team leaders, and to make sure that sufficient resources for team development are available for the teams they oversee.

When working with each team level, four team dimensions need to be addressed: relational, task, strategy, and personal wholeness. For the Kola Team, it would be important to help the members work through their interpersonal relationships, clarify the group and individual tasks they want to pursue, harmonize the overall team strategy, and develop ways for individual members to continue to grow as persons.

The combining of team levels with team dimensions (see Table 1) reveals several facets of team nurture. The resulting matrix can be used as an analytical tool for identifying areas that need attention for either team development or team building.

## A Strategy for Team Development

Team development is designed to foster the systematic growth of both the team as an intercultural missionary group and its individual members. As with all growth, team effectiveness usually comes with consistent

## Table 1. Nurturing Matrix: Relationship Between Team Dimensions and Team Levels.

| Team Dimensions | Team Levels | | |
| --- | --- | --- | --- |
| | Team Leader | Team Member | Team as Unit |
| Relational | With team members, family members, local church, and host community | With team members, family members, local church, and host community | Internal Relationships: Impact on team dynamics and members External Relationships: Impact on other teams, local church, and host community |
| Task | Understands leader's role Facilitates team vision, direction, strategy, and growth Understands team's stage and dynamics | Understands personal role in team Knows resources and colleagues Gives and receives feedback | Has common purpose, goals, and direction Has agreement on ministry values |
| Strategy | Team ministry strategy Growth plan for team and its members Personal growth plan Understands team's norms, procedures, and type of team | Understands personal part in team strategy Identifies personal development areas for intercultural and team effectiveness | Common perspectives and expectations: -communication -decision making -vision/direction -host culture -ministry strategy -personal growth, etc. |
| Personal Wholeness | Impact of ministry roles: -personally -family/house mate Sense of fulfillment | Impact of ministry roles: -personally -family/house mate Sense of fulfillment | Team impact on members Sense of God's corporate direction and blessing |

attention and incremental steps. Like farmers who tend their crops, field leaders such as George (as well as team leaders) must become committed to consistent nurture of the team and not wait for crises to catch their attention.

Consistent nurture requires developing a systematic plan, or *cycle of nurture*. The plan needs to provide regular opportunities for reflection, evaluation, encouragement, and planning for ministry and growth (Vogt & Murrell, 1990).

One way to implement a team development plan is to set aside a day on a periodic basis for each level of the team: team leader, individual member, and the team as a unit. Each level meets with the field leader or possibly another field coach, preferably at least every six months. These meetings, referred to as *focus times* (discussed below), are an important part of an overall cycle of nurture. Additional activities in this cycle usually include prayer, Bible study, discussion, teaching, ministry review, and planning.

## Focus Time

*Focus time* is a specific team development event that is planned into the team schedule on a regular basis. The purpose is to provide personal care, ministry direction, and focused growth. It can be used with individual members, couples, and the team itself, and requires up to six hours so as not to rush the process. Focus times are used to reflect on the past events, present realities, and future direction that affect one's personal life and ministry.

The agenda for focus times is straightforward, and is based on the following five stage process.

1. *Sharing*. This is a time to catch up on general information regarding personal, family, community, and church events. This stage encourages the focus time leader and team member to tune into the lives of each other.

2. *Reflection*. In light of the ministry and personal goals, the missionary reflects on the recent past. The goal is to gain perspective on relationships, events, ministry, oneself, the host culture, and God.

3. *Adjustment*. Here the process moves to learning from the past in order to understand the ministry, the people, oneself, and the ways God is working in the context. This encourages the missionary to adjust the way he/she views the situation, plans and implements his/her ministries, lives in a family/household, and relates to the local church and community.

4. *Direction*. Using information and insights obtained in the previous steps, the missionary with the mission leader will try to gain a sense of God's direction in specific enough ways to make contextually appropriate plans for ministry and personal/family life.

5. *Growth*. Finally, each missionary identifies two to five specific areas for growth. These areas can range from cross-cultural ministry issues to personal issues of family or personal life.

The focus time requires a coaching leadership approach if it is to be effective (Megginson & Boydell, 1986). Through a coaching style, the field leader, field coach, or growth facilitator encourages missionaries to reflect on their past experiences and relationships. Using their own reflections the missionaries can develop understanding which can be immediately incorporated into their ministry and personal life plans. When the reflective process is performed with empathy, the missionaries involved experience a sense of care and encouragement.

## Focus Time and Team Nurture

How can field leaders find enough time to nurture the team leader, each team member, and the team as a unit? With the Team Nurturing Matrix (Table 1) in mind, let's look at some ways that a team leader can provide the necessary help.

*Team Leader*. The most important level of nurturing for field leaders is with the team leaders. By helping team leaders grow, field leaders can multiply their nurturing efforts through the team leader to each member and the team as a unit.

The focus time with team leaders would look at four major areas of life: personal ministry, family life, team leadership role, and church/community relationships. Having heavy responsibilities, the team leader needs help in maintaining marital/family and ministry balance. A strong marriage and family is not a luxury, but a cornerstone for communicating the Gospel as well as nurturing the team.

Another function of the field leader is to help the team leader identify personal gifts and strategically match them with ministry involvement. Again the focus time becomes an event which promotes the realistic matching of priorities to the demands of intercultural service and life.

The agenda of a team leader's focus time includes the ministry and growth needs of the team. It is easy for ministry needs to consume all one's time, leaving none for development of the team or individual members. Working together, the field leader and team leader can plan the team's focus time by discussing the present functioning and the stage of the team's development. Together they can identify ways to help the team reach the group goals and maintain healthy team dynamics. The team leader can then raise issues with each team member and as a group plan the upcoming focus times.

*Team Members*. A focus time for each team member or couple/partner unit is the responsibility of the team leader. It would be helpful to schedule this every six months and to follow the five stage reflective process previously described. Together they explore four areas of the team member's or unit's life: personal ministry, family/couple life, team role/dynamics, and community/church life.

In addition, once a year the field leader needs to have a time when members can share individually, or as a couple/partners, the joys and concerns of their missionary life. Each team member needs to feel he/she has access to the field leader, while not allowing it to short-circuit the authority and nurturing responsibilities of the team leader.

*Team as a Unit.* The focus time for the team is separate from regular team meetings. Holding them twice a year allows the team to corporately reflect on ministry issues and team dynamics. Although usually led by the team leader, external resource people can be also used for specific team building or development issues. The perspectives of such "outsiders" can help the team look at itself more objectively, especially in problematic areas.

### Focus Times and Team Retreats

Each year, a team focus time can be conducted as part of a two to four day retreat. It is usually better to hold such a retreat in a location away from normal, daily interruptions. Be sure to include each team member as the retreat schedule is being planned. Depending on the team's needs, the retreat schedule should allow for times of team ministry review, team planning, recreation/fun, worship, Bible study, and personal rest. The informal times for recreation or rest are important for developing friendships and bonding together as a team. Worship times can be informal, allowing each person to participate. Using outside resource people can be particularly helpful to bring fresh encouragement to the team.

Involve the children too. The older ones also benefit from special group times with one another and with the larger group. In addition, wives need time away from their usual daily responsibilities so they can provide input, renew themselves, and fully participate.

George, the field leader, and Tom, the team leader, could use a retreat setting to tackle the issues facing the Kola Team in a positive manner. Beginning the team retreat with worship and praise would help the team members to focus on God and put their life in better perspective. Allowing members to share significant growth and ministry experiences will help them to tune into each other's world, something often overlooked in the business of daily life. George could administer a short team building instrument—such as one described by Francis and Young (1979), Parker (1990), or in chapter 14 of this book—to identify areas of team stress, conflict, and poor performance. Once identified, the team could begin to discuss and prayerfully work through these problematic areas. It would be important for both George and Tom to acknowledge how they have contributed to the team's struggles and commit to changes in their own behavior before expecting other team members to change.

# Conclusion

The development of an effective missionary team takes significant time and energy, beginning with the team's formation. Ongoing coaching and nurture by a mission's field leadership is a necessity, as is a systematic plan for team development. Regularly scheduled focus times for team and team member growth can strengthen teams for their evangelistic tasks. They also help to build a team ethos that values mutual care and mutual accountability, both of which form the bedrock of any effective team.

## Questions for Discussion

1. Which supportive structures and services should be in place before a team is sent to a field?

2. How does your mission agency provide systematic, periodic nurture for your teams, team leaders, and field leaders?

3. How knowledgeable should team leaders and team members be about team formation principles, team stages, team models, and team dynamics?

4. What are some creative ways for mission agencies to provide care to teams that are geographically isolated, or where there is no field leader in place?

5. What are other useful types of team development events besides the focus times described in this article?

# References

Francis, D., & Young, D. (1979). Improving work groups: A practical manual for team building. San Diego, CA: University Associates.

Gradin, D. (1980). A design for cross-cultural orientation. *Emissary, 11,* (2), 1-6.

Grove, C. & Torbiorn, I. (1985). A new conceptualization of intercultural adjustment and the goals of training. *International Journal of Intercultural Relations, 9,* 205-233.

Harder, K. *(1986). Team development: Stages and issues.* Unpublished instructional material, Farmington, MI: Author.

Harder, K. (1990). *The transition model: Entering a new culture.* Instructional notes for the "Pre-field Orientation Program" of Missionary Internship. Farmington, MI: Author.

Kinlaw, D. (1991). *Developing superior work teams.* San Diego, CA: University Associates.

Megginson, D. & Boydell, T. (1986). *A manager's guide to coaching*. Boston, MA: McBer.

Nuechterlein, A. (1989). *Improving your multiple staff ministry*. Minneapolis, Minnesota: Augsburg Fortress.

Parker, G. (1990). *Team players and teamwork*. San Francisco, CA: Jossey-Bass.

Reddy, W. & Jamison, K. (1988). *Team building: Blueprints for productivity and satisfaction*. Alexandria, Virginia: Institute for Applied Behavioral Science.

Schien, E. (1985). *Organization culture and leadership*. San Francisco, CA: Jossey-Bass, 1985.

Smalley, W. (1966). Emotional storm signals: The shocks of culture, language, and self-discovery. *Evangelical Missions Quarterly, 3*, 146-156.

Torres, C. & Spiegel, J. (1990). *Self-directed work teams: A primer*. San Diego, CA: University Associates.

Tuckman, B. & Jensen, M. (1977). Stages of small group development revised. *Group and Organizational Studies, 2*, 419-427.

Vogt, J. & Murrel, K. (1990). *Empowerment in organizations*. San Diego, CA: University Associates.

# 14

*Kelly O'Donnell*

# Tools for Team Viability

Missionary teams are groups—specialty groups—which exist to perform specific tasks. They come in all shapes and sizes, and vary in their focus, composition, life-span, and scores of other variables.

Some teams are long-term, highly selective groups, such as a Bible translation team living with an Amazon tribe. Other teams, like a relief ministry in a war-torn area, may eagerly take on qualified short-termers, or be willing to include staff belonging to another organization. Planning committees are teams; so are personnel departments. Teams can be comprised of multinational workers, children, home office staff, computer specialists. The point is that when we refer to teams in missions we are referring to entities which are as varied as the individuals which actually make up the teams.

My purpose in this article is to strengthen missionary teams by equipping them with tools to increase their viability. A viable team, literally, is one which is "likely to live." Viable teams are healthy, able to endure hardship and remain effective. I describe some 40 team-building exercises that most teams can use, and then discuss several guidelines for team development. The article closes with a case study highlighting common issues faced by church planting and other teams.

## Team Dimensions and Viability

Teams share three basic characteristics: they have members who must relate together (interpersonal dimension), they have specified purposes (task dimension), and they have a preferred way of doing things (ethos dimension). These dimensions are inseparable and constantly interact.

Team viability requires the careful development of the interpersonal, task, and ethos dimensions. The team ethos is especially key, as it influences how team members relate to each other (interpersonal dimension) and how they go about working on their goals (task dimension). The ethos also functions to integrate the interpersonal and task dimensions. This is an ongoing, precarious, sometimes frustrating process. For instance, at times the focus may need to be more on the development of members, as in pre-field preparation or dealing with a crisis situation on the field. Other times the focus shifts to the task; for example, when there is a project deadline to meet. Viable teams must be flexible, able to place their emphasis on any of the three team dimensions according to situational demands.

Viability also requires commitment, cohesion, and resiliency. These characteristics do not always come easily. For many teams it takes lots of hard work—harmonizing different goals, clarifying unspoken expectations, and dealing with relationship conflicts—to reach a point of viability. Teams become viable by going through the various ups and downs of team life and ministry. By God's grace they learn dependence on Him and on each other, and become more effective in carrying out their tasks. Viable teams are made, or better grown, step by step.

## Tools to Help Build and Develop Teams

There are many creative ways to strengthen missionary teams. The various tools that I describe in this article can be used by consultants, team leaders, and team members. Most of these tools involve team-building or team development exercises, the former which attempt to correct deficits in team function while the latter are less remedial in nature and provide opportunities for ongoing team growth (Kinlaw, 1991). The exercises call for group activity, self-disclosure, personal reflection, problem-solving, and mutual feedback.

Some of these tools I have developed myself, others I have borrowed from colleagues, still others I have picked up from some book or article and adapted it for use among missionaries. Feel free to modify them in order to fit the needs of your team.

These tools are not cure-alls. They are catalysts to encourage change and growth. While most are engaging and even fun, some can entail a lot of challenging work and a sense of personal risk. It thus behooves the person using these tools to be sensitive to the feelings of team members, to have a good sense as to which dimension of team life to focus on (interpersonal, task, ethos), and to have a clear understanding of the process of team building and development.

## Tools Primarily Focusing on Team Relationships

### *Introductions*

Getting to know each other is an important first step in blending together as a team. There are many effective approaches for doing this apart from the usual format of asking questions about where someone is from, how people met, and so on.

*Autobiography.* Have people write up a table of contents as if they were authoring their life story. What would the titles be for the sections and chapters? Include chapters for any future dreams and aspirations. Each team member can then use this table of contents as a springboard to briefly share significant aspects of his/her life history with others.

*Wallets.* Split up into pairs and look through each other's wallets. Ask questions about what you find and what you expected to find but did not, such as pictures, credit cards, and business cards. The goal here is not to learn everything about the other person, but to enjoy the process of getting to know one another. Switch partners a few times and repeat the above.

*Personal Descriptions.* This exercise helps people examine how they present themselves to others. Write down 10 things you typically say about yourself when you meet someone new. Next, change your self-descriptions to represent something that really does not fit you. For example, replace the usual "I am an engineer, grandparent, bilingual, and sports fan" with something like "I am a plumber, single, English is my third language, and I prefer opera and museums over sports." After this, have group members introduce themselves to each other using their new descriptions. Discuss this exercise as a group, focusing on what the members have learned about themselves and others.

*The Seven C's for the Seven Seas.* This exercise explores seven important factors (selection criteria) needed to become part of the mission and team. Each criterion begins with the letter C, hence the name of this exercise. I primarily use it for newly formed teams as a point of departure to discuss who they are, their backgrounds, and their motivations and expectations for the team. It can also be useful for teams going through a major transition period, such as a change in ministry focus or the addition of several new staff.

Directions: Team members describe themselves to each other in terms of one or more of the selection criteria listed below. Questions for clarification are encouraged. An alternate version is to have members write out their responses beforehand, keeping them anonymous, and then circulate them during a team meeting. Members then try to figure out who wrote each set of responses. A discussion can follow.

1. Calling—by God, to work area, people group, and the mission.
2. Character—personality, temperament, strengths, weaknesses.
3. Competence—gifts and skills; preparation, training.
4. Commitment—to calling, team, the mission agency, missions.

5. Christian experience—relationship with God, past ministry.
6. Compatibility—doctrine, organization, culture, goals.
7. Confirmation—from family, church, the mission, and friends.

## Drawing Tools to Build Relationships

Drawing tasks are primarily non-verbal experiences to encourage people to express themselves in new ways. As such they are often a welcome addition to the more cognitive team-building approaches that rely on a discussion format. Here are some samples that are easy to do and can help team members better understand one another.

*Family Trees*—Participants create a picture of their family of origin by drawing and positioning their parents and siblings in some type of tree. They are asked to be as creative and as spontaneous as possible. The activities of family members, their relative position to each other, and the type of tree that is drawn all yield important information about one's family experience and background. After all have finished, participants describe their trees to each other.

*Current Family Trees*—This can either be a family or a team exercise. Family members, including children, do the same exercise as above, but the subject to be drawn is the current family. Trees are then compared and discussed.

*Team Trees*—This can be a bit more challenging, as it requires team members to disclose some of their feelings about the group. Have staff draw trees and place the members in them. Share the drawings with each other, noting the distinguishing and interesting features of each drawing. Sometimes the drawings can be hung up to be viewed and reflected upon for a few days.

*Reconstructing Your Family House*—This is a fascinating non-verbal approach for team members to re-experience and share selected childhood experiences. Have each person draw the main house they lived in before age 12. Include as much detail as possible: rooms, furniture, colors, yard, and so on. Jot down what the rooms were used for and any significant memories or feelings associated with a room. Note the areas that cannot be drawn or else are not complete. After people finish their drawings, allow them to share what this drawing experience was like, and then let members talk about their drawings.

*This Is My Life/Team*—Participants draw a picture of their current life or of their team. It can be abstract, impressionistic, realistic, metaphorical. Give it a title. Discuss these and hang them up.

## Cross-Cultural Orientation

This group activity is particularly useful for exploring cultural differences on multinational teams. Each person takes a brief inventory developed by Lingenfelter and Mayers (1986) to assess his/her position on six important value dimensions: time and event orientation, task and person orientation, dichotomistic and holistic thinking, status and achievement focus, crisis and noncrisis orientation, and willingness to expose vulnerability. The goal of this exercise is to help team members recognize and appreciate each other's differences and in so doing to work together more effectively. Additional exercises for understanding culture and cross-cultural differences can be found in Pierre Casse's (1981) excellent book entitled *Training for the Cross-Cultural Mind* and in *A Manual of Structured Experiences for Cross-Cultural Learning*, edited by Weeks, Pedersen, and Brislin.

## Supportive Group Experiences

Team members, including children, can occasionally or regularly break up into smaller groups according to their different needs and areas of interest. Here are some examples.

*Study Groups*—These are occasional or regular gatherings of team members interested in studying certain topics. Articles can be chosen to be read beforehand and then discussed. Teaching tapes can also be used. Some examples of topics would be the education of missionary children, world events, contextualizing the gospel, and the care of staff. Consider using some of the articles in this book as a point of departure. Keep these times informal and responsive to the concerns of team members.

*Devotions*—Take turns overseeing group devotions. Different people can rotate giving short Bible studies and leading group prayer and worship. Let people minister to one another through prayer and encouragement.

*Prayer Partnerships*—Prayer partnerships involve committed relationships between two or three members of the same sex for the purpose of encouraging each other's relationship with God. They usually occur anywhere from a few times each week to once a month.

*Fun Times*—These involve leisure activities to help team members relax and unwind. Some ideas: exercising together, playing team sports, having meals together, doing crafts and board games, attending cultural events and athletic activities, making home improvements, and traveling together. Don't forget to throw a party. Celebrate something good that happened.

## Past Relationships

Team life, at both the conscious and unconscious levels, stirs up many associations with one's family of origin. This is a normal experience. For instance, leaders, in some ways, can be related to as if they were one's parents. Other team members can be viewed as if they were siblings. Teams thus serve as forums for "recreating" one's original family, stirring up past feelings and providing opportunities to work through unresolved family areas. It is helpful to discuss these factors as a team and to try to be aware of how one's family may in fact be influencing the current group context.

Doing family and team trees (previously described) can be effective ways to get at this process. It is also helpful to discuss some of the previous team experiences and personal relationships that members have had. Here are two exercises to try.

*Previous Teams*—Team members describe their experiences on three different teams. What did they like and dislike? How cohesive, resilient, and effective were these teams? What have you learned about teamwork and yourself as a result of your team experiences?

*Previous Roommates*—List a few roommates that you have had. How did you get along? How did you manage household tasks? How did you deal with differences? What did you learn about yourself and the way you relate to people?

## Conflict Resolution

Interpersonal difficulties are inevitable and a normal part of the team experience. Team life, like family life, involves ongoing adjustments, compromises, and joint efforts to remain strong. Here are some exercises for helping teams deal with conflicts in a healthy way.

*Affirmation*—Most of us appreciate all the encouragement we can get. During times of conflict, the tendency is to confront and highlight the negative. This exercise has the participants starting out the session by listing five positive things about the other parties involved. The purpose is not to minimize differences, but rather to create a more congenial atmosphere by affirming the good and contributions of others.

*Critical Incidents*—Form small groups and identify a significant past episode of conflict or difficulty on the team. Explore this incident in some detail. How was it handled? You could even try to role play the situation if it is not too threatening. Include this exercise as part of an annual review process for the team.

*Proverbs for Reflection*—I like to use the book of Proverbs to stimulate discussion about team life, especially in the areas of conflict and stress management. The use of Proverbs can get at concerns that have not yet been expressed.

I have found it helpful to start off with a discussion of Proverbs 24:3,4, "By wisdom a house is built, and by understanding it is established; and by knowledge the rooms are filled with all precious and pleasant riches" (NASB). The house here can be used as a metaphor for the team. We then go over a few previously selected verses from Proverbs, based on my assessment of the team's felt needs. Participants frequently share related verses. Here are some starters that are relevant to most teams: Proverbs 15:2, 16:2, 16:32, 18:13, 19:20, 19:22, and 20:25.

*Principles*—Have team members come up with a list of conflict resolution principles that work for them. Another approach is to go over the list below as a team and add to it. Periodically review the list and give each other feedback and constructive suggestions.

a. Differences are opportunities for growth.
b. Never assume you fully understand someone; vice versa.
c. Most people have good reasons for what they do.
d. You can seldom change anyone.
e. Emphasize understanding and areas of similarity.
f. Criticism must include constructive suggestions.
g. Be aware of how you use the words *always* and *never*.
h. Agree to disagree in an agreeable fashion.
i. Keep short accounts with others.
j. Uniformity is not necessary for unity.

## Tools Primarily Focusing on Team Ethos

### Team Culture

Team culture, also referred to as *team ethos*, refers to the assumptions, values, and patterns of behavior that characterize a group. It is both visible and invisible, and significantly impacts the ministry, lifestyle, and levels of satisfaction of team members. One of the most important ways to prevent the development of problems on a team is by assessing how one's background culture (social, ethnic, family, occupational, denominational) fits into the overall ethos of the team. Here are some of the main components of team ethos, along with some exercises to help explore them.

*Expectations.* List some of the spoken and unspoken, written and unwritten rules of the group. Explore things like the type of group people really want, the level of intimacy desired between team members, or preferences for leadership style. Many expectations shift with time, and need to be periodically clarified.

*Values.* How does the team spend most of its time? To what extent do stated values reflect team behavior? For example, if a team values language learning and social contact with a targeted people group, how much time do they actually set aside for these activities?

*Communication.* Identify the ways in which information is usually shared (memos, phone calls, verbally). Who serves as the main source of information? What types of self-disclosure are seen as appropriate? Discuss one important time in the last few months when communication broke down.

*Participation and Commitment.* To what extent are members engaged in and devoted to their work? Do they really like what they are doing? Some possible indicators include punctuality at work and meetings, rate of staff turnover, and involvement with each other outside of work. Any implications?

*Boundaries.* This refers to the different invisible parameters that influence the level of contact that team members make with themselves and with others. What types of people are allowed to be part of this team? Who has access to leadership? How much privacy do individuals and families on the team have? How much time do members spend with other groups within the mission and the local community?

*Accountability.* To whom do people formally or informally report? Have team members list the people on the team or outside the team to whom they report, with whom they can communicate at a deep level, and to whom they would talk to in time of need.

*Feedback.* How is staff performance and well-being monitored and evaluated? Is this system effective? Do members feel the freedom to give each other suggestions? One way to explore this is to let members briefly describe the last time they received some significant input from another team member. Can any team patterns be recognized?

*Development.* What types of opportunities are available for staff care and growth? In what ways are the mission and the team committed to the development of the skills, character, and spiritual life of its staff? As an exercise members can identify the helpful services they have utilized and list any additional ones that they believe would be helpful.

### Process Observation

It is important to look at both the content and the process of communication on a team. The content deals with what is said, while the process deals with how the content is expressed. Process also involves the invisible interactions which go on in a group setting, and sheds light on the team ethos.

Directions: This technique looks at 15 process areas that influence a group or team experience. One member of the group is selected to act as a "fly on the wall" during a team meeting. This person remains silent, observes the group, and listens carefully to how things are said and what is not said. He or she takes notes, and then reports back to the group at the end. This can be done every few meetings, using a new observer each time. Here is a list of some of the main areas to observe and a few examples.

1. Physical set up—temperature, noises, seating arrangement.
2. Type of communication—languages used, questions, clarity.
3. Frequency of communication—those who speak much or little.
4. Transitions—changing topics, opening and closing process.
5. Decision-making—by consensus/leader, influential members.
6. Alliances—sub-groupings, coalitions, mediators.
7. Roles—those who confront, harmonize, question, distract.
8. Tension points—differences and how they were handled.

9. Emotions expressed—laughter, frustration, body language.
10. What did not get expressed—anger, preferences, opinions.
11. Values reflected in the experience—loyalty, openness.
12. Team dimensions—focus on relationships, task, and/or ethos.
13. Unresolved areas—concerns that were avoided or not resolved.
14. Themes—the topics, their order, and any patterns.
15. Additional observations—any other areas that seem important.

## Tools that Address Team Relationships, Tasks, and Ethos

### Sentence Completion

This exercise can be used at almost any point in the team's life cycle. It is especially helpful when a team is stuck in an area and when a moderator or consultant is available to help.

Directions: Team members are to complete the following sentences by writing down some of their spontaneous thoughts and feelings. Responses are confidential although members are encouraged to share some of them with the group. After everyone has written down their answers, volunteers share their responses to the first item, discuss it, and then do the same with the remaining items.

1. Life for me right now
2. Our team is good at
3. It is hard to
4. I am most fulfilled when
5. Our team needs
6. My best coping strategy
7. Our biggest team problem right now
8. I am anxious about
9. Three years from now
10. Team communication
11. If only they knew
12. If I were in charge

### Consolidation

This tool is used to periodically review a team's group experience and ministry. It gets at the essence of who the team is, why it exists, and how members want to work with each other. I start off the exercise with a discussion of Ephesians 2:10: "For we are His workmanship, created in Christ Jesus for good works, which God prepared beforehand, that we should walk in them" (NASB). I then draw the diagram below, and as a group we relate this verse to three areas central to team life: identity, goals, and strategy. Identity relates to the interpersonal dimension, goals to the task dimension, and strategy to the ethos dimension.

INTERPERSONAL————————ETHOS——————————TASK

| Who are we? | How will we work? | What will we do? |
| (identity) | (strategies) | (purpose, goals) |

*Identity.* We are God's workmanship. What type of team are we? How has He fashioned us as a team? What skills and personality characteristics do we have as individuals and as a group? List these. What have we gone through together as a team? Draw a time line and plot the key events in the history of the team.

*Goals.* We have been created in Christ Jesus for good works. What is it specifically that we are to do? Have each member develop a two or three sentence purpose statement for the team. Compare these. What has been accomplished in the last six to twelve months? Discuss the ways in which members think they are on course or off course with the team's objectives.

*Strategy.* We are to walk in the works that God has prepared beforehand for us. How are we to do these works? Do a "SWOT" matrix. That is, as a group identify your strengths, weaknesses, opportunities for, and threats to accomplishing your goals. Also look at the procedures, policies, and work-styles that you have adopted to facilitate your task. Divide up into pairs and write down the roles of your partner as you see them, discuss these roles, then change partners until each member has interacted with everyone else.

### Group Enactments

Enactments involve novel activities that can add zest to what would otherwise be a routine team meeting. They shed light on important aspects of team relationships and build understanding between team members.

*Sculpting*—This exercise comes from the family therapy field. It can be used with teams to look at different members' perceptions of the team. One person is chosen to be the sculptor. He or she then places every person in the group in a certain stationary position as if they were doing something, and in relationship to each other. There is no talking until each person has been "sculpted." Participants then discuss their feelings and reactions. When the discussion is finished, another person can volunteer to be the sculptor. This exercise works best with an outside consultant directing it.

*Role Playing*—Team members take on a variety of roles and act them out. They can become each other, neighbors, leaders, other mission workers, or almost any person. The purpose is to try to experience what life for another person is like, and to give each other feedback by the way the roles are acted out. Typically two or more people act out the roles in front of the other team members. Each role playing session usually lasts from five to 10 minutes. A director can also be used to oversee or intensify the drama.

*Trust Walk*—Members pair off. One person is completely blindfolded. The partner that can still see leads the other on a five to ten minute walk, holding his/her arm or hand. Partners then change roles and repeat the exercise. For a variation, blindfold most of the team, have them join hands, and then have one or two people lead the team on a walk. Still another variation is to do the trust walk with no verbal communication. Debrief at the end.

*Group Stories*—Gather an assortment of about fifty large pictures from magazines and place them face down in the middle of the group. The facilitator starts off by saying the first three lines of a story. Members then take turns adding to the story by picking up the top picture and spontaneously coming up with two or three sentences based on the picture. Hold off making comments until the end of the story. Story lines can be chosen according to the needs of the group or just for the fun of it. For example, the team could pretend that they were delegates at an important council of the early church, Franciscan monks in Europe during the Black Plague, exiles at a refugee camp in Africa, or a group traveling together on a caravan. They could also try to envision what the team will be like five years from now, or chose a story with an issue similar to one they are trying to resolve on their team.

*Panels*—Have a few people volunteer to serve on a panel at the next team meeting. This is a chance for people to express their ideas and share their wisdom with the team using a different format. A topic and a moderator is chosen in advance. The moderator asks the panel members several questions related to the topic. Comments are permitted from those listening to the panel, and interaction is encouraged. Here are some possible topics: stress management, time management, maintaining a successful devotional life, friendships, raising children, conflict resolution, understanding the host culture, performance appraisals, building strong teams, and spiritual warfare.

## Team Stages

Most teams go through fairly predictable stages during their life cycle. Some teams cycle through these stages several times during their life span. This is especially true for long-term teams or teams that experience several major transitions. Other teams never make it through the full cycle, as in the case of the team which gets stuck at stage two (adjustment) and disbands before it works through member differences. Note that working through stage two is essential before a team can really function together effectively.

1. Beginning
   a. forming—setting up the team, admittance, initial norms

b. warming—developing relationships and a sense of team
2. Adjustment
    a. differing—experiencing and struggling with differentness
    b. harmonizing—working through basic areas of difference
3. Viability
    a. working—doing the team task and relating together well
    b. developing—maturing as a team and becoming effective
4. Ending
    a. debriefing—reviewing the team experience and phasing out
    b. moving on—leaving the team or disbanding all together

I like to have teams assess which stage they are at, discuss what past stages have been like, and anticipate future stages. What will the team look like one year or five years from now? It is also interesting to have members modify these stages if they feel they can come up with a set that more accurately represents their experience.

## Testing Tools

There are a wide variety of tests available to assess interpersonal characteristics, personality, workstyle, and group dynamics. Most of these tests need to be administered by a mental health professional, and are normed for only a certain population group, such as North Americans. Here is a description of six tests that can be particularly helpful for the members of missionary teams to understand themselves and each other. They are most useful when done as a group and the results are shared and compared.

*Fundamental Interpersonal Relations Orientation (FIRO-B)*—This test assesses three basic characteristics of interpersonal relationships: inclusion, control, and affection. It also measures how comfortable one is with expressing these characteristics and how comfortable one is when others express them.

*Myers-Briggs Type Indicator (MBTI)*—This test explores the way individuals take in information and make decisions, how they focus their attention, and how they orient themselves to the external world. The test results yield one of sixteen possible profiles, referred to as *types*.

*Personal Profile System*—This tool examines work styles and the type of work environment that is needed for maximum productivity. It is especially useful for understanding the different motivational environments required by those with different work styles.

*Personal Style Indicator and Job Style Indicator (PSI and JSI)*—These are informal, self-report questionnaires to help match people with jobs. The *PSI* produces a self-appraisal of one's preferred modes of responding to people and the environment in most situations. The *JSI* explores the work style requirements of a particular job, as well as the strengths and difficulties that one experiences in a particular work role. Both tests require computer scoring and interpretation.

*Work Environment Scale and Group Environment Scale*—These scales look at the "personality" of a particular work setting, and how the social climate (ethos) affects people's behavior, feelings, and morale. They are objective means to get at how team members perceive their work situation.

## Stress Management

Dealing with stress is a major concern of most missionaries and teams. There are various tools that can be used to help teams manage stress more effectively. Here are four that I regularly use.

*CHOPPSS*—This exercise identifies the major sources of stress for missionaries, and requires them to think of strategies to deal with stress. CHOPPSS is an acronym for seven common stressors: cultural, human, organizational, psychological, physical, support, and spiritual. A fuller description of this tool is found in chapter eight of this volume.

*The Lord's Strategies*—How did the Lord deal with stress? There are at least 25 practical ways in which He balanced the demands of His life and ministry. See how many the team can identify. How do these strategies relate to your life and team?

*Burnout Scale*—Burnout refers to the state of physical and emotional exhaustion resulting from chronic exposure to stressful experiences. One way to assess how close one is to burnout is to use the inventory found in Myron Rush's (1987) book *Burnout: Practical Help for Lives Out of Balance*. It consists of 20 items and can be completed in about five minutes. Take this inventory about once each year and compare your scores.

*Family Inventory of Life Events (FILE)*—This tool assesses the impact of changes on a family's coping resources. It is basically a type of checklist which each parent fills out on the family experiences during the last 12 months. Responses are compared and any differences in perceptions of family strains can be discussed. It is available in McCubbin and Thompson's (1987) edited work entitled *Family Assessment Inventories for Research and Practice*.

# Guidelines for Working With Teams

How do teams go about using these and other tools effectively? Here are some perspectives and suggestions that can help.

To begin, team development is something to regularly plan into your schedules. It is an ongoing process, involving much more than the initial orientation period or annual performance appraisals. A team development event every one to three months should be standard for most teams.

Team development helps prevent major problems erupting within the team by dealing with issues that may otherwise not be discussed. They are a necessary complement to regular times of prayer together, fellowship, annual retreats, and conferences. Some teams benefit from special team sessions that are extended over two to three days, even when there is not some kind of crisis.

Team exercises work best when the team ethos encourages openness and speaking into each other's lives. Team members, especially leaders, must be willing to take some risks with each other and be willing to show weaknesses.

Choose one or more "growth facilitators" on the team who can coordinate team exercises. These should be individuals who are sensitive to the needs of others and to group process. Facilitators usually serve as moderators for these times, drawing people out and keeping things on track. They need not be the team leader nor a pastoral counselor to be effective.

Be aware of the team's *current focal point*—that is, the area which is the immediate concern of the group at any given time. This is the point of interest that a team would usually move towards if there were minimal resistance or reluctance to do so. It also represents the next step towards growth as a team seeks to become more viable. Sometimes the real focal point only becomes apparent during the middle of a team session or series of sessions.

The focus of the sessions will change as the needs of the team change. Make sure that you are really dealing with felt needs of the team members, not just someone's good ideas. Frequently an issue or particular theme needs to be addressed over a period of time.

One important goal in almost any session is to help people speak and listen to one another in new ways. Another goal is to encourage people to make contact with each other at fairly deep levels. People usually want to put aside their work roles and be themselves. Effective team exercises allow the real person to emerge from the role.

Keep team development and team building times as practical and enjoyable as possible. Experiential approaches can produce more insights and change than simply sitting around and talking about "things." Use some novelty to keep people motivated and engaged. Make sure everyone on the team is included and contributes without feeling forced.

Find ways to elicit group competencies and call on the collective wisdom of the team. No one should dominate. Important resources lie within the group, not just in some outside specialist.

Encourage people to try new behaviors. Respect any hesitations to do an exercise. Sometimes people may need to be gently challenged; other times it is better to modify or change the exercise.

Children are members of teams too. Do not overlook their need for growth and involvement in team exercises. They can also contribute a lot to the overall group.

When giving feedback, be an encourager. People need to know their contribution. Avoid using generalities, so be specific and direct. Avoid making statements about intentions. Try using statements prefaced by "I think" or "I feel" rather than "You are."

Always debrief at the end of the session. Discuss what it was like, what was helpful, not helpful. Let people express their thoughts and feelings and put closure on any unfinished matters.

Consider using a coach or consultant from time to time, preferably someone with an ongoing relationship to the team. This person helps to clarify issues, gives permission to look at hard questions, mediates, brings in fresh perspectives, encourages, and equips.

# Case Study

This fictitious case highlights several aspects of the interpersonal, task, and ethos dimensions of team life. Many of the issues affecting the church planting team discussed in this case are also relevant for other types of teams.

The case study can be used as a team exercise. Read through the case and discuss it together as a team. Refer to the questions at the end. Another approach would be to do a role-play. For example, your team members can become any of the eight team members described in the case, and interact with each other in these new roles. A third idea is to discuss this case or do a role play from the perspectives of a home office administrator, personnel director, team leader, or visiting pastoral counselor.

## Team North Africa

For the last two years a five person missionary team has been working as tentmakers in the capital city of a North African nation. The purpose of this team is to plant a house church for Muslims which could then plant other churches around the country. The original goal was to plant a church within three years, which has subsequently been extended to five years due to minimal response to the gospel.

The team members belong to the same mission agency and include:

**Tom and Mary,** the leaders, both aged 35, Americans, spent 10 years working with Muslims in Manila. They run a travel agency and have three daughters, ages six, three, and one.

**Robin**, aged 42, Australian, is an engineer by profession, was divorced four years ago, and has a burden for students in the university where he teaches.

**Laura**, aged 28, is single, has a call to work with Roman Catholics as well as Muslims, and has previously participated in several short-term outreaches to a tribal group in South America. She is from Chile, and is trying to find a new job before her current visa expires.

**Joan**, aged 22, is an American who recently joined the team after having finished her bachelor's degree in international studies. Joan works with Tom and Mary in their travel agency.

Before departing for the field, each team member went through a three week program in language and culture learning principles in the United States. They also met regularly for six months to strategize and pray about their upcoming work. Besides English, the languages spoken by the team before their arrival were Spanish (by Laura) and some Tagalog by Tom and Mary. Their initial goal as a team was to immerse themselves in the culture and learn as much French and Arabic as possible.

The first two years have proved to be tough ones. Progress in Arabic has been slow although everyone is at least conversant in French. Team members live on their own with the exception of Laura and Joan who live with local families. They all live within a 20 minute walking distance from each other.

The team has met once a week for prayer, worship, and discussion of their work. The basic church planting strategy has three parts: to make friends with Muslim families who are respected in the city; to participate in "salat, zakat, and sawm" (prayer, almsgiving, and fasting); and to eventually hold a weekly Bible study. Tom and Robin have tried to pray in the mosques but each time have been asked to leave since they were not Muslims. The team also has agreed to abstain from pork, alcohol, and to dress like the nationals. Laura and Joan attend a weekly Bible study for expatriates held at the Catholic church.

There have been several "converts" from among the more marginalized of the city—i.e. the very poor and homeless. Three others have professed faith in Christ but are fearful of being rejected by family members if they openly share their faith.

Team relationships are generally good, although sometimes marked with tension. One of the basic problems seems to be that Robin and Tom have different views on the direction for the ministry. Some team members also feel that Tom and Mary are too involved with their kids, that Robin is too task oriented, and that Laura is distant from the others. Tom and Mary are considering going on a three month furlough, which has also stirred up some concern among the team.

There are a few other issues of concern to the team. These involve how to make decisions with less friction, whether to have a team of university students from the USA work with them for one month next summer, whether to become more involved with the local Catholic church, whether to try to live together in community as a way to make their finances go farther, and how to improve their Arabic and spend more time with their contacts.

In spite of some of their struggles and challenges, each team member is committed to the team and the church planting goals. Robin, however, is the only one who says he is really satisfied with the work he is doing. The others feel satisfied occasionally but usually need to really work at persevering on the field.

### Questions for Discussion

1. What are some of the issues for this team?
2. What are some of the sources of stress?
3. Which team tools would be useful?
4. What recommendations would you make?
5. How does this case relate to your current team situation?

## Suggested Readings

Adler, N. (1991). *International dimensions of organizational behavior (2nd ed.).* Boston: PWS-Kent.

Casse, P. (1981). *Training for the cross-cultural mind (2nd ed.).* Washington, DC: The Society for International Training, Education, and Research.

Dyer, K. (1985). Crucial factors in building good teams. *Evangelical Missions Quarterly, 21,* 254-258.

Foyle, M. (1985). Missionary relationships: Powderkeg or powerhouse? *Evangelical Missions Quarterly, 21,* 342-351.

Hofstede, G. (1980). Motivation, leadership, and organization: Do American theories apply abroad? *Organizational Dynamics,* Summer, 42-63.

Kinlaw, D. (1991). *Developing superior work teams.* San Diego: University Associates.

Lingenfelter, S. & Mayers, K. (1986). *Ministering cross-culturally: An incarnational model for personal relationships.* Grand Rapids: Baker.

McCubbin, H. & Thompson, A. (Eds.). *Family assessment inventories for research and practice.* Madison, WI: University of Wisconsin-Madison.

Reapsome, J. (1988). Choosing a mission board. *Evangelical Missions Quarterly, 24,* 6-13.

Rice, W., Rydberg, D., & Yaconelli, M. (1977). *Fun n games: A sourcebook of games for the whole family*. Grand Rapids, MI: Zondervan.

Rush, M. (1987). *Burnout: Practical help for lives out of balance*. Wheaton, IL: Victor.

Sundstrom, E. (1990). Work teams: Applications and effectiveness. *American Psychologist, 45*, 120-133.

Weeks, W., Pedersen, P., & Brislin, R. (Eds.). *A manual of structured experiences for cross-cultural learning*. Yarmouth, Maine: Intercultural Press.

# 15

*Frances J. White*

# Guidelines for Short-Term Field Consultants

Every November since 1980 a group of member care workers in missions assembles to discuss ways in which they can contribute to the overall emotional functioning of missionaries. The setting is the informal Mental Health and Missions Conference, held near Angola, Indiana.

Many of the participants work part-time in various ways with mission groups. Some are active on the home front doing the psychological screening of candidates, counseling prospective missionaries, debriefing and helping those on home assignment, conducting sessions during candidate orientation or reentry institutes, organizing MK conferences, and carrying on consultations with mission leaders. Others have responded to field needs and have spent periods of time on the field assisting missionaries through team development, family counseling, and crisis intervention services.

What has promoted this relatively new openness in missions to professional member care services—especially those of a psychological nature—that a short time ago were considered superfluous and even suspect? The answer to the question lies in the very reasons why there is a growing interest in and even cry for counseling in North America. The growing number of changes taking place in the social and moral structures of our society are creating an emotional upheaval that is resulting in an increasingly wounded populace. We see the causes and effects of the emotional wounds manifested in the many dysfunctional families that expose their children to situations as impactful as physical violence, depression and suicide, sexual abuse, substance misuse, and broken relationships.

Some of these children, now adults, have become Christians and have experienced the healing grace of our Lord. Yet they have gradually realized that our grasp of sanctification is an ongoing process throughout our lives. This is especially evident where the effects of generations of sin inflicted deep wounds very early in the developmental cycle. In spite of treatment they tend to re-erupt, particularly under stress, continuing to cause emotional distress in such forms as depression, a sense of emptiness, inordinate anger, deep humiliation, feelings of inadequacy, crippling anxiety, or a multitude of other possible effects. Painful feelings such as these generate behaviors that hurt the individuals involved, their families, associates, or those to whom they might minister.

Member care specialists who work with mission agencies recognize that any subgroup (in this case missionaries) reflects the characteristics of the society of which it is a part. Therefore it is no surprise that missionaries, whether candidates or on the field, are not exempt from the ill effects of an increasingly post-Christian value system with its subsequent lifestyle that tends to result in emotional wounds.

When struggles from emotional hurts occur in North America, people can go to a mental health professional or possibly a minister to get further help for a problem with which they may have been dealing. However, when the scar starts to fester again where help is not available—such as on the field—they are caught in a difficult situation.

## Member Care Services

With the growing number of hurting people, including missionaries, one can understand why mission agencies are increasing their requests for help from those trained in emotional healing. The more careful screening of candidates, for example, has aided mission leaders to better ascertain who probably will not survive emotionally intact under the stresses of cross-cultural living especially in the absence of skilled help. This process spares both the candidate and the mission much trauma and undue expense. In other cases mission leaders have directed candidates into counseling before they leave for the field. This has enabled them to overcome their struggles or develop constructive ways to cope with the occasional eruptions of old wounds.

Deep hurts are not limited to candidates however. A growing number of missionaries are experiencing the need for emotional relief. Our Lord understands the cumulative effects of generations of sin with the problems they produce for all of us. Yet, this is the generation through whom He must build His church. He knows that missionaries more often than not work in areas where personnel who could carry them through a difficult period do not exist. Is this part of the reason why a growing number of Christians are sensing God's direction to the mental health field? Although very much in its initial stages, an increasing number of mental health professionals and other member care specialists seem to be responding to the need to serve on a full-time basis in selected geographic areas.

Member care specialists have been instrumental in giving the kind of help that has enabled many missionaries to complete their term of service rather than experiencing the trauma of aborting their commitment. In addition they have been able to conduct on-field seminars in response to the felt needs of missionaries, teams, and mission communities. Since Christian member care workers are not abundant enough to meet all of the home or field needs, the potential for serious problems including staff burnout is very real.

One way to meet this need is to utilize part-time member care specialists who can contribute their skills in a focused, well-planned, time-limited manner. These consultants recognize their calling to work in their profession within their own country but sense God's calling to serve in an adjunctive, supportive role among missionaries. Hesselgrave (1987) points out that, historically, the mission enterprise has been facilitated by those well trained in a field offering their services to missions as consultants when a need for their expertise arises. This is becoming increasingly true of member care specialists. They can assist and supplement the work of those serving full-time on the field or even serve in areas where no other help is available.

Field consultation, by adjunct workers on a short-term basis, demands the close cooperation of mission leaders who are well aware of the uniqueness of their situation and the consultant who has the specialized skill. In my own experience of working with several mission groups I have found that there are particular guidelines that make a time-limited contribution a profitable experience for all parties, both the mental health consultant and mission personnel. I will elaborate on these guidelines in the remainder of this chapter, in response to two questions I frequently hear: How can mission personnel and teams best utilize the services of member care consultants? What must member care consultants know and do to work effectively on the field?

## Guidelines for Short-term Service

*1. Adjunct mission service is done most effectively when the invitation comes from the on-field group with whom the consultant will work.*

Many examples exist in which consultants have enthusiastically gone to an area only to meet resistance by being ignored, by receiving cynical comments or jokes, or by sensing a lack of commitment to the activities. Generally, this results when the invitation comes from the home office, from the field leaders only, or from no one in particular. However when the visit is in response to a felt need on the participants' part, at least a core group is receptive and often serves as the energizing force for the others. Even when the initial contact is from another source, such as a home director, a field leader, or a board member, the missionaries at large need to be in agreement with the request for help to alleviate a recognized need. This assures far more motivated participants.

Occasionally consultants will arrive without a clear invitation perhaps because a missionary friend expressed a desire for what they have to offer, or they themselves would like to add a ministerial component to their holiday travels, or perhaps they received a vague sort of invitation. In such cases they must be prepared to go as learners, listening and observing, letting any ministry on their part grow naturally out of the circumstances. Missionary schedules are full and unexpected visitors and events can put additional, unwelcomed pressure on their time and energy. Also, a group can experience a normal resistance and suspicion of motives toward those who want to minister to them but are not missionaries per se.

## 2. All matters pertaining to finances need to be clarified in advance.

Financial arrangements can be awkward and an emotionally disruptive area if not clearly agreed upon beforehand. Who is going to pay what expenses? In some cases a budget exists to cover consultation expenses. In other situations the missionaries themselves must contribute to defray costs. Often times consultants pay their own transportation viewing the time and expenses as part of their tithe while the field takes care of living expenses.

Honorariums may or may not be part of the expectations. The essential factor is for both sides to clearly communicate expectations and arrive at a satisfactory agreement for all in the very initial stages of planning.

A very interesting and effective arrangement followed by four teams of physicians known by the author is the practice of sending one or two team members to an agreed upon mission site for a determined time where their skills are needed. The group practice covers expenses and in some cases at least a portion of what the lost salary would be. An added bonus for those who go or give support lies in the excitement of being able to share experiences together and learn from each other. As Christian group practices of mental health workers continue to form, could not the same pattern work? Certainly it would give more continuity to such a ministry since one team member would almost always be there.

## 3. Working with a partner rather than alone has definite advantages in cross-cultural situations.

How true the Chinese proverb is that sharing a difficulty cuts its seriousness in half; sharing a joy doubles its pleasure. The potential number of joys and distresses for the novice in cross-cultural settings is vast. Tension is greatly reduced when someone is there to see humor in the unpredictable whether it's a flight cancellation with no hope given for a booking in the near future, a closed border due to a political crisis with no phone service to inform waiting parties, or cockroaches and bedbugs as your evening companions.

I recall one field consultation in which I had to sleep on a narrow couch, and tumbled to the floor each time I moved in my sleep. Fortunately the colleague with whom I was traveling laughingly reminded me that our hosts had given us the best beds they had in a very deprived region! Her comments humored me and helped me not get too frustrated.

In addition, time for relaxation to break the tensions of a situation is more apt to be taken when someone is there to point out the interesting things that could be missed in the midst of so many new stimuli. Finding ways to relax is more easily done when someone is not alone. My delightful memories of swimming along the rocky coast in a Mediterranean area probably would not exist were it not for a colleague who not only insisted on a break but loved adventure! Furthermore the strain of a people-helping ministry is greatly reduced when the requests for counseling can be distributed. It is also helpful to be able to keep each other on track by mutually checking out perceptions and sharing repertoires of possible interventions.

### 4. Member care consultants need cooperation from the home front and from the field to learn as much as possible about the mission picture before they arrive.

The more accurate a picture consultants form of their prospective place of service, the better they can plan. The field and home office should make the participants aware of the political situation, the financial condition, recent traumas (e.g. earthquakes, droughts, floods, famines, hostage situation, religious persecutions), church problems, laws and regulations, or any other tension-producing event.

Understanding the background of a mission and how it operates is extremely helpful to give an overall picture of the field. For example, information could be obtained from home office leaders on how they process candidates, debrief and care for those on home assignment, meet MK needs, assign missionaries to a field, allocate support, pay benefits, plus a host of other factors that would enable the visitors to have a better grasp of problems.

Other valuable information about the field situation would include the length of a term, the furlough policy, field government, MK education, field expenses and money exchange. Also important to know are what contingency plans exist in the event of an emergency and what the policy is on language acquisition.

Obtaining the mission's magazine and reading publications like the *Evangelical Missions Quarterly* can be very helpful in enabling the consultant to be attuned to possible sources of tension. The more consultants are aware of the realities of the mission setting, the more pertinent their choice of topics, illustrations, responses, and understandings can be. Mission personnel could be very helpful to consultants by alerting them to any negative emotional reactions that certain topics may generate.

### 5. The more cross-cultural awareness that mental health professionals acquire the more effective their ministry will be.

Our ethnocentrism is not obvious to us until we try to function as more than a tourist in another culture. What is more distressing for a member care worker is that one cannot assess healthy functioning without taking into account the total environment in which a person functions. This can be a real challenge, especially as a behavior that might seem dysfunctional in one culture may be a healthy adaptation in another geographic area.

Here is an example from one of my field experiences. An American administrator of an African church school was meeting with the regional council that was to decide if, when, and how a new school would be constructed. Although ostensibly the administrator was the leader, he said very little, outside of presenting the need for the building, for the first half of the long meeting. In fact, after his presentation silence reigned for at least twenty minutes. Finally the head pastor, also the chief village elder, spoke. More silence! Then someone a bit younger but also an elder made what might seem to an American to be a flowery speech. Eventually everyone present had spoken. The administrator filled in some requested information but gave no opinion. After five hours the meeting ended with no definite action as yet taken.

Later the school administrator expressed his frustration to me, stating with a resigned air that he wished he could make things move faster. At this point I could have mistakenly concluded that the administrator needed some assertiveness training in order to be comfortably active and less passive. However, having previously worked in this area myself, I was aware of the social rules and meeting protocol.

There was a definite hierarchical etiquette concerning the accepted order of expression. Opinions were not in order at a fact finding meeting. Had the administrator not respected the rules he could have sabotaged the possibility of building a new school. Nonetheless he still needed to express and process his frustration and look at ways to minimize it even though he too understood that in this case he must act in a way appropriate for the culture. Expressing his reactions and feeling understood by someone who was familiar with both the local and American cultures had a tension reducing effect.

Member care consultants offering services in another country could benefit greatly from some understanding of the culture in which the missionaries function. Augsburger (1986) in his excellent volume, *Pastoral Counseling Across Cultures*, points out, "The culturally encapsulated counselor has disregarded cultural variations among clients. A counseling focus on the individual, a preference for examining internal dynamics, and the dismissal of social, environmental, and situational forces as equally significant all contribute to seeing persons as having little significant variations" (p.22). Augsburger's comments are particularly relevant for consultants ministering in multinational missionary settings.

Greater awareness of a particular culture could be acquired in several ways. Reading books on cross-cultural issues is helpful, such as those by Augsburger (1986), Hiebert (1985), Kohl (1979), Dodd (1987), and Brislin (1981). I find many of the articles in the *International Journal of Intercultural Relations* to offer much insight. Magazines put out by different mission organizations are also useful. There are relevant cross-cultural courses at universities and colleges, perhaps offered by a missions, sociology, or anthropology department. Developing a relationship and/or dialoguing with missionaries on home assignment is valuable. In general, a combination of reading and dialogue with those who have cross-cultural experience is the most beneficial.

However, no amount of discussion or reading can replace the actual experience of having been a missionary. Those who hope to do consultant work would gain invaluable understandings as well as immeasurable credibility by programming some missionary experience into their career plans. In fact, some mission groups would see this as part of the required training to do consultation in member care.

**6. An educative approach in the form of seminars, particularly in the initial stages of ministry at a particular setting, has definite advantages over an immediate plunge into personal counseling.**

Holding seminars during the beginning part of a ministry fosters mutual understanding and trust, thereby paving the way for a more positive response to any personal help. There are several reasons for this.

One reason is that the message is clearly given that the consultant is interested in everyone and has not come because a few individuals have problems. Secondly, seminars give the opportunity to present universal principles related to healthy functioning. Some of the participants' struggles are thereby normalized enabling them to be willing to talk more freely about issues rather than fearing that problems will be seen as deviancy.

One example is the normal anxiety that missionaries experience during periods of change and transition. Explaining and discussing the typical reactions to change, in a seminar format, can free individuals to talk more openly about its effects without wondering if they are being viewed

as unstable or unspiritual. The consultant and missionaries can then identify ways to cope with the various anxieties inherent in change. At the same
time it signals to the group that anger, anxiety, sadness or even depression
are okay to talk about.

Thirdly, seminars permit all parties, consultants with missionaries
and missionaries with missionaries, to become acquainted in a non-threat-
ening way. Non-intimidating group activities are needed (e.g., questionnaires, discussions, role plays, games). An *esprit de corps* can be developed
that may continue to expand.

For example, I once conducted a field seminar on "Handling Strong
Feelings," which helped one team with many conflicts begin to grasp the
reasons behind the reactions of its members. Realizing how helpful this was,
they met regularly during that year, following a step by step guide that I had
presented in the seminar. One year later I received a letter from the team
leader who reported the continued improvements in their team relationships.

This leads to a fourth advantage. While helping individuals to better
know themselves and others, the seminars also enable the consultant to
assess the underlying dynamics of the participants, identify strengths and
struggles, disarm sources of stress, and better understand the context in
which the group functions. In short, the seminar is as educative for the
leaders as it is for the missionaries.

I have found that a seminar experience stirs up many issues and
generates requests for private sessions. Providing time slots in which
individuals, couples, or families can sign up for a personal time is a vital
component of a short term visit. Care must be taken though, to insure that
those counseled are not overwhelmed, and that their coping strategies are
adequate to help them remain intact once the consultant has left.

*7. Specific preparatory steps need to be followed in which field
leaders and consultants clearly communicate together in order to
assure a smoother functioning of the consultation process.*

Preparing the field for a consultant is two-fold in scope. First, the
logistical needs must be clearly communicated. Secondly, bridge-building
with the participants must be adequately done.

In the logistical vein, it is important that the consultants clearly
communicate their needs and make advance arrangements. What equipment do they desire? Is it available? What kind of space might be desired?
Does the particular location have electricity? Will missionaries be able to
take the time to attend any seminars? Will everyone live and eat at the same
place? What about baby-sitting arrangements? Contingency plans are wise,
especially as not everything works out as planned.

Having handouts available saves the participants a lot of note taking
while providing them with a clear outline of the material and copies of any
activities that they could later adapt to their work situation. Consultants

will find it helpful to send any handouts ahead of time to be photocopied if possible on the field. Having the field do the copies saves extra luggage weight and can free up extra space to bring other materials and resources.

Missionaries gain more from a seminar or workshop to which they can devote fairly undivided attention for that period of time. This allows them time together to process what has been covered. It provides more opportunity to ask questions or to talk personally with the visiting leader. Participants often have a topic with which they want particular help and can request an extra session. Even the rest and recreation times help them assimilate the material and put things in perspective.

The second vital area that needs clear communication in advance is that of preparing the participants. Mission personnel must communicate clearly what the field wants; consultants must communicate clearly what they intend to give.

A helpful procedure is for the consultants to write a general letter to the group introducing themselves. They could include a short questionnaire to assess needs and preferences for topics. This letter could be followed up with a more specific one that suggests and includes some reading to be done beforehand. Missionaries are busy people often with little time for extra reading. Therefore shorter books and concise materials that effectively translate technical concepts into simple terms are more apt to be read. This is especially true for missionaries where English is not their first language.

### 8. A collegial egalitarian approach rather than an erudite professional tone creates a more receptive atmosphere.

This guideline takes some doing to put into practice, as consultants are not always aware of how they are coming across. There is no room for any tone superiority in the consultant, not even if it is unintentional. Consultants need feedback. Further, mutual feedback is also important, and can lead to more relaxed communication and therefore a greater responsiveness.

One team of consultants, for example, started with an exercise that reviewed several general stressors for missionaries. Noting a sense of frustration among the participants, the consultants asked for feedback and learned that in that culture many of the stressors listed were not applicable. This led to an in-depth discussion about stress-inducing situations for these missionaries, as well as the formulation of some realistic strategies for stress reduction. Humility and feedback won the day!

### 9. The consultant needs to remain flexible, prepared to change the agenda regardless of prearranged plans.

Even a brief overview of world events reveals the unpredictability of life anywhere on earth. What seemed to be the greatest felt need during preparation time may change drastically before the consultant's arrival. I have experienced at least three cases of this.

The first was when an especially sensitive problem surfaced that emotionally affected many families attending the seminar I was conducting. Dealing with this previously concealed situation was essential although it changed the content and tenor of the sessions.

A second radical change in plans occurred when the currency of the country in which I was consulting was suddenly declared void. Many were suddenly bereft of any financial reserve they had been saving for their work. Not only the missionaries but the entire national population experienced turmoil. My seminar content and methods again had to be readjusted to meet the needs emanating from this very current situation.

A third unexpected change occurred when the borders closed in the country where our team was to consult. We had arrived at the airport of a contingent country with plans to take a small plane to our intended destination. No hope was given that the border would reopen before our team's departure date to return to the United States. Rather than lose out on the time and expenses involved, we arranged to minister at a large central area in the country where we presently were. Although this change tended to necessitate a more tentative "stop, observe, listen" approach, it proved to be a profitable time and a response to a problem that had just arisen in the particular place. As it turned out, we were able to enter the intended neighboring country for the last week of our allotted time. This called for further flexibility since we had to shorten and adjust the seminar we had planned.

When I do a consultation, I always bring a large notebook with me, filled with outlines on various topics and activities in order to be prepared for special requests or unexpected needs. This increases my options and helps me be more flexible.

### 10. The member care consultant and field personnel need to clarify the way follow-up will take place after the consultant has left.

A consultation is never finished until the agreed-upon follow-up has transpired. Consultants are often faced with a myriad of follow-up tasks which are hard to get to due to the heavy schedules that usually await consultants when they return home. Keeping a clear description of any requests for books, tapes, articles, or addresses, can make this whole process go more easily, especially if a secretary or friend can help out.

Follow-up is essential when a complex problem becomes apparent that will require additional attention. Member care consultants must be prepared to make an extra effort in proportion to the seriousness and ethical implications of a problem. In one situation several MKs had been traumatized when monsoons swept away six national playmates. The consultant sent several practical materials (books and workbooks) to guide parents as they helped their children work through pain, a sense of loss, and anxiety.

A vital element in follow-up procedure is a letter written by the consultants to all the participants. Graciously thank them for your time together. Remind the group of their plans for follow-up—such as their meeting together in a small group, ordering and circulating specific books, meditating on suggested Scripture passages. Update them on the status of any materials you have promised to send them. Summarize any suggestions or feedback they have given you, especially if you included a time for brief written evaluation at the end of your stay with them.

Another area of follow-up includes a letter of evaluation to the leaders. Care must be taken not to betray confidences. However, general comments giving your impressions of the situation, what was accomplished, on-going needs, and practical suggestions could be very beneficial.

A final factor to consider in follow-up is the possibility of the consultant returning for another period of time. Once a consultant gains the confidence of the missionaries and better understands the setting, a lot of time and energy can be saved on a follow-up visit. This, of course, calls for collaboration on everyone's part.

**11. Missionaries, teams, and mission communities continue to gain from member care consultants' efforts when "growth facilitators" are designated and trained to oversee ongoing mutual care.**

Although consultants can offer several helpful experiences through their skills, the missionaries themselves are primarily responsible to maintain a nurturing ambience and provide supportive care to each other. Certain missionaries can be appointed to serve as part-time "growth facilitators" either alone or in teams, in order to stimulate member care on the field. These individuals have good interpersonal skills and can encourage others to develop their strengths, give support in times of crisis, conduct team development sessions, help others manage stress, and provide some accountability. Consultants may find it profitable to work more intensely with these facilitators who could then impart their learning to others.

## Conclusion

Short-term consultations require careful planning, considerable time, and lots of hard work. A one week consultation trip, for example, can easily involve an entire week of preparation beforehand, and an entire week to do follow-up and get reorganized after the trip. Do not underestimate the energy and emotional costs that go into making a field consultation successful.

All the effort is not without its benefits. One experiences a broader, richer perspective on the world. Cultural differences are appreciated more.

Friendships can develop. There is usually a keener awareness of world news and their impact. Greater empathy for the struggles of missionaries and the people they are serving is experienced.

Not least of the gains is the satisfaction of playing a part in helping missionaries to resolve some of their stresses, to learn new ways to cope in the midst of pressures, to understand themselves and others better, and to be freer persons to give to those to whom they minister. Consultants also realize afresh how God's sovereignty works through an individual's humanness at the point of growth where he or she is, in accomplishing His purpose worldwide. Consultation can indeed be an enriching experience to all those involved!

### Questions for Discussion

1. As a prospective member care consultant how could you acquire cross-cultural experience while living in your present geographical location?

2. What are three problem areas in your mission setting that you think could be helped by a member care consultant? What type of consultant would be necessary?

3. What are some of the advantages and disadvantages of using short-term field consultants for team development? Outside consultants versus in-house consultants?

4. How can children be included in and benefit from times of field consultation?

5. What are some of the special concerns when conducting field consultations for a multinational missionary audience?

## References

Augsburger, D. (1986). *Pastoral counseling across cultures.* Philadelphia: Westminster Press.

Brislin, R. (1981). *Cross-cultural encounters: Face to face interaction.* New York: Pergamon Press.

Dodd, C. (1987). *Dynamics of intercultural communication.* Dubuque, IA: W.C. Brown.

Hesselgrave, D. (1987). Can psychology aid us in the fulfillment of the Great Commission? *Journal of Psychology and Theology, 15,* 274-280.

Hiebert, P. (1985). *Anthropological insights for missionaries.* Grand Rapids, MI: Baker.

Kohls, R. (1979). *Survival kit for overseas living.* Chicago: Intercultural Network/SYSTRAN Publications.

# PART FOUR
## MISSION AGENCIES AND MEMBER CARE

# Part Four
# Mission Agencies and
# Member Care

*Richard Gardner and Laura Mae Gardner*

Consulting Editors

What can mission agencies do to support and further develop their people? How do organizational structures, policies, and ethos affect the quality of life and member care practices within a mission agency? Part Four addresses these two crucial questions from the vantage point of both mission administrators and member care professionals.

The first article, by Dr. Hans Finzel, discusses nine organizational essentials to help mission leaders steer their agencies in a healthy and effective direction. Writing from the perspective of one who has been both a missionary and a mission executive, Hans orients his comments to fellow mission leaders, gently challenging them to consider their leadership practices in light of staff needs. He emphasizes the importance of leaders facilitating the care and ministry of staff, maintaining a clear vision and consistent though flexible policies, communicating regularly with staff, stewarding finances carefully, pursuing excellence in their agencies, and above all staying close to Christ.

Dr. Frances White's chapter on "The Dynamics of Healthy Missions" is a diagnostic tool to explore how mission agencies function. As a psychologist who regularly consults in Africa and Europe, Fran calls upon her many experiences to discuss five central patterns, or dynamics, that influence the overall health of an agency: cohesion, boundaries, adaptability, regulation, and communication. A system's perspective is used in which organizational problems are understood in the context of the overall agency rather than as originating within a single department or individual.

The next article outlines the various components needed to set up or improve a career development program. The author, Peter Shedlosky, sees career development as part of the organization's responsibility to "disciple" its members. Pete's background in human resource development provides him with a wealth of insights on how to help people make an important contribution to their mission agency while also feeling professionally fulfilled and growing as a person.

Drs. Kelly and Michele O'Donnell discuss five basic and sometimes tricky ethical principles which must be considered when providing member care services. Their chapter is a practical application of an earlier article written by Kelly (published in *Helping Missionaries Grow: Readings in Mental Health and Missions*) in which he proposed several ethical guidelines for mental health professionals working in missions. Kelly and Michele use a hypothetical but true-to-life case study to approach the ethical parameters of organizational responsibility, confidentiality, counselor/consultant competence, use of testing, and personal values and legal standards. The final chapter identifies specific ways that member care workers, especially counselors, can support mission leaders—why different leaders need support and the type of support they need. Richard and Laura Mae Gardner, in their roles as both member care providers and administrators, offer several suggestions for interfacing leaders with care-givers. They also include three illustrative situations highlighting (a) the struggles faced by a newly appointed leader and his wife; (b) the challenges of being "parents" at a children's home for missionary kids; and (c) the issues encountered by leadership when intervening in an isolated, dysfunctional family.

Each of the five articles in Part Four focuses on a different aspect of the member care picture. Leaders and staff are challenged to pursue healthy agency practices, understand the dynamics of their agency, participate in a career development program, anticipate some of the ethical issues involved in member care, and make use of supportive resources. Perhaps the underlying theme connecting these articles is the emphasis on the responsibility of the organization to support and nurture its people. The more proactive we are in developing our people, the more effective and God-honoring we will be in the task of world evangelism.

# 16

*Hans Finzel*

# Nine Essentials for Organizational Development

During my ten years of experience in missions in Eastern Europe I have rubbed shoulders with missionaries from many different agencies. I have seen some wild tales of mission mismanagement that would amaze you! My goal here is not to point fingers or criticize any one agency, but to prod all of us who help lead the mission enterprise. We the mission leaders have a sacred trust in the lives of the missionaries God gives us to shepherd. And which one of us cannot improve our performance in providing the best leadership possible?

I have been observing mission agency leadership with intense interest throughout most of the past two decades. I began as an outsider, then a missionary myself, and now I find myself in mission agency leadership. My bent is looking at how mission leaders lead and what sort of organizations they build. Consider this chapter an aid in recognizing what elements make an agency of excellence—an organizational report card for mission agencies, so to speak. My objective is to also advocate for some self-administered member care for those of us in leadership positions.

## Missionaries Slipping Through Member Care Cracks

I recall a bright, enthusiastic young couple I met in Vienna who had been rigorously recruited by one of those fiery-eyed campus mission recruiters that we all like to put on the road. They came to the mission field like most young recruits, with stars in their eyes and a passionate dream of what strategic things God was going to do through them. This couple landed in Europe only to find that the receiving missionaries had no job for them. In fact the mission team was not even aware that this couple was coming to their field. It seems that there was a "mix-up" about which field was to receive them. The home office scrambled. Faxes flew. They were sent from their original destination to the Vienna branch of the mission. Could the missionaries maybe figure out a job for this couple in Austria? When the answer was, "Not really," they came to our mission group and asked if we could use them on loan. We agreed and gave them a couple of years of meaningful service before they left the field—discouraged, disappointed, and disillusioned with the whole mission enterprise.

Who is to blame here? The recruiter? Not really. He did his job faithfully. But recruiters should make an effort to see where their fresh faces end up and how they pan out over the long run. What good is it if our back door is busier than our front? If we lose more long-term workers than we recruit, we have a big problem. Even if the flow is balanced both ways, it is not good. We should heed the messages that are sent out by those who leave our missions. Do we listen to those who resign? Are they debriefed? Our own mission tries to perform exit interviews on all those who resign and retire. It can be very enlightening if we have the courage to ask the right questions and listen. They may tell us a great deal they never dared to whisper to us when they were "under" our authority.

Are the mission leaders the guilty ones in the scenario I described? In general yes, for they did not care for the basic infrastructure and organizational systems that insure that people are properly placed and cared for once they get into the "system." This couple literally fell through a big organizational crack in the mission agency. We in mission leadership have not only to build roads to overseas service assignments, but carry a bucket of cement to fill in the dangerous member care cracks along the way. This couple should never have boarded that initial flight for Europe.

## Is it Enjoyable to Work in Your Mission?

In the late 1970's I cut my ministry teeth in my first assignment out of seminary in a local church in California. While I was the senior pastor of this flock of 700 believers, my wife Donna was working for an oil company in Long Beach. This may sound simplistic and unspiritual, but she had more fun and better friends at her work than I had at mine.

Twelve years later it is not at all strange for me to see that for many Christians it is more fulfilling and enjoyable to work in well-run secular organizations than in the poorly organized, stressful environments of many Christian organizations. It is time that more attention was given to the details of shaping the organizations God has appointed us to lead, so that the people whom he calls to work within them will indeed find long-term productivity and fruitfulness in a fulfilling environment.

I know, some of us will immediately argue that the point of mission work is not *enjoyment*, *fulfillment* or *fun*, but servanthood for Jesus sake. My perspective, though, is that it is not an either/or proposition, but a call for both. On the missionary's side, there should be a willingness to sacrifice and serve even in situations of great hardship. But on the mission agency side there should be effective organizational leadership that provides as fulfilling and meaningful service as possible.

Our Lord Jesus told a parable that points to this issue. He claimed that the world is often better at its respective tasks than the Christian community is at doing what God has called the Church to do well. In the parable of the shrewd manager, Jesus discerned that the world's sons often make wiser leaders than the sons of the kingdom:

> *The master commended the dishonest manager because he had acted shrewdly. For the people of this world are more shrewd in dealing with their own kind than are the people of light (Luke 16:8 NIV).*

It was the steward's *astuteness* and not his morality which was commended. One commentator rewrites the passage like this: "The children of this world look further ahead, in dealing with their own generation, than the children of light" (Morris, 1974, p. 248). It was the wisdom, not the corporate ethics, that was commended here, and that is the point to bring home to Christian leaders.

Christian organizations are distinct from secular ones in that they are a community of God's people doing God's work in the power of God the Holy Spirit. Yet Christian organizations—including mission agencies—are also human institutions that have much to learn about how humans work together. It is my conviction that there are many principles of knowledge and truth in God's universe under the heading of "general revelation" that are available to all mankind. Organizational dynamics, leadership skills, and management training all fall under that heading.

Christian organizations have a spiritual dimension as well as a human side of their enterprise. Mission agencies should be distinct in their values and beliefs from their secular counterparts, but they could stand to learn a few lessons from their shrewd worldly neighbors about running the business.

## Organism or Organization?

Is a mission agency an organism or an organization? One of my missionary colleagues and I had an ongoing debate over this issue for many months. He questioned the validity of management principles used in Christian work. "Organism is what is key, not organization," he argued. This dear friend and brother in Christ really believes that organizational theory applied to the body of Christ is wrong: it takes the life out of the movement. We are the body of Christ, he holds, an organism that is governed only by spiritual relationships and biblical guidance.

The problem is, my friend is half-right. If we add management and take away the dynamic of the Spirit's influence we are in big trouble. The best mix is a leadership team made up of godly praying men and women who have good managers and leaders in their midst. We need a blend of visionary and administrative talent at the top. Too much of one without the other is deadly.

Unfortunately my friend's mission went too far in their evolution from organism to organization, and practically turned the mission over to a group of young Harvard MBA's armed with their calculators and computers. In his opinion that move took the heart and soul out of his mission—quenching the ability of the Spirit to empower and lead. And it turned off my friend from considering sound organizational leadership practices.

When it comes to understanding what is actually going on in our mission agencies *organizationally*, Christians are at times guilty of putting their collective head in the sand. I have heard people rationalize that the spiritual dynamic will most certainly care for such details as how our organization is structured and managed. In the real world in which we must operate, this simply is not true. We must strike a strategic balance in giving ourselves to the Spirit's work and attending to the practical human dimension of organizational life. We are both organism (part of the body of Christ) and organization (a human enterprise), and must work within the realities of both dimensions.

## Nine Organizational Essentials

It is this issue of the organizational needs of mission agencies that we want to look at now. Just what does a mission agency need to be and do in order to fulfill its responsibility to its members? What are the key provisions that the leaders must make to insure a healthy and happy organizational life? One interesting way to phrase the question is from the point of view of the missionary: "What do I have the right to expect from my mission agency?" And from the point of view of the leader, you might ask, "What areas need to be considered if I want to improve my organization?"

Here is my list of nine organizational essentials to be seriously considered by the leadership of today's mission agencies, all beginning with the letter "C."

### 1. Connection to Christ the Head

If my board of directors asked me to make a short list of my essential activities week in and week out, I would put cultivation of my spiritual life at the top. Without that foundational activity covered, the mission and I are in big danger of going adrift. The first and foremost responsibility of mission leaders is to maintain a close personal relationship to Christ.

The trouble is, when missionaries get thrust into agency leadership things can get very crazy. Gone is the relatively quiet life out on the mission field. In my own case I was immediately thrown into a torrent of activities, including reading, writing, speaking, phoning, traveling, and meetings, meetings, and yes, more meetings. Add to that my demands as husband and father of four and there is just too much to do and not enough time to do it.

During a recent conversation one of my mentors warned me of the danger of neglect in the spiritual realm. His observation was that every young emerging mission leader he knew—and he is connected to many—experienced this problem of the squeezing out of the former personal habits of Bible study and prayer. That which is more essential than ever is the first to go in the hectic pace of mission leadership business.

Rule number one of mission leadership: stay connected to the Head of the Church, Jesus Christ, who is our commander in chief of the mission enterprise. Before all else we are to be examples to our flocks (Phil. 3:17; I Cor. 11:1; I Tim. 4:12). Without a vital spiritual life, the work becomes routine, the spiritual edge is gone, and the dangers of carnality lurk around every corner. We have to be careful not to neglect the gift of God that is within us (I Tim. 4:14); quite the opposite, the responsibility to fan it becomes greater the higher one goes in spiritual leadership (II Tim. 1:6).

## 2. Commitment to Members

How does a mission agency view its missionaries? Do they exist to help the mission fulfill its objectives, or is it the other way around? My conviction is that the mission agency is a vehicle that God has raised up to *facilitate* the ministry to which God has called the missionaries. The agency exists to help the missionaries, not visa versa.

I have a lot of trouble with the attitude that praise and recognition is not really necessary in working with missionaries. We should celebrate the performance of our missionaries as they serve in faithfulness and excellence. Affirmation can only help the mission enterprise, as each player is encouraged for his or her value. We need to bury the notion that Christ's reward is the only motivation our missionaries need.

The mission I help lead is not perfect, but one thing we do believe is that our missionaries are our most precious resource. Just as airlines give a great deal of attention to their aircraft we try to be as committed as possible to the missionaries who serve under our banner.

Several years ago we adopted a set of core values for our mission. Two of them express our commitment to our members, out of which has grown our Missionary Development Department, an entire division devoted to the care and growth of our missionary personnel (CBFMS, 1989):

*Individual Dignity: We diligently maintain and promote the dignity and worth of each individual within CBFMS ministries world-wide. People with a proper sense of spiritual and emotional well-being are freed for productive ministry that is committed to goal oriented planning and team accountability.*

*Personal Development: We are committed at all levels of leadership to create an organizational climate conducive to continuing personal growth and development in missionary service.*

Mission agencies should have comprehensive mission-wide goals and plans. And yes, the missionaries are asked to make them happen. But the missionaries should be a vital part in making those plans, and the agency must realize that without the missionaries the plans will never work.

As a leader I do not like to admit this, but which of the following two scenarios would be worse? Option one: something happens to the home office and it is wiped out. No more home office. Option two: something happens to all the missionaries. No more missionaries. Under which option would mission work continue and under which one would it come to a screeching halt? If the home office were wiped out the missionaries would appoint new leaders and continue their ministries in the far-flung corners of the earth!

I am thrilled at the development of the relatively new field of missionary member care. The subject of this entire book, member care, is something to which the leadership of every agency should be committed. The field includes a commitment to such areas as training, personal development, lifelong learning, counseling, career guidance, continuing education, and missionary children's care.

Commitment to the members of the mission is an issue of attitude. We in leadership have to keep our servant role in perspective: we exist to serve them in facilitative leadership.

## 3. Clear Vision, Goals, and Strategies

We have to be careful that our mission agencies avoid the experience of Christopher Columbus. When he started off, he did not know where he was going; when he got there he did not know where he was; when he got home, he did not know where he had been. That may be fine for explorers, but it is complete irresponsibility in the cause of world missions.

Leadership must be always devoting itself to the issues of goals and strategies: where are we going next and why are we going there? "We are more in need of a vision or destination and a compass (a set of principles or directions) and less in need of a road map," says Stephen Covey in *The Seven Habits of Highly Effective People.* Covey clarifies the difference in management and leadership when he says, "management is efficiency in climbing the ladder of success; leadership determines whether the ladder is leaning against the right wall" (Covey, 1991, p. 101). We need both in missions today: a balanced dose of good visionary leadership and an effective management team.

Developing vision and direction is one of the primary tasks of leadership. A mission agency is responsible to take the lead in planning for the future. It must develop organizational goals, plans, and strategies that flow out of its purpose statement. And as I noted in point number two above, the mission personnel should be an integral part in shaping that vision and making those plans. When the missionaries have a stake in goal formulation on their fields then they have a vested interest in goal ownership and seeing the dreams fulfilled. One of the very best books I have found on leadership and vision is *Leaders*, by Warren Bennis and Burt Nanus (1985).

How clear are the goals of your mission in the minds of your missionaries? I recall a management consultant that spent several days with a mission leadership team of which I was a part. We were a group of about 12 leaders who represented the various divisions of our mission enterprise in Eastern Europe. The consultant went around the conference table and asked each one of us to articulate the purpose and core goals of our mission. To our surprise and frustration, no two of us had the same purpose statement or set of goals. As a result, we were not "singing out of the same hymnbook" and it was causing frustration that made itself felt all the way down the ranks. Conflicting agendas within a leadership team reap havoc throughout an organization.

Leadership must give itself to articulating a clear purpose statement and set of corporate goals that the top leadership can embrace. Then the organization can focus and concentrate its resources on doing specifically what God raised it up to do, instead of dissipating its energies by dabbling in a little bit of everything.

Not a week goes by that I am not confronted with another great opportunity that our mission could pursue. After my initial excitement—I tend to get excited when I first hear of these great schemes—I sit back and ask myself this question: "How does this square with what God has called us to do in the world?" If it is not going to lead to the fulfillment of our basic goals, we should not get involved. "Concentration is the key to economic results," says Peter Drucker, "...no other principle of effectiveness is violated as constantly today as the basic principle of concentration....Our motto seems to be: 'Let's do a little bit of everything'" (Drucker, 1967, pp. 110-112). I have seen the same hold true in missions.

One final piece of advice on goal setting. When you put together a set of goals for your mission, they should be SMART goals:

S—specific
M—measurable
A—attainable
R—relevant
T—trackable.

## 4. Consistency with Policies and Procedures

Policies and procedures are one of those areas I call good news, bad news. The good news is that they are essential for a large group of people to work effectively together within one organization over a long period of time. The bad news is that they tend to stifle creativity and innovation which is so desperately needed in missions today.

What is the purpose of having a policy manual for a mission agency? Why must there be standard policies? Simply put, *policies and procedures are formed to solve recurring problems consistently.* Instead of reinventing the wheel every time the same issue comes up, a guideline is written to handle this situation if it comes up again. That guideline becomes a policy.

Policies and procedures also serve to assure fairness among the members of the group. For example, one missionary family wants to spend half their time on the field and the other half at home. This translates to quite a bit of international flying and short stints with the nationals. The other family senses that this is a bad stewardship of the donor's money, and that a missionary belongs on the mission field. Solution? A furlough policy developed by the agency to bring consistency, fairness, and the right values into the disagreement. Our agency uses the 80/20 policy, meaning that for every 80% of you time overseas you earn 20% in your home country for furlough (which we call home assignment).

*Consistency.* Mission agencies owe it to the missionaries to have policies and procedures in writing. The cultivation and management of that set of guidelines is hard and tedious work, but is a must to assure that members are treated fairly.

Policies also help assure that everyone embodies the corporate values of the mission, and that no one goes too far out on a limb into an area or practice that would embarrass or damage the mission as a whole. Having said that, I caution my fellow keepers of the policy manuals not to use them as police clubs to come down harshly on missionaries. Negative motivation via police tactics never works. If there is a problem missionary, he/she needs positive personal attention, not chapter and verse from the policy manual.

*Flexibility.* Let me end this section with a plea for *flexible response* amid policies and procedures. We must avoid the danger of trying to make everyone "equal" with no chance for true personal initiative. Do not allow your policies and procedures to stifle your brightest stars. Be flexible. Bend the rules if you believe that someone needs more space.

Never be in bondage to your policy manual. Do not allow it to become the issue that drives away the most promising young candidates and missionaries. Take risks and let people soar. Take this advice seriously: goals should never rise out of corporate policy, company tradition, or religious heritage. Goals should always transcend these.

Organizations go through many stages in their life cycles. Most move from inspiration to institution, from an apostolic vision to mechanistic bureaucracy. Unless we're careful, we'll follow these four stages in the devolution of a fresh movement of God: (a) Men, (b) Movement, (c) Machines, (d) Monuments. The key to arresting or reversing this trend is to keep it a Holy Spirit led and inspired movement. How is that done? By allowing room for flexibility—give God room to breathe amid your policy and procedure manuals.

## 5. Chain of Command

If your missionaries have a question or problem, do they know who to approach in your mission? If they have a serious complaint, is there a clear path for their issues to rise up to the top? When you have a project to assign within the agency, do you know who's job it should be? If there is a major problem, do you know who is in charge of that area? These are all issues of chain of command. *Chain of command clarifies the questions of who reports to whom, who supervises whom, and who is in charge of what.*

*Organizational Charts.* The idea of an organizational chart is not really new. Moses has a very detailed one for how to organize the Hebrew nation. Does your agency have an organizational chart? The organizational chart is a *people map* that shows relationships within the organization. *Basically the purpose of an organizational chart is to show the lines of authority and responsibility in an organization.*

Organizational charts help leadership see the way that the ministry is organized in a quick visual overview. The charts also help the members of the organization know where they fit and where to go "up" the organization for help, resources, permissions, clearances, complaints, and grievances. And they are very helpful in explaining the corporate culture to the new members of your mission.

Organizational charts show relationships in organizational life. Since those relationships change often, the charts should change as necessary. They should be simple and they should be flexible, but most of all they should *be.*

*Job Descriptions.* Does your agency have job descriptions? There are a thousand ways to write them, with some quite complex and others very simple. I like job descriptions that lean toward simplicity. They need to be flexible and should outline three basic ingredients of any job: (a) What are your primary responsibilities in the organization? (b) What key activities and tasks are you asked to do to fulfill those responsibilities? (c) To whom do you report? With a clear job description, there can be no confusion about expectations between the missionary and the agency over what that person is supposed to be doing. It also becomes a good tool for evaluating effectiveness.

*Delegation of Authority and Responsibility.* No single issue creates more frustration in management than fuzziness in the issue of delegation. I have seen many of my fellow missionaries frustrated to the hilt over this issue. Let me paint a typical scenario.

Jack is asked to work up a plan to reach a new area of his city with evangelistic Bible studies. His team leader Bill (official mission supervisor) has asked him to work on this project. Jack gets very excited and pours weeks of effort into research, thinking, praying, and planning. He has even taken the time to write up a serious proposal for the team to consider. Because he and Bill live in different towns, they do not always communicate in a typical week or even month. One day Jack opens the mail to find a copy of Bill's most recent newsletter home and is shocked at the contents. In this letter Bill shares a detailed plan for doing the job that Bill had actually commissioned Jack to plan. Jack has actually found out by accident that the rug was pulled out from under his pet project. How does Jack feel? Angry, frustrated and ready to quit.

Another variation of this theme includes reversals of decisions that undermine prolonged efforts to put programs and strategies in place. My rule of thumb is this: *the one who is asked to do the job plans how it will be done.* We can check their progress but should not (a) constantly look over their shoulders, (b) tell them how to do their work, (c) reject their work in favor of our "expert" approach, nor (d) reverse strategy decisions that our workers have come to believe in simply for a different preference that we might favor as leaders.

This issue of delegation is an issue of respect. With responsibility must come the authority to do a job. I believe in the 80/20 rule of success: 80% of the time I'll make the right decision, and 20% of the time I will make mistakes or not do it as well as it could have been done. I allow my subordinates the freedom of the 80/20 rule as well, and give them the grace to fail.

One of the best books I have come across on the fine art of how to delegate and supervise effectively is Hersey and Blanchard's *Management of Organizational Behavior* (1982). These authors show that there are four ways of delegation and keeping up with those to whom work has been assigned, based on the workers' own maturity and motivation: *delegating, participating, selling,* and *telling.* The greatest mistake we can make in the arena of supervising our subordinates is to treat them all the same.

## 6. Communication with Staff

Some years ago Francis Schaeffer wrote a significant book entitled *No Little People.* In that book he argued that in God's kingdom there are no little people and no little places. I think the same principle should be practiced by mission agencies in their attitudes about the far-flung corners of their mission enterprises. Everyone is important. Everyone has a right and a need to know what is going on in the organization—the big news and the little details. The more people are informed the more they feel a part of the whole organization and the less chance for misunderstanding.

How do you feel if others know something that you do not know? Have you ever learned significant news about your own organization from an outsider? How does it make you feel? Try words like little, insignificant, hurt, forgotten, and unimportant, to name a few. Keep your people informed. Have a passion to communicate, communicate, communicate. One really cannot overcommunicate. Listen to the advice of Max DePree (1989), from *Leadership Is An Art*:

> *The right to know is basic. Moreover, it is better to err on the side of sharing too much information than risk leaving someone in the dark. Information is power, but it is pointless power if hoarded. Power must be shared for an organization or a relationship to work. (pp. 104, 105)*

At the root of many conflicts is a disagreement about expectations. The members have a right to know what is expected of them, and if and when they are not fulfilling their expectations. Realistic and appropriate expectations should be established between the home office and all fields and missionaries. And this should be a two-way street. If the missionaries have a major problem with the agency, they should not let resentment or bitterness simmer. Speak up and speak out in respect for those whom God has placed in authority over you (I Thes. 5:12,13).

One mission that has put a good deal of energy into communication with its members is Fullerton, California based Church Resource Ministries. They have developed a statement called, "The Expectations and Privileges of CRM Staff," which includes the following points (CRM, 1991):

> *As a staff person with CRM, it is fair for me to expect the following from those whom I follow throughout the organization. I can expect:*
>
> *To know those who lead me and what they believe*
> *To have leaders who will explain to me their vision*
> *To never be left in isolation*
> *To be heard*
> *To be trusted*
> *To be provided a context for growth*
> *To be held accountable*
> *To be the object of grace.*

## 7. Credibility in Financial Stewardship

Money makes missions happen. Without adequate finances there will be no continuation of the fulfillment of our zealous mission goals looking toward the 21st Century. How we handle the funds that God provides our missions is of utmost importance.

In thinking about how we can be good stewards of the money that our donors send our way, three important areas must be addressed: adequate provision for missionaries, honesty with donor gifts, and integrity in public relations.

*Adequate Provision for Missionaries.* There is a great deal of talk going on in mission circles about the high cost of sending North Americans overseas in the 1990's. The purpose here is not to enter that debate but to argue for caring for those we do send.

Young recruits that come to our agencies have to put a great deal of faith in us, that we know what we are doing and that we will not send them overseas to perish. Developing a comprehensive financial package is our responsibility before God.

I have known missionaries that struggled greatly with lack of adequate finances because their pre-field planning was not given enough consideration by their sending agency. One family in our group had to repeatedly come to the other missionaries with outstretched hand as we took collections to pay for their rent and utilities at various times. It was not a case of undersupport, it was a case of being sent overseas with an inadequate financial package to care for all that was needed for effective ministry in our context.

It is my conviction that the financial package of a career missionary should include adequate provisions for salary, housing, work and equipment funds, children's education, travel to and from the field, health and life insurance, and retirement provisions. Without the resources to do ministry and to care for the family, the mission is asking for a short-lived career from the units they send overseas.

*Honesty with Donor Gifts.* An issue that made big headlines in the 1980's is the issue of financial integrity among Christian organizations. Because missions send most of their money overseas, they are less likely to be scrutinized and "caught" using finances in a way that is not quite legitimate.

Here is a short list of grey and downright black areas that missions should be vigilant to avoid in their dealings with financial matters:

- Lack of full disclosure of budget and financial details.
- Using Mission reserves for ongoing regular operating expenses.
- Engagement in financial practices that are not in accordance with laws and regulations.
- Diverting designated gifts to expenses other than what the donor intended.
- Charging missionaries with expenses that are the responsibility of the home office to cover.

An excellent booklet that addresses this subject of integrity in donor relations is *The Ministry of Fund Raising*, by Whitney Kuniholm (1990).

*Integrity in Public Relations*. In the arena of what we communicate to our donor base through our magazines, newsletters and brochures, we need to be careful to avoid these traps—all of which I have seen done in my years of watching missions operate:

- Overselling a financial need that is not really as great as the promotional material implies.
- Overstating a financial crisis to play on the emotions of the donors.
- Stretching the truth when relating stories from the fields.
- Continuing to raise money for a popular project that has already been fully funded.
- Sensationalizing news from the fields, especially from restricted access areas, for the sake of playing on donor emotions.

## 8. Care in Crisis

During the past six months, our mission has had three major crises in three different continents. First, one of our missionaries was killed in a terrible car accident. Then at about the same time on another continent a team of our missionaries found themselves in an area of the world where live bullets were flying around them during a coup attempt. Shortly after that experience, in another area several of our missionary personnel were the objects of violent crime and terrorism.

How do we respond in the time of crisis in our mission family? The answers are as varied as the situations. The real necessity is that we *do* respond, with as much action as we can muster to help our missionaries in time of need.

A responsible mission agency should have a *crisis intervention plan*. A careful procedure of reaction and response should be planned out in advance for each area of the world in which you work. The missionaries in dangerous areas should have evacuation plans and drills. Your mission should have policies in place for how to deal with hostages and ransom demands. And your missionaries must be trained in how to respond in hostile situations or cases where there is extreme and sudden political unrest.

Our mission works with Contingency Preparation Consultants (P.O. Box 4792, Ventura, CA 93004) which aids us in assessing and planning for all types of dangers on our fields. We also subscribe to the new S.A.F.E. (Security Assessment for Evangelicals), a service of Evangelical Foreign Mission Association that keeps our mission abreast of imminent dangers around the world.

One final necessity for caring for missionaries in crisis is counseling. Whether they think they need it or not, missionaries do indeed go through trauma and disorientation in such cases. It should be the responsibility of the mission to either allow the units to come to home base for regrouping or to send counselors to the field to aid in recovery. Do not ask if they are coping, assume that they could use some encouragement and help. The cracks may not show immediately, but they will show eventually if emotional care is not provided.

## 9. Concern for Quality and Excellence

The "quality movement" is sweeping the secular organizations of North America. It was born out of necessity in an environment where the competition is forcing American companies to rebuild their commitment to quality from the ground up. Without a commitment to excellence, says Joel Barker, in *Future Edge* (1992), there will be

no future for most American companies in the competition of world markets. The same goes for organizations in other countries.

Christian organizations should be committed to total quality for spiritual reasons: "Whatever you do, work at it with all your heart, as working for the Lord, not for men" (Colossians 3:23 NIV). Whatever we do should be done with excellence to honor and glorify God. I personally feel that there is no room for shoddiness in mission management. I agree with Barker's analysis, that the organization that is on the constant quest for excellence will experience, for the most part, the following:

- Everything works right the first time
- Everyone quests for doing it better tomorrow than today
- Customer's (constituents and members) needs are constantly met
- Products (and services) work better, last longer
- Waste disappears from the system
- People love their jobs

In speaking with young potential missionary recruits around the country I always tell them this: "*Who you go with is more important than where you go.*" If you plan to spend a long time overseas, carefully investigate the management practices of the potential agency. Make sure you ask the hard questions about how they are organized and what kind of leadership they will provide you.

Young missionaries should go with a group that will look after them, lead them with integrity and excellence, and keep their best interests at heart. It is a question of stewardship—missionaries stewarding their gifts and agencies stewarding their people.

# Conclusion

Let me finish with a word of caution. Baby Boomers—a term used to describe Americans born after World War Two—tend to expect more from mission agencies than any previous generation. While I applaud the innovations of my generation (Boomers), I warn them of expecting too much (see Finzel, 1989). Do not let the age of entitlement in which we live get into your blood. Your mission agency can only do so much. It is neither your parent nor spouse, and cannot provide the personal support that only close family members and friends can. Missions get in trouble when they create expectations that they cannot deliver. Most of us are not capable of being a mission "family" as much as we wish we could be; we are a mission "agency." Our responsibility before God as mission leaders is to make our agencies the best they can be with the resources we have available to us.

"Great necessities call forth great leaders," said Abigail Adams in 1790, in a letter penned to Thomas Jefferson. The great necessity of our day is to finish the task of reaching the unevangelized and unreached who have yet to hear the good news of Jesus Christ. What our mission agencies need today is strong, resolute, humble, and yes, *great* leaders to accomplish this great task. And since great leaders are developed not born, agencies would do well to make an ongoing, substantial investment into the training, mentoring, and care of their leaders.

## Questions for Discussion

1. In looking over this list of *nine organizational essentials,* where are the greatest strengths in your mission organization? List them. And conversely, what areas need the greatest improvement?

2. Mission Leaders: What actions could you take to work on the list of improvements that you created under question #1? How can you approach your leadership to help solve some of these problems if you are not the chief executive officer?

3. Missionaries: What actions could you take to graciously approach your mission to work on the list of improvements that you created under question #1? Without alienating yourself from the leadership, what issue do you feel is most important on your list?

4. Are there other organizational essentials that you feel the author has left out? List them. Do you feel that perhaps some of the concerns that the writer has expressed are overstated? List them.

5. What one action point can you take as a result of reading this chapter to help make your mission a better place in which to work for the glory of God and the fulfillment of the Great Commission?

# References

Adizes, I. (1988). *Corporate lifecycles: How and why corporations grow and die and what to do about it.* Englewood Cliffs, NJ: Prentice Hall.

Barker, J. (1992). *Future edge.* New York: William Marrow.

Bennis, W., & Nanus, B. (1985). *Leaders: The strategies for taking charge.* New York: Harper and Row.

CBFMS. (1989). *Core Values of the Conservative Baptist Foreign Mission Society.* Wheaton, IL: Author.

Church Resource Ministries. (1991). The expectations and privileges of CRM staff. *CRM's statement of corporate values and beliefs.* Fullerton, CA: Author.

Covey, S. (1989). *The seven habits of highly effective people.* New York: Simon & Schuster.

DePree, M. (1989). *Leadership is an art.* New York: Dell.

Drucker, P. (1967). *The effective executive.* New York: Harper & Row.

Finzel, H. (1989). *Help! I'm a baby boomer.* Wheaton, IL: Victor Books.

Flamholtz, E. (1990). *Growing pains: How to make the transition from an entrepreneurship to a professionally managed firm.* San Francisco: Jossey-Bass.

Hersey, P., & Blanchard, K. (1982). *Management of organizational behavior.* Englewood Cliffs, NJ: Prentice Hall.

Kuniholm, W. (1990). *The ministry of fund raising.* Washington, DC: Prison Fellowship.

Morris, L. (1974). *The gospel according to Luke.* Grand Rapids: Eerdmans.

# 17

*Frances White*

# The Dynamics of Healthy Missions

This chapter presents criteria for understanding and evaluating the quality of the dynamics of a mission organization. By *dynamics* I refer to the interpersonal patterns that determine the way the group maintains its equilibrium in the midst of change. Does its mode of functioning as a body result in a more wholesome growth-producing adjustment or in a more dysfunctional adaptation to the many transitions, and their consequent stresses, that it constantly faces? The criteria I discuss are used by many counselors who evaluate and treat families as a unit or system. My underlying assumption is that the same interrelationship processes that one can observe within families are applicable to mission groups.

In a very real sense a mission, made up of a home staff, varying levels of field leaders, and missionary families, functions as an extended family. Missionaries in a particular geographic area form a more nuclear family. These new relationships are strengthened by the unique cross-cultural experiences with its stresses that no one but that group can really understand and share, as well as the fact of the members' geographical distance from their own families. Similar "family" dynamics can be seen in schools, churches, medical clinics, camps, and other organizations that are made up of closely functioning individuals (Friedman, 1985).

## Systems Approach

What is a systemic or holistic way of examining how mission agencies and groups function? An approach is systemic when the interrelationships among a given set of individuals are studied in their total context. This holistic approach permits a more accurate picture than one that conceptualizes a mission as a composite sum of discrete individuals since the dynamics of the whole mission are greater than the sum of those of the individuals, family units, and administrative units that make up the organization. The reason is that each unit affects and is affected by every other unit. This principle comes through in Paul's analogy of the Body in I Corinthians 12. Looking at a mission as a system in this way forces one to recognize how the entire system is related as well as the functioning position of each individual who comprises it.

Systems thinking, then, views problems as originating within the overall context as opposed to residing in one individual or group. For example, if an individual missionary is suffering from inordinate stress, these questions would be asked: "What in this system's way of functioning has created or contributed to the stress? What is perpetuating it? Why is this particular individual manifesting the stress? How can this mission's way of functioning be modified to keep the symptom from recycling?" He or she would be seen as the carrier or symptom bearer of some dysfunction within the total system.

In this chapter I will explore five main patterns of systemic functioning, and discuss their relevance for mission agencies. These patterns are cohesion, boundaries, adaptability, regulation, and communication. My goal is to shed light on the healthy and unhealthy aspects of how mission agencies function. I draw upon several of the major concepts that researchers have identified (Kantor and Lehr, 1975; Lewis, Beavers, Gossett, and Phillips, 1976; Oliveri and Reiss, 1982; Olson, Sprenkle, and Russell, 1979).

Each of the five patterns is presented on a continuum with counterbalancing forces as end points or polarities and the integrated balance of the two as the ideal center point. The two slash marks on the continuum indicate the theoretical parameters for health. To function outside of these boundaries toward the end points indicates possible dysfunction.

## Patterns of Cohesion

| Enmeshed | / | Connected Separate | / | Disengaged |
|---|---|---|---|---|

Cohesion is the glue that holds the mission system together. It consists of the emotional bonding members of a mission have with one another and with the nationals. This includes both the degree of togetherness and the degree of autonomy that the individuals experience in the system. Healthy cohesion fosters a harmonious balance between the more enmeshed and disengaged polarities thereby permitting members of the mission to develop their own uniqueness and yet experience this sense of unity with one another.

Healthy mission organizations fluctuate toward more connectedness or separateness along the continuum according to their need to adjust to the changing developmental and situational circumstances of life. New missionaries, for instance, are generally more dependent upon their relatively experienced co-workers until they become more enculturated. Or, in times of crisis, there is a need to function towards the connected or even enmeshed end. Also, different segments of a total mission group or national church may function at different points between the polarities according to the cultural, political, or work environment. This flexibility is a vital component of a healthy system.

An important factor to remember is that the more to the extreme a system goes, the more precariously fine is the line between health and dysfunction. For example, mission groups that foster excessive sharing and closeness with excessive accountability may succeed in reducing present anxiety but concurrently risk creating a deeper level of anxiety when individuals must act more independently. On the contrary, those that promote excessive self-sufficiency with minimal sharing may succeed in reducing dependency but risk creating lonely individuals with many unmet needs.

Carnes (1981) elaborates five dimensions which he sees as characteristic of a healthy family's cohesion: closeness, support, decision-making, commonality, and unity (p. 64). Closeness is defined as warm and caring feelings between the system's members. Support is the affirmation given to and received from other mission members. Decision-making is the degree of involvement mission members have one with another in order to make choices. Commonality consists of the elements a mission family can share in common such as time, space, interests, activities, and friends. Mission unity emanates from the meaningful, healthy type of pride individuals take in their mission membership.

Any of these dimensions carried to the extreme contribute to problems. For example, an overdose of support can be smothering and manipulative. Too little support, though, fosters discouragement with a sense that no one really cares. Further, a lack of healthy pride or appreciation in the mission to which one belongs can lead to a disloyal critical attitude on the disengaged side or a naive simplistic trusting stance on the enmeshed end.

## Enmeshment

Missions that function most of the time toward the enmeshment end experience a "pseudo-closeness" to others that does not give a sense of the right to be an individual. To the extent that this is practiced, dependency is fostered. Separate units such as individuals, families, and teams are deprived of growth. Differences are perceived as disloyalty. Guilt messages often are communicated to anyone expressing something new or questioning aspects of the old. An attitude of exclusiveness can prevail, tending to produce isolation from others. A solid boundary seems to exist around the group, which keeps new ideas, people, and methods from entering the inner ring. Yet the boundaries between those already in the circle are too permeable, eliminating privacy and individuality. People are simply too close!

When church planting missions, for example, function primarily on the enmeshed polarity, they tend to build their own enclaves. There is a tendency for missionaries to function in parental roles thereby keeping the national church more dependent. Both nationals and missionaries are not encouraged to see themselves as part of the church worldwide. They become ingrown and insular. Less latitude exists for even healthy forms of contextualization. The national church, therefore, is more apt to be a photocopy of the mission group rather than have its own truly national flavor. Cooperation with other organizations is minimal. Furthermore, nationals or missionaries who try to enter a new area, geographically or work-wise, often do so with a sense of guilt for their independency. A high level of anxiety, a general suspicion of the world and a feeling of having betrayed others is often prevalent.

Enmeshment often is visible when missionaries tend to be totally absorbed in work involving all the same people—spending spare time together and talking almost exclusively about work. Encouraging them to develop side interests and mix with other groups (Christians, non-Christians, nationals, other missionaries, business people), can increase enthusiasm, enlarge vision, refresh and correct perspectives. Too much exclusiveness in relationships tends to create petty behaviors that can grow into major problems.

## Disengagement

The mission organization that functions toward the other polarity, disengagement, would experience the opposite effect. Autonomy tends to reign with each person doing his or her own thing. Competition serving self-interest may be rife. The effect of one project upon another is ignored. In short, too much "I-ness" and "mine-ness" exists as opposed to the extreme "we-ness" and "our-ness" of the enmeshed group. Connectedness to each other and the nationals is minimal. Consequently roots are not put down and true commitment is lacking.

The effects can be seen in the national church that does not truly jell. The caring supportive function is not there on an emotional level. Members may not even be aware of their loneliness. They become very vulnerable to respond to the overture of any group that provides the emotional fulfillment that is lacking. Changes are pursued without considering the effects of separation and loss upon others.

## Patterns of Boundaries

| Rigid | / | Structured Flexible | / | Under-defined |
|-------|---|---------------------|---|---------------|

Just as countries have invisible boundaries that define and protect their territory, human systems also have boundaries that determine their space and regulate the access their members have to outside influences. Boundaries therefore refer to the invisible lines around the mission-at-large as well as given groups within the mission. The smaller groups within the larger circumference of the mission can be called *sub-systems*. Each sub-system is a unit within the overall system.

The healthy mission group forms clearly defined sub-systems. Each sub-system is a unit responsible for carrying out distinct functions within the overall system. The task, privileges, and limitations are well understood.

Members often belong to several sub-systems simultaneously. For example, just as a man can be a husband and a father within the family system, so also on the mission level he can be a business manager in the executive sub-system and a member of the team in a particular project sub-system. In healthy missions, a person's role in each sub-group is unambiguous. Along with this, though, there must be access to and communication among sub-systems (e.g., a mission school director having input into policy formulated by field leaders), and within sub-systems (e.g., an executive in charge of business functions hand-in-hand with an executive in charge of personnel).

When the boundaries of sub-systems are too closed, it becomes difficult to shift roles and move from one sub-system to another. Communication with those outside the system breaks down. Reasons for actions are possibly misunderstood. Suspicion could

result. Those within the boundaries would tend to become authoritarian and legalistic.

On the other hand, boundaries that are too loose or open can produce insecurity with confusion about roles, responsibility for decisions, or respect. Members feel leaderless and powerless.

The need for flexible well-defined boundaries is particularly evident for missionary children who attend boarding schools. Houseparents step into the parental sub-system yet must be ready to relinquish that role when parents come back into the picture. Both parents and houseparents must respect each other, keep communication open, and be emotionally prepared to adjust to the needed intensity of their level of involvement with the children as they go to and come from family and school.

Flexible clear boundaries are particularly important in a mission system because members are exposed to more frequent changes and transitions than they normally would experience in other systems. In systems terms, the way a mission responds to change is referred to as adaptability.

## Patterns of Adaptability

| Homeostasis | / | Stability Transition | / | Morphogenesis |
|---|---|---|---|---|

Adaptability is the ability of a mission system to change in response to situational and developmental pressures. The task of the healthy mission system is to develop an equilibrium between the amount of constancy (homeostasis) it maintains and the degree of change it fosters. Nonetheless, in today's rapidly changing world where upheavals are taking place in basic social and political structures, institutions, technology, methods, and scientific concepts, openness to change is essential not only for growth but for survival. However, no stable system can function healthily for extended periods of constant flux. Excessive or prolonged periods of change break down common meanings, values, and expectations, all essential for the survival of a cohesive system (Wertheim, 1973, p. 365). Enough stability must be present to permit an adequate period to accommodate new elements into existing structures in order to enable members to assimilate them with the least amount of trauma. These more static periods also provide periods of respite from ambiguities, risks, and anxieties that often accompany change. Thus, balance is indeed essential.

Church planting teams, for example, that function too exclusively on the homeostasis end can fail to prepare the church to realize the need to examine changing cultural norms in the light of biblical truth. Nor do they provide opportunity to influence the directions and consequences of new developments. A tendency would exist to create an impermeable boundary around the mission and church systems to protect them from the new. Without the stimulation of the new, an apathetic attitude could easily develop.

### Feedback Loops

Interestingly, living systems have inner controls that automatically regulate the amount of constancy and change they can tolerate in a given period. In systems theory they are called *feedback loops*. The analogy often used to explain this is the home thermostat that regulates the temperature of a house. When the house gets too cold the thermostat signals the furnace to turn on, but only until the temperature reaches a determined point. At that point, the furnace shuts off and the cycle begins again. Likewise, when the dynamics of a mission system are healthy, members tend to respond with constructive behaviors that enable the group to grow, create, and innovate. In short, the mission changes as the need arises. This is a process known as *positive feedback*. On the other hand, when change is inappropriate or excessive, negative responses from the members occur (frustration, poor morale, lower performance), and will tend to pull the system back to its previous level of functioning.

A poignant example of the adaptability dynamic is the case of one group of missionaries in northeastern Zaire who evacuated to Kenya during a period of extreme political unrest. All their coping strategies for dealing with change came into play as they carried out the evacuation. After being in Kenya for about a month they realized that the amount of change the children were undergoing was unhealthy. An MK school in exile was set up by the parents and administrators with the same teachers they had in Zaire in order to get the children back to the familiar. The reactions of the children to too much change pushed the system back into a healthier, more homeostatic state.

During this time the Zairian church had suffered tremendously from the prolonged sociopolitical instability. When the missionaries eventually returned after the rebellion, they encountered nationals who longed for stability and the reestablishment of what they had known and with which they were comfortable. Although both the missionary and national church systems knew corrections had to be made to remedy faulty relationship styles of the pre-evacuation period, the church's readiness to adapt and absorb health-promoting changes had to be a gradual self-directed process. Any attempt on a national or missionary's part to bring about changes before this would have been resisted.

## Patterns of Regulation

| Rigid | / | Structured Flexible | / | Chaotic |
|-------|---|---------------------|---|---------|

A mission's adaptability to change is greatly influenced by the way it regulates or governs itself. Regulation refers to the way a mission organizes and monitors itself in order to fulfill its objectives. Differing circumstances and philosophies can lead to more flexibility or more structure. Either direction can be healthy. Each has its own advantages and disadvantages. Nonetheless, the mission that can fluctuate between the two as the need arises will experience less tension when change is required.

When a mission's regulatory functions are overly rigid it will not be adaptable. Too many specific rules eliminate degrees of freedom. Excessive external control diminishes the development of internal values. Adjustment to changing circumstances is hindered. Creativity is stifled. Everything becomes absolutized with a strong authoritarian approach. As in enmeshment an unhealthy degree of dependency exists. Leaders are not developed. More often than not, an undercurrent of anger, criticism, or negativism develops.

On the chaotic end where there is too great a degree of flexibility, bedlam exists. Too few rules, unexecuted ones, or unclear ones fail to give direction and security. Core values that serve as guidelines either remain unidentified or never develop. A sense of disorganization, lack of responsibility, and unpredictability offer too little sense of security. Everyone does his own thing with little accountability.

## Factors Influencing Regulation

There are five basic factors, or dimensions, that are intricately related to how a system regulates itself: leadership, discipline, negotiation, organization, and values (Carnes, 1981, p. 27).

The *leadership dimension* directly influences the way tasks are carried out. Missions that function more to the left on the continuum have a more stable but restrictive executive system. Those who function more to the right tend to be quite democratic with more room for input and variety.

The *pattern of discipline* determines how limits are set. In more structured mission systems, more rules tend to be explicit and detailed. Their application is monitored more, usually by the leadership. In the more flexible group, principles are the explicit focus with the exact rules that grow out of them being more open to interpretation according to the situation at hand.

*Negotiation* is the way missions solve problems, make decisions, and plan. In more structured missions the process, carried out by the executive sub-system, is faster and more concrete, offering a sense of efficiency and reliability. On the more flexible side, particular sub-systems are responsible for the issue under discussion and are given more freedom to work through their own problems, though not to the exclusion of considering the effect they have on the rest of the mission.

The *degree of organization* present in a mission group depends to a large extent on its particular need for predictability. The more highly structured the group, the more logistically organized it will be, thereby affording a greater sense of routine and security. In the face of major changes, however, more time may be needed to readjust the organizational infrastructure. On the other hand less organized groups would be more flexible during times of change and will probably readjust quicker as needed.

*Values* too are well defined in more structured groups. This could give a greater sense of stability to a mission. Flexibly regulated missions also appreciate value identification but are more open to put them into a hierarchy from the more absolute to the more relative. They are thereby prepared to modify some as the felt need arises.

## Relating Cohesion and Regulation

Olson, Sprenkle, and Russell (1979) combine the dimensions of cohesion and regulation, and believe these to be the most important dimensions in a system. These researchers use two-term descriptors in which the first word characterizes the regulatory dimension and the second word the cohesion dimension. They consider systems with balanced levels of both regulation and cohesion as healthy. Such systems are either flexibly separated or flexibly connected or else are structurally separated or structurally connected. Those that reflect the most dysfunctional dynamics are either chaotically disengaged or chaotically enmeshed or are rigidly disengaged or rigidly enmeshed.

The impact of these combined dimensions can be illustrated from the history of church-mission relationships in underdeveloped areas. When missions first founded churches in such areas, a more structurally connected type of functioning between the national and missionary may have been necessary. Missions were in effect parenting babies in the body of Christ, teaching basic skills such as reading, simple math, doctrine, and the application of biblical truths. As the environment in which the new churches functioned developed politically, socially, educationally, and spiritually, the churches entered into an "adolescence" period and were ready for and needing more autonomy and flexibility. The relationship between mission and church systems had to gradually become more open, more democratic, and more flexible. Rules, role relationships, and power bases had to be redefined. The problems associated with change were prevalent and at times ambivalence or ambiguity created greater tensions. Both mission and church systems often slipped into the more unhealthy categories. Ideally, bit by bit relationships changed until today the pattern of cohesion and regulation is characterized by one of the combinations that indicates mature, healthy functioning between church and mission systems.

## Patterns of Communication

| Dogmatic | / | Literal Figurative | / | Diffuse |
|----------|---|--------------------|---|---------|

Communication is a tool that not only enables relationships to form but also determines the form that they will take. Communication can be verbal or nonverbal; but to be healthy it must be a clearly delivered, easily understood and empathic exchange of information among mission and church members.

Healthy communication also includes ways of verifying understandings and clarifying intentions and meanings where necessary. Feedback in the form of expressing favorable reaction or disagreement without defending or attacking is necessary. Suggestions can be made or alternatives offered. Statements are neither overly critical nor patronizingly nurturing. The empathic part means that communication is made with the attempt to understand the receiver. This also involves active listening so as to hear the content and sense the feeling. Recipients of this quality of communication tend to feel understood and confirmed.

Receivers of unhealthy communication on the other hand are prone to feel misunderstood and unconfirmed. Diffuse or unclear responses tend to ignore, belittle, or distort statements made by others. These types of "fuzzy" communication patterns also leave the receivers puzzled about the intents and expectations of the speaker. Their confusion, in turn, can elicit defensiveness, anger, or withdrawal, all of which minimize the possibility for mutually enhancing relationships.

On the dogmatic end, receivers of messages can feel trapped, stifled, and depreciated. Rebellious or antagonistic behaviors—subtle or overt— may result. Wholesome relationships are again hindered.

Good communication is at the heart of any healthy system. It binds the group together. Through it new relationships are made, existing ones sustained or modified. It provides the acknowledgement and endorsement that all human beings need.

## Summary Comments

Two words stand out when considering the characteristics of a healthy mission system: balance and flexibility. These two characteristics are most apparent in missions that encourage clear communication with those outside as well as within the system; that have clear stable boundaries that adjust themselves as occasion demands; that are internally connected without being enmeshed; that have a reasonable degree of structure that is neither too rigid nor too chaotic; and that are open to change yet recognize the need for periods of stability.

Systemic health is contagious and will certainly impact the people targeted for ministry. Unfortunately dysfunction is likewise contagious and will also be passed on. How important it is then for mission agencies to promote balance and flexibility in their patterns of cohesion, boundaries, adaptability, regulation, and communication.

### Practical Suggestions

How can leaders and other members of a mission agency get a clear picture of the overall health of their organization? What steps can be taken to help develop and maintain organizational health in each of the five dimensions discussed in this chapter?

Start with a commitment to regularly assess your organization—at least on an annual basis. Involve the staff. Questionnaires, surveys, and discussion times are useful avenues for getting at how members perceive the organization. Open, frank comments are to be encouraged, as are constructive suggestions for change. Concrete activities to explore the organizational dimensions discussed in this chapter can be found in Carnes (1981). Some missions include a member care track in the program of their annual conference to encourage and process such activities.

In addition, consider inviting an expert in member care who is experienced in working from a systemic perspective to participate in the assessment process. He/she could also provide practical training for recognizing and assessing system patterns. It may also be appropriate to recruit personnel with training in organizational development to work as full-time colleagues.

Another option is to set up a special team or department that can study the organization, help monitor how it is functioning, and make suggestions for change to the leadership and staff. This might best be overseen through a pastoral care or personnel development department. Be sure to include members from different cultural backgrounds to insure that the perspectives and needs of all members can be adequately represented and understood.

The book of Proverbs says: "By wisdom a house is built, and by understanding it is established; and by knowledge the rooms are filled with all precious and pleasant riches" (24:3,4 NASB). This is certainly true of mission agencies, as wisdom, understanding, and knowledge are needed to maintain organizational health. Healthy functioning is not to be taken for granted. Rather, it is something to work on, pray through, and openly dialogue about on an ongoing basis.

### Questions for Discussion

1. How did each of the five dimensions identified in this chapter manifest themselves in your family of origin? In the local church in which you were/are a part?

2. How might these background experiences influence the way you presently function in your team, department, or mission setting?

3. What specific behaviors in each of these dimensions would you like to see modified in your mission setting?

4. How would you go about seeking to change an organizational dimension that was out of balance?

5. In what ways might the dominant culture or cultures influence the way your mission agency functions in these five dimensions?

## References

Carnes, P. (1981). *Family development I: Understanding me.* Minneapolis: Interpersonal Communication Programs.

Friedman, E.H. (1985). *Generation to generation: Family processes in church and synagogue.* New York: Guilford Press.

Kantor, D., & Lehr, W. (1975). *Inside the family: Toward a theory of family process.* San Francisco: Jossey-Bass.

Lewis, J., Beavers, W., Gossett, J., and Phillips, V. (1976). *No single thread: Psychological health in family systems.* New York: Brunner/Mazel.

Oliveri, M. and Reiss, D. (1982). Family styles of construing the social environment: A perspective on variation among nonclinical families. In Walsh, F. (Ed.). *Normal family processes* (pp. 94-113). New York: Guilford Press.

Olson, D., Sprenkle, D. & Russell, C. (1979). Circumplex model of marital and family systems: I. Cohesion and adaptability dimensions, family types, and clinical applications. *Family Process, 18,* 3-28.

Wertheim, E. (1973). Family unit therapy and the science and typology of family systems. *Family Process, 12,* 361-376.

# 18

*Peter Shedlosky*

# Career Development and the Mission Agency

In this article I would like to explore how career development plays an integral part in assisting mission organizations to achieve their stated purpose. I present a conceptual framework for understanding career development, discuss a specific career development program, and make suggestions for establishing or improving similar programs. Let's start off with a foundational question: What is the purpose for your organization's existence?

In the for-profit sector, the bottom-line goal is to provide the best possible goods and services for the customer while making a fair and honest profit. The non-profit organization has a slightly different bent, in that acquiring money is a means to an end, with the end being the effective and efficient completion of that organization's stated purpose. For mission agencies, the underlying purpose is to fulfill their particular part in God's mandate to make disciples of all the nations (Matthew 28:18-20).

One of the basic challenges of a mission agency is to find a balance between its commitment to accomplishing evangelistic tasks and its commitment to care for and develop staff. Too frequently, the emphasis falls more on the side of the task, to the near exclusion of the people who are needed to work on the task. Organizational practices which place task attainment over staff development is considered a non-acceptable operating procedure in today's business world, and rightfully so. This should be especially true within the mission agency, considering the biblical exhortations to care for and honor one another (e.g., Romans 12:10, Galatians 5:14). Not surprisingly, industrial research, in line with Scriptural principles, has shown that the care and development of people within the organization facilitates task/goal accomplishment (Argyris, 1957, 1964; McGregor, 1969).

In organizations today, the practice of caring for and developing personnel is referred to as Human Resource Development (HRD). The missions community can glean much from this important field.

## Human Resource Development

Let's look at a definition of HRD, as outlined by the professional society of HRD practitioners called the American Society for Training and Development (McLagan, 1989).

> *HRD is the integrated use of training and development, organizational develop-ment, and career development to improve individual, group, and organizational effectiveness. It's the combined use of all developmental practices in order to ac-complish higher levels of individual and organizational effectiveness than would be possible with a narrower approach. (p. 7)*

This definition sees HRD as being composed of three parts: (a) training and development (T&D), (b) organizational development (OD), and (c) career development (CD). Each of these parts and their respective compo-nents are diagrammed in the human resource model found in Figure 1 (p. 250).

Figure 1 relates HRD to a larger system referred to as the "human resource system" (HR). As can be seen in this model, HR is divided into two areas of emphasis: human resource development (HRD) and human resource management (HRM). HRD focuses on the development of human resources while HRM is concerned with the policies and procedures needed to effectively use human resources.

Human resources are to a mission agency what blood and the circu-latory system are to the human body. Whether the agency is in its infancy or has reached full maturity, once the circulation is restricted or cut off to other parts within the organization, its functioning will be diminished or eliminated.

HRD can be viewed as the arterial part of the agency circulatory system that brings the nourishment necessary for staff development. Ca-reer development, the specific focus of this chapter, is one of the three main arteries or paths that act as a conduit in providing that nourishment. The other two arteries would be organizational development and training and development.

Leaders and managers can err by not taking into account the interre-lationships between the various parts. Further, when numerous smaller parts or one larger part within HR is eliminated or dysfunctional—for instance, overlooking the need for regular training and development for staff—the organization's effectiveness in achieving its stated purpose is threatened or even curtailed.

## The Four Systems of an Organization

Let's take the human resource system (HR) described in Figure 1 a step further by relating it to the overall organization. HR is actually one of four main systems that form organizations (Bolman & Deal 1984). These systems are based on the major schools of organizational research and theory, and are also useful ways to understand mission organizations.

1. *The structural system* is what we commonly see represented through organizational charts. This system emphasizes the importance of formal roles and relationships. It identifies the connection between line and staff workers and the way individuals, departments, and management are related (the division of labor).

2. *The human resource system* (described in Figure 1) focuses on the care and development of the people that make up the organization. It is a constantly changing and dynamic part of the organization. The challenge is to create a good fit between the organization and the people who work in it—to find an organizational form that will help people be the most productive and satisfied with their work.

3. *The political system* is one that is frequently minimized or overlooked by Christian organizations. It deals with the power/influence needed to allocate limited resources (e.g., people, money, vehicles, computers) to accomplish certain prioritized tasks. Conflicts are expected due to different individual and group needs, as well as different perspectives, and are a normal part of organizational life. Bargaining, persuasion, compromise, and the formation of special interest groups are also involved.

4. *The symbolic system* holds an organization together through shared values and the type of organizational culture that is created and reinforced. Rituals, stories, and unwritten protocol exert strong influences on organizational life; sometimes even more so than rules, policies, and managerial authority.

All four of these systems need to be functioning in some sort of balanced manner for an organization to be considered healthy. Different mission agencies, for example, may emphasize a particular system, but that does not mean the other three systems should be neglected. The mission I belong to (Youth With A Mission) has a very influential symbolic system which requires that our structural system receive continual attention and adjustment. Our organization is highly flexible, and in many ways our structure shifts according to our present missionary involvement. Over the years some parameters have been introduced to channel this flexibility towards fulfilling our overall objectives. Such flexibility, nonetheless, is part of our organizational distinctiveness, and is an important ingredient in making our ministry effective.

# Human Resource Model

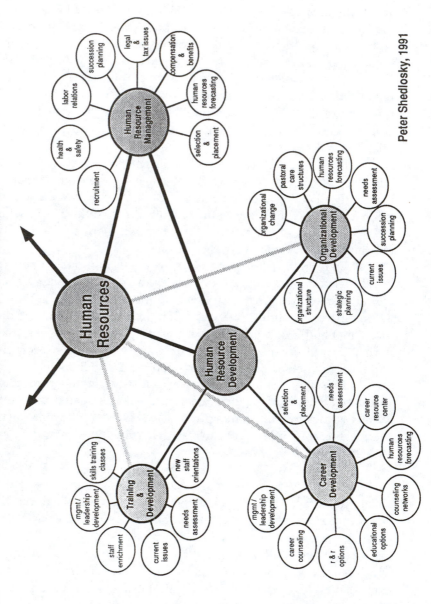

Peter Shedlosky, 1991

# Career Development Programs

People in leadership have a primary role within the agency to help staff achieve the stated purpose of that particular organization. Leaders also serve to release others to exercise and develop their respective gifts. In addition, the leadership position is one of oversight and care of staff workers. In other words, mission leaders, in one form or another, are actively involved in the development or *discipleship* of their staff.

Previous chapters in this book have discussed how leaders and others can help care for mission personnel through pastoral care, clinical care, stress management, crisis intervention, and team building. Another area I would like to introduce is organizational career development, and how its implementation benefits the organization's bottom-line goal. I consider career development to be an important part of the discipleship process for mission workers. Let's take a closer look at career development and how a career development program can be of service to a mission agency.

Leibowitz, Farren, and Kaye (1986) define a career development program as being:

> An organized, formalized, planned effort to achieve a balance between the individual's career needs and the organization's work-force requirements. It integrates activities of the employees and managers with the policies and procedures of the organization. It is an ongoing program linked with the organization's human resource structures rather than a one-time event. It also serves to refine and develop present human resource activities. (p.4)

Career development thus focuses on both the development of individuals and improving the match between individual career interests and specific organizational career opportunities (Gutteridge, 1986; Gutteridge, Otte, & Williamson, 1983). It addresses a variety of areas, such as the level of competency needed to perform certain jobs, the time frame for skills to be acquired, and the type of training required to become proficient in a job or task.

Initially, career development was considered by both employee and management to be the individual's concern and responsibility, not the organization's. This perception has been changing, as both the individual and organization are now seen to play important roles: the individual's responsibility (referred to as *career planning*), and the organization's responsibility (referred to as *career management*). Table 1 (Gutteridge, Otte, & Williamson, 1983) points out the different responsibilities of both individuals and the organization in the career development of staff.

In the secular world, career development does not always mean advancement; it might mean moving laterally to assume another position or a short-term cut in status and pay for long-term career growth (Segalla, 1987). Currently, there is a more participative atmosphere between man-

## Table 1. A Working Model of Organizational Career Development

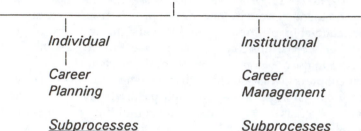

Organizational Career Development

| Individual | Institutional |
|---|---|
| Career Planning | Career Management |
| *Subprocesses* | *Subprocesses* |
| * Occupational choice | * Recruitment and selection |
| * Organizational choice | * Human resource allocation |
| * Choice of job assignment | * Appraisal and evaluation |
| * Career self-development | * Training and development |

agement and employees in organizations, a fact which has allowed the career development process to take on a more congenial flavor in meeting the goals of both individuals and organizations.

### A Model for Career Development

Gutteridge (1986) has constructed a career development model that is applicable to many mission settings. It posits five general areas that need to be included and integrated into an organization's career development program: (a) self-assessment tools, (b) individual counseling, (c) internal labor market information/placement exchanges, (d) organizational potential assessment processes, and (e) developmental programs. Table 2 expands these five components.

## Table 2. Career Development Components

A. *Self-assessment tools*
1. Career-planning workshops
2. Career workbooks
3. Pre-retirement workshops

B. *Individual counseling*
1. Personnel department staff
2. Professional counselor (internal and external)
3. Outside placement
4. Supervisor or line manager

C.*Internal labor market information/placement exchanges*
1. Job posting
2. Skill inventories
3. Career ladders/career path planning
4. Career resource center
5. Other career communication formats

D.*Organizational potential assessment processes*
1. Assessment centers
2. Promotability forecasts
3. Replacement/succession planning
4. Psychological testing

E.*Developmental programs*
1. Job rotation
2. In-house human resource development programs
3. External seminars/workshops
4. Tuition reimbursement/educational assistance
5. Supervisor training in career counseling
6. Dual-career programs
7. Mentoring systems

How might a mission agency go about applying this model? Here are some ideas. To begin, it must be understood that establishing or improving a career development program depends on the size, monetary resources, and the member care commitment of the organization. It is better to start small and grow as the needs and demands within your organization dictate. If the agency has 75-100 members, I strongly recommend establishing a career development department. This requires a significant financial investment. For smaller agencies or ones desiring to transition into a full-time department situation, hiring a qualified career consultant should be considered. Either way, on your own or with outside assistance, a career development program is competent stewardship of your agency's financial and human resources.

Consider assigning a special task force to assess the elements in Gutteridge's model that already exist in some form within your agency. Next, discuss which elements you need to also include or further develop. At this point you may want to call on the services of an experienced career development consultant. After determining the aspects of the model that your organization will use, discuss them with several members of staff. Get their input. Then incorporate the new elements of the program formally into the structure of your organization. If a program is brought in without the involvement of the staff, or if it functions on an informal basis, then its chances for acceptance, utilization, and survival are greatly reduced.

When a mission agency wants to develop or improve a comprehensive career development program, the tendency can be to focus on the first two components of this model: (a) self-assessment tools and (b) individual counseling. These are fine and necessary elements, which HRD specialists tend to concentrate on, but it is the other three components that will generate the greatest impact on staff development. All five components are necessary to insure that the right people are in the right place at the right time. No singular component can be expected to do it all.

Remember, Gutteridge's model is just that—a model or guide. This means that an agency does not need to match point for point with the model. Most mission agencies can identify at least some career development components within their organization. Trying to develop a thoroughly comprehensive career development program though, is idealistic. Resources are always limited, so agencies must be as creative as possible. As an example, I will outline and describe the career development program at our Youth With A Mission base in Sunland, California. Each of Gutteridge's five components occur at varying levels of intensity; there is certainly plenty of room for improvement.

## YWAM-Los Angeles Career Development Program

A. *Self-Assessment Tools*
   1. Career-planning workshops.

We have initiated a practical *career development workshop* for our candidates called "The Gift of You." The participants are trainees in YWAM's entry level program called Discipleship Training School. The workshop consists of two to three hours of teaching on the biblical foundation of natural gifts and abilities. This is then followed by eight to nine hours of testing and feedback on the test results. Participants are tested in four areas typically used by career development specialists to determine a person's career profile: (a) *personality*, using the Myers-Briggs or Personal Style Indicator, (b) *interests*, using the Self-Directed Search, (c) *work cluster abilities*, using the Career Development Placement Survey, and (d) *work values*, using the Values Scale or Career Orientation Placement and Evaluation Survey. The last two hours are spent walking the participants through a career plan developed by them, based on their career profile and sense of God's long-term call for ministry.

B. *Individual Counseling*
   1. Personnel department staff.
   2. Professional counselor (internal).

Our human resource department consists of one person (the author), so the two roles listed above are fulfilled by that one staff member. On our base, *personnel counseling* addresses individual staff issues concerning job performance and satisfaction, while *professional counseling* looks more at personal issues predominantly in the area of career development, as this is where the author's expertise resides. Referrals to outside professionals are usually made should someone need individual, marital, or family counseling. Therapeutic counseling is often needed before effective career counseling can take place.

C.	*Internal Labor Market Information/Placement Exchanges*
	1. Job posting.
	2. Career resource center.

*Job posting* is simply listing the opportunities for service within a particular organization. This is pretty straightforward for smaller agencies, but can present much difficulty for large organizations with position openings all over the world. For Youth With A Mission, with close to 400 ministry locations worldwide, we publish a catalogue every two years listing present and potential ministry openings by location and type (e.g., street evangelist in Paris, executive secretary in Seattle). As one can imagine, parts of this publication become quickly outdated. This is partially rectified by informally exchanging letters and faxes between ministry locations to update each other.

The *career resource center* is basically a reference style library of assorted books and information pertaining to careers and career development issues. This information ranges from the theoretical to the self-directed "how-to" book. Staff members are encouraged to check out appropriate items to better prepare and plan for ministry and career decisions. Our library is fairly small, with only one hundred books or articles collected over the years.

D.	*Organizational Potential Assessment Processes*
	1. Promotability forecast.

This is one of the least developed elements of Gutteridge's model for us. *Promotability forecasts* identify the personnel who are capable of functioning in more complex ministry positions. They usually involve a formal evaluation process (e.g., performance appraisals, spiritual maturity assessment, individual career plans, peer evaluations). Many areas—not just spiritual vitality, for example—need to be looked at when someone is being considered to take on additional responsibility and challenges. Presently at our YWAM base in Sunland, this process involves our Leadership Council subjectively discussing who they believe is prepared for advanced ministry placement. This usually works out fairly well, although it is clear that a more objective and systematic approach would be helpful.

E.        *Developmental Programs*
          1. In-house HRD programs.

There is a strong *in-house HRD component* within YWAM worldwide with regards to staff training. Our staff can take a variety of courses and workshops at scores of locations around the world through YWAM's training arm, the University of the Nations. The University offers courses in such areas as community development, biblical counseling, frontier missions, and early childhood development, to name a few. YWAM staff can request a leave of absence to pursue further training through the University.

## Benefits from Career Development

What are some of the benefits of an effective organizational career development program? Well, for one, mission personnel will probably feel more fulfilled and will be more engaged in their work. Turnover rates are likely to decrease (Segalla, 1987). The agency can then avoid the significant financial costs involved in the search, hiring, training, and lost productivity when having to replace just one staff member.

Second, your mission agency's reputation of being a good and desirable place to work will improve. We all know of Christian organizations that are deemed outstanding places to work and some that are not. Your organizational reputation of how well you care for your staff goes a long way in attracting the necessary human resources to reach your organizational objectives.

A third major benefit of organizational career development is increased staff motivation. When staff comprehend the possibility of their achieving career/life goals within the organization, the result is felt needs being met, which increases their productivity (Vroom, 1964). Both the mission agency and the individual end up winners.

There are, of course many other pluses to implementing or improving a career development system. A summary of additional benefits, taken from Segalla (1987) and Barkhaus (1983), is found in Table 3.

## Table 3. Career Development Benefits

*Organizational benefits*
- Improved person-job match
- Increased productivity and profits
- Decreased employee turnover/absenteeism
- Improved communication of career opportunities for employees
- Identification and development of high potential employees

- Adequate supply of qualified, promotable employees
- Accelerated work force adaptation to change
- Improved cost-effectiveness of human resource decisions
- Strong managerial support of career development process

*Managerial benefits*
- Productive performance appraisal discussions
- Improved communication between manager and employee
- Larger inventory for special projects
- Better staff development and planning
- Enhanced reputation as a skilled manager

*Employee benefits*
- Better understanding of organizational career opportunities
- Clearer identification of career goals, options, needs, and plans
- More effective management of career development plans
- Greater visibility in the organization and profession
- Higher job performance

## Individual Career Development

My emphasis in this chapter has been to help mission leaders mentor and disciple their human resources by establishing and improving career development programs. However, as pointed out in Table 1, the responsibility for career development also lies with the individual member. I would be remiss if I did not include some brief guidelines to help individuals understand how they can contribute to their own career development.

Here are four basic steps for career development which can be pursued on one's own and hopefully also with the support of the mission. They are intended to help individuals identify their gifts, develop their skills, and find satisfying positions within missions. These steps are particularly useful for candidates and those considering significant ministry/job changes.

*Step 1*. Obtain objective assessment and feedback on your particular areas of gifts and characteristics (e.g., occupational interests, personality profile, work values, work style, and motivated abilities).

*Step 2*. Begin a determined and detailed exploration of different career/ministry occupations that may interest you. Read career reference books, try out some short-term involvement in areas of interest, interview with others about the work that they do. The key is to do relevant research!

*Step 3*. Select a career/ministry by prayerfully discerning which of the careers/ministries that you researched best matches your interests, corresponds to your personality, is consistent with your values, utilizes your abilities, and is intrinsically satisfying.

*Step 4.* Develop a realistic career/ministry plan that fits your individual profile, needs, and options. Include your goals, the education/training needed, finances and other resources required, and time frame. This fourth step is the most important of the four, because it requires you to set up a specific, step-by-step plan for your career development. Share this plan with others, get their input, ask them for support and to hold you accountable.

## Concluding Thoughts

Career development is not just another great "missions management" idea, to be overshadowed when another great idea comes along. Rather, it is a long-term program which requires an ongoing commitment to its administration and growth if it is to yield positive results. A career development program reflects the level of investment that the organization is willing to make in its people. It is worth the time and effort!

We in Christian missions should be involved in the career development process of our staff, not only for its benefits to our organization, but because it is part of our responsibility to disciple and nurture the people whom the Lord has given us. We need to set high standards for staff care and development within our mission organizations, as we seek to touch the nations with the love and truth of the Lord Jesus.

### Questions for Discussion

1. What type of career development program does your mission agency have? Refer to Gutteridge's model in Table 2. Which components need to be further developed?

2. How does your organization view the individual's role in his/her career development?

3. In what ways do the three components of HRD interact in your mission agency (training and development, organizational development, and career development)?

4. Why is career development an important part of the discipleship process?

5. Which of Bolman and Deal's organizational systems are most influential in your organization (structural, human resource, political, symbolic)?

## References

Argyris, C. (1957). *Personality and organizations.* New York, NY: Harper & Row.

Argyris, C. (1964). *Integrating the individual and the organization*. New York, NY: Wiley.

Barkhaus, R. (1983). Career development in the corporation—The purposes and benefits. *Journal of College Placement*. (September): 29-32.

Gutteridge, T., Otte, F., & Williamson, B. (1983). *Organizational career development—State of practice*. Washington, DC: ASTD Press.

Gutteridge, T. (1986). Organizational career development systems: The state of the practice. In Hall, D., & Associates. (1986). (Eds.). *Career development in organizations* (pp. 50-94). San Francisco, CA: Jossey-Bass Publishers.

Kaye, B. (1985). *A guide for career development practioners: Up is not the only way*. San Diego, CA: University Associates,Inc.

Leibowitz, Z., Farren, C., & Kaye, B. (1986). *Designing career development systems*. San Francisco, CA: Jossey-Bass Publishers.

McGregor, D. (1960). *The human side of enterprise*. New York, NY: McGraw Hill.

McLagan, P. (1989). The models. *Models for HRD practice*. Alexandria, VA: American Society for Training and Development.

Mirable, R. (1987). New directions for career development. *Training and Development Journal*. (December): 31-33.

Segalla, E. (1987). *Best ideas for career development systems*. Info-Line. Alexandria, VA: American Society for Training and Development.

Vroom, V. (1964). *Work motivation*. New York, NY: John Wiley & Sons.

# 19

*Kelly O'Donnell*
*Michele Lewis O'Donnell*

# Ethical Concerns in Providing Member Care Services

Member care is a central and indispensable aspect of mission strategy. It ranks in importance with pre-field preparation, language acquisition, and church planting strategies. Member care services such as in-serve training, reentry orientation, and pastoral counseling, promote staff health for greater effectiveness. It thus makes sense for mission agencies to prioritize and integrate such services into their overall mission strategy.

Member care, however, is more than just a strategic practice. It is an ethical necessity. That is, it is a means of valuing and investing in the development of staff because it is the right thing to do. An important theme of Scripture is to care for the flock with which we have been entrusted (John 21:16, Acts 20:28, I Peter 5:2), a command which is as applicable to mission agencies as it is to churches. This biblical theme reflects the heart of member care—to faithfully pursue the growth and well-being of mission agency staff.

## The Relevance of Ethics

The way in which member care services are provided is as significant as the actual services themselves. It is an astute mission agency which periodically examines the appropriateness, or ethical quality, of its services. By "ethical" we mean in accordance with recognized standards which promote responsible care. An example of this would be the ethical guidelines for counseling developed by the American Association of Pastoral Counselors.

Most mission agencies do not have well-defined or formal ethical standards in writing. While there may be every intention to provide member care services which are helpful and appropriate, mission agencies may still encounter some perplexing ethical issues. Resolving such issues may not be as easy as one would think!

Consider, for example, the compassionate missionary who informally counsels a couple and then prays with his wife about some of the couple's struggles. Is this appropriate? That is, is this an ethical approach to handling confidential information?

Or take the experienced consultant who makes recommendations to a mission agency based in another culture while being only vaguely familiar with that culture. Is this person acting competently? Is this appropriate?

Finally, think about the needy mission agency which abbreviates a family's field preparation so that the husband can take over a crucial and vacant overseas position. To what extent is the organization being responsible, and this appropriate/ethical?

## The Case of Jean-Le-Fidele

One useful way to explore the relevance of ethics in the care of staff is to use a case study approach. The following fictitious account includes at least 25 unethical or potentially unethical practices. Read through this study and try to identify as many of them as possible.

The remainder of the article discusses this case in light of five ethical principles—organizational responsibility, confidentiality, counselor/consultant competence, the use of testing instruments, and personal values/legal standards/ These principles can be used as a helpful reference point for mission agencies to explore their own set of ethical and member care issues.

### The Fidele Family
### Jean—Anne (parents)
### Angela, Jerome (children)

Jean is a 28-year-old member of a European mission agency. On the average he works nine- to ten-hour days and is almost always available to help out when there is a need in the ministry. He is the type of person who

---

This chapter is a revision of the authors' article, "How to Avoid Ethical Traps in Treating Hurting Staff" (1991, *Evangelical Missions Quarterly*, 27, 146-151). Used by permission.

doesn't say no to those over him. sometimes at the expense of his own needs. He often uses part of his vacation time for ministry abroad.

Jean was raised in France and went to a university in England for two years where he met his wife, Anne. He married at age 24 and has two healthy children, Angela (aged 3) and Jerome (aged six months). Currently he and his family live in Prague and are involved in ministry to Eastern Europe.

During the last three months Jean, who is usually very friendly, has become increasingly irritable with his colleagues and somewhat withdrawn with his family. His supervisor notices these changes and talks to Jean's wife about what he views as "pride and independence" in Jean. She confides in him that they both feel apathetic and that she has little energy to take care of her home and work responsibilities. The supervisor shares some Scripture with her. He then encourages her to talk to Jean about taking some time off to "get back into work shape" and for him to talk to someone about his problems. She follows his advice.

Jean is too busy to take time off but he does agree to contact the Director of Training, Ms. Bartell, for counseling. She is an American woman who has taken some counseling courses at a Christian university and is recognized within the agency for her ability to listen and offer appropriate advice. She also provides counseling to Christians from some of the local churches to supplement her income.

Ms. Bartell works on a fund raising committee with Jean and three others which meets once a month. Jean approaches her after a meeting and schedules a time with her to talk and pray about his problems. She also begins to pray regularly for Jean with the Pastoral Care Committee.

Ms. Bartell obtains Jean's files from the temporary secretary in the Personnel Department to better acquaint herself with his background. Jean had taken a personality test as part of the screening process to be accepted on staff. He scored high on the "depression" scale, so she wonders if he had tendencies towards a serious emotional disorder.

Ms. Bartell also decides to speak to Jean's wife and supervisor to better understand his struggles. The supervisor recommends that Ms. Bartell borrow a "temperament analysis" test and administer it to Jean in order to further explore his personality. She administers the test and then speaks with the supervisor, recommending that Jean be placed in a department where he can have less paperwork and more people contact.

Jean and Ms. Bartell meet for four counseling sessions. They spend most of their time talking about the challenges of raising his two children, his past relationship with his father, and his apprehension to openly talk about his work frustrations with leaders. Ms. Bartell spends time listening for what might be the "root" of his problems, and subsequently advises him to work fewer hours, spend more time with his family, and be more assertive with colleagues.

After the fourth session, Ms. Bartell tells Jean that she feels led to send him to a mission leader who has come to the Prague base to give two weeks of seminars. She feels this person can encourage him and possibly give him more insights into his current situation. Jean gives her a small honorarium for her services, and a few days later approaches the mission leader.

## Case Discussion

### Organizational Responsibility

Basic Principle: Mission agencies acknowledge responsibility for the quality of care they provide staff. They seek to develop integrated, comprehensive member care services which are periodically reviewed to determine their effectiveness. They also make reasonable efforts to ensure the appropriate use of these services.

1. Perhaps he central ethical issue in this case is that the organization seems to have no set policy or protocol for care to which the supervisor or Jean can refer. Rather it appears to take a reactive, hit-or-miss approach, with little prevention emphasis.

2. The organization also had a responsibility to the Fidele family during the selection process. Did it adequately assess such areas as Jean's emotional stability, family well-being, work style, and motivation? Psychological assessment in this contect can be an important preventive measure and a stimulus for personal growth.

3. The supervisor avoids his responsibility to confront and talk with Jean directly. Instead he speaks to Jean's wife and then suggests that Jean somehow obtain help. The supervisor, though, wisely avoids taking on the dual roles of supervisor/counselor with Jean, as this would probably confuse their relationship. Supervisors nevertheless have a duty to be aware of the needs of staff and to link staff with the appropriate resources.

4. The staff in Jean's department did not seem to have met during the last three months (and possibly longer) for regular feedback times to discuss personal and work matters. Problems build to the crisis point before they receive attention.

5. When and how is the organization responsible for tracking Jean's progress in counseling and providing supportive follow-up? The agency does not seem to be very thorough in these areas.

### Confidentiality

Basic Principle: Mission organizations and member care workers have clear policies based on the legal and organizational limits of confidentiality. Ownership and accessibility to counseling and personnel records must be clarified in advance with staff. In general, staff have the right to determine how information which they have disclosed in confidence can be shared. Confidentiality procedures must be clarified for in-house consultants and counselors who are responsible to protect the interests of the organization in addition to the individual.

1. This case is filled with questionable confidentiality practices. First, the supervisor talks to Jean's wife, Anne, without his prior permission. Jean should be consulted about his "problems" and the supervisor should only speak wih outside parties,including Anne, with his consent.

2. The temporary secretary has access to Jean's files. This may or may not be appropriate, depending on the agency's policies regarding who has current and future access to important/confidential information.

3. Ms. Bartell has access to Jean's files without his knowledge. If counseling records are kept, it is important for him toknow how they will be stored and who will own them. For instance, will they be kept in the Personnel Department files or kept separate in Ms. Bartell's counseling files?

4. Ms. Bartell talks with Jean's supervisor and wife without his permission—Jean is bypassed again.

5. Ms. Bartell prays with the pastoral care team about Jean. The problem with this is that both the fact of counseling and the content of counseling are generally considered confidential unless policy states otherwise. It would have been well for Ms. Bartell to have Jean's permission to share in this team contect and then to disclose only material relevant for prayer while avoiding in-depth details about the case.

6. Ms. Bartell probably never discussed the legal or organizational limits of confidentiality before she rendered service. Some of these limits might include: a) being a danger to self (suicidal) or a danger to others, b) suspected child abuse and neglect, c) serious moral failure in the areas of sexuality or money, and d) serious problems which significantly impact one's job such as severe marital discord or chronic depression.

## Counselor/Consultant Competence

Basic Principle: Member care workers are dedicated to high standards of competence in the interest of the individuals and mission agencies which they serve. They recognize the limits of their training, experience, and skills and work only in those areas where they are qualified. They also endeavor to maintain and develop their competencies.

1. A fundamental issue in this case involves identifying where the actual problem lies. Does the real problem reside in Jean's internal struggles, his marriage, the way his department functions, and/or the organization's marginal member care services? So who really does have the problem after all? Furthermore, who in this organization can accurately assess and work with the problems which may exist at various levels of the organization?

2. Ms. Bartell listens and gives good advice. This is often necessary but usually not sufficient for more serious problems. She means well, but needs to consider her skill limitations. Consequently she appears to have little direction to her intervention and no treatment plan. Ms. Bartell's counseling strengths are probably more in the areas of support and encouragement.

3. Competence in one area or setting does not imply competence in another. For instance, with people from a different culture it is important to understand the limits of one's competence. Is Ms. Bartell familiar with French culture or issues relevant to cross-cultural marriages? She recommends that Jean be more "assertive" at work. Does she know how to assess or develop this skill in Jean in a culturally appropriate manner? Consultation with an experienced colleague is necessary when working outside of one's area of member care expertise.

4. There is another "dual relationship" issue here. Is Ms. Bartell's competence (objectivity and judgment) as a counselor impaired by virtue of her serving on a fund raising committee with Jean? Personal relationships and friendships are not necessarily incompatible with counseling—in many mission settings they are inevitable or possibly seen as appropriate, depending on the type of counseling services rendered—but they must be clarified.

## Use of Testing

Basic Principle: Only qualified individuals are to administer and interpret psychological, education, and vocational tests. Those who provide testing services safeguard their tests and take precautions to prevent the inappropriate use of test results. Individuals have the right to receive feedback on their test results and to know the basis for arriving at any recommendations and decisions.

1. There are many misuses of testing in this case. To begin, Ms. Bartell refers to the personality test results from the initial screening process done six years ago. Are the results still applicable?

2. In addition, did the personality test have norms for French or Europeans? In other words, with whom is Jean being compared on the test?

3. What does the depression scale on this test actually measure and what does a high score mean? Confirmation from other tests is needed to confidently determine serious maladjustment. Only one test was given in the screening process. Hence Ms. Bartell's *tentative* interpretation of the depression scale is accurate, although her attempt at interpretation is inappropriate.

4. Tests need to be administered, scored, and interpreted by a trained professional. Ms. Bartell's background does not qualify her to use tests. The supervisor's recommendation to borrow and use a temperament analysis test was also inappropriate.

5. Was the temperament analysis test valid with cross-cultural populations, given Jean's French background? How relevant would the information it provides be in Jean's situation even if there were French norms?

6. Tests can help guide decisions regarding candidacy, promotion, and transfers. Jean, though, should be apprised of what Ms. Bartell recommends to his supervisor and the basis for this recommendation. He should also receive feedback by a qualified person concerning the results of his temperament analysis test.

### Personal Values and Legal Standards

Basic Principle: Member care workers and mission leaders are aware of the values and standards held by the organization and the society in which they work, They are sensitive to how these values, as well as their own, might impact the agency and its staff.

Legal regulations regarding the provision of mental health services are understood and followed.

1. There may be a "quick fix" value operating within the agency. Evidence for this is seen in the suggestion that Jean take some time off, in trying to get at his root problem in four sessions, and in his being referred to a visiting leader. Mission agencies which value and rely primarily on quick approaches to change and healing (prayer, repentance, short-term counseling), may be doing their staff a disservice in cases where more intensive and lengthy care is needed.

2. Anne's "apathy and home responsibility struggles" raise a red flag which need to be explored by the supervisor. These symptoms may be an indication of depression or another serious problem. If there is serious dysfunction here, what are the legal obligations to report suicide potential or possible neglect of her children?

3. The supervisor seems to value Jean's job performance more than his adjustment and health. Perhaps Jean too! Is this a reflection of the organizational culture? Both values involving work effectiveness and individual well-being need to be emphasized and balanced.

4. Can Ms. Bartell legally receive payment (an "honorarium") from Jean for her services? Was the idea of payment even agreed upon in advance? In addition, can she represent herself as a counselor or provide counseling services within Czechoslovakia to nationals and charge a fee?

## Conclusion

Providing ethical member care is often a matter of applying a specific ethical principle to a particular member care situation. Would that it were always so simple, though! Many gray areas also exist, as the case study reveals. For example, what should be the balance between Jean's ultimate responsibility for his own well-being and the organization's responsibility for his well-being? Should Ms. Bartell provide services that challenge her to go beyond her sphere of competence in response to crises or the non-availability of others more qualified? And how should Jean (and other missionaries) balance their pursuit of personal fulfillment and growth with the call to sacrifice and suffering?

These are the types of ambiguous ethical questions faced by mission agencies today. Dealing with such inevitable ethical concerns is best accomplished through careful reflection, through regular consultation with mission leadership and colleagues, and through reference to written policies and ethical guidelines for

member care developed within the unique context of the mission agency.

### Questions for Discussion

1. How would you go about dealing with this case? List three things that you would do to help Jean and his family?

2. What suggestions would you make to the mission agency in this case to improve its member care program?

3. How important is it for a mission organization to have written ethical guidelines for its member care services? Does you mission organization have any written guidelines?

4. Are there other ethical principles besides the five discussed in this article that also need to be considered? What might these be?

5. Which ethical issues are mission agencies most likely to face? Which issues are most common within your organization?

## Suggested Readings

American Association of Pastoral Counselors (1986). *Code of ethics.* Fairfax, VA: Author

Augsburger, D. (1986). *Pastoral counseling across cultures.* Philadelphia: Westminister Press.

Board of Professional Affairs, American Psychological Association. (1987). *Guidelines for psychological practice with ethic and culturally diverse populations (draft).* Washington, D.C.: Author.

McGoldrick, M., Pearce, J., & Giordano, J. (Eds.). (1982). *Ethnicity and family therapy.* New York: Guilford Press.

O'Donnell, K. (1988) some suggested ethical guidelines for the delivery of mental health services in mission settings. In K. O'Donnell & M.

O'Donnell (Eds.). *Helping Missionaries Grow: Readings in mental health and missions* (466-479). Pasadena: William Carey Library.

O'Neill, PO. (1990). Responsible to whom? Responsible for what? Ethical issues in community intervention. *American Journal of Community Psychology, 17,* 323-342.

Pedersen, P. & Marsella, A. (1982). The ethical crisis for cross-cultural counseling and therapy. *Professional Psychology, 13,* 492-499.

Spitzer, R., Gibbon, M., Skodol, A., Williams, J., & First, M. (1989). International cases. *Diagnostic and statistics manual of mental disorders III—Revised: Case book.* (363-430). Washington, DC: American Psychiatric Press.

# 20

*Richard Gardner*
*Laura Mae Gardner*

# Supporting Mission Leaders

Mission leaders are people who have responded to God's call to be part of the world-wide evangelization effort. In addition to the mission agencies they serve, they are usually responsible to and supported by a local church or churches. Like pioneer missionaries, they need to be strong, hardy, disciplined individuals, who are creative, devoted to the Lord, willing to take risks, and eager to serve others.

As with other missionaries, leaders may have come from dysfunctional family backgrounds. Such individuals often bring considerable personal pain with them, and may compensate with dysfunctional coping behavior. In spite of personal strengths and talents, mission leaders, whatever their family backgrounds, are not immune to personal characteristics and problems which can lead to conflict, misunderstanding, and frustration on the part of their staff and other leaders both on the field and at home.

Mission leaders are constantly faced with some difficult challenges. Apart from overseeing and supporting their staff, they must also concern themselves with an assortment of ministry and logistical matters. One survey of North American mission executives (Johnston, 1988), for example, identified several of these challenges. Some of these included maintaining a good relationship between the mission and churches, working in nations where there is governmental and social opposition to the gospel, finding appropriate personnel for ministry needs, utilizing untrained field leadership, educating MKs, developing effective church planting approaches, redeploying staff, training national leaders, and raising financial support.

In our efforts to fulfill the requirements of our position as International Coordinators of Wycliffe's Counseling Services and Personnel, we find ourselves having to balance several areas: counseling and administration, private life and ministry, and the demands of being responsible for over 6,000 adult members and their over 4,000 dependent children scattered around the world while still keeping ourselves sane and healthy, and our marriage intact and thriving. It's a challenge! We have personally had to learn the importance of self-care, time with God and friends, a therapeutic network of consulting professionals and caring colleagues, and an emotional network for debriefing and support after heavy outlays of energy. So we speak with first-hand awareness of the draining nature of mission administration and also with experiential awareness of the needs that mission leaders have for supportive care.

The thrust of this chapter, then, is to discuss ways to support mission leaders in the difficult jobs they have embraced. Practical means of encouragement and care are explored to support them both as people and in their roles as leaders. The chapter also includes three brief case studies, two of which involved the Wycliffe Counseling Department, to illustrate how field leaders can benefit from the services of a mission agency's member care program.

## Why Support Mission Leaders?

Every mission leader needs sympathetic, concrete support from friends, colleagues, member care workers, and family members, in order to be effective in leadership. Supportive care is essential to weather the many challenges that leaders face. Let's take a closer look at what these challenges look like for different types of leaders and settings.

1. There may be a strong and individualistic, often opinionated, usually diverse mission team, department, and community. Diversity on every parameter may exist in a single location: age (old and young); experience (new staff and old-timers); marital status (singles and married); country of origin (some fields have up to 20 nationalities represented in their membership); job description (support services, evangelism ministries, training responsibilities); organizational hierarchy (top-level administrators to short-term clerical workers); spiritual experiences (fundamental, charismatic, liturgical denominations) and so on. Managing such diversity takes grace, skill, and cooperative efforts from others.

2. A leader who may be new to his job, untrained for it, and overwhelmed by it. In some small entities, the group of missionaries chooses their leader by popular vote. It could be (and often is the case) that an innovative and hard-working missionary is chosen to be the next field superintendent, such choice based on the respect the membership extends to this member rather than administrative experience or managerial skills.

Further, there may be little warning that one will be asked to take on a new job assignment involving greater leadership skills.

3. Secular management principles developed for business and industry in the home country often do not fit an international team context. Few management books, for example, cover the effective use of multinational teams, especially those whose members are spiritually motivated and who technically are classified as volunteers. It is seldom easy to get a job done in a foreign country through a team of workers from many cultures.

4. Field leaders are often alone. They may have an assistant or an associate, or an executive committee which meets a few times each year; but they seldom have an experienced administrative team around them to serve as a sounding board or to distribute the responsibility and minimize the pressure.

5. The complexity of situations facing field leaders is daunting. For example, how can a leader send a struggling field member back to his/her supporting country when great harm and set-back will come to the field program by the member's loss? Or how does a leader help a mission community work through a significant crisis or trauma? Further, how does a leader find quality time to attend to staff needs, work requirements, family life, and the local community? Leaders are called upon to make difficult decisions that will affect others' lives.

### Special Needs

Extra measures of support are needed for leaders who carry multifaceted responsibilities. An example is the leader who has final responsibility for staff welfare and ministry effectiveness as well as for the continuance of the organization in a given region or host country.

The leader who is responsible for the care of members and their children is likely also to need personalized support: house parents at boarding schools, personnel officers, pastoral counselors, field coaches, and so on. Young leaders, leaders who work in isolated areas, and leaders entering into new roles and positions need special support.

In addition, supportive care is needed for leaders who tend to work too hard and carry out responsibilities to the detriment of their own person or family. They are likely to need help in identifying and responding to family needs and personal health needs.

Who then, is likely to require additional supportive services? There are several: those who bear the responsibility for the welfare of the members, responsibility to the host country, and accountability to the organization as a whole and the organization's constituency; those whose primary task is the care of others; those who are in new positions or in isolated areas; and those whose tendency is to care for others before self and family.

## What Type of Supportive Care is Needed?

Leaders such as mission executives, department heads, supervisors, and ministry directors need to be aware of and have access to all the resources available to them. Setting up a solid network of member care services is one of the most important ways to provide supportive care. Sometimes these services may involve contacting outside agencies, such as obtaining legal counsel in an international matter. Usually, though, these services can be provided through in-house staff, such as sending in a member care team to help a leader work through a conflict at a mission station. Mission agencies would do well to periodically assess the needs of their leaders and staff, and to make sure that relevant member care services are in place to support and nurture them. Here are some examples of services which we provide through our International Counseling Department in Wycliffe.

Our counselors can offer a variety of services to Wycliffe leaders. These services range from preventive activities (leadership orientation that includes personal care, time and people management, maintaining spousal and familial relationships) to counseling (individual leaders and their families) to responses to crisis and disaster.

A counselor can add insight to the assessment committees who are considering the health and hardiness of candidates and potential leaders. If psychological testing is done at the point of entry into the organization, a specially trained counselor can interpret the instrument(s) and provide skillful feedback to the candidate.

Counselors may be called upon to serve as consultants to their administrators or mission leaders, giving input into organizational policies pertaining to personnel, or providing understanding in diagnosis of problem situations (low production, conflicted relationships, communication difficulties, authority problems, personal issues having to do with work stress, depression, burnout) or family concerns (developmental issues such as reentry, furlough, retirement). A mission leader may have a member needing therapeutic help but may be wondering what kind of help to provide, how long a time must be granted to obtain such help, or how to evaluate whether healing has occurred at the end of therapy. A staff counselor may be his/her best source of advice.

Counselors are also equipped to do team building to support team leaders and their teams. They can help teams work together more productively by increasing their awareness of personality differences, communication and learning styles, job issues, and cross-cultural perspectives.

Not to be overlooked is the fact that many counselors are good researchers who can scrutinize trends, populations, and literature, adapting materials to the mission team, and advising leaders in proactive ways. They can also resource leaders with important articles and materials related to the needs, care, and effectiveness of staff.

### Additional Supportive Resources

Here are some suggestions for further developing member care services for mission leaders and their staff.

1. Train and provide more counselors for closer-to-the-field services, perhaps located in large cities or port cities where many missionaries pass through, or on large field centers. Counselors who are bi-lingual and bi-cultural are especially needed.

2. Establish counseling departments on the field, staffed by two or more mental health workers, including a male and female counselor. The ideal is to have sufficient staff so that one counselor is always available for field trips without sacrificing ongoing contributions. Such staffing would make case consultations possible as well as collegue support, joint workshops, and the development of written materials. It would also decrease the counseling load of field leaders.

3. Include member care workers as part of the staff of mission schools. Counselors are needed, for instance, who are skilled in working with adolescents, children, and parents. They could also provide written resources, present seminars on family issues and personal growth, and be available to the school leadership for counseling or consultation.

4. In general, develop additional services and member care-related materials: bulletins, seminars, workshops, and retreats on topics such as marriage enrichment, conflict resolution, parenting, singleness, stage-of-life issues (new-baby workshops, parenting adolescents, letting the children go, parenting adult children, menopause, final reentry to the home country, retirement, death of a spouse), and topical materials for specific situations (infertility, grief issues, transitions). Recording selected seminars on video can increase the range of services.

## Illustrative Situations

The following three stories describe some of the personal and work-related problems that affect mission leaders. These accounts illustrate how leaders can use member care workers and resources to deal with and prevent problem situations. The first two stories are based on situations which required services from the Wycliffe Counseling Department. Each story is disguised so as to assure confidentiality. The third story is hypothetical and one which we use as a teaching tool.

### Story One: A Marriage Is in Trouble

Frank and Jessie felt God's call to missions, paid off their debts, joined Wycliffe, took all the linguistic, cross-cultural and survival training, and went off to Africa with their children. Assigned to a language group, they made friends, completed a preliminary analysis of the language, and were off to a good start on their linguistic and literacy tasks. Several from the host culture were interested in helping them because of their desire to have the Scriptures in their own language.

Frank and Jessie went on furlough; just before their return, the missionaries from that region had their field conference and elected Frank to be their director. The reasoning was that Frank was a self-starter, good organizer, friendly, and able to motivate others—in short, an obvious leader.

Frank had to take office immediately, and there was so much that needed to be done that he could not get back out to the village to pack up the family house and bring their living goods into the central city. Jessie tried to explain to the villagers that they did not know when they would be back. She brought all their language materials to the city, hoping she could continue working on the translation project.

No one thought about Jessie—what she would do as part of Frank's new role. A shy but very competent linguist, she found that she was expected to do what no one else wanted to do—be hostess, secretary, confidant of all, and interpreter of Frank to those who disagreed with him. At times she functioned as both parents, since Frank had to travel a lot both within the country and to international meetings. He had little time for her and the kids. Household repairs did not get done. Jessie was expected to oversee all the family business plus do the correspondence and record keeping.

Filled with grief over the lost language role and relationships, Jessie had no time to grieve because she was trying to keep up with "dynamo-Frank." She sank into depression. Frank got further behind in his work responsibilities, as he dealt with member conflicts, pettiness, low production, crises of machinery as well as people; he was becoming more and more cynical.

Many times Jessie thought of giving up, running away, quitting. She and Frank started out as partners and colleagues in the village and the language program; now she was shut out of his life, and it seemed there was no future for her.

*What happened?* The Area Director who was over Frank realized what was happening and called for help from the Counseling Department, located in the United States. The Department sent a counselor team (husband and wife) to the field to hold retreats for directors and their wives, and to spend time with Frank and Jessie and other couples. The counselors spent several sessions with Frank and Jessie: they listened long, heard and understood the problems, opened communication channels between husband and wife, and helped them come to new understanding of each other. Frank and Jessie made a new commitment to their marriage and family, and developed some realistic strategies for coping—things the wife could do for herself, what she could do for her husband, what he could do for her, what the administrator could do for both, and what both needed to seek God to do for them. As a result of the retreat and personal counseling, Frank and Jessie readjusted their priorities and lifestyle so as to work together and enjoy each other again.

### Story Two: Children's Home Parents

Joe and Jane had two small children. Believing that raising their children as well as ministering to others' children was one of the greatest jobs they could do for God, they applied and were accepted as children's home parents. After membership procedures and minimal orientation, they were assigned to one of the nine children's homes in an area of Africa. The high rate of turnover due to burnout meant that new home parents were always needed.

They took on the job of parenting 10 teen-age boys, four who were adopted, and all of them children of parents who were part of language teams. It took exactly two months to convince Joe and Jane that they were in the wrong job—two of the boys were depressed, one was utterly uncommunicative, two were failing in school probably due to loneliness and not fitting in, and two were rebellious and acting out. In addition, their three-year-old daughter had become afraid of one of the boys and was having nightmares. Joe and Jane had little experience with teenagers, did not understand the emotional issues associated with being adopted, and were not really sure of what they were supposed to do as home parents.

*What happened?* Joe and Jane called the local Wycliffe counselor for help as well as the Counseling Department in the United States. Specific issues were identified which helped Joe and Jane see that they required additional background experience and preparation to do their work effectively. They were motivated to read up on childhood development and needs, to understand problems from the perspectives of MKs, and to consult with others more experienced than themselves.

Joe and Jane realized their most urgent need was to minister to the seven boys who were struggling with their feelings, behavior, and/or school performance. Another urgent matter was to find out what was going on with their three-year-old daughter who was displaying strong fear toward one of the teenagers. Had she been molested, or teased in a malicious way? Was she reacting to having less time with her parents, and to having her home "invaded" by ten strangers? The counselor on-site helped Joe and Jane deal with the pressing and urgent issues, and a visiting member care team helped to identify broader issues for attention by both children's home parents and those who oversaw the various children's homes.

As a result of these interventions, the screening process for home parents was revised, the pre-field orientation for the job was improved, and closer supervision in the early stages of house parents' field assignments was provided. In addition, the entire children's home situation would be monitored more closely.

### Story Three: What's This About Holiness?

Theft, substance abuse, violence, sexual deviance, spousal abuse, and unfaithfulness: Do these occur among missionaries and leaders? Yes, they do. Few things demoralize and discourage members and leaders more than to learn that these things have happened within one's mission community. Consider the following hypothetical case.

A husband-wife team was working in a very remote part of the country, and received little supervision. When the husband asked for a tutor for their four school-age children (ages 6, 7, 9, 11) the regional mission administrator felt he should provide such assistance. The couple had not been very productive and were strangely resistant to requests for reports, assignments to attend linguistic workshops, and never participated as an entire family in field conferences. Thinking that a tutor would not only provide needed service, but a window into the family's field practices, the administrator sent out the only person available, a 23-year-old, first-term Australian teacher, Susan.

Eager to contribute to Bible translation in this way, Susan quickly attracted and won the affection of the children. Almost as quickly she noticed that 11-year-old Grace was deeply troubled about something. After confidence had been built, Grace confided in Susan that the primary language helper for her father, a respected evangelical in the community, had molested her when she was nine years old. She had told her parents, who told her to keep still about it so as not to offend this man. Grace was displaying abnormal fears toward the nationals, and spent most of her time in her room. Her essays and poetry seemed bleak and spoke often of death.

In spite of these hints of trouble, Susan tried hard to fit into family life, and helped out with housework as much as her time allowed. One day while cleaning in the husband's study, she uncovered a stack of pornographic magazines that showed signs of constant use. Not knowing what to say or to whom, Susan decided to say nothing. After all, she was not married, and didn't understand men very well—she was brought up with sisters and a very protective mother. That night, though, she went to the kitchen for a glass of water around 10 p.m., found the husband and wife arguing, and observed that the husband's voice was quite slurred. They stopped talking while she drank her water, but as she was walking down the hall, she heard the wife cry out as if in pain. The next morning, the wife's face was swollen, but no one said anything. Susan didn't either.

Susan finished up the school term and returned to the field headquarters. She was debriefed by the school director and found herself confiding in him the story of Grace's fears and preoccupation with death. Then the school official, a mission leader himself, asked if she had observed other behavior in the family that troubled her. Susan told about the pornographic materials and what she thought was drinking and abusive behavior on the husband's part toward his wife.

*What happened?* The following steps were taken in response to this situation.

1. The school director asked Susan to write up for him each vignette that had troubled her, being as specific, factual, and complete as possible. The school director took this document and went to the leader of the work in that country; together they prayerfully considered their next steps.

2. They informed the Vice President for Personnel (VPP) in the home country, and requested the latest legislation and guidelines for moral conduct of members. They reported to the VPP that their next efforts would be an on-site attempt to determine true details, seriousness of the problem(s), and openness to intervention and help. They had a long-distance conversation with the counselor assigned to their continent, who guided their proposed plan of action.

3. The school director and the director for the work in that country went together to the village location to meet with the husband and wife. They carefully but courageously asked the hard questions to determine the extent of the problem.

4. At first angry and defensive, full of denial, then rationalizing, the husband and wife broke down and confessed their discouragement and despair, their battle with loneliness and isolation, his violent behavior under the influence of alcohol, his pornography, and her depression and suicidal gestures. Both expressed grief over Grace's being the victim of sexual abuse and molestation by the national worker, but had little idea as to how that had impacted her. They had not been intentionally naive or neglectful, but honestly thought they had no alternatives and that Grace would forget the experience.

5. The school director and the director of the work in that country confronted the national who allegedly abused Grace. They informed his pastor and the local authorities.

6. A tentative plan of action was drawn up whereby the family would be returned to their home country, and be assigned to receive individual and family therapy from the mission counselor. For Grace's sake, the mission leaders and the parents were willing to consider a change of assignment rather than insist that the family return to the setting that had caused her so much grief. The services of the mission counselor provided perspective in what might have been addressed in primarily a disciplinary fashion, allowing acknowledgement, confession, and the process of healing to begin to take place. Additionally, the mission counselor arranged for therapy for all members of the family, and stood by to help the family choose the next assignment after completion of therapy.

While this hypothetical story turned out well, there could have easily been a negative outcome. Consider the following two alternate sequels. What would you do if you were the mission leaders?

*Alternate Sequel One.* Arriving at the village home of the couple, the leaders found their gentle queries met with hostility, denial, and threats against Susan and against the organization's education department. As a long-term result, the family withdrew even further from mission activities in that country, resisting even more administrative attempts to elicit information or to supervise their life and work. At this point, the mission leaders needed help to decide on how to minister to Susan, how to intervene administratively, and whether to take disciplinary action.

*Alternate Sequel Two.* The leaders find that the situation in the family has deteriorated noticeably by the time of their arrival, and that the family has made the decision to resign from the organization and continue in their indigenous setting as independent (therefore unsupervised) workers. The leaders reluctantly accept this decision, and withdraw their involvement which is clearly unwanted. The next news the mission leaders have about the family is the report that the wife has left home, having run away from the husband during an abusive event, and is living with another man in a nearby village. Reports begin to come to the leaders from an angry constituency, demanding to know why the leaders had not been more vigorous in getting help for this couple.

## Final Thoughts

A wise worker knows how to use and take care of the tools of his or her trade. Similarly, mission leaders are called upon to skillfully develop and utilize supportive resources for both themselves and the mission community they oversee.

> There must be a prevailing attitude of commitment to growth, to maturity, and to excellence throughout the mission. This would be expressed intellectually, spiritually, socially, and technically by encouraging the reading of specific books, by attendance at retreats and seminars, by in-service training, by guidance and counseling, and by regular vacations. Such a commitment, modeled and verbalized by mission leaders, would move an entire mission into a proactive sphere where people/members become important as individuals and not just producers. (L. Gardner, 1987, p. 313)

Leaders then, must take the initiative to see that appropriate member care resources are available and that all members of the mission—including themselves—are taking advantage of these resources.

## Questions for Discussion

1. What are some of the greatest sources of stress for leaders in your mission organization?

2. Which supportive services do leaders who work as local administrators and those who work as regional directors need, to make their job easier and keep their lives in balance?

3. What can be done to encourage leaders to utilize the supportive services that are available?

4. How would you have handled the problems described in the third story at the end of this article?

5. What would be important items to include in a leadership development program? How would you set up such a program?

# References

Gardner, L. (1987). Proactive care of missionary personnel. *Journal of Psychology and Theology, 15,* 308-314.

Johnston, L. (1988). Building relationships between mental health specialists and mission agencies. In O'Donnell, K. & O'Donnell, M. (Eds.). *Helping missionaries grow: Readings in mental health and missions* (pp. 449-457). Pasadena, CA: William Carey Library.

# PART FIVE
## FUTURE DIRECTIONS

# Part Five
# Future Directions

*Michele Lewis O'Donnell*

Consulting Editor

This final section looks at some of the ways in which member care services can be strategically developed and provided. The essence of this section can be summarized in Proverbs 20:18, which instructs us to "prepare plans by consultation, and to make war by wise guidance." Member care, like warfare, is a serious matter, requiring mutual consultation, wisdom, and cooperative endeavors to be successful.

The first article highlights many of the existing needs and opportunities for further developing the member care field. As such it serves as both an introductory article for this section and a summary challenge for the entire volume.

The author, Dr. Kelly O'Donnell, begins by pointing out that on an inter-agency and more global level, the field of member care is relatively unorganized. This is followed by a brief overview of the member care resources that are currently available. The bulk of the article concentrates on suggestions for expanding and improving member care through planning, mobilization, training, innovative services, and research/writing. Kelly also discusses how member care as a coordinated endeavor might be launched and monitored and what trends the field might expect in the future. The article closes with both a caution and a charge: member care must never become an end in itself; moreover, it must keep pace with the rapidly growing missions force, especially that of the Two-Thirds World.

In the second article, Dr. Gary Strauss and Kathy Narrramore provide an encouraging example of how churches can actively partner with mission agencies to care for their missionaries. Based upon the model of the Antioch church in the book of Acts, the authors develop several helpful guidelines for the policies and practices of the sending church. This is followed by an account of how their home church is working to apply these concepts in each of the developmental phases of the life of the missionary from candidacy to retirement.

One of the striking aspects of this article is the emphasis given to the various stages of pre-field preparation. Gary and Nancy emphasize that the sending church is in a unique position to nurture potential candidates and oversee the personal and relational well-being of those being appointed—areas often overlooked or incomplete in formal training. In addition, they describe how the sending church can provide missionaries with mentoring and accountability in the context of a committed relationship. Many churches may not have the wealth of material and personnel resources available to them like the one described in this article. Nevertheless, the authors present a practical model from which other sending churches can gain useful insights.

The third article in Part Five deals with the utilization of mental health professionals in the member care endeavor. Richard and Laura Mae Gardner examine the preparation and use of member care workers with a particular emphasis on the role of the professionally trained counselor or therapist. Students and mental health professionals interested in member care involvement, along with mission administrators, will appreciate the practical approach the authors take. Richard and Laura Mae discuss selection factors, training and preparation, guidelines for in-house and outside providers, suggestions for mission administrators, and the continuing growth and education of member care workers.

Next, Dr. Brent Lindquist, in his article on missionary support centers, describes and builds upon his experience with this specialized and, as yet, relatively unique member care approach. His article is infused with realism regarding the challenges and potential obstacles facing those who would attempt to establish similar centers. At the same time he is undaunted in his challenge to the missions and mental health community to develop this type of resource. He emphasizes that both a clear philosophy of ministry and a pragmatic development strategy which includes a sound marketing plan are essential to the success of such an effort. The strength of this article is contained in the thoughtful and thought-provoking questions Brent raises with respect to the planning, development, and maintenance of missionary support centers outside of North America. The article closes with two proposal summaries for setting up such centers.

The final article describes a structure for facilitating member care at both an intra-agency and inter-agency level. The "member care consultation," as outlined by Hans Ritchard, provides a forum for dialogue which calls upon representatives from the whole missions community—from mission leaders and missionary personnel to member care providers. Hans views this people mix as critical in order to adequately identify and resource the needs of missionary personnel.

This article will be of real service to those planning a consultation, on whatever scale, as it offers many practical examples and suggestions for setting up such an event. At the same time it addresses some of the conceptual and theoretical underpinnings of consultations. I am convinced that the type of member care consultation envisioned by Hans has the potential to be a dynamic tool for organizing member care on a more global level. Further, it would be particularly valuable in the efforts of Western and Two-Thirds World missionaries as they collaborate in the development and delivery of member care.

Where then is the field of member care headed? And where does it *need* to head? I believe the most strategic direction can be summarized as follows: To pursue cooperative endeavors between mission organizations—especially including mission agencies and sending churches from the Two-Thirds World—which can develop additional, innovative member care resources that are prioritized and channeled towards missionary personnel working in the least evangelized areas and people groups. As Todd Johnson (1990) points out:

> If the "whole world is to be filled with the knowledge of the glory of the Lord," a major change in direction is needed in the present method of locating missionaries both at home and overseas. It can be summed up in a phrase: deploy them among the least evangelized. (p. 105)

A similar charge might be aimed at current and potential member care workers. As the number of member care providers expands in the coming years, where and how can they be most strategically placed? What types of specialized training and experience will be needed to deal with the unique challenges of particular frontier settings and the burgeoning numbers of missionary personnel from the Two-Thirds World? And when will mission support centers, inter-agency consultations, and other member care resources be established to serve missionary personnel who have prioritized work among unevangelized areas and people groups? These are the crucial questions—and the directions—which the missions community must pursue as it seeks to both adequately care for its people and faithfully fulfill the Great Commission.

## References

Johnson, T. (1990). Editorial: The fatal attraction of pseudo-frontier mission. *International Journal of Frontier Missions, 7,* 105-106.

# 21

*Kelly O'Donnell*

# An Agenda for Member Care in Missions

One of the pressing issues facing the missions community today is the care of its people. This is especially true of those who are pioneering work in areas where isolation, social opposition, political unrest, spiritual warfare, and a lack of supportive care can incapacitate even the most robust, committed missionaries. Missionaries need, and usually appreciate, all the supportive resources they can get. It is not enough to simply send out strong workers into the fields. These workers must also be maintained and nurtured, and not only for their own sakes, but ultimately for the long-term impact on the people who are the focus of their ministry.

Missionary care, referred to in this article as *member care,* is being increasingly recognized as an essential ingredient of mission strategy. Member care can be defined as the investment of resources by mission agencies, sending churches, and related mission organizations to nurture and develop missionary personnel. Services which help prevent problems, support staff, and aid in restoration lie within the member care domain. Some examples include leadership training, pastoral counseling, reentry orientation, crisis intervention, prayer groups, and the overall encouragement that missionaries provide each other. Member care focuses on everyone in the mission, on adults as well as children, on candidates as well as those retiring from the field (O'Donnell and O'Donnell, 1990).

Member care, at the more global level, remains a relatively unorganized practice and an underdeveloped mission strategy within the missions community in general. For example, apart from the previous three International Conferences on Missionary Kids (1984, 1987, 1989), which largely emphasized the needs of missionary children and families, there has been no major inter-agency gathering at an international level for member care providers. Neither has member care received much attention at such influential conferences as Lausanne II in Manila (1989) and the Congress on the Holy Spirit and World Evangelization in Indianapolis (1990). Yet member care should be a core ingredient of any global missionary strategy. It is to be a standard feature, not an optional luxury (O'Donnell and O'Donnell, 1991).

Shifting to the individual agency level, however, there are several noteworthy member care programs—Wycliffe Bible Translators, the Southern Baptist Convention, and The Evangelical Alliance Mission, to name a few (described in chapter one). Most mission boards, agencies, and mission leaders are in fact quite committed to the care and nurture of their people. There are of course exceptions to this, but on the whole the importance of member care is receiving greater recognition within most mission organizations.

My purpose in writing this article is to explore some of the ways to further develop and coordinate member care services. Careful planning and mutual consultation will be needed between mission organizations, sending churches, and member care workers. It is my conviction that most of these additional member care resources need to be developed and deployed to support those missionaries and agencies working with the least evangelized people groups. Filidis (1990) aptly puts it this way:

> The sheer quantity of need vying for the attention of committed missions-minded Christians, requires a ranking of global mission priorities....To deploy large numbers of mission personnel in areas where viable churches already exist, or in harvest fields where Christian workers have already been sowing, reaping, and re-sowing year after year would therefore be strategically unwise. (p.3).

The goal then, is not just raising up more member care resources. Rather the goal—or *agenda*, if you will—is to strategically raise up and direct these resources so as to put greater closure on the Great Commission.

## Member Care Update

It is encouraging to note the many contributions to member care that have already been made. Here is a quick overview of some of the key materials, organizations, and other resources that are available.

1. *Books*. Many books have been written to address the various challenges of missionary life and missionary development. Some titles include Marjory Foyle's (1987) *Overcoming Missionary Stress, Manual for Today's Missionary* by Marjorie Collins (1986), Bill Taylor's (1991) edited work *Internationalizing Missionary Training*, and the compilation of readings edited by Kelly and Michele O'Donnell (1988) entitled *Helping Missionaries Grow*.

2. *Articles.* Several journals and magazines regularly publish articles on missionary care topics. Included here are *Evangelical Missions Quarterly, Journal of Psychology and Theology, Journal of Psychology and Christianity,* and the *International Bulletin of Missionary Research.*

3. *Conferences.* The International Conference on Missionary Kids (ICMK) has met three times since 1984 to discuss the needs of MKs and their families. There has been considerable interest in holding future meetings at a regional level throughout the world, an example of which is the 1992 "European Children of Missionaries Education and Training" conference held in the Netherlands. The Interdenominational Foreign Missions Association (IFMA) and the Evangelical Foreign Missions Association (EFMA) periodically address member care items as part of their conference programs. Each year Missionary Internship offers a workshop where personnel directors in missions can meet together. In addition, the annual Mental Health and Missions Conference in Indiana, now in its eleventh year, and the recently established Enabling the Missionary Consultation in California provide forums to network and discuss member care issues.

4. *Courses.* Several courses exist to train member care providers who have a call to missions. Youth With A Mission in England has developed a three month Pastoral Support School. Both Rosemead School of Psychology and Fuller School of Psychology have graduate elective courses entitled Mental Health and Missions, and Regent College has a master's program in counseling and missions.

5. *Organizations.* Several independent groups provide training, counseling, and orientation services to missionaries. Link Care in California and Missionary Internship in Michigan are two of the most utilized. The Narramore Christian Foundation, Interaction, and Barnabas International are also noteworthy. Makahiki Ministries provides housing for missionaries on furlough or who need a period of rest. Mu Kappa is a fraternity organization on university campuses to support MKs. Several Christian mental health professionals donate part-time consultation services to mission agencies, with some regularly traveling overseas to consult.

6. *Research.* The MK Consultation and Resource Team (MK-CART) is a group which coordinates research on MKs and their families. According to Dr. Leslie Andrews (1989) of MK-CART, between 1985 and 1989 there were over 35 graduate theses from American universities and seminaries in areas relating to the missionary family alone. There is also considerable research being done by mission consultants and mission agencies themselves on member care topics.

7. *Mission Agencies.* Many mission agencies have set up specific departments to oversee the provision of member care services. The names of the departments vary—such as personnel development, personnel services, pastoral services, and international counseling ministries—yet their existence reflects the priority which mission agencies have placed on the care of their people.

## Cooperative Endeavors

The above seven areas point to the increased attention being given to missionary care and development. Building upon this foundation, I believe the next step should be in the direction of inter-organizational endeavors to develop and coordinate member care resources around the world. The time is right for this to happen.

Why is this so? There are three reasons. First, I believe the Lord is calling the missions community to prepare for what may very well be the final evangelistic thrust into the unreached peoples of the earth. God is raising up and developing a variety of supportive ministries to help reach these peoples—for example, intercessory prayer, spiritual warfare, Scripture translation, financial resources, and member care. In light of this, member care is best understood as playing a significant part in the broad, integrated, and Spirit-inspired plan to fulfill the Great Commission.

Second, the phenomenal growth in the number of missionaries in general requires a similar rise in supportive services and personnel. Barrett (1990) estimates that in 1990 there were 3,970 foreign mission agencies and 285,250 career foreign missionaries (Protestant and Catholic). By the year 2000 the estimate is up to 4,800 mission agencies and 400,000 missionaries. This growth is certainly good news! Yet keeping this new wave of missionaries healthy and effective will take some doing. It will necessitate the development of additional member care resources—such as field coaches, in-service training, and missionary support centers—born out of cooperative efforts between agencies.

Finally, there is a sufficient "critical mass" of member care resources with which to work. The last several years have witnessed an unprecedented increase in personnel, consultants, written materials, conferences, seminars, and organizations committed to the care and growth of missionaries. In fact, member care as a practice (though needing additional coordination and direction) has reached the point where it can now be considered a specialized field within missions.

# A Proposed Agenda

I would like to outline several ideas for further developing member care resources and services. What follows is part visionary statement, part needs assessment, describing some of the major cutting edges of this field. My suggestions are just that—suggestions. They are intended to stimulate additional discussion and hopefully be expanded and modified by others. They are also as applicable to the general missions community as they are to those working in frontier missions. I address five basic areas: planning, mobilization, training, innovative services, and research/writing.

*1. Planning*

One of the most important initial steps for promoting and coordinating member care would be to form an inter-organizational task force. This would be a planning team comprised of seven to twelve people who are respected and actively involved in member care. This planning team could possibly be set up as one of the Task Forces for the AD 2000 and Beyond organization. Individuals from such groups as Link Care, ICMK, IFMA, EFMA, the Mental Health and Missions conference, graduate training programs, and others, would be represented within this group. The intent would be to include a diversity of people who represent different disciplines and member care perspectives—mission leaders, mental health professionals, human resource specialists, and professors.

The task force would meet two or more times a year to pray, plan projects, and make recommendations for the overall member care field. Clerical support would be a must to help carry out the chosen projects. Participants would serve for a few years and then others would be periodically rotated into this group. Here are a list of important projects that this group could help oversee.

a. Develop a referral list of individuals and organizations who can provide professional services to missionaries around the world. Put this on a data base and have it available at key places. Keep this updated. Possibly write up a resource and referral manual based on this information. There would be some security issues involved in compiling such a list, and safeguards would be in order.

b. Oversee the writing of occasional papers to help give greater direction and clarity to the field. Some examples would be papers on the current status of member care in missions, member care practices in mission agencies from the Two-Thirds World, cross-cultural issues in member care, member care opportunities for sending churches, services available for missionaries at different stages of missionary life, and annotated bibliographies on member care areas which draw on articles form non-Western countries.

c. Plan a regular international conference on member care. This would serve as a strategic forum to exchange ideas, network, and coordinate member care efforts. Be sure to encourage the attendance and participation of missionary personnel from the Two-Thirds World. Also encourage member care topics to be an integral part of mission conferences. Plenary sessions, workshops, and poster sessions would be excellent avenues to highlight and discuss such topics.

d. Send out a regular newsletter to inform and link the member care community together. The newsletter would be a means to exchange ideas and share information.

e. Explore ways to set up regional, inter-organizational task forces at key locations around the world, especially areas within the "10-40 Window." These would meet together regularly to pray, plan, and further develop member care in each respective region.

f. Consider setting up a "Member Care Association" which can support and provide networking opportunities to member care workers. This type of association may start off as a regional chapter and expand into a larger organization (Rogers, 1991).

## 2. Mobilization

There are many potential member care workers who are currently either studying or working in a related area. Many have an interest in missions, but are not sure what steps to take to become more involved either part-time or full-time. Opportunities and guidelines for involvement could be shared with them through articles, brochures, at conferences, and through personal contact.

a. Focus on undergraduates in Christian universities who are preparing for the behavioral and human service fields. There are many opportunities to speak in classes about missions and member care. Having member care representatives at student conferences like Urbana and Europe 90 would be key. Students need to be challenged and understand how they could practically prepare for involvement in this field.

b. Focus on graduate students in Christian schools who are pursuing degrees in psychology, counseling, and related areas. Conduct chapels, visit classes, provide information, give ideas for research, and encourage the formation of a support group for students committed to missions.

c. Encourage professionals around the world to be more involved in services to missionaries. Do not limit this to just North Americans or Westerners. Professionals may also be encouraged to financially support other professionals working in member care areas.

d. Recruit retired missionaries and current personnel to provide member care services. Writing letters of encouragement, running a Bible study, being available for counseling, and doing some work for the personnel department would be examples.

e. Explore practical ways in which sending churches can increase their involvement in member care. Using materials from the Association of Church Mission Committees or having church leaders do field visitations are examples. Cooperation with mission agencies in the preparation and on-field support of staff is key.

## 3. Training

Training programs in member care areas are needed, as are continuing education opportunities for member care workers. It would be helpful to develop a missions component or track within several existing graduate programs in counseling, psychology, and human resources. Likewise it would be important to include a member care track in seminaries and mission departments.

a. Develop member care tracks in Christian graduate schools. Identify several key programs in which to develop such a track. Some possible schools would be those represented at the Rech Conference, which focused on training issues for Christian graduate programs in psychology (Tan & Jones, 1991).

As part of the training, include a core course on "member care in missions" as well as the "Perspectives on the World Christian Movement" course. Where there is no specialized track available, consider offering a three day seminar, or better, an elective course on member care. Also develop practicums and internships with supervision for students wanting to prepare for work in member care. Include practical short-term experience overseas in a missionary role as part of the training.

b. Organize seminars and workshops on member care areas at conferences where there is an interest in member care in missions. Examples would include the conferences sponsored by the IFMA/EFMA, the Christian Association for Psychological Studies, the Association of Christian Schools International, and the International Conference on Christian Counseling. Also continue to provide workshops at ongoing conferences related to member care, e.g., Enabling the Missionary, Mental Health and Missions Conference, and ICMK.

c. Encourage and provide workshops for member care workers within mission agencies themselves. Train missionaries in basic people-helping skills, either pre-field or else while they are on the field. This would strengthen their ability to offer mutual support to each other. Team, department, and ministry leaders would be strategic candidates for this training. Training could be done in coordination with several programs, such as the Pastoral Counseling Institute or YWAM's College of Counseling and Health Care.

d. Hold member care consultations and conferences at different places around the world. Include nationals as part of the steering committee. Regional consultations will provide a sharper focus and greater opportunity for specific issues to be discussed.

## 4. Innovative Services

Mission agencies usually wrestle with the realities of finite resources—funds, staff, office space, and services. Creativity and lots of perseverance are called for when trying to provide member care within mission agencies as well as for the missions community at large. Member care personnel are encouraged to channel their current skills and strengths in new ways, to experiment, to innovate, and to initiate helpful changes.

a. Start missionary support/care centers around the world. These would be places where missionaries could go for rest, restoration, and further training without having to return to their home country. They would also hopefully be staffed by multinational and multilinguistic individuals, representing different organizations and different disciplines.

Some strategic locations would include the West and East coast of the United States, New Zealand/Australia, and Europe (due to the amount of missionaries they send out). In addition, locate centers in Cyprus and Southern Spain for the Islamic world in the Middle East and North Africa respectively, South Korea for East Asia including China, Singapore for Southeast Asia, perhaps two locations in India, one in Kenya and in southern Africa, and a place in Brazil and Spanish-speaking South America.

b. Form member care consultation teams that are either formally or informally associated. These teams could concentrate on one part of the world, such as missionaries working with Hindus in southern India, or focus their work by providing services to only a few mission agencies.

c. Establish or make available houses for furlough, retirement, or rest at different locations around the world. Put together a description of these places and make them available to the missions community.

d. Develop programs in conjunction with mission agencies to support missionaries during transitions such as during pre-field training (e.g., Missionary Internship, Link Care) and reentry (e.g., Mu Kappa, Narramore Foundation).

e. Set up special supportive coaching services for tentmakers who work in restricted access countries and who may not be part of a mission organization. Some of this may be done in conjunction with the churches that send out such workers.

## 5. Research and Writing

There can never be enough solid research and insightful, practical helps for missionaries. The member care field would greatly benefit from additional articles, books, and research projects. Those with expertise and experience can build upon the materials that have already been written, by authoring materials on stress management, cultural adjustment, missionary preparation, and missionary families. Especially useful would be materials on organizational development, multinational teams, and cross-cultural applications of member care. Empirical research is also needed to further identify member care issues, evaluate the effectiveness of member care programs, and study the nature of the missionary experience.

a. Continue to encourage articles to be written in journals like *Evangelical Missions Quarterly, International Bulletin of Missionary Research, Journal of Psychology and Theology, Journal of Psychology and Christianity*, and others. Be sure also to keep the general Christian community informed by writing articles for magazines such as Christianity Today, Destiny, Moody, and Decision. In addition, continue to write in-house articles within mission agencies and circulate relevant member care materials. It would be timely to begin publishing a journal specifically devoted to member care issues.

b. Periodically organize the key articles in this field into a compendium, perhaps every five years. Include an annotated bibliography of the research and articles in different member care areas. Be sure to search out articles written by missionaries and member care workers from the Two-Thirds World.

c. Prepare and distribute video and audio tapes from teaching and seminars on member care areas for the missions community.

d. Encourage students to write doctoral dissertations and masters' theses on topics related to missionary care and quality of life.

e. Form specialized research groups and projects which focus on different areas of the missionary experience. Key areas needing research would be identified and then research strategies would be designed. The MK CART group, which coordinates and conducts MK-related research, is a good example of what can be done to encourage individual and joint research projects.

f. Begin a special journal on member care in missions. Include innovative, practical, and scholarly work. Make sure the editorial board includes people from a variety of mission organizations, disciplines, and nationalities.

## Check Points For Member Care

How do we begin implementing some of the above suggestions? I believe there are three necessary steps for launching member care in a more coordinated direction.

First, a few seasoned leaders in this field must initiate the formation of the inter-organizational task force previously described. I would encourage this group to begin by spending some considerable time in prayer, seeking the Lord's heart and direction for member care. Depending on the Lord's leading, this task force could then oversee the next two steps.

Step two is to convene a major member care conference which will attract participants from various countries and organizations. This conference could be held in conjunction with another global evangelization conference, such as the Global Conference on World Evangelization to be convened in Seoul, Korea in June, 1994. Another option would be to have it be a main track at a major inter-organizational conference.

Third, a regular newsletter must be sent out to update the member care community and link workers together. Upcoming conferences and special events can be announced. The newsletter could be eventually expanded into a magazine which would include brief articles. All three of these steps will be keys to consolidating and stimulating member care as a field.

After this launching period, it will be important to monitor the ongoing impact of both individual and coordinated efforts at member care. Here are four areas to periodically review which can help keep us on track. Together they can be used as a grid to examine our contributions to missions through member care.

1. *Cooperation.* To what extent are we working on our own as independent workers, or as separate departments, or as individual agencies within this field? Suppose we are providing pastoral coaching services to teams in North Africa. Who else is involved in a similar ministry? Let's keep networking and finding ways to work more closely together.

2. *Priorities.* To what extent do we provide our services with a clear sense of which needs and requests to target? For example, how important is it to support mission agencies whose members may be more at-risk? A case in point would be missionaries working in an isolated and oppressive frontier setting who have less access to important member care resources. Which guidelines are we using to help determine the specific direction of our work?

3. *Availability.* To what extent are our services accessible to those whom we want to serve? Do we wait for missionaries to take the initiative and come to us? Are other responsibilities crowding out the actual direct services we would like to provide? It is important to scratch where missionaries really itch, and not just when and where it feels good for us.

4. *Building.* To what extent are we helping to establish something more permanent through our services? There is a difference between providing services and setting up ongoing member care ministries and structures. Consider a group of mission agencies, for instance, engaged in the burn-out-prone work of medical relief for refugees. How could a long-term, supportive ministry be organized for this and similar mission settings?

Reviewing these four areas is not always a comfortable task. They are reminders, indeed challenges, to think and act as strategically as possible in our service to missionaries. The basic strategy thus becomes clearly identifying which services to provide, for which groups of missionaries, in cooperation with which other member care providers, and with a view towards building which types of long-term ministries. Regular appraisals of our ministry and mutual accountability are keys to maintaining the strategic impact of our work in member care.

## Member Care in the Future

Member care, as we have seen, is an emerging field that is increasingly becoming "mainstreamed" into mission thinking and mission organizations. Given this reality, what are some of the implications for the future?

First, mission agencies and sending churches will have access to additional strategic resources needed for their mission programs. Missionaries will not only be healthier, but more effective as well.

Second, expect to see the entrance of additional culturally sensitive, member care workers—especially missions-minded mental health professionals—into the member care field. This will involve a significant increase in the individuals and member care teams who are willing to relocate overseas to serve the missions community.

Third, member care will be seen as a prerequisite for missionary effectiveness. The notion, for instance, that pre-field orientation with a dab of on-field pastoral counseling equals member care will be expanded to include a much broader perspective focusing on ongoing staff development. Mission agencies will therefore continue to release more finances and develop more resources for missionary care programs.

Fourth, member care will be seen as the responsibility of everyone involved in missions rather than being charged to only a few specialized ministries. Mutual care between mission personnel will be increasingly encouraged, complemented by the development of additional member care resources and services.

Finally, expect to see greater cooperation between mission organizations. Agencies, sending churches, and related mission organizations will coordinate their efforts and share resources to support the mission personnel working within a specific region or a particular people group.

## Putting It All Together

The member care momentum in missions today is most heartening. Yet there must be a direction for this momentum: to prioritize and channel member care resources towards those working among the least evangelized.

Ultimately, the adjustment and development of missionaries is God's concern. Member care must be kept in this perspective. It is important to plan, to implement new programs, and to seek to further organize this field. Yet we must be careful not to get ahead of God and do anything simply because it sounds like a good idea.

Member care must also never become an end in itself. All the focus on adjustment and personal growth must not detract us from the sacrificial call to take the gospel to all peoples. Member care is to remain in its proper place—as a servant to the missions community and to the mission task.

Further developing this field is not something to be left up to chance. Neither is it the responsibility of a single conference nor a periodic meeting where member care issues are addressed. Rather, mutual consultation, coordinated efforts, perseverance, and interdependency are to be the guiding principles.

Cooperative endeavors, like any team effort, are seldom free from interpersonal friction and misunderstandings. People and organizations are different, and this difference can create obstacles when seeking to implement coordinated member care programs. We need to anticipate such obstacles, discuss our differences, and trust God to hold us together to accomplish His purposes.

Member care must keep in stride with current missions thinking and realities. The missions force is rapidly expanding, a fact which is especially true for missionaries from the Two-Thirds World. This expansion must be mirrored within the global missions community by developing appropriate, comprehensive member care programs and services.

We must not forget the spiritual nature of our work in missions. Intercessory prayer, worship, spiritual warfare, and member care services are all required as we work together to reach the peoples of the earth for Christ.

Finally, I am convinced that the time has come to actively pull together the various pockets of member care workers around the world. It is also time to systematically train and mobilize many others for this strategic ministry. And the time is here for anointed leaders to step forward and help steer this field in response to the Lord's direction.

### Questions for Discussion

1. What would be some strategic ways to encourage greater member care involvement among frontier missionaries, member care personnel, and mission agencies?

2. What topics and issues would be important to address if an international member care conference were organized?

3. What other areas would you want to add or emphasize as part of this proposed agenda?

4. What types of obstacles are likely to be encountered when trying to coordinate member care within a geographic region?

5. What is the place of intercessory prayer and spiritual warfare in the development of member care services?

## References

Andrews, L. (1989, November). State of the art in missionary family research. Paper presented at the third *International Conference on Missionary Kids*, Nairobi, Kenya.

Barrett, D. (1990). Overall status of global mission and world evangelization, 1900-2000. *International Bulletin of Missionary Research, 14*, 26-27.

Collins, M. (1986). *Manual for today's missionary*. Pasadena: William Carey Library.

Filidis, P. (1990, December). Not where Christ has already been named. *World Christian News*, 3.

Foyle, M. (1987). *Overcoming missionary stress*. Wheaton: Evangelical Missions Information Service.

O'Donnell, K. & O'Donnell, M. (1988). *Helping missionaries grow: Readings in mental health and missions*. Pasadena: William Carey Library.

O'Donnell, K. & O'Donnell, M. (1990). The increasing scope of member care. *Evangelical Missions Quarterly, 26*, 418-428.

O'Donnell, K. & O'Donnell, M. (1991). How to avoid ethical traps in treating hurting staff. *Evangelical Missions Quarterly, 27*, 146-151.

Rogers, M. (1991). Preliminary proposal for the establishment of a regional missions-mental health association. Unpublished program proposal, Seattle, WA.

Tan, S., & Jones, S. (1991). Christian graduate training in professional psychology: The Rech conference. *Journal of Psychology and Christianity, 10*, 72-75.

Taylor, W. (1991). (Ed.). *Internationalizing missionary training*. Grand Rapids, MI: Baker.

# 22

*Gary Strauss*
*Kathy Narramore*

# The Increasing Role of the Sending Church

Over the years we have witnessed the missions enterprise becoming increasingly sophisticated and relatively autonomous from the local church. With these developments, we have observed that much of the responsibility for the preparation and the spiritual and emotional support of missionaries has been assumed to be the domain of the mission agency. This has left the sending church a rather narrow, though vital role: financial and prayer support, occasional contact via letters, field visits, and during furlough; and some supply of clothing and other material needs.

It is imperative that the local church play a larger role in world missions, particularly in the care and development of missionaries that they send out. But the question is, just what role should the sending church play? The following personal testimony from a missionary suggests some answers to that question.

> I was so angry when I heard what our church mission's pastor had said to my wife Evelyn about our marital and family needs. If he had critical comments to make about me, he should have said them to me directly. Not many days later he confronted me with the same stinging truth, and I was stunned. "The relationships of the people in the church you plant will reflect your relationship with Evelyn and your daughters."

> The mission's pastor knew how I had dreamed—for 25 years—of planting a church among a previously unreached people group. All of a sudden my dream froze. I knew that my weaknesses had been discovered. There was no way around this. The only path that I could take would lead through much pain to

*great change, and that is the road that God wanted me to take.*

*Since I was twelve, I had dreamed of taking God's Word to a people group who had never tasted the bread of life. Establishing a New Testament church was my strong desire. My training had prepared me for this mission. For seven years my wife and I had worked together to prepare for the next step in our missionary venture. And now this.*

*But how could I change the deeply ingrained ways in which I related to my wife and children? How could such a change take place—making our family a positive model of Christian love—so that new believers, modeling their relationships on ours, would grow to be powerful examples to others?*

*We needed counseling. It was obvious and unavoidable. We began to learn to face the pain. It helped to have a supporting network of committed friends around us. Part of this network was a missionary support group that met each week. Within this group, we learned to honestly share our lives, accept one another, and support each other in prayer. I had never dreamed that such a situation was possible. I thank God for a church that helped us through the process of change. (**We will return to this story later.**)*

The experience of this missionary family in the context of their sending church has implications for a number of the responsibilities traditionally fulfilled by the mission agency. Issues of selection, readiness for ministry, training, ongoing care and support, and facilitation of intervention as needed should also be the concern of the sending church. We have been encouraged by the emergence of multifaceted church missions programs. These programs demonstrate the relevance of sending churches and mission agencies partnering together to develop and maintain resilient missionary personnel (Borthwick, 1991). Church programs currently exist that include such activities as:

1. Candidate selection and training (which also includes internship experiences).

2. The building of spiritual/emotional support networks in which the members are personally selected by the missionary candidate(s).

3. Active concern by designated subcommittees for the ongoing well-being and effective functioning of the missionaries.

4. Field visits by church staff and/or members.

5. Coordinated furlough schedules.

6. Reentry experiences provided by the local church.

It is vital that local churches carefully examine their role in sending out and caring for missionaries and especially how they could develop and implement some of the activities listed above. Every church varies, of course, in the type and amount of resources it has to train and support its

missionaries. Nonetheless we believe a planned, concerted effort is necessary to see the development and provision of supportive resources for the
missionaries which a church sends out.

We would like to share some of our thoughts and experiences concerning our missions program at Whittier Area Baptist Fellowship, located
in California. Our active involvement in this church and its missions
program has taught us many things about the preparation and care of
missionaries. Additional suggestions can be found in the materials published by the Association of Church Missions Committees (PO Box ACMC,
Wheaton, Illinois 60189), and in Neil Pirolo's book (1991) *Serving as Senders*.
Before we discuss our mission program, however, let us first explore some
biblical reasons and biblical principles for the role of the local church in
sending, supporting, and nurturing missionaries.

## Biblical Rationale and Principles

The Acts of the Apostles provides several foundational concepts for
the development of missions policy and practices. Peter, Barnabas, Paul,
and Silas are all clearly recognized for their respective efforts in sharing the
Gospel with those beyond the confines of the towns or cities in which these
men lived. What is commonly identified as the first missionary journey had
its source in the development and vision of the church in Antioch.

In Acts 11:20 we find the first reference to believers, now living
outside Palestine, "speaking to the Greeks also, preaching the Lord Jesus."
As word of God's blessing on this ministry reached Jerusalem, the "mother"
church sent Barnabas as a support to this new work. Witnessing the fruit
of the efforts of unnamed believers with the Greeks, Barnabas first encouraged them himself (v. 23) and then went to look for Paul to come and assist
him (vv. 25 & 26). As a result of this work, a church was established in
Antioch. We see a precedent here—church planting. Thereafter, Barnabas
and Paul were sent by the Antioch church to carry a gift of monetary
support for the financially needy "mother" church in Jerusalem, evidence
of the maturity that had been nurtured among the new believers in the
Antioch church during the ministry of Barnabas and Paul. It is this very
church that provides a model and rationale for the involvement of the
sending church in the missions enterprise.

Having fulfilled their mission in Jerusalem, Barnabas and Paul, taking
with them John Mark, returned to Antioch. It is sometime after their return
that the Holy Spirit spoke to the leadership of the church regarding the
setting apart of Barnabas and Paul "for the work to which I have called
them" (13:2). Following a time of prayer and fasting, hands were laid on
them and they were sent on their way.

An initial observation that can be made from the biblical text is that
the local church (not even the "mother" church in Jerusalem) was the

sending agency. This stands in sharp contrast to the prevalent model of today in which the local church has become, at best, a secondary agent in the life of missionaries. While the organizational structure of the church has changed much since the first century A.D., including that of the missions function, the role of the local church may well have been diminished by default rather than by thoughtful application of a biblical model.

Winter (1981) observes that, following the Reformation, Protestantism, unlike Roman Catholicism, had established no mechanism for missions for almost three hundred years, until William Carey's proposal to utilize "means for the conversion of the heathen." Beginning with the formation of the Baptist Missionary Society, twelve missionary societies were organized in the span of thirty-two years. It was not until the nineteenth century that Protestants became actively engaged in missions. The mission societies that were formed, whether denominationally based or independent, assumed primary responsibility for the mission enterprise with the local church taking, at best, a rather weak supportive role. We believe, however, that the local church needs to be actively involved (though not necessarily the exclusive or primary agency) in the preparation and sending of laborers into the field.

Two additional observations can be made concerning the missionary role of the Antioch church. First, this church had an active ministry and a corporate devotional life. We note that it was while the body of believers was engaged in "ministering to the Lord and fasting..." (13:2) that the Holy Spirit communicated His desire concerning Barnabas and Paul. This would suggest that missions-minded churches need to invest in a sincere devotional life so as to be sensitive to the leading of the Spirit regarding their role in setting apart and sending out missionaries. That is, they need to be devoted to meaningful experiences of participative worship and corporate prayer, experiences within which the Spirit of God can speak to the local body concerning His will for those He is calling to ministry.

The second observation is that prior to sending out Barnabas and Paul, the church fasted, prayed, and laid their hands on them (v.3). This suggests that it is important that the church as a body actively enter into a process of seeking God's affirmation of the call, praying for their missionaries and their ministry, and bestowing the blessing of the local fellowship upon the ones it sends. This activity of the Antioch church is an early example and model of the common commissioning service observed in many churches upon the departure of the sent ones.

As the biblical narrative is pursued, we see that Barnabas and Paul returned to Antioch, the sending church, upon completion of their mission. Once again the significance of the sending church is noted as being the source "from which they had been commended to the grace of God for the work that they had accomplished" (14:26). "When [Barnabas and Paul] had arrived and gathered the church together, they began to report all things that God and done with them and how He had opened a door of faith to the Gentiles. And they spent a long time with the disciples" (vv. 27, 28). The important role of the sending church is reflected in the fact that Barnabas and Paul returned first to the sending church, gave their first extensive report to the sending church, and then spent considerable time with the sending church.

Likewise, today's missionaries returning from the field need a supportive fellowship where they can debrief, report, rest, and give and receive encouragement. Here are three important experiences to provide, following the Antioch example.

1. Missionaries should receive a warm and supportive reception, affirming their identity as loved members of the local body and their role and work as missionaries.

2. Missionaries should be given adequate time to fully report their mission experience, enabling their experience on the field and their resulting thoughts and feelings to be sufficiently heard and understood. This will also enrich and further promote the missionary vision of the sending church.

3. Missionaries should have sufficient opportunity to spend time renewing relationships and experiencing extended fellowship. They should also have ample time to rest and recover, to reenter the daily life of the sending church, and to make further contribution to the church beyond their report while being nurtured by the church in return. To accomplish this, the sending church and the mission agency must cooperate to plan schedules and activities.

As we are considering some biblical roles and principles for the sending church, it is clear that the current missions situation is a significant departure from the Antioch pattern. Most sending churches take a back seat to the more extensive involvement of mission agencies. Attempts on the part of the sending church to unilaterally implement practices more akin to what transpired in the first century could lead to a competitive spirit between the sending church and the missions agency as to who has the greater authority and to whom missionaries owe the greatest allegiance and/or investment of time and energy. Clearly, the sending church and the mission agency need to work toward a balanced, trusting partnership to facilitate the sending, the ongoing support, and the return of missionaries, teams, and families.

In summary, it is important that the sending church be recognized by the missionaries, the mission agency, and by the church itself as a vital and fundamental element in (a) the identification of those who are called to be missionaries, (b) the preparation of its missionaries for their work, and (c) the development of a relatively comprehensive spiritual and emotional support system for its missionaries. This third element begins with nurturing individual church members as they consider God's call to missions involvement, and continues through every phase of missionary life culminating in assisting those who are retiring or transitioning to some other calling.

## Examples of Roles for the Sending Church

We now move to a consideration of the roles of the sending church in each of the developmental stages of the life of missionaries. We begin with the pre-field stage, including its several substages, and then look at the on-field, furlough/home assignment, and retirement stages.

### The Pre-Field Stage

*Nurturing the potential missionary candidate.* We see the first step to be taken by the local church is to nurture potential candidates by teaching its members to become world Christians. Many missionaries first develop an awareness of and interest in missions within the context of their local, missions-minded church. Some of the ways in which this step can be promoted include:

1. Special services of missionary commissioning and reporting.

2. Missionaries on home assignment spending time with Sunday school classes, youth groups, Bible study groups, and with vacation Bible schools.

3. Individual families inviting missionaries over for dinner and other family activities.

4. Ongoing dialogue and teaching about missions and what the entire enterprise entails.

The sending church also plays a part in nurturing the openness of MKs to a career in missions. Although many MKs follow in the footsteps of their parents in pursuing missions involvement, we recognize that the life of the MK is sometimes negatively impacted by the stresses that typically accompany missionary life. These negative experiences can harden the MK to any consideration of missionary involvement, and can leave scars which result in dysfunctional patterns of behavior that can significantly interfere with his/her future success, whether or not missions involvement is pursued.

*Short-term missions experience.* Both young people and adults from our church have richly benefited from short-term missions experience. Such opportunities can provide important experiential learning about the nature of missions activities and about a person's suitability and readiness for missions involvement. For those whose lives are involved in other career endeavors, short-term missions can provide opportunities to come alongside to assist, support, and encourage career missionaries, and to invest individual gifts and abilities for a limited time that would not otherwise be available to the missions enterprise. While short-term programs do not require nearly the investment of time and resources in preparation and support as career missions does, the returns of a carefully planned and executed short-term missions program can be substantial to the people targeted for ministry, the career missionaries, the short-termers, and for the life of the local church. For more information on setting up short-term missions programs, refer to Steve Hawthorne's (1987) edited handbook, *Stepping Out: A Guide to Short-Term Missions.*

*Candidate preparation programs.* Systematic preparation of candidates is a must. Personal testimonies of career missionaries can speak powerfully to the benefit of candidate preparation programs. Let's return to the family whose experience was introduced at the beginning of this chapter.

> *What did our church do to help us? First of all, there was the willingness to confront us—to say, "You may not know it, but you have a problem." That took guts, love, and commitment. Being part of a church that doesn't shoot its wounded is a beautiful thing. As we got into counseling there were some ugly truths to be faced. We were able to share these with our missions pastor and senior pastor. That they were willing to accept us as we were was a major part of the healing process. The missions committee provided funds to help pay for the counseling that would become a key piece in God's provision of healing and change.*

> *The general positive attitude at our church toward getting counseling helped a lot in our being able to share our own neediness with others, such as in our Sunday school class. The unspoken but clear message is, "Counseling isn't just for sick people. Counseling is for people who want to grow. We are all needy in some way."*

> *Knowing that our church leadership accepted and valued us, even though they were quite aware of our struggles and weaknesses, helped us on the field to accept our fellow missionaries and minister to them. We were able to expose our weaknesses, and so pass on some of the things we had learned: foremost, that the Christian life was meant to be lived in community, not all alone. So we found friends that we could meet with each week for encouragement and accountability—individually and in small groups—with whom to share and pray. In addition to our own involvement in a couple's sharing group, we also helped to start small groups for others in the mission community. As we interacted with national Christians, God gave opportunities to pass on more of what we had learned.*

> *In closing, I ponder on what the church can do to help care for missionaries. Building up missionary candidates while they are in the church seems to me the most positive care the church can give. Since relational problems rank high as reasons for missionary failure and attrition, whatever churches can do to promote emotional well-being and healthy relational skills in their candidates is a*

*wise form of "preventive maintenance." Creating the expectancy that Christians live in community, not as Lone Rangers, by modeling interdependency throughout the church, is a must. This includes placing missionary candidates in supportive small groups in which transparency, accountability, and encouragement thrive, and promoting the health and growth for missionaries over the long haul.*

This testimony highlights what we have come to see at Whittier Area Baptist Fellowship as the central focus of our pre-field candidacy program—namely, concern for personal and relational well-being. Specifically, this concern includes the dimensions of spiritual and emotional personal health along with constructive and growing relationships with God, family, and fellow believers. Finding and filling gaps left incomplete by formal training is another important concern of our program. To help meet this need, we include experiences designed to increase knowledge and skills in cross-cultural relating, evangelism, and personal and family life planning and development. The specifics of the program are as follows:

*Stage One—Candidate*: Designed for those who are seriously considering missionary service as a career. This person has crossed the threshold from "willing to go, but planning to stay" to "planning to go, but willing to stay."

During this stage, the candidate is asked to read certain recommended books, work out a plan to meet his/her educational requirements for the next three to five years (including 30 units of Bible training and the taking of the three month "Perspectives on the World Christian Movement" course offered by the U.S. Center for World Missions in Pasadena), and to be involved in the life of the church, particularly various elements of the evangelism program. In addition, the candidate meets with the psychologist member of the Candidate Subcommittee for psychological testing and interpretation. It is also during this stage that a discipling relationship is established with a mature individual for single candidates or married couples to provide a more personal and intimate level of mentoring during the course of the candidate program.

*Stage Two—Apprentice*: Designed for those who are convinced that God is leading them to vocational missionary work. God's leading has also been confirmed through the leadership of the church. This individual should now have a clear path in view for getting "from here to there."

During this stage, the candidate continues the recommended reading program, takes a course dealing with cross-cultural sensitivity, pursues a local cross-cultural experience that is coordinated to fit the candidate's ministry goals, and is involved in a short-term or summer missions project. Personal development is encouraged through attending a weekend missions retreat and at least a 12 session small group dealing with issues such as personal adjustment, personal relationships, marriage, parenting, discipling, financial management, and using the Bible for personal nurturing. With the approval of the Candidate Subcommittee, the candidate applies to mission agencies.

*Stage Three—Appointee*: Designed for those who have been accepted by a mission board. They will be involved in mission orientation and deputation.

During this stage, regular meetings are held with the Missions Pastor and the Candidate Chairperson. A cooperative relationship between personnel from the church's candidacy program and the mission agency is sought to facilitate the candidate's involvement with both. The candidate fills out a church support application, meets with the entire Missions Committee upon recommendation of the Candidate Subcommittee, and meets with the church Board of Overseers. A support team made up of close friends within the church is selected by the candidate. This support team meets periodically with the candidate for sharing, emotional/spiritual support, and prayer. Books specific to the candidate's field and ministry are read and a paper on the assigned country and ministry is written and presented to the Missions Pastor. Deputation is pursued and upon completion, a formal commissioning service is held by the church prior to leaving for the field.

While the pre-field program as outlined provides structure and designated activities, it is through personal contacts during the program that the candidate becomes known more intimately. Feedback and specific recommendations are made to further the growth of the individual, couple, or family. Two-way communication between the church and the mission agency to which the candidate has been appointed provides further opportunity to exchange perceptions of the candidate, to make recommendations both for pre-field preparation and on-field placement and job assignment, and to plan ahead for the ongoing relationship between the missionary, the sending church, and the mission agency.

A good church/agency relationship is essential for the pre-field program of the church. Without it, the missionary can become vulnerable to incompatible and possibly competing perspectives, recommendations, and requirements of the church and the agency.

### The On-Field Stage

Most missionaries seem to appreciate personal visits from friends and other members from their church. One missionary from our church wrote:

> We are often put in a pastoral/leadership role and have no one who can really understand to turn to when we need help. Some missions try to overcome this situation by putting people to work in "teams", but this doesn't always work out either. What if the problem is with the team? Or what if like me, you need some one who really knows you to help you look at the situation from an out-

*side perspective to help you decide what action to take?"*

*I think the key factor in pastoral visits to the mission field is not just to hear the missionaries' problems and help them to cope on a personal basis, but to take the responsibility to go to those in authority about issues that need to be dealt with…As a supporting church, you had both the authority and right to do that. And I'm sure it made a big difference in the way I was listened to and treated from that time on…I think if more churches would take responsibility and hold mission agencies accountable for treatment of the missionaries they support, the agencies would sit up and take notice. And perhaps some very needed changes would take place.*

As Missions Pastor, I (Kathy) try to go overseas once a year. In addition, missionaries sent out from our church are visited by either our senior pastor or another staff person, as well as an Overseer or other church representative.

We see a biblical precedent for these pastoral visits to mission outposts in the Philippian church who sent Epaphroditus to visit Paul. He brought Paul needed gifts, as we do to our missionaries, often returning with letters, just as Epaphroditus returned with Paul's precious letter to his church of Philippi (Phil. 2:25-30; 4:18). The mutual ministering that occurs is important.

Our field visits last a minimum of three days at each location. The purpose is to spend time talking with the missionaries, getting to know their family better, and gaining a sense of their ministry. We are there to learn, encourage, comfort, pray, confront, and be helpful in any way we can. When we return we can be a far better advocate for them to our sending church. We have been a part of their cross-cultural setting and have observed their financial, health, emotional, and spiritual needs first-hand. These we can share with the church as fresh news and urgent needs or victories we need to celebrate and thus enlarge the church's giving and involvement. Here are two examples of how field visits have helped our people overseas.

Jan was a very gifted and capable person but emotionally and physically breaking down when we arrived. This was due in part to a faulty job placement. She was in administration and being effective but her heart was in evangelism and discipleship. We were able to be an advocate for her to her national and American director. It encouraged them that her church cared this much about her. We were also able to put her in touch with an on-field counselor for missionaries. This enabled her to last longer on the field and identify personal issues that could be worked on later.

Josh was uncertain about our coming since we had previously confronted him when he was on home assignment regarding the structure and administration of his mission. But as his trust in us grew during the week, the sharing went deeper. As feelings of fear, confusion and guilt surfaced, healing began to take place. This resulted (in time) in a new and expanded vision for the ministry. He said at parting, "You came as committee members; you left as friends."

The benefits that a traveling team can offer to the missionaries include identifying stress points, giving encouragement, providing resources (from counselors to cars), and being their advocate to the home church or to their mission. There are also blessings for those at the home church. Members of the home church are often stretched in their own vision of the world and of God's greatness as they hear the first-hand reports of what He is doing. Their praying is more urgent and focused, their identification with the missionary's struggles and humanity is more real, their giving is more liberal and compassionate, and sometimes others are moved to visit and get involved personally in their missionary's ministry. An example of this follows.

I (Kathy) returned from a four-week visit with our missionaries throughout Africa and Europe. I reported on my trip in the Sunday morning services and in the adult Sunday Schools. In response, two adult classes joined forces, raised $3,000, and with our missionary's help was able to place a desk top computer printer in a strategic Eastern European city so they could print desperately needed materials in their own language. Then the couple who initiated this project took part of their vacation to visit the Christians there. What a blessing they were to us when they returned.

## Additional Contributions from the Home Church

Besides visits to the field, what else can the home church do for its missionaries who are on the field? In our church the Care Committee sends cards, our weekly church publication, and the Sunday morning service tapes. There's also a line-item in the budget for missionary children in the States to call their parents overseas at least once a quarter. This was especially meaningful when an MK was able to call his dad about his engagement to an old-time family friend.

Sunday Schools "adopt" two or three families each and send them cards, letters, tapes, and gifts like special food and clothes. Missionaries are especially thankful for mail. "We both put in full eight to 12 hour days in the field," writes one couple in a large urban center, "so when we get home the first thing that we do is to go through our mail. Usually the first letters that we open are those that are from our church. This is a great break from the long day, to reminisce, and think of those who really care enough to send off a personal letter."

The church also sends out an annual questionnaire to its missionaries. The purpose is to help the missionaries reflect on their past year and plans for the future, as well as to discuss ministry and support needs.

Younger Sunday School classes adopt the MKs, writing them while away and inviting them to camp and social events when they come home. In this way when the MK returns he or she feels a greater level of belonging.

Each missionary unit is encouraged to develop a small network of church members who know them intimately. Missionaries need people who can pray for them in the very personal areas of their lives and keep in close communication by phone, fax, and letter. A couple working with a difficult unreached people group wrote regarding their support group, "We have gotten many assurances of prayer and love, and even several phone calls since leaving [our church]. This has convinced us that the church cares for us personally and is also actively interested in the task here!"

The following recent account describes how one of our missionaries has been encouraged by her small group.

> We had gathered to greet and support one of our young missionaries. She had flown in from her mission field to attend a conference on "recovery." She had spent most of the previous furlough time working on issues from her past—issues that caused her to question and doubt.
>
> As she spoke and felt the loving response from the small group, she became more vulnerable—more willing to speak freely. She did not know all of us well. But she did know that her airfare and fees for the conference had been paid by someone in the group though that person remained anonymous. The questions posed to her were gentle and loving. There was no critical spirit present. She told us later that she felt our love and concern and was so very relieved. It was hard for her to talk of her background and the present doubts of her faith.
>
> She is back on the mission field now. We, as her support group, have agreed to help her return every six months for a week of intensive therapy. Hopefully, we will be able to gather again at those times, not just to have an update on her progress, but to come alongside and experience mutual ministering. God chose each of us very carefully. We are part of her life, a part of her recovery. She is very much a part of God's blessings to us too.

## Furlough and Home Assignment

Reentry for furlough can cause as much or more stress than going to the field. Debriefing becomes extremely important, in which we set up a time as soon as possible to meet and talk without interruptions or feeling hurried. We listen deeply to our missionaries' needs and joys, their victories and struggles. How frustrating it must be for those missionaries who, by contrast, are only given a few minutes to tell their story in a Sunday School class or when few really ask or want to hear about their work.

Meeting the physical needs of returning missionaries is also important. Often missionaries are exhausted from the stress of packing, tying up loose ends and leaving. The church can help them set up house and transition back into life back home. When Charlie and Kristi first arrived home for furlough they were able to walk into a nicely furnished two-bedroom apartment—a triplex purchased by a missions-minded physician and his wife just for missionaries. Their rent was low. They were able to use a car donated for missionaries by an MK from our church. Money was provided for each of them to buy new clothes. There was a mission's closet that helped them set up housekeeping with kitchen, cleaning, and other household supplies.

More and more, mission agencies are giving reentry seminars for their missionaries and families. To supplement such experiences or help fill the gap when there are none, we give our missionaries articles on reentry to read and discuss (e.g., Austin, 1983; Pollock, 1987).

We see the sending church as having a significant opportunity to provide support to the children of missionary families (MKs) sent out by the church through efforts directed specifically toward enhancing their growth and well-being. For example, the church can make it possible for MKs coming to their parents' home country (while their parents remain on the field) to attend reentry programs such as those offered by the Narramore Christian Foundation. A support group for MKs can also be provided within the context of the local church to enable them to discuss their thoughts and feelings as they adjust to the new situation. At the very least, church families can reach out to MKs to provide a surrogate family for them while they are separated from their parents and siblings.

Furlough is also a time for review and honest confrontation if a problem has developed. If this is done with love and sensitivity it can be very helpful for both sides. Professional counseling may be necessary. A good resource in such situations are the Link Care Centers in Fresno, California and in Mount Bethel, Pennsylvania. This agency is especially set up to care for a whole missionary family for one to six months at a time, helping with problems involving burnout, marriage, or parenting issues. Sending churches would do well to also call on the services of Christian professional counselors in their area who are familiar with missions and the church's mission program.

Putting money in the missions budget for this kind of ministry to the missionary is essential. Close cooperation with the missionary's agency is also necessary so that the church and the agency are working together for the best interests of the missionary, rather than pulling two different ways and catching the missionary in the middle. Another way our church has been able to enrich and nurture the furloughing missionary is involvement in the annual church missions conference. While the missionaries are busy that week sharing and meeting with people, there are also two mornings specifically set aside for their spiritual/emotional enrichment. The conference speaker or pastor feeds them from the Word. In addition there is time for sharing personal issues faced on the field or helpful breakthroughs. Small groups are formed for personal mutual prayer. Sometimes a couple under great stress is placed in the center in chairs. Then many gather round to lay hands on them and pray.

Our women's ministry organizes a beautiful Christmas dinner for the ladies of the church and the returned missionaries. Several of these missionary ladies share what their Christmas times overseas have been like. A large offering is taken at the end and divided among the missionaries we support for a bonus Christmas present. This event is greatly appreciated by both missionaries and the church.

## Home Assignment

Home assignment is part of our missionaries' furlough experience. It too can be a stressful time. Just when missionaries on home assignment are most in need of rest and renewing, they have to think about the additional money they need to raise and the 30 or more churches and individuals they need to visit. It is hard on their children: constant traveling and meeting new people, having little stability and no place to belong and become known.

One answer to this problem is to set up a consortium agreement between churches. For example, churches within one region can cooperate together to take on at least 70% to 80% of a missionary's support. They need not be part of the same denomination. But their cooperation makes a major difference in the quality of life and ultimate health and effectiveness of the missionary. By staying in one main area they can minister to these churches and be nurtured by them. There is more stability to the home life—the kids can stay in one school and one church and they do not have to constantly travel or have a parent that is frequently gone.

For these same reasons we believe in giving more money to fewer missionaries, rather than spreading the missions budget among a large number of missionaries. This increases accountability and gives the church a more meaningful relationship with its missionaries.

Our missionaries on home assignment are viewed as an extension of the church staff. Therefore they are invited to sit on the missions committee, attend staff meetings, fill the pulpit, speak in Sunday School, and so on. The greatest blessing and returns are in the area of recruitment—often it is the people who know missionaries who became missionaries!

# Retirement

Retirement is as important a stage in missionary life as the other stages. Sending churches need to be prepared to help their missionaries with at least three aspects of the retirement process.

First, we need to challenge and educate our missionaries to prepare financially for retirement. Our Candidate Training Program devotes a special section to finances, including financial planning for retirement. As Norm Frisbey (1987) puts it, "Individual missionaries need to realize that [government] benefits plus mission pensions need to be supplemented by personal assets acquired through savings and investments" (p. 328). The sending church thus has a responsibility to help its missionaries think realistically about their financial needs in their retirement years.

Second, sending churches need to decide if or how they are going to continue their financial support of their missionaries during retirement. As a general rule, it seems that if a church has been a major supporter of a missionary, and if that missionary has been active in the sending church when he/she has been on furlough, then the sending church has a responsibility to continue supporting the missionary during retirement.

Finally, sending churches need to be prepared to help their missionaries continue an active and productive lifestyle during retirement. Although each missionary and missionary family is different, retired missionaries can be a tremendous help to new candidates and younger missionaries as well as to the entire missions program in the local church. One of our retired missionary couples has provided some very helpful leadership to our missions committee and our Candidate Training Committee. The wisdom, perspective, and encouragement they bring to our program has greatly enriched our candidates and has kept this couple active and productive well into their seventies.

## Conclusion

We believe it is important for sending churches to become actively involved in the training, care, and nurturing of its missionaries. This is not the exclusive domain of the mission agency; in fact most mission agencies would welcome sending churches to take an increasing role in supporting missionaries.

We also believe the sending church and mission agency are called to cooperate together to support missionaries throughout their entire life—from candidacy through to retirement. The sending church through its members, support groups, missions pastor, and missions committee can serve as a stable reference point for missionaries as they go through the multiple transitions and the ups and downs that are such a central part on the missionary life. The challenge is for sending churches to embrace a long-term commitment, provide compassionate care, and develop practical, supportive resources for their missionaries.

## Questions for Discussion

1. Why has the care of missionaries been largely assumed by mission agencies rather than sending churches?

2. What problems can occur when sending churches send out missionaries independent of mission agencies, and vice versa?

3. In what ways does your church support the missionaries it sends out?

4. What could be done to increase your church's involvement in missions and the care of its missionaries? Which other churches in your area might be candidates for a cooperative mission effort?

5. How would some of the suggestions and programs described in this article apply or not apply to sending churches from the Two-Thirds World?

# References

Austin, C. (1983). Reentry stress: The pain of coming home. *Evangelical Missions Quarterly, 19,* 278-287.

Borthwick, P. (1991). A love affair that must be cultivated three ways. *Evangelical Missions Quarterly, 27,* 48-55.

Frisbey, N. (1987). Retirement of evangelical missionaries: Elements of satisfaction and morale. *Journal of Psychology and Theology, 15,* 326-335.

Hawthorne, S. (1987). (Ed.). *Stepping out. A guide to short-term missions.* Evanston, IL: SMS Publications.

Pirolo, N. (1991). *Serving as senders.* San Diego, CA: Emmaus Road.

Pollock, D. (1987). Welcome home! Easing the pain of MK reentry. *Evangelical Missions Quarterly, 23,* 278-283.

Winter, R. (1981). The two structures of God's redemptive mission. In Winter, R., & Hawthorne, S. (Eds.). *Perspectives on the world christian movement: A reader* (pp. 178-189). Pasadena, CA: William Carey.

# 23

*Richard Gardner*

*Laura Mae Gardner*

# Training And Using Member Care Workers

The global missionary force is expanding, estimated to reach nearly 300,000 full-time, Protestant workers by the year 2000 (Pate, 1991). There is also a growing movement among churches and mission agencies around the world to prioritize and send workers into the approximately 12,000 people groups—representing some two billion people—that have been virtually untouched by the Gospel (Bush, 1992). These are encouraging indications that God is at work through His people to help us fulfill His command to make disciples of all nations (Matthew 28:18-20).

Nevertheless, as the number of missionaries increases—especially those entering into complex and demanding frontier settings—so also does the need for their support and care. Additional member care services must be developed and provided. This will necessitate raising up hundreds of new member care workers who are both professionally trained and familiar with the challenges of missionary life. Included would be human resource specialists, pastoral counselors, personnel directors, mental health professionals, field coaches, outside consultants, cross-cultural trainers, and others. Each of these types of workers plays an important role in the supportive care of missionary personnel. They are a necessary complement to the mutual care between colleagues that is foundational for missionary resiliency and effectiveness.

This chapter addresses the training needs of workers who are either currently preparing for or actually involved in member care ministry, with a primary emphasis on therapists or counselors. In addition to training considerations, the focus will also be on how best to utilize these workers. We consider two main questions: What types of training programs are needed to equip member care workers in counseling and other related mental health skills? How can member care workers provide their services in an effective manner?

We will explore selection factors for member care counselors, identify different levels of training, discuss several guidelines for using in-house and outside member care professionals, and make suggestions for continued personal and professional growth. We approach these subjects from our perspectives as the International Coordinators for the counseling programs and personnel of Wycliffe Bible Translators (WBT) and the Summer Institute of Linguistics (SIL). The suggestions in this chapter are born out of our 20 years of field work as well as our responsibility to oversee the Wycliffe Counseling Department which consists of 23 full-time or part-time counselors.

## Selection Factors

What characteristics are needed by individuals who want to work as member care counselors? Two factors that must be examined with potential counselors are their motivation to counsel and their level of self-awareness.

### Motivation

Why does a person want to counsel and help others in this agency? Here are some appropriate motivations:

1. The person is responding to a keen sense of God's calling to this ministry which is in line with his/her gifts and abilities.

2. Past experience as a people-helper confirms his/her servant heart. Documentation is needed by impartial observers of one's spiritual giftedness; character qualities of genuineness, warmth, integrity, and empathy; as well as emotional health and stability.

3. The person is interested in people, respects their ability to grow and serve, and has an appropriate desire to facilitate that growth. People have already sought out him or her for emotional, practical, or spiritual guidance and help.

There are also some unhealthy motivations, and persons displaying these should not be encouraged toward a counseling career.

1. The need to be needed and to "parent" or nurture others (codependency). Such a person hopes to vicariously get his/her needs met through the counseling process.

2. Inordinate curiosity that revels in intimate knowledge of another without respecting personal boundaries.

3. Desire for control over people that accrues from being in a position of influence.

4. Wanting to help others as a way to avoid resolving one's own problems. One focuses on others' needs rather than his/her own.

5. Wanting to help others in the same way that one has also been helped through counseling. This is not necessarily inappropriate, yet must be a minor motivating factor for pursuing a counseling ministry.

### Self-Awareness

Proverbs 14:8 says, "The wisdom of the prudent is to understand his way, but the folly of fools is deceit (NASB)." An awareness of the strengths and limitations of one's technical training, personal assets, and life experience and skills is essential. The healthy person maintains and displays attitudes of non-defensiveness, openness to input from trustworthy people, and insight when faced with new information about him/herself. He or she demonstrates a commitment to godly, continued growth, and willingness and energy to implement personal growth plans. Mission agencies should look for these characteristics in the people who counsel their staff.

## Levels of Training for Member Care Counselors

Training is needed for all types of member care workers, from those who provide informal peer counseling to the mission psychologist or psychiatrist. We see four levels of counselor training that can equip missionary personnel and prepare professionals to work in mission settings.

### Level One

This level is for those who have demanding people-related tasks and wish to increase their understanding of people and interpersonal skills. This might be a medical doctor, mission administrator, personnel officer— anyone whose job it is to accomplish mission goals through teams of people or to care for fellow staff. As an example, the Counseling Department of Wycliffe offers basic workshops annually to improve the interpersonal skills of mission administrators. Teaching, discussion, and opportunities to practice core skills are provided. Information can be obtained by directing queries to the International Counseling Department, 7500 W. Camp Wisdom Road, Dallas, Texas 75236.

### Level Two

This level provides training for informal people-helpers—those who desire on a collegue or peer basis to minister more knowledgeably to others. Such training is offered by Stephen Ministries (8016 Dale Street, St. Louis, Missouri 63117), the video courses offered by Liberty University (PO Box

11803, Lynchburg, Virginia 24506), Youth With A Missions's counseling courses offered through the University of the Nations (75-5851 Kuakini Highway, Kailua-Kona, Hawaii 96740), the "Skilled Helper" training offered at Burnaby Counseling Group (7325 MacPherson Avenue, Burnaby, British Columbia V5J 4N8), and the week-long Institutes in Biblical Counseling offered by Dr. Larry Crabb (16075 West Belleview Avenue, Morrison, Colorado 80465).

## Level Three

Level three, "associate counselor" training, is for those who want to become more seriously involved in helping their colleagues, but do not have the time to take formal studies. This level ideally includes both levels one and two, plus an additional mini-practicum such as that developed by Tim Sieges, Wycliffe counselor in Papua New Guinea. This 30 hour program spread over ten weeks offers both classroom teaching and group process experience. Topics include foundational principles for helping, family of origin issues, emotional states, anger management, grief and bereavement, behavior management, addictions, counselee resistance, diagnosis, and referrals. One of the distinctives of this program is that it takes place in a field setting, is designed for field workers, and is taught and supervised by field counselors.

We suggest that spouses of mission counselors and all counseling department staff should have this level of training. Such training will increase their supportive understanding of their spouse and enable them to serve that spouse in a debriefing capacity allowing the spouse to "unload" personal feelings. Further, this training will assist the non-counselor spouse to meet counseling challenges that come his/her way by virtue of being married to a counselor.

## Level Four

This level addresses people pursuing graduate degrees who desire to or actually provide therapeutic services to mission agencies. These individuals are trained to function as mental health professionals who can offer the full scope of therapeutic, preventive, consultative, and educative services, as well as crisis intervention and referrals. Services may range from growth and enrichment guidance, life management skills, and helping people get unstuck at transition points in their development, to analysis of dysfunctional family or organizational systems and intervention in cases of severe pathology.

Such training is almost always obtained through an accredited university program. A significant part of the training can include a three month practicum experience at a mission setting under the supervision of an experienced member care provider (O'Donnell, 1988). Another possibility is doing a one to two year counseling internship in a mission setting which could count towards the hours needed to obtain professional licensure as a therapist. An example of such an internship will be discussed in the next section.

## Preparation for Member Care Professionals

The remainder of this chapter will focus on the preparation and utilization of "Level Four" workers—professional member care workers who provide therapeutic services to the mission community.

### Technical Training

The technical training for professional member care counselors and therapists must include at least masters-level training in a reputable school. Course-work should include actual participation in courses as opposed to merely taking correspondence courses that do not involve personal interaction, feedback, contact, and practice. Basic courses include human development, dysfunction and pathology, testing and measurement, learning, personal growth, counseling, and personality theory. In addition Biblical Studies courses and courses on the integration of Scripture and psychological concepts are foundational for the Christian member care professional.

If possible, a specialty program in mission psychology or mission counseling which includes a relevant practicum or supervised experience within a given mission organization would be beneficial. Any additional training that might be available (such as organizational and community psychology, cross-cultural counseling, and missions courses) will also be useful and can be part of preparation.

### Missions Experience

A member care professional, both for personal credibility and a sense of adequacy, would greatly benefit from time overseas in a mission's apprenticeship or from working with an experienced missionary or missionary team. There is no substitute for going through the same experiences—the joys and the sorrows, the challenges and the victories—as those to whom one intends to minister. Such experiences expose a person's tendency to ethnocentrism, increase one's appreciation for diversity and the perceptions of others, and help a person become more aware of personal strengths and limitations. Prior to such field experience, we recommend participation in a mission's orientation program such as through QUEST (Wycliffe) or Missionary Internship.

## General Cross-Cultural Experience

A variety of background experiences in different cultural settings is very useful (e.g., involvement with people in multi-ethnic neighborhoods, studying abroad, living overseas). These experiences increase one's observation skills, respect for difference, tolerance for ambiguity, and ability to relate to others from different cultures. These are skills needed for any cross-cultural worker, but have special implications for care-givers preparing to serve an international mission.

## Organizational Compatibility

We strongly encourage a member care worker to familiarize himself/herself with the organization which he or she wants to serve. Mission agencies vary greatly in their policies and practices, their views of the limitations and/or privileges of power, roles of males and females, opportunities for women in ministry and leadership, control of funds, decisions with regard to the welfare and education of children, freedom of action and self-directed activities, member care needs, work expectations, and ministry foci. In order to work compatibly within a mission organization, one needs to know the organization and subscribe to its policies and practices (Reapsome, 1988).

## Internship and Supervised Experience

An internship carried out in a missions atmosphere with supervision provided by experienced practitioner-missionaries, offers the new care-giver the opportunity to gain experience, make mistakes, ask questions, and shape theories and conceptual data into practical services. One example is the internship offered by Wycliffe located in Dallas, Texas.

The Wycliffe Counseling Internship generally involves two years of hands-on experience under supervision. Dr. Phil and Mrs. Barbara Grossman, founders and pioneers of Wycliffe's counseling services, realized the need for a mechanism such as the internship to permit screening and evaluation of potential mission counselors. Additionally, it allows the intern to experience the intricacies of missionary counseling and thus build a body of memories, techniques, and materials that will serve him/her in an eventual field assignment. Much counseling is done by modeling—so the internship provides an opportunity to work with and observe the intern and his/her spouse and see if their lifestyle, interpersonal skills, and marital and family relationships will support their counseling contribution—or negate it.

The internship has six goals:

1. Developing relationships with other counselors within the Counseling Department for professional and collegial support; awareness of and ease with department policies and uniquenesses.

2. Interacting with the mission agency to familiarize interns with the people and policies of the organization; knowing what is unique about our organization and able to live non-critically and compatibly with those factors.

3. Interfacing with the organization's administration so the therapist knows how to work in tandem with administrators while at the same time retaining his professional separateness.

4. Working with cross-cultural problems to complement any previous professional training and experience.

5. Providing external evaluations by experienced counselors and supervisors to assess compatible and sturdy personality traits, professional skill and competence, biblical awareness and integration, and a balanced and godly lifestyle. The intern can receive corrective input and non-defensively integrate that input.

6. Encouraging self-awareness and self-evaluation as both a person and a professional counselor in the light of this organization and the missions task.

The actual components of the two-year internship program fall into four parts: prerequisites, technical expectations and experience, evaluations, and concluding procedures.

*Prerequisites* that the intern comes with include a master's degree (or equivalent) with a broad technical base, and validations from within and outside the organization. *Technical expectations* include using skills in a mission setting that have been obtained during the internship and from prior training. *Evaluations* are carried out in the beginning, at midpoint, and at the end of the internship. *Concluding procedures* of the internship involve presentation of one's counseling model, a time of oral examination by all counselors present, and submission of a personal program for ongoing growth.

The internship program is quite thorough, as such preparation is essential for the protection and preparation of the intern, and for the confidence of the mission membership. Ten interns have completed this program in the last five years and most are in field locations, serving competently in difficult and often isolated settings.

## Guidelines for Involvement

The following guidelines are presented to help member care professionals (both in-house workers and outside consultants) work with credibility and more effectively within a mission agency. Professional training and experience provide sufficient credibility in some organizations and in some tasks—but they are usually not enough in the member care field. Credibility must be earned. It is a necessary complement to the areas of competence that a member care professional has.

### Personal Relationships

Know and be known. Johnston (1987) suggests that mental health specialists need good interpersonal relationships, especially with mission leaders, in order to increase the acceptability of their services. The same applies to member care professionals in general, who must know the leaders and in turn must be willing to be known by the leaders. This means time must be spent together; missions meetings, field conferences, and inter-agency conferences are attended; and professionals stay updated by reading relevant mission publications.

### Long-Term Service

Sustained contribution is key. There is value in short-term contributions in the areas of training, crisis intervention, and consultation. However, significant changes in people's lives (and agency health) by means of therapy, coaching, organizational development, or preventive ministries normally takes place over longer periods of time. The opportunities for service are vast. A member care professional could choose a particular area of the world, or a particular organization, and devote his/her efforts to this focused audience. Such efforts might include living on a field, making regular visits to the field, being available to furloughing members as a referral source, and/or serving as an ongoing consultant to field leaders.

### Building a Network

Identify a comprehensive referral base. Member care workers do well to establish a network of services in both sending and host countries, as they cannot meet all the needs of their organizations by themselves. The network ideally consists of specialists in individual, marriage, and family counseling; physicians and medical clinics; psychiatrists and psychiatric facilities: pastoral counselors and school psychologists; legal advisors and support groups. A referral network will help direct missionaries to specific services which the in-house member care professional cannot offer due to limited training, time constraints, or lack of availability within the mission agency.

### Building a Team

Work with like-minded colleagues. The formation and building of teams for service to missions personnel is an idea whose time has come.

Some of these teams could provide services from an overseas office as well as make trips to different fields. For example, a small team of three or four care-providers could make regular trips to offer counseling, career guidance, team development resources, and educational aids to parents and teachers. A pastor who could bring spiritual refreshment to field people would enhance such a team.

The team could also be available for crisis intervention. Team members need to understand normal and abnormal responses to stress, know how to do short-term therapy and guide those with longer-term needs to additional resources, be able to serve as consultants to a highly stressed mission leadership, and minister peace and encouragement through teaching from Scripture. Such a team should be skilled in working with both adults and children, in communicating spontaneously and appropriately with groups, and in organizing activities promoting group cohesion and stability.

## Suggestions for In-House Member Care Workers

It is not always easy to find a comfortable niche in the mission agency and settings where one provides services. This is especially true for member care workers who are new to the mission. Here are several practical guidelines (adapted from O'Donnell & O'Donnell, 1990) to help in-house member care workers tailor their services and professional style to fit into the organizational ethos. Many of these suggestions are also relevant for outside consultants. Member care workers would do well to discuss these suggestions together, and to seek out accountable relationships and confidants who can give them feedback as to how they are coming across to mission personnel.

1. Let yourself be known as a real person and as a true servant of Christ. Show your love for Scripture, people, and the ways of the Lord.

2. Use the same terms as the groups with which you work. This includes theological or Scriptural terminology, as well as special terms for colleagues and ministries (e.g., language helpers, personnel officers, mission stations). Avoid technical, psychological jargon and "buzz" words.

3. Contribute in ways beyond your professional services. For instance, one of our Wycliffe counselors is skilled at remodeling; every apartment he lived in for any length of time was vastly improved by his presence. Take your turn proof-reading a publication, collating papers, or cleaning up after tea.

4. Avoid dichotomizing spiritual and psychological approaches to care. Emotional health and spiritual living are not mutually exclusive. For example, psychological problems, interpersonal relationships, or authority issues can be addressed from Romans chapters 12-15.

5. Providing effective treatment to staff, especially leaders, can increase credibility (Proverbs 22:29). Try offering educative or preventive seminars on stress, burnout, and team relationships; serving as a consultant in personnel matters; developing written materials for specific issues such as reentry or family adjustment packets; and having a voice in leadership discussions which deal with personnel issues, when invited to do so.

6. Develop relationships with influential people who can help increase the acceptability and availability of your services. Examples include evaluators, trainers, ministry and department heads, and others who are respected in the agency.

7. Do not attack the organization or be critical toward its practices. If there are concerns, seek out the appropriate leaders and discuss the situation or practice privately. Every organization has strengths and weaknesses—do not be overly alarmed when you uncover unhealthy practices. Every organization also has its own ethos—know what it is, understand it, and work with it.

8. Move slowly. It takes time to develop credibility, respect, and a reputation of trustworthiness (Zechariah 4:10). It also takes time to develop relationships with busy leaders.

9. Anticipate a "learning by doing" experience. Much of your training has to be adapted to a cross-cultural or in-house agency setting and may need revision. Be prepared to encounter issues and problems no one ever anticipated during your training program.

10. Expect to make some mistakes (the organization will too). You will probably make some errors as you set up your services, apply ethical principles, and handle the myriad of logistical matters (agency policies, budget, phone calls, reporting system, record keeping, and so on).

11. Adjust your expectations from having worked in private practice and non-mission settings. Adequate pay, professional respect and courtesy, adequate facilities—none of these may be true for your field experience. Expect to reach out to people, rather than waiting for them to come knocking on your office door.

12. Get personal support from confidants—develop an emotional and relationship network for personal health and balance. Involve yourself with the mission community and friends, and maintain healthy, wholesome relationships.

13. Understand and anticipate some of the ethical ambiguities of practice in mission settings. Holding the line on ethical and professional standards while at the same time maintaining and building trust and confidence between yourself and administrators is not easy, but it is essential. One area of ambiguity is the matter of dual relationships—the people you see in counseling are those with whom you socialize, worship, and discuss organizational business. Another is the matter of making referrals when you are beyond your skill level when there is no one to whom to refer.

# Suggestions for Outside Member Care Providers

We realize that many times a deeply committed Christian member care professional wants to give a portion of his/her time and skill to the missions effort. Here are several ways that these professionals could serve the missions community and some cautions to observe.

1. Serve as a referral source in your own location. Make your availability known to mission agencies and your willingness to see furloughing members. Clarify guidelines for the nature of your involvement, especially confidentiality issues.

2. Serve as consultants to mission leaders and mission counselors in your areas of expertise. This can be done at your home location as well as through short-term visits to different fields.

3. Serve as supervisors, if trained and certified to do so, for mission counselors and therapists with whom you have established a relationship. We have found that adequate supervision can also be provided by telephone for therapists in remote areas with no access to such input in their location.

4. Give workshops or seminars in your areas of expertise to groups of missionaries. For instance, develop seminars on family life, marriage enrichment, and stress management. Make this known to mission leaders and counselors, and volunteer your services.

5. Offer short-term counseling services on the field. Make sure that appropriate follow-up services can be provided as necessary, whether it be through phone calls and letters on your part or additional services by other member care workers.

6. Become part of a mission effort yourself. The hardships and rewards of field work will not only add to your credibility, but also be a source of blessing to the people with whom you work.

## Cautions for Outside Professionals

There are a few basic cautions to keep in mind when providing services to missionary personnel. Here are some of them.

1. "Normal" functioning means something vastly different for a cross-cultural Christian worker than for someone working and living in North America, Britain, or Europe. It demands a much higher ability to cope with stress, to live compatibly and closely with people very different from oneself, and to have resolved old issues and patterns of behavior which can impair one's effectiveness.

Therapists, for example, can err by recommending a potential worker or furloughing worker for continuing service, deeming him/her ready for mission activity when in fact the person needs more time for restoration and care. The failure to understand the isolation, stringencies, and demands of missionary life is one of the reasons mission leaders are reluctant to utilize the services of consultants and therapists who are not experienced in missions.

It takes time to solidify and test new growth. New coping skills and patterns of communication must be tested and solidified in an environment that is familiar and supportive. A minimum of three months is desirable between termination of therapy and reentry into the field task.

2. Long-term therapy is usually not an option. Missionary personnel are not free agents; they are on the field or in the home office as part of an organization, having made a commitment to contribute to that organization's goals. Normally they are supported by churches and individuals in their sending country. They do not have the luxury of long-term therapy at others' expense.

On the other hand, there can be problems with short-term therapy. Most missionaries are eager to resolve problems and get back to their task quickly. This may push them to premature resolution of problems; and it may push a therapist to premature solutions and closure of therapy. At the same time, there will be little patience with therapy (by either the member, supporting constituents, or the organization) that extends over a lengthy period of time.

3. Aim for independent, practical self-care. Many mission workers must take care of themselves because there are few if any support services around them. It may not be possible for them to get involved in a support group, or weekly meetings with their pastor, or set up an accountability relationship with a local friend, as these resources may not be available. Avoid making suggestions, then, that are not feasible. Workers need practical tools and ideas for maintaining their own emotional health.

Do not overlook the major role of spiritual resources. Missionaries all have access to the Scriptures. Most derive a significant part of their strength through reading and meditating on the Bible. Encourage this, and incorporate Scripture explicitly into any services you render. Member care consultants and therapists need to be able to practically apply Scripture and help others do the same. A therapist should not assume that this resource is obvious for the member.

## Suggestions for Mission Administrators

Both in-house and outside member care professionals must be prepared to adjust their lifestyles and work styles so as to fit into the organization. In most cases, the burden of change is on the member care professional, not the organization. Nonetheless, it behooves mission leaders to be aware of the special needs and backgrounds of these professionals, so as to help them fit more readily into the organization and utilize them more effectively. Here are some guidelines (based on O'Donnell & O'Donnell, 1990) for mission leaders to consider.

1. Dialogue on mutual expectations, practices, and apprehensions. How will services be rendered? What are the fees, if any? Do members really want to utilize these services? To whom is the member care professional accountable? These and other questions must be openly addressed, making it necessary to interact with each other on a regular basis.

2. Be merciful if confronted with the member care professional's "disciplinary culture." A consulting psychologist, for example, has been trained in a discipline as stringent as that of a medical practitioner; he/she will have to observe the discipline's ethical guidelines, may use technical terms specific to the profession, and perhaps not think of problems from an administrative perspective. The health and welfare of an individual member or a family may have a higher priority than organizational goals. They may also push to obtain office space which is private, peaceful, and nicely furnished to see missionary clients, even though such space is at a premium. Try to see things from their perspective.

3. Clarify any plans to use the member care professional as "an arm of the administration." While the member care worker does indeed serve the mission leadership, he or she cannot and should not be viewed as part of the administrative structure, nor used as a disciplinary measure—"If you don't shape up, I'll send you to the counselor and he'll fix you." Most professionals function best when they can retain a neutral posture that supports both administrator and member. Allow them to stay out of the administrative structure, and off certain decision-making committees.

4. Find ways to increase the acceptability of the services offered by member care professionals, especially for these types of people: (a) Rugged individualists—"We toughed it out; why can't others do the same? Who needs a counselor to tell us what to do?—we never had one in the old days." (b) Overly spiritual people—"We have Christ, the Holy Spirit and God's Word—why do we need any psychological help?" and (c) Those who are out of touch with their own needs—"I am too busy to get distracted with introspection; we must decrease and Christ must increase."

A field leader could help these and others utilize member care services by announcing these services well beforehand, preparing an introductory meeting to discuss what the member care professional(s) will do, and publicly endorsing (when possible) the member care professional. Having member care professionals give a testimony or share a devotional message can also lower resistances and relax apprehensions.

5. Involve mental care workers in the planning and revision of member care policies and services. They are not only service providers, but service developers. Many have training and experience in setting-up services, so tap into all of their skills.

6. Encourage interaction with other member care workers and mental health professionals. The job of "caring for people's souls" is extremely stressful and draining of emotional energy. One of the ways to renew

member care workers is to encourage them to attend conferences, make time to read professional materials, and meet with professional colleagues.

7. Provide an "organizational/administrative bridge" to the member care worker. Workers need to feel connected, understood and appreciated, especially by those over them. Find someone with whom they can easily relate who can help them fit into the organization's ethos and connect with leadership.

8. Distribute member care responsibility. One member care professional or department cannot take on the sole or even primary responsibility for member care. It is a corporate responsibility. Professionals may provide specialized services, but the backbone of any effective member care program involves an organizational ethos which encourages the ongoing, informal, mutual support between mission personnel.

## Opportunities for Continuing Growth

Egan (1986) states that effective people-helpers "are first of all committed to their own growth—physical, intellectual, social-emotional, and spiritual—for they realize that helping often involves modeling the patterns of behavior their clients hope to achieve" (p. 28). A commitment to ongoing personal and professional growth is requisite for maintaining effectiveness as a member care worker. Personal growth comes through such things as healthy relationships, fellowship, prayer, and recreational activities. Professional growth is obtained through interaction with colleagues, ongoing formal and nonformal education, reading, and so on.

Certain types of professional growth, though, can be hard to find. This is certainly true for the member care workers who serve in field assignments. For example, where is a field therapist to find quality supervision? Within Wycliffe, our answer has been supervision by telephone, provided by experienced missions counselors who can quickly grasp the issues without having to have organizational ethos, administrative field practices, or environmental stressors explained. When the phone call is originated in the United States, for example, the cost is considerably less than when placed from an overseas number. Monthly or biweekly calls of one hour have been sufficient, and not unduly expensive.

Another possibility is to utilize mental health professionals who are located in large cities around the world—Hong Kong, Singapore, Manila, Guatemala City, Nairobi, for example. These could certainly be approached in order to develop some type of supervisory or consultative relationship.

What are some other ideas for personal and professional growth? Books, videos and audio tapes, book reviews, a quarterly letter to all the counselors in the department, and subscriptions to professional journals and magazines are some of the ways the Wycliffe Counseling Department seeks to encourage and stimulate field counselors. As another means of stimulation, consider holding a biennial retreat where all counselors and spouses gather for extended debriefing, reports, and encouragement. Annual visits by an international coordinator or counselor are also useful.

For member care workers located closer to growth options (such as those who reside in the United States), we encourage a minimum of 25 contact hours of professional seminars per year, as well as a planned program of reading and professional interaction. A requirement for field counselors, or those planning to serve on the field as counselors, should be an articulated, written, and demonstrated commitment to continuing professional, personal and spiritual growth (and follow-through on this). We believe this is essential to maintain stability, perspective, and freshness.

## Conclusion

Member care is neither a discrete entity nor a task that can be relegated solely to the professional. It must permeate the organization as an articulated value and be practically demonstrated in the ethos. An important part of this ethos involves the skillful utilization of competent professionals who are dedicated to the evangelization task and to the goals of the mission organization. Respect for the mission membership and for the task of reaching the world for Christ should prompt us all to be as thoroughly prepared as possible if we are providers of member care—and to utilize professionals as wisely as possible if we are in the role of administration.

If mission organizations want to attract and keep high quality missionaries, they/we will have to consider new directions, techniques and contributions to meet member needs. According to Barrett (1991), there are 4050 foreign mission sending agencies contributing to world evangelism. Those considering missionary service have many options of organizations to join. We believe the kind of member care provided by a given organization is something these prospective missionary personnel will consider.

We would like to propose four member care components that can help mission organizations support their staff more effectively:

1. An adequate member care ethos permeating the mission organization with leaders subscribing to and participating in member care. This ethos must consider care of whole families as well as individual adult members and encourage members to care for one another.

2. A sound corps of member care givers within the organization who are equipped to provide such care through educative, preventive, therapeutic, and consultative means.

3. A trauma team that is trained, funded, and able to respond immediately to calls for help. This trauma team need not come from a specific organization, but can be jointly utilized by many organizations. However, it is comprised of missions-experienced care-givers.

4. A network of counseling centers on the fields located in large cities or centers, staffed by a variety of specialists, serving the total mission community in that area.

We believe responsible care of our members reflects a conscientious use of resources, honors God, lowers attrition rates, and demonstrates the gospel in relational and God-glorifying ways. Providing such care—through member care professionals and through fellow missionaries—is essential for the long-term effectiveness of our staff.

### Questions for Discussion

1. What are the pros and cons of using care-givers who are not members of the organization versus those who are serving within that organization?

2. What types of member care workers does your organization utilize?

3. How might an organization raise money to pay for additional member care services and professionals?

4. Which of the four levels of counselor training described in this article are most relevant for your mission organization?

5. What changes could your organization make now in order to begin to establish a more caring environment?

## References

Barrett, D. (1991). The status of the christian world mission in the 1990s. *Mission in the 1990s.* New Haven, CT: Overseas Ministries Study Center.

Bush, L. (1992). (Ed.). *AD 2000 and beyond.* San Jose, CA: AD 2000 and Beyond.

Egan, G. (1986). *The skilled helper: Model, skills, and methods for effective helping (3rd ed.).* Monterey, CA: Brooks/Cole.

Johnston, L. (1988). Building relationships between mental health specialists and mission agencies. In O'Donnell, K., & O'Donnell, M. (Eds.). *Helping missionaries grow: Readings in mental health and missions* (pp. 449-457). Pasadena, CA: William Carey Library.

O'Donnell, K. (1988). A preliminary study of psychologists in missions. In O'Donnell, K., & O'Donnell, M. (Eds.). *Helping missionaries grow: Readings in mental health and missions* (pp. 118-125). Pasadena, CA: William Carey Library.

O'Donnell, K., & O'Donnell, M. (1990). *Suggestions for involvement in missions as psychologists.* Unpublished manuscript. Amsterdam: Youth With A Mission.

Pate, L. (1991). The changing balance in global mission. *International Bulletin of Missionary Research, 15,* 56-61.

Reapsome, J. (1988). Choosing a mission board. *Evangelical Missions Quarterly, 24,* 6-13.

# 24

*Brent Lindquist*

# Missionary Support Centers

This chapter will focus, to a large extent, on my personal experience working at and more recently leading a missionary support center based in the United States (Link Care Center). First, I will provide a brief description of this center. Then I will cover some guidelines on the planning, development, and maintenance of similar centers in overseas contexts. The article closes with a summary of two proposals—one actual and one hypothetical—to set up a missionary support center.

## Brief Description of Link Care

Twenty-seven years ago Link Care Center was established as a support ministry for the comprehensive restoration of Christian workers in cross-cultural contexts. The founder, Dr. Stanley Lindquist, had been in Europe on sabbatical leave from his position as a Professor of Psychology at California State University, Fresno, in order to work on a book. During that time he and his family (myself included) visited many missionaries throughout the European continent in 17 countries. Through times of fellowship and chatting around the dinner tables, missionaries would find out that my father was a psychologist. Sensing a low degree of threat and a high degree of acceptance, they began to open up to him about the problems with which they were struggling—problems that they did not see as readily solvable, either on the field or at home, due to a lack of resource people who were sensitive to the needs of those in cross-cultural ministry. At that time the vision seed was planted in my father's heart, and grew to fruition a couple of years later with the establishment of Link Care.

Link Care initially only included Stan Lindquist in his private practice office in central Fresno. Missionaries would come, stay as guests in homes, and go through individual counseling with him. He provided the bulk of the psychological services. Outside consultants were used as necessary. A board was soon established. A few years later a piece of property, a retirement complex, was purchased.

From these humble beginnings, Link Care has grown to an 8.5 acre complex with 107 apartment units, 28 guest rooms, 10 counseling offices, meeting rooms, seminar rooms, food service, and administrative buildings. Approximately one hundred seniors live on the campus in 85 of the apartments. The remaining apartments are kept available for occupancy by missionaries and ministers during their time at Link Care. These apartments are fully furnished, with as many comforts as can be available.

While not an in-patient facility, Link Care has a unique residential flavor to it. At any given time there may be 20 to 25 adults from up to 10 or 12 mission agencies and approximately 20 children living on campus. There is a library, basketball court, volleyball court, playground, and swimming pool for the families to utilize. In 1990 a smaller office was started in eastern Pennsylvania as Link Care East.

The focus of our work has been primarily psychological and pastoral, with pastoral care staff working with the counseling staff to meet the needs of the missionary. Concerted attempts are made to move away from an individual-based model of care to a more systems-community-based model of care. In addition, we are endeavoring to integrate the linguistic and anthropological disciplines as they relate to the healing as well as learning process. Link Care also offers pre-field orientation seminars, psychological assessment services for candidates, an MK program to assist MKs and their families, and language learning and cultural adaptation workshops. Currently there is a staff of eleven counselors: intern level; marriage, family, and child therapists; psychologists; and pastoral counselors. A typical week for a missionary might involve anywhere from two to five hours of individual or couple sessions with a therapist, one or more pastoral care sessions with the pastoral care staff, a community group meeting, and a men's or women's group. The remaining time is spent in reading, study, recreation, and the usual responsibilities for daily living.

While the program has been somewhat flexible in that a missionary could come for anywhere from two weeks to a year for help, the changing economic environment of the world today, as well as the ways in which health care benefits are paid, is causing some significant changes in the delivery of health care services. What this basically means is that we are having to decrease the length of time that we have available to work with missionaries. Link Care has usually been able to provide intensive services over a short period of time, and while the average length of stay has been from three to five months, we are finding that this might be beyond the resources of increasing numbers of mission organizations and missionaries.

Consequently, brief programs of as little as a week or two weeks are being developed and are in operation.

## Setting Up Missionary Support Centers

Over the last ten years we have received increasing inquiries into how to set up missionary support centers (MSCs) like Link Care in various parts of the world. So far I have seen six concrete proposals set forth with strong, at least verbal, backing from mission organizations that would like to see such a center come into being. While there is a lot of good will being passed around, there is little follow through in terms of making an effort to see something happen. I have talked with numerous people who have been trying to raise funds for a year or years for their support center, based on the initial positive response they received from a number of mission executives. Emotional support, though, is not the only factor that is needed. Financial commitments and other resources are also required to back up these embryonic proposals.

The problem is that most missions do not have money for such MSCs. It is hard to see the frustration on the part of people who, in good faith, sacrificed greatly to try to raise interest and support for an idea that the missions themselves have not been able to bring to fruition in any sort of tangible way. As a result, the six proposals of which I speak have never come to pass. One of the disadvantages of that is that there is somewhat of a reputation in the missions community of us mental-health-types always putting forth ideas but never following through with actual programs. This seems to result in some reticence on the part of mission organizations to actively support proposals because so many have come before and have not been realized.

In spite of all the above, I believe it to be timely to continue the effort to set up MSCs overseas. This chapter reflects what I would do if I had the resources necessary to establish the kind of overseas centers I have been thinking, dreaming, and planning about for a number of years. Most of the guidelines I discuss emphasize the need for both a clear philosophy of ministry and a realistic development strategy that includes a sound marketing plan, without which most entities are doomed to either mediocrity or failure.

Once the philosophy of ministry and development strategy have been formulated, there needs to be a phase in which the ideas are shared and seriously discussed with mission executives. It is at this point that the advocates for the proposed MSC will seriously approach mission organizations for ideas, input, funding, backing, and other resources.

## Services

What types of services will the MSC provide? The possibilities include medical evaluation and treatment, pastoral counseling and care, individual and family therapy, cross-cultural and missions training, supervision for member care trainees, and crisis intervention teams. The services emphasized would make a real difference in terms of how an MSC would go about seeking to gather support for its programs. For the purpose of this chapter, we will assume that the desire is to provide some combination of spiritual-psychological services to support and help restore missionary personnel.

The MSC also needs to address its philosophy towards working with the national support services in the country. If one takes the long view that the MSC is there to stay for awhile, it will naturally—if it is planned correctly—grow into something that can also be a viable resource for the national church or local nationals in the surrounding countries. This may include, but not be limited to, having nationals on the staff and being accountable to a local advisory board.

## Prevention Approaches

Will there be an emphasis on primary, secondary, or tertiary prevention? Ideally, an MSC could provide all three types of prevention approaches for the missionary personnel it has targeted.

Primary prevention seeks to limit the incidence of problems by focusing on the development of missionaries and ways for them to live effectively. Conducting on-field seminars to facilitate cross-cultural adjustment would be an example. Secondary prevention helps missionaries deal with the problems that arise (such as the educational needs of MKs or discouragement on the field) and thus decreases the impact of the inevitable struggles of missionary life. Tertiary prevention occurs after the fact, when an accident or illness has already occurred, and seeks to minimize the residual effects of problems. Examples include supporting a staff member following a traumatic event or counseling a couple with marital problems.

MSC planners and organizers need to take into account these different approaches to prevention. Focusing on tertiary prevention means that the MSC will typically be responding to crises, rather than developing strategies to avoid crises in the first place. In the long run, initial costs in primary and secondary prevention help to reduce the much heavier costs of tertiary prevention efforts, while also extending the range of services to a greater number of people.

## Target Groups

Which specific groups will be targeted for ministry and services? Some possibilities: the local missionary population, mission personnel located throughout a large region, administrative levels of missions, national leaders and believers, and the local community.

I believe it is especially important to clarify the degree to which MSC staff are willing to work with nationals. In some situations, maintaining a strict focus on a specific missionary population may be in order, while in other situations it may only alienate national believers and other groups. A national, for example, might argue that he or she deals with stress and strain in ministry and needs the support of other people as well (for instance, the Indonesian national who is church planting among Indonesian Muslims). There is a potential for the national to see a missionary support center as just another resource that the missionary has that he or she does not share with the national. In this way the MSC runs the risk of actually being more of a divisive influence in the larger community, at least from the perspective of the national.

The lines between national missionary and foreign missionary will continue to be blurred as the missions movement expands. Nationals will increasingly work in other countries as well as remain in their own country as missionaries. An MSC, then, might work with people from many other countries who may be in that country as missionaries, or nationals who live in or have returned to their home country and need assistance and support. Therefore, it would make more sense that an MSC starting out now establish a long-term plan to develop and include services for nationals and missionaries from the Two-Thirds World.

### Potential Staff and Reimbursement

Who will work at MSCs? The kind of services that will be provided will obviously determine the staff skills and disciplines that will be required. Examples include psychologists, pastoral counselors, physicians, psychiatrists, and marriage, family, and child counselors. There is a wide spectrum of mental, emotional, and interpersonal problems that require a variety of services.

At Link Care most of our staff have graduate degrees and are licensed in their particular discipline. Sometimes licensure is a lengthy process, though it really pays off in the long-term as regards receiving third-party reimbursement for services. If an MSC does not charge for its services, this point might be moot, although pragmatically one wonders how long an MSC could support itself in that way. If on the other hand an MSC hopes to get reimbursement through other missions' health-care benefit plans, it will have to be staffed by people who will be licensed or qualified for such reimbursement.

## Short and Long-Term Goals

What is a reasonable time frame for an MSC to become operational? To begin, a distinction needs to be made between short and long-term goals as part of the development of a multi-year plan of action. The establishment of MSCs and their various programs will take time. It is entirely realistic to expect that some aspects of the MSC may be ten years in development. This needs to be understood by churches and other supporters who want to invest in these centers. It takes time to plan, time to build, time to gain credibility, and time to become viable in the overseas setting. Five to ten years is an appropriate time frame to consider.

## Relationship with Other Organizations

With whom can the MSC partner and network in providing its services? An MSC will probably be grounded in an existing organization, whether that means one particular mission organization or a joint cooperative effort of a group of mission organizations. Many mission organizations have a history in their target countries. A new group seeking accreditation or permission that is unknown to national leaders is not going to get as far as the group affiliated with the mission organization that is already accepted and established. Being connected with a larger organization is also important for the personal and emotional support of the MSC staff. This connection provides accountability and a sense of integration into larger corporate goals. Furthermore, there should be regular relating to other professionals to facilitate the flow of ideas, research, data, continuing development, and professional support.

## Avoiding Paternalism

What types of attitudes are needed to provide effective care? As I travel around and listen to various mental health professionals explain their vision for serving missionaries, it often ends up sounding rather paternalistic in terms of "we in the mental health profession have solutions for your problems, the answers to all your questions. If missionaries and organizations would utilize us, problems would be greatly reduced." The fact is that there is a lot that mental health professionals need to understand and learn in order to be effective providers of care to people in cross-cultural work as well as nationals in those countries. The best starting place is for those who staff MSCs to embrace learner-servant roles as they seek to minister to their targeted groups.

### Needs and Resource Assessment

What needs do mission personnel have, and what MSC services do they think would be useful? These questions must be researched in order to make sure that the MSC is really providing services relevant to the target groups. Do not assume you know best!

Be sure to also include nationals in the needs assessment process. Very few studies have been done that ask nationals about the kinds of problems that missionaries face. Surveying the nationals can be quite expensive and require some trips to the target area, but it may also serve to forge links into the country.

## Two Proposals for a Missionary Support Center

This section describes two separate proposals for setting up missionary support centers. The first one is currently being pursued by several mental health professionals while the second one is hypothetical. As you will notice, the proposals differ in the location chosen, the range of people served, and the types of services to be provided.

### Proposal One

This first proposal summarizes a plan for a missionary support center which is to be located in the vicinity of Colorado Springs, Colorado (Dodds, Dodds, and Schaefer, 1992). The center will primarily emphasize the care and restoration of hurting, emotionally-wounded missionaries. While I wish such a center were being set up in an overseas context, the fact that so many mission agencies have relocated in this area as well as the plan for this center to send out short-term member care teams and eventually spawn similar centers overseas, makes its development strategic. This proposed MSC is no easy venture. I appreciate my colleagues for the challenges and sacrifices that they are undertaking to develop this center and for their future plans to target geographic areas where missionaries and national Christians have limited access to member care resources.

*MSC Proposal.* As the world becomes increasingly complex and the pressures upon missionaries increase, we expect to see an increase in the number of foreign missionaries with crisis-level needs. Places of respite and healing are needed for the global missions community, free from the usual myriad of responsibilities of both field and furlough, with a staff specifically equipped to minister to their unique needs.

This proposal is to establish a residential center for missionaries who suffer burnout or other serious forms of distress. Healing and growth will occur in the context of a nurturing, loving community in which the fruits of the Spirit and professional skills are utilized. The center will also offer training for missionaries, leaders, and support personnel to help prevent such incapacitating problems as burnout.

The center will be set up as an independent entity, with an advisory board and board of directors made up of persons from different mission organizations and churches. It will be legally incorporated as a non-profit organization which will allow financial gifts to be tax-deductible. The process of setting up the MSC as a legal entity will take up to two years. Other practicalities we are looking into include applying for grants from various foundations, obtaining licenses to provide medical and psychological services, purchasing liability insurance, and providing health insurance benefits for staff.

Staff will include professionals from counseling and related health care fields. Many will be bilingual, and most will have had extensive cross-cultural experience overseas. About 20 such professionals are seriously considering full-time work in the center, hopefully supported by their current mission boards.

Care and therapy will be holistic and include spiritual, emotional, interpersonal, cognitive, and physical components, in recognition of the many dimensions of the human personality and the complexities of the needs of missionaries. Emphasis will be on a team of professionals cooperating together to foster the healing of each individual and family. These professionals will live in community with those in need of care.

Each person will receive a thorough medical consultation and assessment coordinated by a resident physician, and follow-up care provided by a network of local medical professionals. The resident clinical psychologist will work along with resident counselors to determine the most helpful modes of therapy. Individual, family, and group counseling will be provided.

Corporate daily worship and therapeutic prayer will be emphasized as foundational for the creation of a healthy community and personal healing. A resident pastoral counselor will minister specifically to the spiritual needs of the residents and staff. Classes and various educational programs will allow participants to gain greater personal awareness and develop new skills (e.g., interpersonal communication, stress management). A library will be available. Staff will also use the center as a "launching pad" from which to offer training and services to missionaries abroad.

The length of stay will vary, according to the needs of the missionaries. Expenses will be paid on a fee per service sliding scale. Contributions from mission agencies using these services, as well as other outside supporters, will be necessary.

The ideal physical setting seems to be one removed from the pressures of city life, in a rural location in which the beauty of creation and nature are most visible. Distractions would be reduced and participants could focus more on their healing and growth. A camp or resort setting with a lodge or large group-living facility, plus homes or cabins for staff is ideal. Opportunities for different recreational activities, as well as access to a major airport within two hours' driving, are also important features.

The tentative location of the MSC is in Colorado. The major reasons for this location include the restful, rural setting; the availability of funding from local supporters; the fact that many mission organizations are located or are relocating in this area; access to a network of community resources, especially physical health and mental health professionals; and above all, a collective sense of God leading us to this area at this time. It is our hope that this center will serve as a model and training ground out of which other MSCs will develop overseas. We see the need for the missions and member care community to set up at least one such MSC in each continent or major geographic region of the world.

## Proposal Two

In the attempt to incorporate many of the concerns I have expressed earlier in the chapter, the following is a report and prospectus for a possible overseas MSC. I refer to this MSC as an *International Support and Learning Center* (ISLC). While it is entirely fictitious, it does reflect some of the major steps I would incorporate in bringing such a center into reality. The report will undoubtedly raise several questions related to legal, professional, and logistical issues, which will have to be worked out. Central to this report is the philosophical emphasis of service to the wider community and the international nature of staff.

*MSC Report and Proposal.* The International Support and Learning Center grew out of an idea first developed in 1986. At that point interested missionaries and allied health care professionals gathered at Link Care in Fresno, California, to form a Task Force that would oversee the initial plans for an ISLC in what was then an unspecified country. This ISLC was to be a joint venture. Throughout the year meetings and correspondence cemented the relationships between three mission boards, Link Care Center, and some potential staff for the proposed center. The Task Force also developed a ten-year plan for the center. Since the three mission organizations were working in western Africa, it was decided to establish the center in that part of the world.

The Task Force agreed to set up a Board of Directors consisting of members from each of the sponsoring organizations; the proposed ISLC, however, was to remain autonomous. Further, it was to be understood that half of the board members would be nationals from the targeted part of the world. Finally, they made plans to establish an advisory board of local ministry and professional people from the host country who would serve as a guide and a networking vehicle into the local community.

Following the development of partnership documents and memorandums of understanding, the search for a site began. Throughout 1987 potential sites were investigated. It was decided that the location for the

ISLC would be in Abidjan, the capital of Ivory Coast, because of its central location in the region, good transportation network, and political stability. In addition, Abidjan was already the location of a cooperative mission effort by the three mission organizations in conjunction with local African groups. The ISLC was to be located in several offices adjacent to the grounds of the local seminary. It was in an area of the capital that was relatively stable and peaceful, and in close proximity to the mission agencies, sites for potential housing, and the local national university. The site also had space available for construction of future buildings for housing and training programs.

1988 saw the development of a marketing proposal to raise funds for the center and for an initial needs assessment. In addition, key preliminary staff from each organization were identified. Later that year, one of the mental health professionals who did not have extensive missionary or language skills, entered language school in France. This was in keeping with the long-term goal of the center to provide resources to the local community, the nation, the language area, the local church, and the mission organizations. In order to do this, the staff would need to be proficient in the international language of the area—French—as well as develop strategies to become proficient in the local varieties of language that would be important in the ministry ventures.

Following language school, the mental health professional spent the first six months of 1989 working in an orphanage in a different part of Abidjan in order to learn Ivoirian French and immerse himself in the local culture. At this time he signed a contract to teach a few courses related to mental health at the local university. This gave him the opportunity to develop relationships with like-minded professionals in the university system.

By June of 1989 the local advisory board had been identified and was being formed, with the by-laws and rules of behavior being developed. Around the same time the mission groups began raising finances for the long-term goal of providing a revolving fund for the people whose resources were so limited that they would otherwise be prevented from receiving help.

In 1990, another African mental health resource person was identified. This person had experience in the local church and was about to graduate from the local university with a master's degree. Over the next two years, this person affiliated himself with the ISLC and raised financial support.

Upon completing his ministry at the orphanage, the mental health professional worked with the local advisory board of the ISLC to conduct an extensive needs and resource assessment focusing on churches and missionaries in that part of the world. It transpired that there was a national psychiatrist in Abidjan who had received training in France and was a practicing Christian. This person was brought on board as a full member of the resource team, albeit on a consultant basis.

In 1991, after all the appropriate personnel were relocated and settled in the capital, the first programs were offered. These were mainly seminars and were conducted for both the missionaries and the national Christians. In addition, a very productive time was spent at the national university in teaching classes and participating in a budding Christian student movement, particularly involving the students in mental health and medical professions.

Finally, in early 1992 (at the time of this report) the property adjacent to the seminary was purchased and the building program began. Buildings will consist of a 5000 square-foot counseling and training center with appropriate housing to follow at a later time, hopefully within the next four years. Future plans include remodeling the existing buildings on the property and moving staff into the new housing by the middle of 1994. Early 1995 is the projected date for the establishment of a full-fledged counseling center for all of the various target groups.

Although funding has been a real struggle, a number of sources have been identified. First of all, the sponsoring organizations have been able to fund the administrative expenses. The North American staff are partially supported, like missionaries, with the remainder of their support coming from fee-for-service from the clients' organizations. Additional finances will be derived from project funds within the various supporting agencies.

One of the special ministries of the ISLC will be to train and mentor Christian graduate students from the national university, some of whom could go to work for the agency as member care workers and counselors. Hopefully by 1994 the first African staff person will be able to spend time at Link Care for further training, and to teach at the local seminary and graduate school of psychology. This person will also stand for licensure in California in order to provide accredited supervision to North Americans and others at a future training program to be developed in Ivory Coast.

In 1996, at the end of the ten-year plan, the facility with its various ministries will be complete and functional. By this time, the expatriate workers will have been in the country for several years and will have developed proficiency in the language and culture. There will be a professional group comprised of expatriate and national resource people affiliated with the ISLC. Missionaries coming to the center will thus have options for being treated and trained by expatriates and nationals. The entire staff will be respected members of a broad section of various communities, including the missionary community, the church community, and the national professional community. In conjunction with national professionals, they will have developed professional models of treatment that are being utilized throughout the country and will have developed a trauma team ready to respond to regional crises and disasters. In addition, they will have become resource people for training health and allied health care professionals in Ivory Coast as well as in surrounding countries.

## Conclusion

So how do we go about setting up a missionary support center? Where is the definitive plan? Well, there is none—at least not at this time! Actually, there are so many options and details to consider that there can be no real step-by-step plan except to plan well. No amount of vision or zeal for this type of work will ever take the place of good planning, careful attention to detail, regular review of progress, and the development of new or alternative plans in the face of lack of progress.

Missionary support centers are but one small part—albeit a vital part—in the development and care of mission personnel. Such centers are especially needed to support the growing number of career missionaries from the Two-Thirds World. Those of us from Western countries must be careful to take on a more global frame of reference to reduce the ethnocentrism and paternalism that might be inherent in our efforts.

There is a rising group of Christian professionals around the world who want to provide help to missionaries as well. Many are multi-lingual and understand the culture of the nationals and missionaries from their respective countries and regions. We need to diligently seek out and link up with these Christian professionals.

It remains to be seen just what will happen with the different desires and plans to set up MSCs overseas. Their time is coming. The handwriting, so to speak, is already on the wall. Who will rise up to the challenge? Missionary support centers are a strategic, worthwhile investment. May the Lord give us grace to persevere and trust Him as the missions and member care community seek to establish such centers around the world.

### Questions for Discussion

1. What are some of the predictable challenges and hindrances that would be encountered when establishing missionary support centers in different countries?

2. Where would be some strategic locations to set up missionary support centers?

3. What are some of the advantages and disadvantages of providing services exclusively to missionary personnel?

4. How would you develop long-term funding for a missionary support center that you want to start?

5. What practicalities would need to be considered if staff from missionary support centers were to regularly travel to different fields in order to provide their services?

# References

Dodds, L., Dodds, L., & Schaefer, C. (1992). *A proposal to establish a residential center for the restoration and healing of missionaries who suffer burnout or other serious difficulties, using multimodal therapy and a holistic approach*. Unpublished manuscript. Santa Barbara, CA: Author.

# 25

*Hans Ritschard*

# The Member Care Consultation

Member care must be a collective endeavor. The participation of the whole missions community is required, from key leaders to care providers, to ensure the full benefit of member care services. We must gather and build upon the experiences of others, depending upon them to share their wisdom and expertise, and especially involve those who have provided care for many years.

One means of gathering this expertise might be termed the "member care consultation." Several of these have sprung up over the past decade or so, and have begun to connect member care providers with mission agencies, missions personnel, and ultimately, with missionaries themselves. This chapter will discuss these consultations from several perspectives, including their theoretical underpinnings, their history, and their salient (and hopefully most helpful) features. Finally, some pragmatic suggestions will be included to aid those who would plan similar meetings in the future.

A word about the term *member care consultation* seems an appropriate place to start. Although *consultation* has been less widely used in connection with member care than the term *conference,* it seems more descriptive of the actual content of these meetings. A conference is usually understood to be a series of meetings where various speakers present their ideas, insights, and knowledge for the benefit of the hearers, presumably in a somewhat didactic manner. A consultation, on the other hand, is conceived as a

The author wishes to thank the members of Enabling the Missionary for their helpful comments and suggestions, especially Cynthia Bloomquist, Jeff Ellis, Laura Hurston English, and Meng Toh. Many of the concepts described in this article originated at Enabling the Missionary planning meetings.

discussion or dialogue, where participants present personal insights with the goal of formulating an overall plan or strategy; the emphasis is on interactive sharing, rather than on teaching and taking notes. The use of the term *member care* in connection with a consultation is more obvious, since member care—defined as the ongoing commitment of resources to develop missionary personnel—provides the focus of the interaction.

So taken together, the member care consultation refers to a series of meetings or discussions where invested participants share their perspectives, insights, and visions, for the purpose of bringing member care to the missions endeavor. To do this, several groups of people are necessary: those who provide the services (member care workers), those who make decisions about the implementation of the services (mission leaders), and those who will benefit from the services (missionary personnel). The discussion alternately revolves around the relevance of or need for member care services, the resources and services that are available or need to be developed, and the feasibility of applying those services to the task of world missions. Consultations can be set up to include participants from several organizations or convened by individual mission agencies to address the member care needs for their own people.

Before specific member care consultations are discussed in more detail, however, it is helpful to consider some essential concepts that provide a context for such meetings. The purpose of the next section will be to consider the theoretical underpinnings of the member care consultation.

## Theoretical Considerations

Community psychology is a mental health discipline which seeks to provide services and create change at the community level. The focus is usually on working with groups of people rather than individuals. Interestingly, community psychology embraces a variety of perspectives that are either similar to or relevant for those used in missions and the member care field (O'Donnell, 1986). Member care consultations can be conceived as a vehicle by which some of these community perspectives may be applied.

For example, a primary perspective within community psychology is that services and resources within the community should be made available to all community members, especially to those who are underserved for one reason or another. These reasons might include lower socioeconomic status, geographical location, or age, to name a few. Similarly, adequate access to all services by all members of the mission community should be an important concern in providing member care. The tribal missionary in the Amazon or the tentmaker in Mongolia, for instance, probably have less access to member care resources than church planters located in Europe. Member care consultations, in the spirit of community psychology, can help to disseminate services equitably, provided that (a) the participants seriously address the disparity of resources that exists, and (b) that consultations are held in those areas within the global missions community where member care services are less available and developed.

There are several additional perspectives from community psychology that can serve as guidelines in conceptualizing the member care consultation. Three perspectives that stand out in particular are the need for citizen participation, empowerment, and alternative settings.

### Citizen Participation

Citizen participation refers to the important roles that all community members can play in the planning, development, and delivery of needed resources and services. The term points to the fact that often the most effective service providers, within any system, are the members of the system themselves. For the member care context, citizen participation means the involvement of a variety of people, already in place within the world missions movement, who can plan, develop, and provide member care services. It is particularly concerned with finding practical ways to stimulate mutual support between missionaries, as well as to encourage opportunities for those interested in member care to work together.

In short, the "citizens" of world missions are the immediate starting point for an effective member care effort. As such, members from all mission levels should be invited to the member care consultation. All are needed, from the top leadership of the organization to the newly recruited missionary. When member care workers are few, as they are, and when the task is large, as it is, the citizens of missions must be mobilized to care for their own. This necessity provides the bedrock on which is built the foundation of any member care consultation.

The concept of citizen participation can also be a major topic for discussion at a consultation: how might missionary personnel be involved in member care, and what are the possible hindrances to providing services? Heller (1990), writing from a community psychology perspective, has delineated several such impediments: (a) finite resources can discourage wide involvement; (b) competing agendas and intergroup conflict can prevent broad participation within the community; and (c) feeling powerless to change a community or impact an organization may detract from greater involvement. Thus, for instance, a barrier to participation in member care which can be explored at a consultation might be a shortage of time on the part of over-worked staff; or limited funds to train missionaries in caring skills they can use with each other; or staff apathy which tolerates unhealthy aspects of organizational ethos.

## Empowerment

To community psychologists, empowerment refers to a commitment to give people the skills, competencies, and structures they need to live effectively in their community. Empowerment is prevention taken a step further: the frequency of problems decreases because community members have developed the means they need to assure their own well-being and that of their community. Member care consultations may be used to similarly impart new skills and competencies to the missions community.

There are several ways that consultations can apply the goal of empowering missions personnel. To begin, missions leaders from a particular organization might be more fully apprised of the needs of their members, and then take steps to train missionaries to counsel one another or set up a more thorough pastoral support structure. Next, a consultation might be arranged in which a number of member care professionals would train leaders and missionaries in team development skills that could then be taught to team leaders on the mission field. A third possibility for empowerment is to provide practical written resources at consultations on such topics as family life, stress management, and team relationships. These resources could then be distributed by the consultation participants within their organization(s).

Empowerment will occur whenever the ideas, plans, and programs developed at a consultation are directly conveyed to those who will ultimately benefit from the services. This is not necessarily an automatic process, as it frequently takes concerted effort and commitment to implement additional or improved member care services for mission personnel.

## Alternative Settings

In community psychology, an alternative setting is a strategy for social change in which a group of people come together to carry out activities and achieve goals that it holds to be important for itself or others (Sarason, 1972). Alternative settings are created to function alongside more established institutions. The new setting allows for an additional means of implementing new programs and meeting the needs of a community.

Throughout missions history, alternative settings have been needed to complement more conventional mission structures. A recent example is the formation of organizations to mobilize and train tentmakers and non-resident missionaries for work in countries that are not open to traditional missionaries. In the member care context, for example, one such setting is the missionary support center designed especially to care for and restore mission personnel in ways that mission organizations may not be able to do themselves (see chapter 24).

Several types of settings have been described in the community psychology literature (Rappaport, 1977). Of prime interest in the member care context is the *autonomous alternative setting,* so named for its goal of developing and distributing resources without imposing control over those who will benefit from the new services. Instead, the goal of the new setting is to ultimately impart control and ownership of the new programs to those who need the services. A member care consultation may be considered an autonomous alternative setting, in that a central goal is to develop new resources for the mission community, whether it be a particular group of missionaries or an entire organization. The term *autonomy* speaks of the desire to leave control in the hands of those who will utilize new member care services. It also reflects the desire to identify new structures or services which the participants themselves see as relevant to meet member care needs.

### Summarizing Community Psychology's Perspectives

The ultimate goal of the member care consultation is to "prepare God's people for works of service, so that the body of Christ might be built up..." (Ephesians 4:12, NIV). A consultation endeavors to prepare God's people (mission personnel) for works of service (member care) to build up Christ's body around the world (missions). In community psychology terms, a consultation is an "alternative setting" which works in tandem with existing mission structures to promote member care, especially for those who are underserved. These gatherings deliberately include a wide range of mission personnel—"citizen participation"—who with God's help can further "empower" one another with new skills and resources for missionary care and growth.

## Examples of Consultations

Perhaps the best way to illustrate what is meant by the member care consultation is to list some representative examples from the past few years. The oldest of these, the Mental Health and Missions Conference, now in its eleventh year, has met annually near Angola, Indiana to discuss ways in which mental health professionals can best be involved in providing services within the missions context. Over the years the annual meeting has been small and informal (by design), ranging from just over twenty in 1980 to about sixty at present. A good cross-section of missionaries, mental health professionals, and mission leaders has attended and has helped create an atmosphere of personal interaction and exchange.

Another group, the International Conference on Missionary Kids (ICMK), has met three times since 1984 to discuss the needs of missionary children and their families. These meetings have generally been larger gatherings planned around a series of related topics, and in that way have resembled other large conferences. The emphasis on interaction and discussion, however, makes these meetings a good example of a successful member care consultation. In addition, compendia of the proceedings of the first two ICMK conferences have been published.

Similarly, the Interdenominational Foreign Missions Association (IFMA) and the Evangelical Foreign Missions Association (EFMA) regularly discuss member care topics in their annual meetings. Although these meetings are not convened for the sole purpose of discussing member care, a growing number of people within these organizations have become interested in establishing member care services within their missions. On a larger scale, the International Conference on Christian Counseling had a track in missions at its first meeting in 1989, although this was more a formal conference than a consultation.

Individual mission agencies have also held member care consultations, although both the venue and the terms used to describe these gatherings are variable. Youth With A Mission in Amsterdam, for instance, held a "Personnel Services" workshop in 1991 for several of its leaders and personnel workers in Europe. Practical ways to set up personnel departments and pastoral support structures were discussed. The fact that this was an in-house event enabled the participants to focus more effectively on the specific issues and needs of staff within their own organization.

Recently there have been two informal member care "consultations" set up as retreats for graduate students who are preparing to work in various areas of member care. The retreats took place at a monastery in Sierra Madre, California, and provided a time to reflect on Christ and His heart for the world and for those who serve Him as missionaries. This type of consultation (in the broadest sense of the term) serves to keep us anchored in Christ and focused on Him as we work in the member care field.

Member care consultations then, can be set up in a variety of ways, and do not always need to involve large gatherings of people. Ultimately, the best way to illustrate a member care consultation is to discuss one in more detail. My association with a group called Enabling the Missionary (ETM) will be the focus. The formation and goals of the organization will be discussed, along with details of the two consultations that have been held.

## The Enabling the Missionary Consultation

Established in 1989, Enabling the Missionary (ETM) was founded to advance the availability and implementation of member care services worldwide. ETM was started by a group of students at Fuller Theological Seminary, and continues to be based in Southern California. It is now comprised of representatives from several area graduate schools (both faculty and students) and mission agencies. One of its prime areas of focus has been to convene member care consultations.

The first Enabling the Missionary Consultation was held in April, 1990 at the U.S. Center for World Mission in Pasadena, California. It was attended by about one hundred people, including missionaries, mission leaders, and member care providers. A variety of topics, ranging from the need for member care services to the selection and care of missionaries, were discussed over a three-day period. The primary mode of presentation was the panel discussion, which allowed those with experience to share their insights and to further discussion and planning.

In addition to the topical panel discussions, the ETM consultation provided written materials pertinent to member care, including a variety of magazines, books, and articles on the subject. Several informal times for personal interaction were scheduled to encourage discussion around common areas of interest. Interest groups were organized on the second day to provide those with specific concerns a more formal way of interacting. In addition, an extensive address list of those interested in member care issues was compiled,and preliminary discussions for the formation of a member care newsletter were held.

Enabling the Missionary convened a similar three-day consultation in February, 1992, held at the U.S. Center for World Mission. About 120 people attended. The topic was broadly defined as "an agenda for member care," which looked at ways to further develop member care services, especially through cooperative endeavors. There was a good deal of interest in organizing a professional association for member care workers, setting up training opportunities for students interested in member care, holding member care consultations overseas, and developing missionary support centers in key locations around the world.

Presentations and panel discussions also took place on crisis care, resources for member care, and establishing a caring environment. In addition, several of the main presenters arrived early in order to speak at a series of pre-conference gatherings at mission and psychology schools and mission organizations. In this way the consultation extended its influence by spreading itself over a longer period of time and by involving additional groups of people.

## Common Features

In considering the above examples, several features seem essential for a helpful member care consultation. First, there are important demographic considerations. There must be good (if not equal) representation from the three groups mentioned—mission leaders, missionaries, and member care providers. There is additional benefit if these people represent the following: (a) a broad geographical area; (b) a variety of missionary visions; (c) diverse backgrounds and training; and (d) a wide range of ages, from students to retirees.

Second, the goal of the consultation should be to further the cause of world evangelization. This involves thinking boldly about how the missionary force might best be equipped and serviced, as well as what services are most strategic to the task. Here are some examples: a mission agency might request that an organizational climate study be performed, using the services of an organizational expert; a group of physicians might decide more formally to serve a particular group of missionaries; a missionary might approach a psychologist for personal help; or a graduate student might find encouragement in being with like-minded servants of Christ. To accomplish this, a generous amount of time is needed for informal interaction as well as for more formal guided discussions.

Further, past consultations have found it helpful to convene around a general theme or issue within the realm of missions, to provide focus to the discussion. Generally, this has meant identifying those who have some expertise in the proposed area, and requesting that they attend the meetings.

## Planning A Consultation

This section will briefly outline most of the steps necessary to plan a member care consultation, and will provide some preliminary comments from personal experience. These remarks are not intended to be comprehensive, but instead are designed to save some time when envisioning what the overall project entails.

To begin, there must be some sponsoring group or organization which is willing to oversee the planning process. In planning the first ETM consultation, it was helpful to contact a few widely-known mission leaders to explain the proposed gathering and to have them write a formal endorsement that could be used with other promotional brochures.

Planning a consultation obviously requires a considerable amount of work; it is extremely helpful to have either one or two people concentrate on it full time, or to have several work on it together part time. Several areas of planning must be undertaken: (a) public relations, to provide brochures, take and make phone calls, provide signs and directions; (b) logistics, to make arrangements for accommodations, food, transportation, lighting and sound, and so forth; (c) programming, to decide upon topics, contact speakers,and to set the schedule; (d) materials, to provide related books, articles, and possibly to record sessions; and (e) worship, to encourage a prayerful and God-centered atmosphere. Again, this list is not comprehensive, but most aspects of the consultation will fall into one of these areas.

In addition, it is helpful for the consultation to be removed from the daily activities of the participants, and for all involved to be strongly encouraged to spend an entire weekend (or longer) together. This will help to provide a sense of community and continuity, and will encourage those in attendance to eat together, to interact more freely, and to embrace wholeheartedly all of the proceedings. The Mental Health and Missions Conference, for example, seems to have benefited repeatedly from being held in the beautiful and quiet surroundings of a state park. Participants should be encouraged not to commute to and from home, if possible.

The benefit from times of worship and prayer cannot be over-emphasized. Worship and prayer place our focus on Christ and unite our hearts together. All member care efforts must be submitted to the lordship of Christ; perspective is quickly lost when we are left to our own schemes and plans.

## Consultations and the Future

As increasing numbers of people become available to provide member care services, the demand for coordinating and disseminating those services becomes greater. Ironically, we may be approaching a time when the availability of willing member care workers begins to outpace our ability to put such help to service in strategic ways. Consultations and like meetings are essential if decision-makers are to effectively deploy the rising number of professionals (including students) who are potential member care workers.

Part Five of this book addresses several key areas that must be developed if member care services are to be expanded worldwide. Consultations, for the foreseeable future, will provide an important forum of discussion and planning. In keeping with the strategic focus of this section, several remarks on the future of member care consultations are in order.

### Location

To date, the majority of member care consultations have been held in North America. Although this serves a great number of member care workers who are either living or training in that part of the world, it does little to speed the delivery of services where they are needed most. Not only must an international member care conference be held on an ongoing basis, but smaller, more informal consultations, such as those mentioned above, must be convened in other parts of the world. Ideally, consultations would be available so that local missions and member care providers could discuss member care as it applies to their unique context.

### Focus

Closely related to location is the need for specific topics to provide focus to discussions. While topics such as prevention, training, selection, crisis intervention, and so on are valuable, discussions must be tailored to those in attendance and relevant to those who will ultimately benefit from the proceedings. There are many topics of general applicability to member care that might be discussed, which require conveners to focus clearly so that future consultations meet real needs.

The list of possible topics for discussion is nearly endless. As examples, member care topics could include: developing and sustaining healthy patterns within the family (including educational options); addressing personal growth and adjustment, both spiritually and emotionally; maintaining and encouraging effective leadership; preparing new missionaries and leaders for service; developing pastoral care and support in all levels of the missions task; creating a network of local member care providers who are willing to serve on a regular basis; addressing the struggles of those in need of counseling service; helping with cross-cultural adjustment, both in entering the field and in returning home; coping with the unique stresses of missionary life; providing member care services to missionaries from different cultures; and the list goes on. Each of these topics in and of itself could provide an agenda for a whole consultation!

## Students

A growing (albeit small at present) number of students in the behavioral science and human services fields are presently training to become member care providers—these people represent a storehouse of energy and enthusiasm that can be effectively harnessed for member care. Although many of them might as yet have limited professional and missions experience, they are nevertheless being exposed to a variety of academic material and ideas that will ultimately be useful to member care. Further, many students are anxious to participate in member care activities while they are in training; their participation in a member care consultation provides an ideal means of establishing a foothold in the emerging member care field.

It should be noted that the greatest of North American missions movements had students as its initial impetus, as Howard (1979) has noted. The Haystack Prayer meeting headed by Samuel Mills at Williams College in August 1806, and other related student movements at Middlebury College, Yale University, and elsewhere, gave rise to a reawakening throughout North America concerning the needs of foreign missions. By the end of the century the prayers of those under the haystack were coming to full fruition, and the Student Volunteer Movement (SVM) was birthed, most notably at Mt. Hermon, Massachusetts, under the teaching of D. L. Moody and A. T. Pierson. Two years later, in 1888, the SVM was formally organized, and by the end of the year more than 2100 students had volunteered for missionary work. Thus began a movement that until the 1920s sent out thousands of students to overseas mission fields.

The contribution of students to member care, then, is not to be underestimated. While it is not necessary to equate those presently training for careers in member care with their counterparts of 1806, it is nonetheless imperative to recognize that God has often used students in pivotal ways within the course of missions history. It is important that this vital resource and well of enthusiasm be channeled into the mainstream of member care.

A final word about students. If they are to be an integral part of member care during their training, they will benefit greatly from encouragement offered by present leaders to take an active part in both missions and in efforts to establish new member care services. The interaction and thought involved in planning a consultation can be invaluable to a student who has the guidance of older, more experienced member care providers. Mission leaders and academicians must be encouraged to nurture, challenge, and support those who are called to train themselves to provide member care.

### Strategy

As world mission efforts become more strategically coordinated, so must member care. Carefully planned consultations might well be the ideal medium for exploring the future thrusts of member care and its personnel. Where are services most needed? By whom are they needed most? Where are missionaries expecting breakthroughs, and where will there rise the greatest need for supportive services? These questions and similar ones demand purposeful discussion and proactive planning. What should training programs provide to be most strategic? What pressing needs should prioritize research efforts? Where should students be sent (for training, for overseas experience, and for mentoring), and with whom should they be associated?

Moreover, member care services need to be coordinated with the efforts of missions strategists, such as those who are researching and mobilizing workers for unreached people groups. These efforts will include thousands of additional missionaries who will go to areas beyond the reach of present member care services. How will these needs be known, who will provide services, and how will the maximum good be done for the greatest number of people?

## Conclusion

The opportunities are rife for the deployment and expansion of member care services within the worldwide missions community. Member care consultations can facilitate the development and coordination of these services by creating an environment where open discussion and prayerful planning can occur. Proverbs 19:21 reminds us that "Many are the plans in a man's heart, but the counsel of the Lord, it will stand" (NASB). May our plans not result from our own counsel! Rather may we be committed to hear from God and diligent to seek His wisdom and timing as we set up future consultations and initiate new cooperative endeavors for member care.

### Questions for Discussion

1. How would you organize a member care consultation in your area? Who might you invite? What goals would you hope to accomplish?

2. Where would some of the most strategic places be for holding member care consultations?

3. What other perspectives (besides those of community psychology) might be useful to conceptualize and guide the development of member care consultations?

4. What are some practical ways to increase member care involvement within a mission agency (citizen participation)? How might any barriers be overcome?

5. What additional settings or structures are needed to provide better care for missionaries around the world?

# References

Heller, K. (1990). Limitations and barriers to citizen participation. *Community Psychologist, 23*, 11-12.

Howard, D. (1979). *Student power in world missions.* Downers Grove, IL: Intervarsity.

O'Donnell, K. (1986). Community psychology and unreached peoples: Applications to needs and resource assessment. *Journal of Psychology and Theology, 14*, 213-223.

Rappaport, J. (1977). *Community psychology: Values, research, and action.* New York: Holt, Rinehart, and Winston.

Sarason, S. B. (1972). *The creation of settings and the future societies.* San Francisco: Jossey-Bass.

# Index